T0311223

An Early Communist

MUZAFFAR AHMAD
IN CALCUTTA 1913–1929

An Early Communist

MUZAFFAR AHMAD
IN CALCUTTA 1913–1929

SUCHETANA CHATTOPADHYAY

 Tulika Books

Published by **Tulika Books**
35 A/1 Shahpur Jat, New Delhi 110 049, India

© Suchetana Chattopadhyay

First edition (hardback) 2011

Second edition (paperback) 2012

ISBN: 978-81-89487-93-5

Typeset in Sabon at Tulika Print Communication Services, New Delhi;
printed at Chaman Offset, Delhi 110 002

Contents

Illustrations

Acknowledgements

This work is derived from my doctoral dissertation. Generous financial assistance from the Felix Committee during 1999–2002 made this research possible. My thesis supervisor Professor Peter Robb's flawless and prompt correction of each draft enabled me to complete what often appeared to be a never-ending process. My second supervisor Dr Subho Basu's comments and friendship reduced the pressure which the prospect of writing more than 90,000 words generates automatically. Professor Richard Rathbone's support during my first year as a research student equipped me to adjust to an alien academic routine. I am grateful to Dr Jayanta Sengupta for his generosity and preliminary supervision in Kolkata. Anisuzzaman, Amiya Kumar Bagchi, Jasodhara Bagchi, Manabendra Bandopadhyay, Sibaji Bandopadhyay, Himadri Banerjee, Himani Bannerji, the late Sanat Basu, Anit Basu, John Berwick, Malini Bhattacharya, Sourin Bhattacharchya, Anuradha Chanda, Anna Davin, Mary Davis, Devleena Ghosh, Heather Goodall, James Holstun, Mortuza Khaled, Mushtaq Khan, the late Sunirmal Moitra, Richard Newman, Avril Powell, Paru Raman, Aniruddha Ray, Marcus Rediker, the late Ranjit Roy, Sumit Sarkar, Tanika Sarkar and Hari Vasudevan offered insight and encouragement. Despite failing health, the late Gautam Chattopadhyay, the late Naren Sen and the late Ranen Sen allowed me to interview them on the communist movement in Bengal. The late Jayanta Dasgupta, David Horsley, Alok Majumdar, the late Subodh Roy and Tushar Sinha suggested some of the sources when I started my field-work. I am indebted to the late Anil Biswas; CPI(M) West Bengal Archives; Arun Ghosh; Bhabani Sen Pathagar; Atis Dasgupta, Director, West Bengal State Archives; Udayan Mitra, Assistant Director, West Bengal State Archives; and Sandhi Mukherjee, DIG, IB, for their help. The staff of the West Bengal State Archives, especially Ananda Bhattacharya, Ashish Biswas, Madhurima Sen, Moumita Chakraborti, Swati Sengupta and Nilmanida, offered utmost assistance. I wish to thank the staff of Bangiya Sahitya

Parishat, Bhabani Sen Pathagar, Centre for Studies in Social Sciences, Muzaffar Ahmad Pathagar, National Archives and National Library in India, and of British Library, Centre for South Asian Studies (Cambridge), Senate House Library (London) and SOAS Library in the UK. My friends Ranjana Dasgupta and Kakali Mukherjee laboriously copied some of the primary sources on my behalf. Saleha Begam and Rajkamal Sil were also helpful. Though I am unable to name each of the kind individuals who supplied or lent books relevant to this research, I thank them all. I also wish to thank Andrew Whitehead for publishing an article that emerged from the first two chapters, and Mubarak Ali for printing its Urdu translation.

My friend Nina Balogh, proof-reader of the thesis, dealt with various technical and non-technical problems. Donatella Alessandrini, Murad Banaji, Saswata Bhattacharya, my cousin Melissa Chatterjee, Bodhisattva Dasgupta, Chirashree Das Gupta, Jim Gledhill, Phil Hutchinson, Joseph Kelley, Rajit Mazumder, George Orton, Costas Pateras, Kelly Scott, Subrata Sinha, Fabien Tarrit, Damian Tobin, Alexis Wearmouth and Andrew Wigglesworth offered crucial assistance during key phases of writing and revision. Isa Daudpota, Kingshuk Dasgupta, Nupur Dasgupta, Soham Dasgupta, Kawshik Ananda Kirtania and Prakriti Mitra helped with some of the images accompanying the text. Indu Chandrasekhar, my publisher, patiently waited for the manuscript to be delivered. Rani Ray, as the reader, made useful suggestions with characteristic affection. Devalina Mookerjee also went over the text, and was helpful and kind.

The intellectual insight and consistent support of my parents, Ratnabali Chatterjee and Tirthankar Chattopadhyay, enabled me to take on and finish this work. I am indebted to them in ways that are too numerous to recount. Taradi, who passed away in early 2008, was a source of love and strength. My aunt and uncle, Chandra Ghosh and Norman Alexander Hindson, ensured that during my stay in London I knew no material hardship in their house. Mariam and Sol Bannerjee, Kaushalya Bannerji, Ansu Basu, J.R. Chatterjee, Julian Chatterjee, Meenakshi and Sujit Sankar Chatterjee, Subhankar Chatterjee, Sarbani Chaudhury, Mrinalkanti Dasgupta, Indrani Datta Gupta, Madhushree Datta, Sipra Datta Gupta, Mita and Prabhat Ghosh, Cathy Grimes, S.A. Hafiz, Michael Kuttner, Hena Mukherjee, Sibani Ray Chaudhury, Amit Roy, Ela Roy, and Suchetana Sengupta showed concern and generosity. Jaya, Jhantuda, Saraswatidi, Sibkumar and Shantidi were supportive in Kolkata. The solidarity from Azeeda, Achmad, Joe, Kipros and especially Mrs S. Raymode, revealed another side of life in London.

I wish to thank all those who offered hospitality and distraction while I wrote my thesis and completed the manuscript, especially Alvaro, Anamika, Andy, Anil, Anirban, Anup, Arnab, Arifa, Arindam, Asad, Bhai, Brenna, Cleo, David M., Diya, Dorothydi, Emily, Florian, Francesca, Ged, Ghayur,

Greg, Hans, Hajime, Hazel, Jane, Jasmine, Jody, Jon, Junzuo, Kafi, Keiko, Kimi, Koli, Konrad, Lorenzo, Madhuja, Malu, Mallika, Mezna, Nasser, Nigel, Nilanjana, Nina O., Pocket, Ratul, Richard, Rinku, Rituparna, Rosy, Rupa, Satoshi, Saugatada, Selvyn, Sobhi, Soumya, Smita, Stewart, Sukanyadi, Swati B., Swati G., Sayako, Talat, Tattu, Titas, Tom, Trina, Tui, Tuli and Urvi. Finally, I salute all the comrades from the SOAS Stop the War Group, especially Foqia, Jacqui, John, Johnny, Sandy and Scott.

All errors are mine.

This book is dedicated to the late Jayanta Mukhopadhyay, veteran radical and parental figure.

Spelling, Translation and Sources

Some of the Bengali and Arabic names and words have been spelt the way they appear in the sources; others in the way they are pronounced or in accordance with rules of transliteration from Bengali. Calcutta has been used to refer to the city of Kolkata. Certain non-English words/terms are italicized when used for the first time in each chapter. All translations are mine unless indicated. For books and articles citing dates in the Bengali calendar, the exact or approximate year in the Roman calendar has been mentioned alongside. Some of the intelligence file numbers were censored. I have referred to their suppressed origins in the footnotes.

Abbreviations

AITUC	All India Trade Union Congress
B	Bengali Year
Comintern	Third Communist International
CPGB	Communist Party of Great Britain
CPI	Communist Party of India
DW	Defence Witness
IB	Intelligence Branch of the Bengal Police
ISU	Indian Seamen's Union
KPP	Krishak Praja Party
PW	Prosecution Witness
PWP	Peasants and Workers Party
RCIU	Resolution on Committee on Industrial Unrest
SB	Special Branch of the Calcutta Police
WPP	Workers and Peasants Party

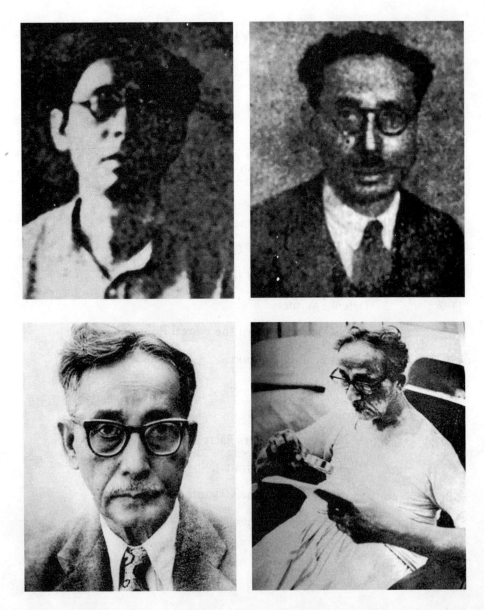

Muzaffar Ahmad: in the 1930s (*above left*), 1940s (*above right*),
1950s (*below left*), 1960s (*below right*)

Introduction

'I will not sleep here tonight. Home also I cannot go.'
— James Joyce, *Ulysses*

Bengal's first communists emerged from the ranks of the region's Muslim intelligentsia in the early 1920s. Their transformation involved a rejection of mainstream politics based on the identities of 'nation' and 'community' — a process that has been little investigated. This book aims to treat this neglected area by focusing on the early life and times (1913–29) of Muzaffar Ahmad (1889–1973), a founder of the communist movement in Bengal and India, and an early communist from the colonial world. Though the left was minute during the 1920s, the shaping of socialist politics in Bengal during 1922–29 marked the beginning of a political tendency which was to leave its imprint on post-partition West Bengal and the struggle for Bangladesh in East Pakistan.

The origins of communism, the core component of the organized socialist movement which emerged for the first time in Calcutta in the 1920s, lay in the appearance of Muslim intellectuals who tried to give shape to a new form of anti-imperialism by stepping out of the confines of mainstream nationalism dominated by the Hindu *bhadralok*, of political movements based on perceptions of Muslim exclusivity, and of secular or ethno-linguistic identities. For these intellectuals, class ideology represented freedom from forms of exploitation and alienation: the other political options did not adequately address these. Class itself was perceived as an identity that would disappear when communist society was attained. Its emancipatory promise and transitory nature could be pitted against the non-emancipatory structure and the transcendental, essentialist claims of mainstream political activism. Class consciousness, therefore, was regarded as a space beyond the politics of identities.

The existing literature on communism in India is silent on this aspect.

Scholars have variously read the Indian communists as remote-controlled by Moscow;[1] misguided opponents of mainstream nationalist politics;[2] upholders of caste divisions[3] and redeployed middle-class hegemony,[4] or prisoners of modernity mediated and tainted by European colonialism and nationalism.[5] None of these readings can serve as adequate tools to unravel the processes of radical transition or to locate the origins of communism in Bengal. For that, a social and contextually grounded interpretation of Bengal politics is required. This can be achieved by looking at the critical transitions undergone by Muzaffar Ahmad in a period of momentous changes. Why was he alienated by dominant identity politics? What were the forms of politics he learnt to reject? What were the social components that were subsumed and marginalized by these dominant forms, and which then induced in him a critical rupture with his own past?

In order to seek answers to these and other related questions, this monograph takes Muzaffar Ahmad's early career (1913–29) as its chronological frame. 1913 was the year of his migration to Calcutta. 1929 marked the end of the first phase of his political life, as a pioneer of the communist movement as it had emerged in Bengal and India of the 1920s. It was the year when leading communists were arrested and their trial began at Meerut. The biographical details of Muzaffar Ahmad between 1913 and 1929 thus converge with a significant phase in the social and political history of India and the world. These years also represent two crisis-points in the history of imperialism and capitalism: 1913 was the eve of the First World War, and 1929 the year of the Wall Street Crash which set off the Great Depression. They enclose a period within which socialist ideas and communist activism became politically familiar in different parts of the globe. The success of the Bolshevik Revolution (1917) and the formation of the Third Communist International directly boosted these currents. Socialism came to be perceived by many in the colonizing and colonized countries as a viable alternative, a solution to the problems posed by capitalism and imperialism in the midst of economic crisis and war. A radicalization of political culture could be felt among the intelligentsia in various urban centres of the world.[6] Calcutta was no exception. Many socially alienated, economically distressed and politically dissatisfied urban intellectuals stood at the crossroads of established and radical identity formations. Among them was a small 'fraction'[7] informed by social radicalism from below, and a leftward turn in literary and cultural fields. They were disaffiliating themselves from the more established political routes open to those from their social background to combat colonialism, and affiliating themselves to a more radical vision of decolonization. The radicalism of the period was not devoid of contradictions. The ideas and aspirations of those with radical potential were often intertwined with social institutions, political movements and cultural norms which could lead to reversal and retreat from left radicalism. Nevertheless, they bore the imprint of the desire for a redefinition of state and society based on egalitarian ideals.

The anti-colonial conjuncture of the late 1910s and the early 1920s made substantial sections of the young intelligentsia, to quote V.I. Lenin on the limits of Russian intellectual radicals, 'revolt against the . . . police tyranny of the autocracy' which hunted down 'thought and action'. Yet their 'material interests' compelled them 'to be inconsistent, to compromise'.[8] This was especially true in Bengal, where, with the waning of the anti-colonial mass upsurge in the early 1920s, many of those who had professed a new faith in widespread popular action retreated to a variety of political positions serving the interests of the elite: revolutionary nationalism, *swarajya*, *praja* politics and communalism.[9] In Gramscian terms, a small minority among these 'traditional intellectuals', though not 'organic intellectuals' of the working class, became linked with the proletariat through the emerging communist organizations.[10] In Bengal, colonial pedagogy had destroyed the residual pre-colonial forms of education and even sidelined the invented 'orientalist' scholarship. As western education, in the course of the nineteenth century, increasingly overwhelmed both the form and the content of learning,[11] the 'traditional intellectual' was constituted and reconstituted under the aegis of colonial rule. All segments of the colonial intelligentsia, though differing on the exact route, were agreed upon setting 'embourgeoisment' as their goal to tide over the colonial system which confined them to land and professions. The general decline in the material conditions of the majority in the colonial and semi-colonial world, glaringly apparent by the early twentieth century,[12] exploded the self-nurturing myth of the bourgeois states that capitalism, mediated by colonialism, was 'unexceptional'; and that capitalist empire formations were like any other in history, to be located as the penultimate link in a long chain of conquests and invasions. Communist internationalism, which gained widespread currency after the success of the Bolshevik Revolution of 1917 and the uncorking of post-war mass protests, was seen as the most effective countervailing weapon to shatter imperialist oppression and the rule of capital in every country of the world.[13] Though Muzaffar and other early left activists came from the ranks of a reconstituted 'traditional' intelligentsia, they represented a break with the past. They no longer shared the vision of embourgeoisment that had enjoyed a hegemonic consensus in nineteenth-century Bengal. Thrust into an uncertain and chaotic urban environment, they were sucked into the vortex of international and local radical tendencies at the end of the First World War.

To grasp the context that propelled Muzaffar and other minoritized and marginalized intellectuals towards communism, this work examines their initial revolt against colonialism, which was then extended to colonial capital and then to capitalism itself, and the social hierarchies and property relations with which it was aligned. It is in this social climate, reflected in the unionization of workers and the socialistic wavering of middle-class intellectuals touched by international left currents, that the political turn of Muzaffar Ahmad could be located. The 'reshuffling'[14] and mutations of self which gave rise to his new politics were rooted in this context. It was related to a complex process of disaffiliation from the existing structures of anti-colonialism, and was linked to a radical conjuncture created by the post-war mass upsurge, material hardship and growing contact with the world of labour. It was underlined by dissociation from the outlook of the main-stream leaders and the dominant ideologies they represented.

This work investigates both the setting and the changes, as represented by Muzaffar. The underlying focus is on the social ingredients of a communist-led left politics as it emerged in the city, rooted in an understanding of class and property, and standing outside or having complicated encounters with dominant identity formations and political movements of the day. Historio-graphic silence on this reality indicates a theoretical occlusion of the com-plexities which characterized Bengal at the time. An attempt has been made, therefore, to trace a part of this radical social history by concentrating on the dialectical interplay between individual and wider consciousness; daily life and changing political praxis; social location and the creation of agency; subjective experiences on the ground; and the making/unmaking of collect-ives.

The first chapter (1913–19) analyses the context and significance of Muzaffar's migration to the city. His rural background in the remote Ben-gal island of Sandwip, and the kind of identity-thinking such a milieu encour-aged, are discussed. His arrival in Calcutta, the only metropolis in Bengal, on the eve of the First World War, and the conditions in the city that contri-buted to his future radicalization are examined – in particular, his experien-ces as an impoverished intellectual and Bengali Muslim cultural activist in a city undergoing war-time privations. The second chapter (1919–21) deals with Muzaffar's political transformation along leftist lines in the context of the working-class upsurge in Calcutta, and the impact on him and some of his contemporaries, of socialist ideas following the success of the Russian Revolution. Muzaffar's entry into political journalism and his growing sen-sitivity to the labour question are shown to have played a vital role. The third chapter (1922–24) engages with the first socialist nucleus in Calcutta, with Muzaffar as the principal organizer. During this period, his links with the Communist Third International, his dissemination of banned socialist literature and his communications with other anti-colonial radicals led to his arrest and trial in the Kanpur Bolshevik Conspiracy Case (1924). Chap-ters four and five examine the growth and activities of the first socialist

organization in Bengal (1926–29), including Muzaffar's role and the attendant constraints. Finally, the transformation of Muzaffar Ahmad's political identity as an example of the evolution of socialist politics in a colonized urban milieu is explained. This includes a discussion of Muzaffar's
prose as 'language of class', and of his autobiographical writings as a prism
through which his early career may be read.

By investigating the roots of early communism and socialist politics in
Bengal through the personality of Muzaffar Ahmad, this book explores a
political space which aimed to transcend dominant notions of politics and
identity. At a time when history is being harnessed to erect new xenophobic
enclosures and imperialism is being projected as a benevolent, 'humanitarian' exercise, this is a way of recording not just the amply documented
strengths, but also the ever-present contradictions which have beset identity
formations under the empire of capital.

Notes and References

[1] G. D. Overstreet and M. Windmiller, *Communism in India*, Berkeley, 1959. David N. Druhe, *Soviet Russia and Indian Communism, 1917–1947, With an Epilogue Covering the Situation Today*, New York, 1959. J.P. Haithcox, *Communism and Nationalism in India: M.N. Roy and Comintern Policy 1920–1939*, Princeton, 1971.

[2] Aditya Mukherjee, 'The Workers' and Peasants' Parties, 1926–30: An Aspect of Communism in India', in Bipan Chandra (ed.), *The Indian Left: Critical Appraisals*, New Delhi, 1983. S. Joshi, *Struggle for Hegemony in India 1920–47: the colonial state, the left and the national movement*, Volume One, Delhi, 1992. B. Josh, *Struggle for Hegemony in India 1920–47: the colonial state, the left and the national movement*, Volume Two, Delhi, 1993.

[3] Dilip M. Menon, *Caste, Nationalism and Communism in South India: Malabar 1900–1948*, Cambridge, 1994.

[4] Rajarshi Dasgupta, 'Marxism and the middle class intelligentsia: culture and politics in Bengal, 1920s–1950s', unpublished Ph.D. thesis, University of Oxford, 2003.

[5] Sanjay Seth, *Marxist Theory and Nationalist Politics: The Case of Colonial India*, Delhi, 1995. Aditya Nigam, 'Marxism and the Postcolonial World: Footnotes to a Long March', *Economic and Political Weekly*, Vol. XXXIV, Nos. 1 and 2, 2–8 and 9–15 January 1999. Also my reply to Nigam: Suchetana Chattopadhyay, 'Misinterpreting Muzaffar Ahmed', *Economic and Political Weekly*, Vol. XXXIV, No. 13, 27 March 1999.

[6] Ruth T. McVey, *The Rise of Indonesian Communism*, New York, 1965. Sepher Zabih, *The Communist Movement in Iran*, Berkeley, 1966. George S. Harris, *The Origins of Communism in Turkey*, Stanford, 1967. Joel Beinin and Zachary Lockman, *Workers on the Nile: Nationalism, Communism, Islam and the Egyptian Working Class*, Princeton, 1987. Arif Dirlik, *The Origins of Chinese Communism*, Oxford, 1989. Hue-Tam Ho Tai, *Radicalism and the Origins of the Vietnamese Revolution*, Cambridge, Massachusetts, 1996.

[7] Raymond Williams, 'The Bloomsbury Fraction', in *Problems in Materialism and Culture*, London, 1980. Williams describes avant-garde intellectuals of the Bloomsbury Circle as a 'class fraction', isolated from the general directions of the English upper classes.

[8] V.I. Lenin, 'The Tasks of the Russian Social-Democrats', in *On the Intelligentsia*, Moscow, 1983, p. 27.

[9] These political formations and their relationships with the left are treated in the following chapters.

[10] See Quintin Hoare and Geoffrey Nowell Smith (eds.), 'The Intellectuals', in *Selections from*

the Prison Notebooks of Antonio Gramsci, London, 2003. For a brief analysis of the relationship between western intellectuals and the communist movement, see Eric Hobsbawm, 'Intellectuals and Communism', in *Revolutionaries*, London, 1999.

[11] For a treatment of colonial pedagogy in the nineteenth century, see Sibaji Bandopadhyay, *Gopal–Rakhal Dwandasamas: Uponibeshbad o Bangla Shishu-Sahitya* (The Gopal–Rakhal Dialectic: Colonialism and Children's Literature in Bengal), Calcutta, 1991.

[12] See Amiya Kumar Bagchi, *Perilous Passage: Mankind and the Global Ascendancy of Capital*, Delhi, 2006.

[13] Eric Hobsbawm, 'Problems of Communist History', in *Revolutionaries*.

[14] Carl E. Schorske, 'Introduction', in *Fin-de-Siecle Vienna: Politics and Culture*, New York, 1981, p. xviii.

CHAPTER ONE

Migration

'Whoever has no house now, will never have one.'
                    – Rainer Maria Rilke, *Autumn Day*

Socialist and communist politics in Calcutta first emerged among a Muslim intellectual fraction. Muzaffar Ahmad, the central figure of the early communist nucleus, represented the turning away of a segment of the urban anti-colonial intelligentsia from the dominant ideological options available in their milieu. Certain aspects of Muzaffar Ahmad's early life contributed to the making of his future politics and may be discerned in his shifting social environment. It will be argued that the constraints of rural living prompted Muzaffar's journey to the colonial metropolis. Migration as a social process and the experiential world of an obscure outsider in the big city formed the critical context for a radical reconfiguration of his political consciousness.

Rural Roots of Migration

When does someone leave the familiar world behind? Those born into genteel poverty in the rural areas of Bengal in the 1880s, imagined the city as a gateway to material opportunities and social advancement, absent in their immediate surroundings. From the second half of the nineteenth century, the middle and lower strata of landed proprietors in the Bengal countryside were increasingly unable to sustain themselves on agrarian income. Only branching out to civil professions could rescue them from the impending loss of class and property. Western education with knowledge of English as its focal point was the bridge that had to be crossed to make one's way in a colonial society.[1] Muzaffar Ahmad, born in 1889 in the remote island of Sandwip on the Bay of Bengal, was one of the many who travelled to the city in search of colonial education. He was also eager to become a part of the urban literati. The rural world he left behind prompted him to undertake this journey.

The Village

Musapur, his village, was indistinguishable from other villages in every respect except for its weekly *hat* (the village market).[2] Despite Sandwip's administrative status as a geographic unit of Noakhali district while Muzaffar was growing up, social dissociation was marked between mainland coastal populations and the residents of the cluster of offshore islands. Separated by river channels flowing into the sea, the physical and psychological alienation of the islanders contained roots of local patriotism. W.H. Thompson, the Survey and Settlement officer of the Noakhali District observed:

> The people of the mainland hold themselves aloof from the islanders. None on the mainland will give his daughter in marriage to a man who lives on the islands; nor, however poor he may be, has he yet shown himself willing to live in one of the new formations with his family and build himself a house there. There is very much of fear as well as conservatism behind this prejudice – fear of destruction by such a cyclone or storm wave as came in October 1876, fear of the actual crossing and the realization that, with the prejudice as strong as it is, the first to go against it will be cutting themselves off altogether from their old associates.[3]

Little traditions, however, could merge with translocal traditions-in-the-making. The tensions between island and mainland residents could be subordinated to a district-based identity, representing wider regional affiliations. Social compulsions dictated such resolutions, doing away with age-old barriers which had survived from pre-colonial times. Formation of districts, such as Noakhali, by the colonizers in the nineteenth century marked the end of pre-colonial rural administration and signalled the firm establishment of colonial authority over the Bengal countryside. The related rise of district-based sub-identities also came to be associated with the emergence of wider provincial and national identities in British India.[4] The social dichotomies linked with the colonial drain of material resources, chiefly in the form of land revenue collection, the destruction of cottage industries, and the consequent decimation of livelihoods and chronic unemployment,[5] were visible in every corner of rural India, Sandwip being no exception. Finding their attempts to achieve embourgeoisment blocked by colonial capital,[6] the Bengali intelligentsia displayed multiple, interchangeable political affinities, not unrelated to their locations on the map of property and social power. This entailed continuous shifts in the boundaries of identity formations during the late nineteenth and early twentieth centuries. The micro-level geographic–organic identities constructed from the hegemonic drives of the local intelligentsia had a necessarily restricted reach, and were absorbed into the emergent identities with wider social and territorial focus.

The chief sources of information on the Noakhali region, including Sandwip, during the late nineteenth and early twentieth centuries, are colonial records and historical tracts by the 'sons of the soil'. The writing process of the latter was underlined by local patriotism, a social tendency embodying the rural intelligentsia's search for self-improvement. *Sandwiper Itihas* (The History of Sandwip), a seminal work by Rajkumar Chakrabarty and Anangamohan Das on the history of the island, uncovers the material dynamics beneath the surface of local pride. A primarily descriptive and laboriously detailed account based on official, unofficial and oral sources, it displays a transcommunal patriotism that never loses sight of middle-class concerns around the theme of 'improvement'. As an exercise in micro-history, it chronicles in detail the myths surrounding the island, its place in pre-colonial history, the material changes generated after the colonial conquest of Bengal, the contemporary social demography, and future prospects of 'regeneration' through education and enterprise.

Author Rajkumar Chakrabarty was associated with *Noakhali*, a literary journal started in 1916 at the initiative of students from Noakhali district residing in Calcutta. The declared aim was to engage in 'self-knowledge', and to remove the barriers separating the educated elite from 'the ordinary people'. An article by Anangamohan Das, in the first issue, was later incorporated into the book. The journal opened with a poem, 'Abahan' (Exhortation), lauding Noakhali's past and present. It was written by Muzaffar Ahmad.[7] The fact that Muzaffar and Rajkumar both ended up in Calcutta reveals the contradictions embedded in ideas of local patriotism, including 'self-knowledge' and 'self-improvement'. Though rich in local history and steeped in folklore from medieval times, providing, by all accounts, a claim of exclusivity, Sandwip was a microscopic fragment in the wider workings of empire. It was a forgotten corner of Bengal, important only to the locals and to the colonial officials sent there to record and retain the territorial integrity of the Raj. The logic of migration to metropolitan centres was thus built into its material life.

Memories of Colonial Drain

From the accounts of the pre-colonial past furnished by British administrators, it would seem that the inhabitants of Sandwip once possessed resources to sustain themselves. In 1569, Cesare Federici, a Venetian traveller, visited Sandwip and described it as 'one of the most fertile places in the world, densely populated and well-cultivated'.[8] A late eighteenth-century colonial report suggested that cheap and abundant grain production attracted migrants from Dhaka and other districts during times of scarcity.[9] The

Mughals, the Arakanese and the Portuguese had established headquarters and settlements in the island, before the advent of British rule.[10]

This picture of self-sufficiency and prosperity, later interpreted by local patriots in search of an elusive embourgeoisment as a 'golden age', was distorted beyond recognition in the colonial period. Salt and cloth manufacture in pre-colonial times had connected the agricultural population of Sandwip with distant lands. Very little of that commercial legacy remained. Complete subordination of trade and production to the interests of colonial capital led to the disappearance of material security for the majority of the island population. In the course of the nineteenth century, with the imposition of one-way free-trade by the colonial state on behalf of colonial capital, salt production was abandoned and cloth production was weakened by the import of cheap English piece-goods.[11] The boatmen and sailors of Sandwip were the only reminder of ancestors whose travels had encompassed the marine and littoral zones stretching from West to Southeast Asia. By the early twentieth century, the islanders were producing rice for export, along with coconuts which grew in abundance; grazing cattle as a way of earning a living; and making boats, which remained a viable profession, though much reduced under colonial rule.[12]

A survey of the material infrastructure in the late nineteenth and the early twentieth century shows that the conditions of social existence in the island encouraged migration. Renewed pressure of population and dearth of resources compelled the islanders to leave. Though Sandwip had lost nearly half of its population during the cyclone of 1876 and the cholera epidemic that followed, little official work was done to improve the civic amenities in the region. By the late nineteenth century, the presence of the state in Sandwip was confined to running a rudimentary and parasitic bureaucracy, revenue collection, and enforcement of colonial law and order through judicial and police functions.[13] A Union Committee was the sole source of local welfare, and although the state determined its composition, it did not financially aid its activities in any way. The committee, consisting of six members, was entrusted with the maintenance of village roads, water supply and drainage, and it raised funds to maintain essential services through contributions and local levies.[14] There were no hospitals or institutions of higher education in Sandwip, and very few schools. The only secondary school, formally inaugurated in 1902, grew out of the Sandwip Middle English School, started at the initiative of the local intelligentsia in the late nineteenth century, with financial support from Hindu and Muslim donors.[15]

Restricted education and job opportunities meant that a section of the male children from genteel families would leave the island in search of livelihood. For them, growing up meant going away from their rural origins. Some from the impoverished peasant families also left. The Muslim *lascars* (sailors) from Sandwip, alongside those from Chittagong, worked as sea-men in ships departing from the Calcutta Port. They were also prepond-erant among the crew of the vessels engaged in inland navigation.[16] The majority of those who stayed back remained tied to the land. During the 1910s, 78 per cent of the island population were involved in agriculture, 8 per cent were dependent on industry and 7 per cent worked as labourers.[17] The island's poor, irrespective of communal categorizations and identity formations, lived in conditions of extreme hardship. According to writers sensitive to the plight of the local peasantry, rural indebtedness was high, and three-quarters of the peasant cultivators did not have enough to eat despite the abundance of rainfall and the fertility of the soil.[18]

A Case of Downward Mobility
It can be argued that alongside the material relationships created under colonial rule, the historic exclusion of sanskritization facilitated the growth of a composite intelligentsia in Sandwip. Sanskritization as an ideological agency of class and caste formations did not thrive. Brahmins, the custodi-ans of caste knowledge, were conspicuous by their near-absence in Sandwip society. Caste Hindus were supposedly non-existent in Sandwip before the seventeenth century. By the twentieth century, the Kayasthas were predomi-nant among the upper-caste Hindus. As on the Noakhali mainland, their ranks were swelled by Vaidya settlers who had merged with them.[19]

Otherwise, the composition of the Hindu community in Sandwip resem-bled that of the East Bengal mainland. The upper castes constituted a minori-ty *bhadralok* gentry, as was evident in Bengal as a whole. They made their living as landed proprietors or as professionals. To a greater extent than any other section of society, the Hindu *bhadralok* sent their children to be for-mally educated. Among the children sent to school, only a few were able to attain higher education.[20] The size of the intelligentsia was minute. Only 6.2 per cent of the Hindu and 2.4 per cent of the Muslim population were literate at the beginning of the twentieth century.[21] During the 1910s, only 2 per cent of islanders belonged to the professions.[22] Lower-caste Hindus who had not converted to Islam were in the majority within the Hindu community, and lived as cultivators, artisans and labourers. The legend of the brigand-king Dillal Khan, who ruled the island in the seventeenth cen-tury and apparently forced his subjects to intermarry without observing caste or religious customs, discouraged mainland Hindus from associating with those of the islands.[23]

In 1901, an official report recorded the presence of 85,175 Muslims and 29,993 Hindus in the island. Only 9 came from other communities.[24] The preponderance of Muslims was true of Sandwip in Cesare Federici's times too; he had described it as inhabited entirely by the 'Moors'.[25] A legend suggested that the inhabitants had been adherents of Islam from medieval times. Twelve Aulia fakirs travelling on the back of a fish from Baghdad to Chittagong, in the fifteenth century, had stopped to offer prayers at a 'shunya dwip' (empty island). 'Shunya dwip' evolved into Sandwip.[26] From the thirteenth century onwards, religious preachers and immigrants from the mainland built settlements and spread the words of Muhammad among the locals. Though the Arab traveller Suleiman visited Sandwip in the eighth century, it was during the Turko–Afghan period that large-scale Islamization occurred through the conversion of the local lower-caste Hindu population. The Muslim population was also boosted by the settlement of large numbers of ex-soldiers of the Mughal army and their descendants, who had been pensioned off with land grants in the region. The Muslims were linguistically divided into 'Chittagong' and 'Sandwip' sub-groups, according to the Bengali dialect they used. Mostly they were poor peasants.[27] Shared heterodox customs between lower-caste Hindus and their Muslim neighbours created zones of social interaction where identity based on religious community consciousness was suspended and blurred. Worshippers at the dargah (shrine) of the twelve Aulia saints came from the ranks of those classified as Hindus as well as Muslims.[28] Before the advent of the British, most of the zamindars of Sandwip were also Muslims. After the British conquest of Bengal, the few who survived the colonial land revenue administration, the Permanent Settlement of 1793, were reduced to the status of talukdars.[29]

The vicissitudes of landownership and tenurial rights under the colonial regime allowed a section of the landed population to prosper, while others sank. The contrasting fortunes of Muzaffar's father and his father-in-law indicated this trend. The Chittagong, Tippera and Noakhali sub-region included an independent peasantry, comprised of occupancy rayats (peasants) and tenure-holders.[30] It has been argued that their regional preponderance made the middle peasantry of Noakhali 'politically active'. They were 'poor but independent peasants' who 'enjoyed the greatest amount of freedom' and 'were in the forefront of the leadership in most peasant movements'.[31] The middle peasants of Sandwip harboured numerous grievances against the absentee zamindars who operated through unpopular agents, and periodically fended off collection and enhancement of rent. In 1890, Courjon, a European who had purchased half of the government estates by auction, tried to forcibly impose illegal cesses and assess land-holdings without the consent of the tenants. The rayats, irrespective of religious affiliations, united under the leadership of Munshi Chand Mian, a local Muslim landowner, who was instantly catapulted to the position of a praja[32] leader. The united resistance forced Courjon to retreat.[33]

Chand Mian became Muzaffar's father-in-law in 1907.[34] The power, property, prosperity and respect this man came to enjoy locally contrasted with the picture of failure presented by Muzaffar Ahmad's father, Mansoor Ali. The two men represented two facets of the Bengali Muslim gentry in Sandwip. Mansoor Ali's wife and Muzaffar's mother, Chuna Bibi, came from a family with minor aristocratic claims. Mansoor Ali was born in 1827, and was educated in Bengali and Persian in keeping with the system of education prevalent[35] during the transition from Persian to English as the official language of government.[36] In the Sandwip law courts, Persian was still used as late as 1883.[37] Muzaffar's father studied law and was examined in Bengali. He practised at the Munsif's Court in Sandwip.[38] Muzaffar writes while he was still a child, his father, a man of advanced age, had virtually retired. He was mostly at home during Muzaffar's childhood and by the time he died in 1905 at the age of 78, his health had broken down completely; Muzaffar was then in his mid-teens.[39]

Legal wrangles were common. Litigation over landed property and rent, a by-product of the Permanent Settlement, made law a viable profession even in remote corners of rural Bengal such as Sandwip.[40] From Muzaffar's descriptions, it would seem that Mansoor Ali's contemporaries in the legal profession could use the existing conditions to their advantage and acquire substantial landed property. Mansoor Ali failed in this respect and deepened the 'indescribable poverty' of the family. Ownership of a tiny plot of land afforded a precarious claim to gentility though not elite status. Besides, all connections with cultivation had stopped in Muzaffar's family while he was still a boy. He would recall that during the time he had stopped going to school, he had nothing to do. He could not even engage in tilling the family land.[41]

Escape Routes

Muzaffar was the youngest child of his parents. His father was 62 at the time of his birth.[42] Muzaffar belonged to the generation born in the island when it was undergoing a demographic boom.[43] Being the youngest had its disadvantages. Family fortunes could not be relied upon even to gain access to education. The situation was possibly a little better for his three brothers before him. All three had acquired enough education to attain lower-grade white-collar jobs available to lower middle-class men in the districts. Munshi Mahabbat Ali was a lawyer's clerk. Moulavi Maqbul Ahmad was a teacher educated at the Calcutta Madrasa. Munshi Khurshid Alam worked in a zamindari estate.[44] Mahabbat Ali was the closest to their father's profession. None of them earned enough to improve the material conditions of the family.

At a significant period of his childhood, Muzaffar's family could not afford formal education for the youngest son. Muzaffar had enrolled at Sandwip Middle English School. He was studying in the Bengali division of the upper primary section when he was forced to leave. His father did not even have the money to pay for his 'meagre school fees'.[45] The distance between Musapur and Sandwip Town also obstructed his education. The school was located in Sandwip Town, the administrative centre of the island.[46] Since he was a child, he could not travel to school alone. There was no one to take him there.[47] This indicates that Sandwip did not have a developed system of transport either. Muzaffar was to claim that no one was particularly worried when his education was disrupted. However, from the same account it would seem that, in his own way, Mansoor Ali had tried to educate his youngest son. Mansoor Ali's early concern for the development of Muzaffar's linguistic abilities increased Muzaffar's competence in Bengali and helped him to emerge as a writer later in life. Like all other Muslim boys of his age and background, he was taken as an infant to the local mosque where a *moulavi* had guided him to write a line from the Koran in Arabic. Soon afterwards, Mansoor Ali introduced Muzaffar to the Bengali alphabet by making him read one of the most popular nineteenth-century primers, *Shishu-Shikhya* (Child Education) by Pundit Madanmohan Tarkalankar. The practice continued at school where Bengali was his medium of learning. Muzaffar did not abandon the study of language even after leaving school. He avidly read Bengali books and periodicals he came across. The periodicals also printed articles encouraging English education. After a while, he was influenced by others of his age to join a local *madrasa* (Muslim religious school) where he started learning Arabic and Persian, thus developing a taste for Persian poetry.[48]

It seems the breakdown of paternal authority within the family led to a loosening of the family's hold over the youngest son. After his father's death, Muzaffar had expressed his desire to study in a school where English was taught. He wrote to his brother, Moulavi Maqbul Ahmad, who taught in a village in Khulna district and occasionally helped him with money. Maqbul Ahmad's silence prompted him to take drastic steps. Muzaffar ran away from home. His aim was to earn and save enough to return to school. The escape enlarged his geographic knowledge, and indicated his need to break away from life and location in a remote island. During his rural sojourn, he was often dependent on the generosity and communitarian spirit of chance acquaintances. A Hindu court *chaprashi* (peon) took pity on him and paid his fare as he did not possess the means to pay for a steamship ticket. From the island, Muzaffar made his way to the Noakhali mainland, where he re-registered at a *madrasa*. After travelling through coastal areas, he crossed the border of Noakhali and entered the neighbouring Bakherganj district. According to Muzaffar's account, even the 'slightly educated' from Noakhali could teach in the 'illiterate villages' there. He stayed at a Bakherganj village with a Muslim peasant family and imparted rudimentary knowledge of the

Bengali alphabet to boys of various age-groups. He was working in this village when Maqbul arrived to take him home. At the time, Muzaffar was thinking of joining one of the high schools in Bakherganj. He was promised that he would be sent back to school.[49]

In 1906, at the 'age of sixteen or seventeen', he returned to his former school, renamed as Sandwip Kargill High School. His linguistic skills helped him to re-adapt. Despite the considerable age difference, his classmates came to accept him. Muzaffar observes: 'The fact that the small boys let me sit in class, and did not throw me out with a whack behind the head, was because I had a far better grasp over Bengali than they did.'[50] In order to develop his linguistic skills, he was forced to read Hindu *bhadralok* writers who were architects of Bengali prose. Muzaffar initially refused to read Bankimchandra Chattopadhyay, the nineteenth-century literary giant and leading ideologue of Hindu revivalism. He was persuaded to do so by his friend Abdul Ahad, a local Muslim youth, who insisted it was impossible for a Bengali to ignore Bankim. Though suspicious of Bankim's ideology, Muzaffar eventually came to read his works.[51] Language and literature were beginning to connect him with the wider social goals of the Bengali intelligentsia.

Proprietorial Vocabularies
The authority enjoyed by Bankim as the greatest Bengali novelist, even over his critics such as Muzaffar, suggests that linguistic skills, including the vernacular, acted as conduits of proprietorial aspirations related to the fashioning of ethno-linguistic identities of the Bengali intelligentsia. The process of transforming languages into hegemonic tools had started from the nineteenth century, revealing a complex engagement of the western educated intellectuals with English as the principal vehicle of colonial power/knowledge and a simultaneous attachment towards vernacular modernization.[52] It was hoped English would open doors to the kind of knowledge, vocation and enterprise that would equip the intelligentsia to equal, and if possible go beyond, the colonial masters. Modernized Bengali, in turn, could become the tool of the intelligentsia to weave hegemonic ideologies facilitating the cooption of materially disunited and diversely placed social classes and class segments into unitary ideological and cultural frameworks. These frameworks combined notions of indigenous entrepreneurship with social identities receptive to the growth of local industry, and projected them as solutions to mass poverty and the travails of the educated underemployed or unemployed.

His grasp over Bengali led Muzaffar to the world of literary productions and generated an ambition in him to become a writer. In 1910, he shifted to Noakhali District School. He successfully sat for his Matriculation Examinations and finished secondary education from this institution.[53] It seems the boundaries of Muzaffar's local patriotism were further extended during these years. Though Sandwip remained his concern, he became more aware of the district it was a part of. His earlier escape from home had already set the stage for this broader identification. While living in Noakhali town, two of his essays appeared in *Prabasi*, a leading Calcutta-based literary journal. In an article published in 1910, he highlighted the beneficial properties of *punnal*, an oil-producing tree commonly found in Sandwip. He hoped its qualities would be commercially explored so that the inhabitants of the island could profit from it and prosper economically.[54] The subject of and response to his article reflected a local patriotic feeling among a section of the Noakhali intelligentsia. They were expressing their social identity not just in communal but also in ethno-linguistic terms. Thus the 'lucidity' and 'elegance' of Muzaffar's prose earned him the appreciation of the Hindu *bhadralok* of Noakhali. A younger contemporary, Gopal Haldar, recalled that his father, a local intellectual, praised Muzaffar's article in these very terms.[55] Muzaffar was emerging as a local boy with promise.

Two years later, his second article, 'A Successful Musalman student', was published in *Modern Review*. Its sister publication *Prabasi* carried the Bengali version of the same piece. The article displayed Muzaffar's faith in the ability of his island to make a mark in the wider world. It was a brief outline of the career of M. Obeidullah from Sandwip, one of the two Muslim Indians with a degree in geology from a European university. Muzaffar highlighted Obeidullah's impoverished yet respectable family background,[56] characteristics they shared. This article reflected the aspirations of the local intelligentsia to gain access to the knowledge-systems of the world, seen as avenues of social empowerment in the urban metropolitan centres. It is not surprising that Muzaffar went away from Noakhali the following year. He made his way briefly to another district town and soon transferred to a college in Calcutta.

The social dynamics of Muzaffar's education in the rural environment resulted in his physical shift from the countryside to the city. The stages of his migration to the city were intertwined with insufficient access to colonial higher education in the districts. 'Traditional' education was not what he was seeking. However, exposure to Arabic and Persian instilled the desire in him to learn more about 'Islamic civilization'.[57] Little of his earlier knowledge remained with him. When he took stock of his linguistic abilities in the city after failing his I.A. exams, he realized he could read classical Persian only with great effort, and that he had not succeeded in mastering Arabic, his second language at school and college. He could read Urdu books and make some sense of them, but the exercise took up a great deal of time. He had an average knowledge of English, enabling him to read and understand books. Bengali was the only language he could write with some competence.[58]

Despite this net result, the social implications of his linguistic training reveal the contradictions embedded in the world he left behind. The rural environment produced, yet could not retain, those members of the intelligentsia in search of higher education, greater exposure to the world and white-collar jobs, which would help them escape poverty and obscurity. The literary promise recognized by others in Muzaffar's prose underlined a middle-class desire for recognition. The subject matters of his early essays focused on this aspect. The spirit of enterprise in 'Punnal Briksha' and the high praise for academic merit in 'A Successful Musalman Student' implied a search for bourgeois modernity. Since the outlet to such a world was restricted in Sandwip and Noakhali, those in the rural areas who had the potential to emerge as its ideological architects had no option but to move to the city, the showcase of colonial capital.

Later in his life, Muzaffar would contest notions of gentility as well as the power of colonial capital. As a young man, however, he sought a vision of prosperity that capitalist enterprise generated. This spirit prompted him to support the economic programme of the Swadeshi Movement. Though an impoverished student, he tried to buy the more expensive Indian-made cloth from the 'Swadeshi Stores' owned by a Hindu *bhadralok* in Noakhali town, whenever his means permitted. He also boycotted foreign commodities as much as possible. Yet his relationship with anti-colonial nationalism was already ambiguous. He could identify with the nationalist economic programme, while the Hindu revivalist ideology of the *bhadralok* leadership alienated him. He stayed away from the anti-partition movement as well as the Muslim opposition it had triggered. The fear of Hindu Bengali proprietors that the partition of 1905 would lead to an end of their domination over predominantly small, marginal and landless Muslim peasants was all too palpable. Muzaffar himself was not free from the influence of Islamic revivalism. He was 'a devout Muslim' during this period. He attended meetings guided by the vision of a political Islam, demanding 'special privileges'.[59]

Intersections
Muzaffar stood at the intersection of different political currents, which contradicted and interacted with each other at the same time. Ethno-linguistic, communal and nationalist visions of social reconstruction clashed and combined to generate aspirations of upward social mobility. These found an echo in the expansion and contraction of solidarities based on the ownership of property regardless of religion. Local patriotism and the logic of

self-improvement in such a context could be read as manifestations of proto-
capitalist thinking. The logic of agrarian improvement and 'improvement
literature' depended on the ethic of profit, productivity and property.[60] They
represented a set of values shared by Hindu and Muslim respectable folk
alike, and arguably, also by the impoverished as well as prosperous rural
proprietors, finding expression in widespread and popular support for movements against 'absentee' landlords. In Muzaffar's immediate social setting,
the permanently settled landlords were perceived as parasitic outsiders
intent on extracting local resources and obstructing 'rural development'.
This attitude contained the seeds of the *praja* (tenant) movement, led mainly
by the Muslim landed proprietors of East Bengal.

In all probability, had Muzaffar remained in the districts, his life would
have been no different from those who came from a similar background.
He would have pursued the professions open to those from the lower gentry. He could have found employment similar to that of his brothers or his
friends from the Noakhali District School. The politics and aspirations of
the rural intelligentsia were being expressed through a 'Bengali Muslim'
identity.[61] Such identity-thinking held out myriad possibilities, and was to
combine variously with anti-colonial, anti-zamindari and sectional movements in keeping with the shifting relationships between colonialism, landed
property and communal consolidations. Muzaffar could have explored any
and each of the available political directions. Men like his brothers were at
the forefront of many of the emergent agrarian political movements. The
material constraints in Muzaffar's immediate environment propelled him
towards the city. In the vortex of metropolitan upheavals, his life would
take a completely different turn. A new political focus, previously absent,
was going to evolve.

In the City

Why did he travel to the city? In 1913, Muzaffar Ahmad was just one more
in the sea of migrants. They crowded the urban space that was Calcutta in
search of a better life. A contemporary, Abul Mansoor Ahmad, visiting the
city nine years later, regarded the journey as a necessary step for aspiring
writers keen on developing contacts in the centre of the Bengali literary
world. While making acquaintances among writers and literary activists
prominent in his milieu, he came across Muzaffar Ahmad.[62] Though Muzaffar had arrived with the same ambition as Abul Mansoor, he gradually
ceased to display a strong attachment to his rural origins. Though a regular
visitor to the city till the partition, Abul Mansoor's political life as a *praja*
leader prevented a severance of social ties with rural Bengal. For Muzaffar,
despite his periodic absences, the city was to become the centre of his social

and political existence. He remained in touch with the milieu he had left behind. Yet it was no longer his world.

Streets Unknown

The familiar, unlit, relatively less crowded, sparsely built villages and district towns suddenly gave way to an alien, luminous, over-populated and densely constructed urban social space. This sharp change in the physical form of the material location could be experientially bewildering and visually staggering. Civic infrastructure gave Calcutta its distinct metropolitan features. By 1913, Calcutta had regained its status as the capital of reunified Bengal. It was no longer the administrative centre of British India. As if to compensate for the fall from its highly ambiguous pre-eminence as the centre of colonial rule, massive projects were being undertaken to spruce up its image as the leading centre of colonial capital. Even this position was to be taken away after the First World War.[63] But in the pre-war and inter-war years, Calcutta was still a showpiece of colonial urban development.

The pride and high hopes of the colonial municipal planners, in 1912–13, in the 'capital of the newly created Presidency of Bengal' found reflection in the following pronouncement: 'Its trade, commerce, industries and its civic amenities have all developed during the year and there seems no reason for doubting that its prosperity will continue or for apprehending that it may forfeit its claim to be the first city in India.' Among the civic facilities expanded in the course of 1912–13, the report focused on the lighting system of the city. Proudly announced was the 'illuminating power' of the 443 new gaslights, bringing the total number of street-lamps to 10,502. The proposal to instal electric lights 'in certain selected streets' was also considered.[64]

City-lights beckoned, though their dazzle could not hide the contradictions of urban existence. Uncertainty immediately engulfed the impoverished migrant upon arrival. 'The transfer of the capital' from Calcutta to Delhi in 1911 was drying up 'major sources of government jobs and patronage'.[65] The racial hierarchy of a colonized city produced its own paradoxes. The groups and classes populating the city were concentrated in different geographic zones, sharpening the existing social divisions. The neighbourhoods lying to the north and the east of the city constituted the 'native' quarters. This area of 'intense density', a maze of narrow alleys and main roads, housed principal Indian-owned markets, shops and business centres. The city-centre, constituting Chowringhee, Dalhousie Square and Park Street, as well as areas lying to its south and west, were well-planned with wide roads. European-owned banks, government and public offices, leading hotels, and spacious residences of European business and administrative personnel were located in these zones. While the densely populated north was overwhelmingly Indian in composition, the 'sparsely inhabited' south was predominantly 'European in character'.[66] Claims by civic authorities of developing the infrastructure were underwritten by hidden disparities in resource allocation. The lighting system, occupying such a pride of place in the Municipal Report of 1912–13, and representing the technological innovations associated with the interwoven structures of the colonial and the modern, demonstrated a spatial hierarchy shaped directly by the priorities of colonial capital. Unreliable gaslights were installed, generating complaints 'particularly' in the northern wards inhabited by Indians that year. As for the proposal to introduce electricity, the area selected was Store Road in Ballygunge, a European neighbourhood in south Calcutta. It was supplied with free electric lights for three months as part of an 'experimental demonstration'.[67]

The civic infrastructure was also not adequate to deal with the substantial and increasing number of deaths from epidemics. Plague, dengue, malaria, smallpox, diphtheria, cholera, tuberculosis and respiratory diseases claimed their share of victims. However, the authorities did try to facilitate better funeral arrangements that year. The dead were classified and care was taken to dispose of their bodies according to religion. Various alterations and improvements of the cremation and burial grounds were effected. Iron railings replaced the old boundary wall of the Gori Goriban Cemetary in Park Circus. A small piece of low land within it was raised and made available for fresh graves.[68] It was here that Muzaffar Ahmad was to be buried sixty years later.

The contemporary images of the city were also associated with impending social catastrophe in various forms. Newspaper reports spoke of traffic accidents, an indication that the ongoing 'transport revolution' made city streets unsafe:

> walking in the Calcutta streets is gradually becoming full of danger. An enormous increase in the number of motor cars in the city is leading to almost a daily occurrence of fatal and serious accidents. In some cases the drivers of the cars running over people are punished in law-courts, but most of them are never detected and punished. Then, besides the motor cars, there are bullock carts, carriages drawn by horses and so forth. It is, therefore, easily conceivable how difficult and dangerous the Calcutta streets have become for pedestrians. The attention of the Municipal Commissioners is drawn to the matter.[69]

Other dangers also lurked in the street-corners. On the eve of the First World War and during the early years of the war, assaults on pedestrians by drunken European soldiers and robberies by organized gangs were also reported in Indian newspapers. A fracas between college students and European soldiers in the Sealdah Railway Station in 1914 led to demands for a government investigation.[70]

Reports reflected the growing involvement of the Bengal intelligentsia with economic and political issues that were coming to the forefront with the outbreak of war. As the colony was drawn more and more into an imperialist war effort, gloomy and dejected forecasts of a regional famine were advanced in a climate of spiralling food prices and unemployment, making way for regular news of scarcity and starvation deaths. The mainstream nationalist leadership had extended its support to the imperial war effort in the hope of future political reforms. No attempt was made to channel popular war-time grievances against the hardships imposed by colonialism into an anti-colonial mass movement. As the conditions kept deteriorating, issues related to the poor received increased focus from sections of the intelligentsia. The attitude towards the poor ranged from a liberal–humanist, paternalistic and genuinely felt 'compassionate protectionist' concern, to impulses of undisguised hatred, terror and loathing. A palpable anxiety centring on proprietorial control over society could be detected. Middle-class voices of fear stridently argued that sections of the criminalized urban poor were about to take over the streets and demanded police protection. At the same time, the colonial state could not be relied upon to uphold justice. An extension of police powers to suppress openly rebellious members of the intelligentsia was condemned. There was outrage over racist attacks, including fatal beatings inflicted on domestic servants and workmen by European officials, officially treated as 'accidental' deaths from 'ruptured spleen'. Anti-colonial sentiments were also expressed on what was perceived as the arbitrary detention of nationalist revolutionaries from a Hindu *bhadralok* background and of pan-Islamic preachers under the war-time security acts. Outside Nakhoda Mosque, the most important monument to Islamic worship in Calcutta, the police picked up Maulavi Imamuddin, a pan-Islamist described as a 'warrior' of faith, in late 1916. The Muslim press claimed that he 'had no political interests whatsoever' and that his indefinite internment 'will produce a baneful influence on the public mind'. The British surveillance and policing networks, throughout the war, were accused of manufacturing suspects to justify the repression of political dissent, officially branded as 'extremism', 'sedition' and 'terror'. Press censorship, imposed as a strategy to prevent anti-colonial opinions from spreading, also attracted strong criticism.[71] These extraordinary war-time social and political anxieties were to merge and pave the way for greater, though temporary, post-war solidarity among the middle and upper classes of Indian society, despite the community identities that had emerged under colonial rule in Bengal.

The configuration and reconfiguration of social classes and class fractions among the Indian population created highly differentiated social identities. They were to leave their imprint on city politics and assume institutional characteristics at various levels. The complicated relationship between
social hierarchy and sectional configurations, phenomena made acute by
the colonial circumstance, shaped the multilayered political culture of Calcutta. Popular politics reflected the volatile connections between nationalism, working-class protests and communal hostilities.

The Flame and the Flag of Islam

Various interconnected tendencies acted as the social stimulus for popular-
izing political Islam in such an environment: official policy, especially the
politics of colonial census, the complexities of mainstream nationalism which
freely borrowed ideological symbols of Hindu revivalist politics, and competition with different ranks of the Hindu community over the restricted
resources available to Indians in a colonial milieu. During the second decade of the last century, Muslim identity politics displayed a confusion of
social attitudes. The ideological fluidity accommodated sentiments both
anti-imperialist and sectional in character. However, during and immediately after the war, the sectional components of identity-thinking were largely
superseded by the widespread grievance against colonial rule. The resurgence of pan-Islamist politics in the second decade was directly linked with
increased western incursions into Turkish territory. This influenced rising
anti-colonial feelings among Muslim populations of the colonial world.
The change in and struggle over the leadership of the 'community' reflected
this political shift in the years immediately preceding the war.

The reunification of Bengal as an administrative unit in 1912 had meant
withdrawal of the social power and privileges the Muslim proprietorial classes
had temporarily come to experience in East Bengal from 1905, resulting in
acute political resentment not only towards the colonial government but
also towards the loyalist, mostly Urdu-speaking aristocratic leaders. The
capture of the leadership of the All-India Muslim League in 1912 by pan-
Islamist and anti-loyalist forces, and the Lucknow Pact of 1916 between
the Muslim League and the Congress (to share seats in the elected bodies
and exert pressure on the government to cede greater power to Indians after
the war), contributed to the popularization of anti-government militant
politics among the city Muslims. A.K. Fazlul Haq and Abul Kalam Azad,
new leaders respectively representing the Bengali and Urdu-speaking intelligentsia, were closely aligned with these developments. The different shades
of Islamist politics they represented ranged from constitutional opposition
to the government, as in Haq's case, to revolutionary anti-colonial resist-

ance, as evident from Azad's actions. During the war, arrests of Indian revolutionaries, mainly from a Bengali Hindu middle-class background, and of pan-Islamists who opposed and tried to subvert the British war efforts, generated extensive joint campaigns for civil liberties. After the war, the Khilafat and Non-Cooperation Movements became the vehicles of this unity.[72] For a small though significant minority, participating and supporting these anti-colonial mass movements evolved into a rejection of the political authority and ideology of pan-Islamist and nationalist leaders. From anti-authoritarian communitarianism they would arrive at communism. 'Reshuffled' in the course of the war and reconfigured during the post-war, anti-colonial mass upsurge, their politics would undergo a radical transformation.

In and Around College Street

Anti-colonial political Islam dominated the world of the urban Muslim intelligentsia when Muzaffar arrived in the city. Initially, between 1913 and 1919, the social milieu in which he lived in Calcutta made him a part of the student community. He also developed closer and increasingly deeper links with the wider, mainly Muslim, middle-class intellectual circles. These literary associations, rather than the student community, were to become the focus of his social existence in the city.

Though Muzaffar's student life in the city was cut short, he became familiar with a mode of social existence and politics associated with the young intelligentsia. A constant interplay between the world of the intelligentsia and larger political developments could be registered throughout this period. Though not everyone was an active participant, politics was a vehicle of social aspirations and interactions between different sections. Students, as young members of the urban intelligentsia, displayed vigorous political interests. From 1905, students from a Hindu *bhadralok* background became visible in nationalist politics. The process was followed by increased recruitment of this segment into the nationalist revolutionary networks and acts of individual terror against European administrators and their Indian collaborators.[73] Muzaffar was acquainted with this form of politics. One of his most prominent classmates in the Noakhali District School had been initiated into revolutionary nationalism and had served time in prison.[74] A climate of admiration and a certain degree of support among students enabled the nationalist revolutionaries to function. The student community sheltered and provided them with new recruits. Neighbourhoods in and around College Street, a central thoroughfare of north Calcutta, provided the physical spaces where different forms of anti-colonial dissent emerged and were sustained. The student lodgings, college residences, top colonial educational institutions for Indians such as Presidency College and Calcutta

University, various institutions linked with the public activities of the intelligentsia as well as College Square, a swimming pool and park, were utilized
to host meetings and discussions.

A concentration of the literati also made the locality a flourishing centre
of the book trade. Apart from the offices of most booksellers and publishers
in the city, including the journals Muzaffar Ahmad came to be associated
with, the second-hand book market was one of the highlights. While the
established booksellers and publishers mainly came from a Bengali Hindu
middle and upper-class background, poor Muslims monopolized the used-
books trade. They would spread their wares on jute cloths and sacks on the
College Street pavements, where middle-class clients came and browsed
through page after page for hours. These traders, and the book-binders, a
profession also dominated by Muslims, created a daily social link between
the urban working class and the Calcutta intelligentsia.[75] The burgeoning
underworld, consisting of hoodlums and pickpockets, with a proportion of
unemployed Muslim working-class people who had been forced to turn to
crime, also enjoyed a presence in this area.[76] Volatile and riot-prone in times
of acute hardship, sections of the so-called criminals could also respond to
the appeal of large-scale anti-state upsurge, as became increasingly evident
in the post-war period.

Student life, migration and the search for the security of a collective
existence in an otherwise unfamiliar environment indicated the dialectic
between *Gemeinschaft* (community of shared values) and *Gesellschaft* (civil
society) in the city.[77] The communities associated with migrants, minorities
and marginalized segments represented a complex mosaic of identity and
difference rooted in the urban social matrix. Out of the contraction and
expansion of various types of communities and networks, intersecting collectivities were being continuously constituted, reconstituted and dissolved.
The migrant-outsiders, who carried these values to the city, still related to
the urban space as their temporary abode.[78] The metropolis was the 'world',
an impersonal environment, where one tried to make a living and improve
one's situation, forging non-familial yet close bonds and solidarities in
order to survive socially. The line of demarcation between the public and
the private, between the external material spaces and gendered domesticity,
could not be maintained here. 'Home' represented a remote rural corner far
away. The rural–urban dichotomy faced by migrants increased their sense of
isolation in the city, and made them search for collectives based on religious, ethno-linguistic as well as regional loyalties.

A vast majority of migrant students stayed together in lodgings on the
basis of these linkages, often sharing with non-students who were part of
the same identity structure. The maze of alleys, bylanes and streets connecting College Street with the surrounding areas of north Calcutta were the

heart of mess life. Wealth and social status divided the mess communities. Lower middle-class students rented the stairwell of a rooming house as a place to sleep at night. A sizeable section of the migrant student community came from East Bengal. Muzaffar was part of this inflow. Religious distinctions and their minority status within the student community often made it difficult for Muslim students from the Bengal countryside as well as other provinces to find suitable living space. The dearth of accommodation could force Muslim students to give up their studies in Calcutta and return home. In 1912, the year before Muzaffar came to the city, the plight of Muslim students who were refused admission to Calcutta colleges and hostels generated controversy. The lack of housing was highlighted in particular. Hindu landlords and mess-keepers often refused to let out their premises. But this was a wider social problem reflecting the communal prejudices of Hindu property-owners that persisted over the years. Some less prejudiced and economically pragmatic Bengali Hindu landlords were willing to rent out their property to Muslims. In 1918, the Bengal Muslim Literary Society, an association Muzaffar Ahmad had joined, was able to rent a portion of a house owned by a Bengali Hindu medical practitioner.[79] A significant section was too poor to rent a room, and earned board and lodging as private tutors, staying with the middle-class Muslim families employing them. Muzaffar stayed with a family continuously for four years during the war, in a predominantly Muslim neighbourhood close to College Street. However he was also familiar with shared lodgings since many of his friends stayed in such accommodation. The Muslim student lodgings in Mirzapur Street, connected to College Street, often hosted the meetings of the Literary Society, indicating a presence of Muslim students within the mess system.[80]

This was Muzaffar Ahmad's material environment when he arrived in Calcutta and enrolled at Bangabashi College for a pre-graduation course. Bangabashi was part of a cluster of colleges affiliated to Calcutta University, set up at the initiative of the Bengali Hindu intelligentsia to provide greater educational opportunities to the increasing number of Bengali middle-class students. These were self-supporting institutions, dependent on tuition fees. Bangabashi was one of the largest colleges and encouraged its students to engage in socially oriented activities. It had a debating club founded in 1909, a drama club, a society for the support of poor students and a night school for disseminating education among local working-class people. Unlike some other institutions, the college admitted Muslims. Muslim lower-middle-class students were attracted to institutions like these because of their low fee structure. However, the Muslims formed a tiny minority within the student-body. Among more than 1,000 students enrolled in 1914, only 27 were Muslims.[81] Muzaffar was one of them.

Having failed to qualify in the pre-graduation examination, Muzaffar

College Square

Coffee House on College Street

gave up his studies. This was not unusual among Muslim and indigent students. The percentage of success was low among Muslim students, and poverty prevented the unsuccessful ones from continuing. A government survey published in 1916 showed that out of the 399 students who replied to the questionnaire, '87 had given up their studies because of poverty rather than any other single reason'.[82] Later, Muzaffar helped fellow-writer Kazi Imdadul Haq to publish the fictional account of a young drop-out whose life closely mirrored the author's own and that of others around him.[83] The eponymous hero of the unfinished novel *Abdullah*, an impoverished Bengali Muslim intellectual with traces of gentility, loses his father at an early age and leaves *madrasa* education in search of western learning. Having failed the secondary school-leaving examination, the unemployed youth wishes to devote himself to the reformation of Bengali Muslim society through the spread of English and female education. His secular, modernizing impulses as well as his inability to procure a job are contrary to his mother's expectations, and invite her disapproval and incomprehension.[84] Though the novel was apparently printed to better acquaint the liberal Hindu *bhadralok* intellectuals with their Muslim counterpart, it was a literary projection of the aspirations and frustrations of the young Bengali Muslim intelligentsia of which Muzaffar had become a part.[85]

Though Muzaffar was a student for only two years, College Street and its surrounding neighbourhoods, associated with the intelligentsia as well as

People's Corner, one among several bookshops in the College Street area

subterranean and prominent political currents, remained his regular haunt. During 1919–20, while residing at the Literary Society office at College Street, he became a habitué of the Book Company. This shop opened in College Square in 1917, and quickly outmanoeuvred older, established European-owned book firms like Thacker–Spinck as the largest importer of foreign books, including banned literature. The owner, Girindranath Mitra, was always welcoming, even though the shop had begun to attract police attention for its stock of potentially seditious literature and its association with early communists like Muzaffar and nationalist revolutionaries. Some of these revolutionaries even secured employment there. The shop was also well known as a meeting-point of Bengali writers and intellectuals from diverse social backgrounds and literary circles.[86]

The spaces traversed and created by the intelligentsia continued to provide the realms of social intercourse for Muzaffar, constituting the public sphere where he circulated. This environment, integrally connected with anti-colonial as well as sectional forms of political consciousness, increased Muzaffar's ambivalence towards nationalist politics. In an age of greater Hindu–Muslim cooperation and widespread Muslim antipathy towards the British government, he felt drawn towards anti-imperialist movements. The Indian National Congress had extended its support to the government with the onset of war. The nationalist revolutionaries comprised the only branch of the nationalist movement not to have done so. They were trying to subvert the war effort and thereby weaken colonial rule in India. Muzaffar's location made him quite close to their field of recruitment. Besides, their individual courage in the face of police torture and state repression made them the heroes of contemporary middle-class youth. But inspired by Hindu revivalist ideology, they often refused to include Muslims. Members of the Anushilan Samiti were openly antagonistic to Muslims. The Jugantar group was less so but, like Anushilan, saturated with Hindu imagery of nationhood.[87] Muzaffar wrote:

> Considering my mental condition in the second decade of this century and the romance that lay in the terrorist movement, it was not impossible for me to join the terrorist revolutionary camp, but there were . . . obstacles. . . . The terrorist revolutionaries drew their inspiration from Bankimchandra Chattopadhyay's Anandamath. This book was filled with [Hindu] communal ill-will. . . . The fundamental message of the book lay in Bankimchandra's invocation *Vande-Mataram*. The song contains the lines:
>
> Thou, as strength in arms of men
> Thou, as faith, in hearts, dost reign . . .
> For, thou hast ten-armed Durga's power . . .
>
> How could a monotheist Muslim youth utter this invocation?[88]

In nationalist political culture, the country was synonymous with a mother-goddess. Since idolatrous and Hindu-chauvinist symbols dominated all branches of nationalism, they culturally excluded Muzaffar and other Muslims. Muzaffar was unable to commit himself totally to this form of anti-colonial politics. However, wider anti-imperialist forums and mobilizations continued to attract him.[89] Instead of direct political engagement, Muzaffar gradually turned to full-time cultural activism.

Literary Activism

While he was a student, like most lone migrants in an alien environment, Muzaffar looked for some kind of an association. He was already a published author and soon turned to literary circles. At the initiative of a group of students like himself, an association had been set up in 1911: the Bengal Muslim Literary Society (*Bangiya Musalman Sahitya Samiti*), devoted to popularization and strengthening of Bengali literature among the Bengali Muslims.[90] This indicates that awareness of being part of a minority intelligentsia, in a region where the Bengali intelligentsia was overwhelmingly high-caste Hindu in composition, prompted the formation of this society. Shunned by the ideological and social prejudices of Hindu upper and middle-class society, the small group of Muslim intelligentsia in Calcutta formed community-based associations of their own. Such associations indicated a reactive desire for religious consolidation along exclusivist lines, bred intra-class competition with Hindus, and became platforms for segments that were better off to advance hegemonic claims vis-à-vis the community. But their appearance also indicated the isolation of disprivileged minority intellectuals. Similar organizations developed among Muslim workers also.

The emergence of the Bengal Muslim Literary Society also signalled the awareness of being a minority within a minority, producing the need to separate from Urdu-dominated literary culture. A mess run by a group of Muslim students living at Choku Khanshama Lane acted as its office.[91] The location itself was significant. Choku Khanshama Lane was one of the oldest streets in Calcutta and one of the many named after butlers (*khanshama*), a profession dominated by working-class Muslims from the earliest days of city formation. From the late nineteenth century, the Municipality became uncomfortable with streets named after lower-class individuals who were among the earliest residents of Calcutta and started changing these names.[92] Choku Khanshama Lane was one of the few to escape this zeal for gentrification. Like Muzaffar, the Literary Society changed address several times during the 1910s. The office would later shift to Mirzapur Street and from there to 32 College Street. Muzaffar was also to move in there during 1919, as the society became the focus of his activities.

Though the Bengal Muslim Literary Society aimed to work within the

Bengali Muslim literate community, it developed a plural character. The organization offered membership to Bengali Hindu intellectuals interested in promoting the Bengali language among Muslims in a province where the majority of Bengali speakers were officially classified as followers of Islam. It acted as a launching pad for budding Bengali Muslim authors. The ethno-linguistic cultural politics of this society made it contribute to, rather than create, a separate space outside the existing Bengali literary scene dominated by Bengali Hindu writers. It was therefore affiliated to the *Bangiya Sahitya Parishat*, the federation of literary societies in Bengal.

When Muzaffar joined the society in 1913, it was in disarray. He con-tributed to its revival alongside prominent Bengali Muslim writers and poli-tical activists who were well known within the Calcutta literary circuit. Soon, Muzaffar became a full-time literary activist. Many leading writers from a Bengali Hindu background, including an author who never donated his novels on principle, gave their works to the society's reading room. Work in the Literary Society helped Muzaffar develop connections with Muslim writers, journalists and political activists, as well as members of the Bengali Hindu intelligentsia. A minor figure associated with this society, Abdur Rezzaq Khan, became his first socialist colleague in the early 1920s. He also met his first recruit, Abdul Halim, in the society's reading room in 1922. A colleague from a Hindu *bhadralok* background who helped out with work in the Literary Society, suggested a visit to a nearby bookstore in 1921 when Muzaffar was searching for socialist literature.

Since this was voluntary work, Muzaffar survived by taking up various temporary jobs throughout the war years. Unable to retain any employ-ment for long, he was forced to shift from one to the next: a *madrasa* teacher, a slaughterhouse clerk, a Home Department translator and finally a full-time journalist. While he was a student, during a summer vacation, he taught at a *madrasa* in the Kidderpore Dock area. No doubt, his earlier *madrasa* education in the village proved useful here. He also worked as a private tutor, teaching young boys from Muslim families. In the course of his career as a tutor in Calcutta, he stayed with the family of a nineteenth-century Urdu writer, Munshi Alimuddin. Alimuddin had already died and Muzaffar never knew him. His family still occupied the same house at 3 Gumghar Lane, at the heart of Chandni, a buzzing Muslim commercial area close to College Street. It was an address where he was always warmly welcomed. Later, when he became a political activist and a police suspect, the house provided both refuge and cover. Muzaffar also worked briefly at the office of the Inspector of Schools. Most of these jobs were probably secured through his acquaintance with members of the Literary Society. Maulavi Abdul Karim, the elderly president of the Bengal Muslim Literary Society, was a retired inspector of schools, and Kazi Imdadul Haq, one of the most active members, was the headmaster of Calcutta Training School. As a well-known figure in the world of education, he had links with the Education Department. Muzaffar was employed for the longest stretch at the Bengal Government's printing facility. His job was to sift through volumes of paper in the cavernous godowns of Writers Building where the press was located. He also worked as a clerk in a slaughterhouse. This entailed issuing tickets for the slaughter of animals. In his own words, he was spared the unpalatable task of 'slaughtering the animals myself'. He also accepted, and soon gave up, another unpleasant job. Despite a reasonable salary and the risk of future unemployment, he did not continue as official translator of Arabic and Urdu material in the Home Political Department of the Bengal Government.[93]

The Realm of Tangled Cultural Politics

The size of the Muslim intelligentsia was minute. According to the Census of 1911, less than 6,000 Muslims belonged to the civil professions. As a white-collar segment they were 'not only outnumbered by the Hindus (in the proportion of 7 to 1)' but 'even less numerous' than the Christians.[94] Yet their literary activities in Calcutta were attracting a great deal of official monitoring and censorship during the 1910s. The Urdu and Arabic Press were acting as vehicles of pan-Islamic ideas, and Urdu journals started by pan-Islamists were facing prosecution. Anti-British and pan-Islamic sentiments were being voiced in the Bengali and English journals, and in newspapers also. They stood for joint Hindu–Muslim campaigns against the government.[95]

Muzaffar's work in the Literary Society transformed him into a prolific writer and facilitated his later turn to political journalism. The subjects he chose and the debates he participated in reflected the gradual shifts in his own intellectual and political positions. The larger political developments played a key role in changing the content of his writings. As a student in Noakhali, he had been interested in politics. After the Lucknow Pact of 1916, when Hindu–Muslim unity was very much in the air, he had attended 'all kinds' of political meetings including a protest rally demanding freedom of political prisoners. Muzaffar was also part of the audience that had gathered to listen to the speeches made at the Congress and Muslim League conferences held in the city in 1917.[96] He knew political figures linked with the Literary Society who were also prominent Muslim League and Congress activists. This connection may have encouraged and enabled Muzaffar's access to these forums.

He refrained from joining either organization. His political position during this period was multi-stranded and reflected a confusion of attitudes. In this sense, he was very much a part of the Muslim intellectual milieu in

Calcutta, experiencing the pull of identity politics from diverse directions. A brief examination of the writings published in Bengali Muslim journals reveals this flexibility of political positions. Muzaffar's own writings from the 1910s, only a few of which survive, were mainly excursions in cultural polemics, conforming to contemporary middle-class notions of a Bengali Muslim socio-cultural identity.

Muzaffar humorously recalled that he was 'like all young boys who dabble in poetry once or twice'.[97] Their very poor quality[98] made him rapidly give up creative writing and by the late 1910s he was concentrating on prose and essays. Between 1916 and 1921, Muzaffar was well acquainted with the Bengali Muslim literati and the leading literary journals printed during these years. He worked as the assistant editor of *Bangiya Musalman Sahitya Patrika* (Bengal Muslim Literary Journal), the organ of the Bengal Muslim Literary Society.[99] Its news pages, composed by him, described the activities of the society and acted as a bulletin board. Muzaffar also compiled brief news-clips informing the readership of developments on the literary scene.[100] By 1919 he had earned praise in the wider Muslim literary circles as a 'skilled writer' whose articles were a 'pleasure to read', and was listed as one of the leading Bengali Muslim essayists.[101]

The periodicals, which flourished during war-time and post-war communal rapprochement and combined political campaigns, advocated Hindu–Muslim unity and emphasized the ethno-linguistic component of Bengali Muslim culture. They also reflected the modernizing social aspirations of the Bengali Muslim middle classes by stressing the cultural politics of 'self-improvement'. The first issue of *Bangiya Musalman Sahitya Patrika*, published in 1918, while elaborating its principles, stated this agenda clearly. The discourse of self-improvement in the Muslim middle-class context included the goal of becoming equal to the Hindu middle classes in terms of education, culture and socio-economic achievements. It was a fragment of the wider ideas on 'improvement' that had motivated both Hindu and Muslim members of the proprietor classes in Muzaffar's rural milieu.[102]

Emphasis on the ethno-linguistic cultural roots of Bengal Muslims plunged these journals into lengthy debates on the language question. A broad agreement persisted that Perso–Arabic traditions provided Muslims the world over with their spirituality and culture, and that Urdu was the vehicle of Islamic glory in India. Yet the intellectuals writing in these journals felt that Bengali, more than any other language, was close to the culture practised by Muslims of the region. These writings projected Bengali as the 'mother tongue' and the language of folk culture rooted among the masses. Muzaffar was heavily in favour of this opinion and, like the other writers in these magazines, stressed the Islamicization of content rather than form. In the article 'Urdu Bhasha o Bangiya Musalman' (The Urdu Language and the

Bengali Muslim), he attacked all those who tried to impose Urdu on Bengali Muslims in the most vehement terms. He declared that no 'Islamic wave' could rob the Bengali Muslims of their language, and that such a move would meet with stiff resistance.[103] In 'Banga Deshe Madrasa Shikhya' (Madrasa Education in Bengal), he acknowledged the need to learn Arabic but emphasized the primacy of Bengali language-teaching.[104] He criticized the popular pan-Islamist periodical *Mohammadi* for wrongly spelling words to project itself as the champion of a pure, Arabicized Islam. He ridiculed the fashion of pronouncing 'Islam' as 'Eslam', arguing that this particular phonic variation of 'E' did not exist in Arabic.[105] Similar sentiments were reiterated in several short pieces written during 1919–20 in praise of Islamic glory and culture. They did not state any new standpoint but repeated the usual argument put forward by many Bengali Muslim intellectuals, the refrain being that Arabic and Persian languages and cultures were the larger heritage which all Muslims shared. Knowledge of these cultures could improve the intellectual conditions and build character. However, they were not to be misused by preventing Bengal Muslims from identifying with their first language, Bengali, and the historical and heterodox roots of the region.[106]

This intellectual position, also a conduit for identifying the hegemonic potentials of languages accessible to Bengali Muslims, further argued against the deliberate suppression of Turko–Persian and Arabic words from the Bengali vocabulary by Hindu *bhadralok* writers. Inspired by nineteenth-century Hindu revivalist intellectuals such as Bankimchandra Chatterjee, they were sanskritizing the Bengali language. But none of the Muslim literary journals employed a consciously non-Sanskritic prose. Muzaffar himself penned 'Premiker Pan' (A Lover's Determination), a few lines of verse translated from the Persian poet Sha'adi's 'Golistan'. A romantic rendition of the spiritual bond between the worshipper and God in sanskritized prose and replete with sentiments of eternal fidelity, it indicated a degree of competence in engaging with Persian and Bengali literary styles missing in his other incursions into poetry.[107] Despite the tensions between the regional and extraterritorial, amorphous claims of Islamic nationhood evident in their pages, famous authors revered by the entire Bengal intelligentsia were invited to write in these journals. Exchange of ideas, debates and dialogues with Bengali Hindu writers was encouraged. This was not a self-enclosed world. Hindu women authors who wrote on the travails of the 'respectable' Bengali middle-class woman contributed to these journals and received praise. Many writers from Hindu Bengali backgrounds wrote on topics of interest to both the Hindu and the Muslim middle classes.[108]

The journals published articles in abundance on the 'past glory of Islam'. The pre-history of Arabs, the might of the Moorish kings in southern Spain, and the literary and scientific achievements of medieval West Asia were some of the recurring themes. Clearly, a usable past for Bengali Muslims was being constructed in these pages. Like the language question, the issue of cultural traditions was tied up with an attempt to create the ultimate definition of the ideal Muslim *bhadralok* in search of an elusive embourgeoisment. Also published were articles on the status of Muslim women. They generally argued that Islam had traditionally accorded a high place to women, emphasizing the necessity of the veil as the marker and site of female and communal 'honour'. Simultaneously, Hindu writers were attacked for claiming that Brahmanical culture had traditionally treated women better than in Islam, while being saturated in customs such as '*sati*' (burning of widows on the funeral pyre of their husbands) and opposition to widow remarriage. Muzaffar also participated in the ongoing debate on gender and argued in favour of female education as well as the veil. Sudhakanta Raychaudhuri, a liberal academic from Santiniketan and a regular contributor to the Literary Society journal, criticized Hindus for maltreatment of women; he also argued that the system of '*purdah*' (veil) prevalent among Muslims needed to be condemned. In a defensive rejoinder, Muzaffar declared that greater self-reflection was expected from the Hindus who failed to acknowledge that Islam recognized women as 'individuals' by granting them the right to property, education, divorce, remarriage and alimony. He stressed the idea of a separate but equal development programme for Muslim women through education. In his second and final reply Muzaffar did not retract these arguments, though apologizing to Sudhakanta and all 'Hindu brothers' for the tone of his earlier response which could have been interpreted as 'offensive'.[109] At this juncture, Muzaffar still saw himself as a devout Muslim and was a contributor to the prevailing patriarchal discourse on the fashioning of the Muslim gentlewoman. Within a couple of years, in the process of becoming a radical activist and disaffiliating from middle-class social concerns, he was to question and then reject this position.

Apart from the 'women's question', other sensitive topics discussed were Christian Anglicist and Hindu revivalist prejudices against Muslims and Islam. All these articles and debates, in turn, could be related to essays focused on the status of enterprise in Islam, and on how Islam itself looked at capital accumulation and usury, as well as the 'empowering' knowledge of modern economics. These could be matched with advertisements of handbooks explicitly intended to advise 'enterprising' Muslims on the intricacies of business investments. These preoccupations revealed the emergence and evolution of a social mentality strikingly similar to that of the Hindu middle classes in search of capitalist modernization. The 'plight' of wealthy tenant-farmers (*jotedars*) and peasants (*rayats*) in the hands of the predominantly Hindu landlords also found a space in the poems, literary pieces and advertisements devoted to agrarian questions affecting the Muslim middle classes.

This encouraged incipient competition with and contestation for the socio-economic power of the Hindu propertied elements.[110] These journals also advanced a critique of mainstream nationalism which deployed Orientalist concepts that were hostile to Muslims, making free use of Hindu-revivalist symbols. Though primarily structured to promote the social interests and shape the identity-thinking of the Bengali Muslim middle classes, this critical perspective had not evolved into an outright rejection of nationalism. Repeated attempts were made to pressurize the nationalist leaders, who came from Hindu upper-caste backgrounds, into accepting Muslims as equals.[111]

The underlying notion of 'community advancement' was not without contradictions. Stemming from overlapping identity structures, hegemonic claims and loyalties, many of the articles reflected a sense of creeping doubt. Scepticism was expressed on the social and conceptual inadequacy of a monolithic identity centred on the idea of community, which never stated how individual freedom was maintained within its boundaries while demanding absolute loyalty, and did not question its own hierarchical structure. These questions were indirectly referred to and left unresolved. This was a grey zone of irresolution, throwing up critical reappraisals of the components of community identity, and advancing ideas ranging from the emphasis on free thought within Islam to heterodox spirituality, to a clear-cut rejection of all identities based on religion. The first part of Azizal Islam's article, 'Nabajuger Katha' (The Story of a New Age) in *Moslem Bharat* (Muslim India), published in 1920,[112] when Muzaffar was closely associated with the journal, tried to combine socialist ideas with community development, nationalism and freedom of the individual. The article did not really succeed in conveying any central ideological position. Another article by Muzaffar published in the same year in the *Bangiya Musalman Sahitya Patrika*, on the Persian Sufi saint Al-Ghazzali, stressed the saint's stimulation of free-thinking. According to Muzaffar, Islamic 'orthodoxy' had been unable to appreciate this aspect.[113] He also condemned any display of prejudice and exclusion regarding such attitudes as unbecoming of Muslims. In his review of Lutfar Rahman's novel, *Pathhara* (The Traveller Who Lost His Way), Muzaffar praised the author for producing something other than 'the sort of rubbish sweeping the market'. But he chided Lutfar for harbouring certain conservative social attitudes that had crept into his writing. The refusal of Lutfar's young Muslim hero to have dinner with a Japanese woman was condemned as an example of 'narrow' intolerance since Islam, a universal religion, had no place for 'untouchability'.[114]

This 'reformist' position was not dissimilar to a bourgeois humanist critique of religion developing among a section of the liberal Bengali Muslim intelligentsia.[115] This particular strand of thinking remained weak and was unable to hegemonize Muslim mass politics in the region since its social content promoted a 'composite' elite formation. Yet, at this particular moment it indicated a lack of political direction at the heart of community-oriented concerns: disquiet with the idea of a closed community as well as the social need to identify with it. Muzaffar's engagement with Bengali Muslim liberal reformism proved to be brief. The pronouncements on gender and community in the essays he wrote during 1918–19 indicate a simultaneous adoption of conservative and liberal positions. Neither yielded a course of political action acceptable to him. In the post-war radical conjuncture, complex interactions between Muzaffar's social location and wider class conflict facilitated the emergence of a new political agency, and solved his dilemma. Reformist individualism, with its promise of a possessive bourgeois selfhood, would no longer appeal to him.

Shadow of Revolution

Though largely conforming to the contemporary preoccupations of the Bengali Muslim intelligentsia, Muzaffar was also feeling increasingly alienated. He was not happy with the name of the Literary Society journal. He had proposed in 1918 that a name free of sectional identity be given. The society president had felt otherwise and stressed the need to attract a Muslim readership. Muzaffar had gone along with this since 'we did not wish to alienate our aged President'. However, two years later he would oppose and thwart such a suggestion made by his then employer and leading Bengali Muslim politician, A.K. Fazlul Haq. Those at the fringes of these societies were being drawn into radical currents unleashed by the Russian Revolution of 1917. This process coincided with, and also may have contributed to, his gradual loss of faith in the leading figures of the community, especially in their social and political judgments. His correspondence with the poet Kazi Nazrul Islam between 1918 and 1919, and their eventual meeting in 1920, can be taken as a case in point. Nazrul had volunteered in the colonial army and became steadily politicized during his stay in the North West Frontier Province of British India. This geographic zone, a source of alarm to the colonial state, was officially viewed as a dangerous meeting-point of Bolshevism and pan-Islamism. News of the Bolshevik victory had reached Nazrul and he felt inspired to write a story, 'Byathar Dan' (The Gift of Pain), which was published by Muzaffar in the Literary Society journal in early 1920. Muzaffar changed Nazrul's explicitly eulogistic references to the Red Army as an unstoppable victorious and revolutionary force to avoid police censorship, even though he was impressed by its sentiments.[116]

Pabitra Gangopadhyay, a writer from a Hindu middle-class background who met him in 1919 and became his friend for life, was struck by Muzaffar's inclination to oppose authoritarian figures. Though they had not met during the war years, their social situations were similar. Like Muzaffar, Gangopadhyay had been dependent, as a struggling lower-middle-class writer, on leading lights of the Hindu literary circles. He too had remained silent or conformed when areas of disagreement had arisen. One such area was the support among a section of Hindu *bhadralok* intellectuals for the British war effort. Gangopadhyay had also been dismayed by the loyalist positions assumed by the Congress leadership. The two men were part of informal political discussions among younger intellectuals in the wake of the Bolshevik Revolution, an event they had welcomed, precisely because the British government was against it.[117]

Fragments of radical ideas could be often glimpsed in their intellectual milieu. These ideas, especially the revolutionary mood they conveyed, may have directly and indirectly encouraged the anti-authoritarian positions taking shape among marginalized figures who could not agree with their elders and betters. Marx and Marxism were making their presence felt in Muzaffar's cultural world from the pre-war days. In 1912, the Bengali and English versions of his article, 'A Successful Musalman Student', were published, respectively, in *Prabasi* and its sister organ in English, *Modern Review*. The same year, *Modern Review* printed an article on Karl Marx by the nationalist revolutionary, Lala Hardayal.[118] Censored images of revolutionary Russia were also seeping in during the closing years of the war, preparing the ground for a more serious engagement of the intelligentsia with socialism. A British film on the February Revolution, celebrating the fall of czardom and the establishment of liberal democracy, was released for general viewing in Calcutta in April 1917. From October onwards, the revolutionary upheavals came to be condemned in the European newspapers, especially in *The Statesman*, the voice of colonial capital.[119] Sensational accounts based on descriptions by western journalists were also in circulation.[120] Muzaffar himself was to notice a tract on socialism written in Hindi, in 1919.[121] *Prabasi* was the first journal to show enthusiasm about the revolutionary events of 1917 in Russia. In 1918, other Bengali journals edited by members of the Hindu intelligentsia also started displaying a positive attitude towards the Bolsheviks.[122] To what extent did these ideas circulate, and influence men like Muzaffar? It is difficult to say. However, these journals were read and many of the articles published in them were reproduced in Bengali Muslim literary magazines. Muzaffar's direct links with *Prabasi* are also recorded.

Other Derooted Collectives

Muzaffar's trans-communal connections with diverse segments of the intelligentsia acted as a source of divergence from any exclusivist identity. The lingering local patriotism of his earliest writings in the urban environment, implying a search for capitalist modernity by the rural intelligentsia, directed him towards his regional roots. This was evident in his attempts to establish a Minor School in Sandwip, requesting Abdul Karim Sahitya Bisharad, Literary Society president and Inspector of Schools, to secure official recognition and funds for the project.[123] It also prompted Muzaffar to develop links with some students from Noakhali and lower-class Muslim sailors from Sandwip. His associate in the Bengali Muslim Literary Society, poet Golam Mostafa, was assistant secretary of *Noakhali Sammilani* (Noakhali Union) during 1916. The society had been formed by some Noakhali expatriates as early as 1905 in Calcutta. Mahendrakumar Ghosh, a youth from a prominent Bengali Hindu upper-caste landlord family, was the secretary when Muzaffar became connected with this association. Ghosh expressed socially egalitarian as well as local concerns, and edited the monthly periodical, *Noakhali*, the mouthpiece of the association.[124]

The regional associations also contained the roots of an identity-thinking that would, in a few years' time, take Muzaffar elsewhere. Certain concerns that were becoming visible among Bengali Muslim writers were also present in the regional associations they frequented. The first issue of *Noakhali* opened with a poem, an exercise in local patriotism and nostalgia, penned by Muzaffar Ahmad. It was followed by an article by Mahendrakumar Ghosh, who criticized the government for setting up the Benaras Hindu University. Ghosh argued that this step could only strengthen Hindu high-caste tyranny, aid 'those who profit from religion-as-business', and undermine the educational drive necessary to improve the condition of low-caste labourers and peasants.[125] These, and other anti-hierarchical and anti-authoritarian views, indicated the emergence of a 'class fraction'[126] among younger members of the intelligentsia, rife with the potential to disaffiliate from the general directions of their class or class-segment. A mono-dimensional interpretation of emerging fractions as mutating exercises to reconstitute, redeploy and perpetuate the hegemony of the proprietor classes needs to be avoided in this context. Such a partial reading can only represent the social as flexible yet locked within certain boundaries, represented by models of 'compassionate protectionism' only, and bereft of potential ideological departure. Instead, it is possible also to see in the fraction formations, the material ingredients of dissent and disaffiliation among alienated segments of the younger intelligentsia. The complex unfolding of this social tendency involved looking for, identifying with and actively supporting the emerging countervailing and potentially transformative self-expressions from below. These intellectuals were being drawn into social maelstroms challenging their own class origins, thereby breaking, in some cases, with the proprietorial aspirations they had been socialized into. The extent of political disaffiliation, mediated through exposure to the hitherto repressed forces, varied and prompted a return to paternalistic 'compassionate protectionism', disillusioned conformity or opportunistic surrender after a period of dissent, as well as radical departure and ideological transition.

Frequent Visitor to the Calcutta Docks

Regional affiliations and overlapping identifications were also pulling Muzaffar towards the direction of workers. He had known working-class segments in the Calcutta Dock area since 1910s. As mentioned, for a brief period during the summer of 1915, he had taught at a *madrasa* in Kidderpore, situated in the port area. Since his native island, Sandwip, supplied a huge number of seamen, his initial aim may have been to keep abreast of news from home. It developed into a concern over the conditions of these sailors.[127] From police reports on post-war trade unionism in the docks, it seems that the majority of seamen, who came from the ranks of impoverished Bengali Muslims of Chittagong and Noakhali in East Bengal, depended on brokers with underworld connections for work and accommodation. These brokers subjected them to extreme exploitation, appropriating the bulk of their wages. The shipping companies in turn tacitly encouraged the brokers. By controlling the work force, the brokers weakened the collective bargaining power of the seamen.[128] Expropriation and abuse encouraged the rise of trade unions in the port area. The sailors fought the shipping companies and the brokers by forming an organization in 1918, and through strike actions in the early 1920s for better working conditions and wages.[129]

Muslims constituted three-fourths of the population in Calcutta Port,[130] which played a crucial role in the British war efforts. The port had been developed as one of the most capital-intensive zones of the city. Established in the late eighteenth century, it was the indispensable organ of surplus extraction from the colony. With the establishment of a state-of-the-art dock at Kidderpore in 1892, its profitability increased rapidly. It was directly connected by water and rail to the rising industrial complex on the Hooghly embankment and the import jetties. An electric tram service and wharves illuminated by electricity made it a modern marvel since the main thoroughfares of Calcutta were still gas-lit. Within eight years of its construction, this valued colonial public facility in Calcutta was being prepared for further improvement. A contemporary account lauded the project and commented upon 'the stupendous strides with which the port of Calcutta has reached in the last 200 years, its present position as emporium of trade of the first magnitude under the beneficent, all powerful and world-pervading protection of the Union Jack, in spite of the ceaseless freaks of a treacherous river.'[131]

But 'the beneficent, all powerful and world-pervading protection of the Union Jack' was not extended to the workers of the port area who kept this gigantic enterprise running. Kidderpore was one of the poorest municipal wards with abysmal living standards. It had the worst public health record in Calcutta, an illustration of desperate material deprivations. The major concern to the colonial authorities was its unplanned growth,[132] interpreted as a hindrance to order and profit. They ignored the population living under the constant shadow of death. Throughout the second decade of the twentieth century, including the war years and their immediate aftermath, Kidderpore remained the unhealthiest ward in the city. It had the highest death rate in Calcutta with a high record of infant mortality. Each year, tuberculosis and other infectious and malignant diseases claimed their victims. The Calcutta Corporation held the 'insanitary condition in the docks' with the 'place swarming with the flies', to be responsible. It recommended that the port authorities take 'immediate steps' to 'remedy the present state of affairs in the locality'.[133] Despite such observations and suggestions the health situation in Kidderpore remained unchanged, indicating a deeper malady.

Not unexpectedly, therefore, Kidderpore's dubious gift to the city during the closing year of the First World War was a global pandemic, the influenza. Alongside plague and small-pox, it struck Calcutta in 1918, arriving by sea. The highest mortality rate from influenza (64 per mille) was recorded 'as usual' at Kidderpore, as the municipal observers noted with resigna-

A building in the Khidirpur (Kidderpore) area of Calcutta

tion. This status placed it 'way ahead' of other disease-prone wards of the city. The pandemic infected Kidderpore and from there rapidly engulfed the rest of the city. Unhygienic living conditions, the highest death rate and high infant mortality were already prevalent. The weak physical resistance of the ward's population made them succumb quickly. Inadequate medical attention and facilities made matters worse.[134] Caught in a web of exploitation, poverty and pestilence, the ward proved to be one of the liveliest centres of labour protest in the city during 1920–21,[135] a period when Muzaffar was turning towards labour politics and socialism. Muzaffar already knew the community of sailors. He also knew some of their leaders, members of the Urdu and Bengali-speaking Muslim intelligentsia, through the overlapping literary and political circles.[136]

The majority of those affected by the influenza pandemic lived in municipal wards dominated by the working class. Peace in Europe meant little to an ordinary inhabitant of Calcutta in 1918. Acute war-induced scarcity thrust the majority of its residents into hardship and made the disease-ridden city desperate. Prices of essential commodities such as rice, wheat, salt, cooking oil and cloth had shot up, making life difficult even for middle-class householders.[137] Violence flared easily in this environment. Marwari business firms were attacked and godowns looted. An irate Muslim mob accused them of hoarding and causing an artificial cloth famine. The cloth riot, begun by the unemployed or semi-employed Urdu-speaking Muslim poor and directed against a section of the non-Bengali Hindu rich, reflected the antagonistic divisions based on ethno-linguistic, class and religious identities among the diasporic communities of the city.[138] The next year, the very same segments would join forces against colonialism, by then identified as the primary source of hardship, and indicating the social convergence of sectional and nationalist mass mobilizations in an altered political context.[139]

Reshuffle and Transition

Exposure to working-class conditions and hardships during and immediately after the war brought Muzaffar closer to direct politics. From the realm of a muted distaste towards colonial authority, he was entering a zone of confrontational activism. This transition would make him oppose the rule of colonial capital, and involve sharp divergences from the politics of mainstream anti-colonial nationalism as well as the claims of exclusivist religious and/or ethno-linguistic identities. 1919 was a turning point in Muzaffar's career. His social milieu was being increasingly drawn into the post-war anti-colonial upsurge. Yet he was reluctant to commit himself to any of the existing political options. Throughout the year, a debate was raging within him: was he going to remain a full-time literary activist or should he

become involved in politics? In 1920 he would decide in favour of anti-
colonial politics and take up political journalism. This in turn would
involve him in the working-class movements being directed against both
European and Indian factory-owners in and around Calcutta. These movements generated an interest in socialist literature and, in 1921, the intention of forming a communist organization. The social networks he had
forged during the war years, especially through socio-literary activism, would
continue to offer him support to a very great extent. Kazi Imdadul Haq, for
instance, despite being a government employee, ignored the possible repercussions, including the threat of police harassment, and sent food to Muzaffar
when the latter was in jail as the sole 'State Prisoner' in Bengal during 1923.
Some fringe members of his literary circle, whom he met through the Bengal
Muslim Literary Society, became his first political colleagues. The lanes, bylanes, lodging houses and addresses in and around College Street continued
to be useful to him as the principal means of diverting police attention.
Unknown war-time visitors to the city appeared as political colleagues many
years later. J.W. Johnstone, a British soldier stationed in war-time Calcutta,
would visit the city as a representative of the Communist Party of the USA
(CPUSA) and the Communist International during 1928.[140]

Muzaffar Ahmad had left behind a rural existence where communal,
nationalist and ethno-linguistic components of social identity had not yet
assumed a coherent political focus. Intersecting experiences in the city, therefore, prepared the ground for a more intensive process of politicization in
the years that immediately followed. This process was mediated by his
urban social milieu and the political trends which touched the Calcutta
intelligentsia during the First World War. In a semi-segregated colonial city
registering material scarcity, state repression and racist violence during the
war, self-awareness as a racialized subject could give shape to an intense and
desperate social hostility towards colonialism. The war years provided an
ideological environment that was complex and multilayered. Changes in
leadership, a direct result of alienation from the policies of the colonial
state, temporarily acted as a bridge between mainstream nationalism dominated by the Hindu proprietor classes and the Muslim intelligentsia. Nowhere were the multiple layers of Muslim intellectual thought more apparent than in the cultural writings of the period, simultaneously revealing
identity formation and identity crisis. In the post-war period, the anti-imperialist mass upsurge and labour militancy in his immediate environment
and beyond would facilitate a dialectical interplay between the two, and
open up various ideological options before the Muslim intellectual, including the socialist alternative.

Muzaffar Ahmad had wished to devote himself to thoughtful essays on
the glories of Islamic culture. He gradually involved himself in political

activities since, in his milieu, culture and politics had become explicitly intertwined. His political experiences as a marginalized figure on the fringes of society had made him focus on the larger anti-colonial struggle. It had also made him support the multi-dimensional political ideology of Bengali middle-class Muslims who were unable to separate themselves from either sectional or ethno-linguistic identities. The contradiction bred by the forms of political consciousness made Muzaffar reject the cultural ethos of nationalism, dominated by a Hindu *bhadralok* intelligentsia. However, opposition to British rule and friendship with non-communal, socially marginalized Bengali Hindu middle-class intellectuals made him oppose the orthodox elements within the so-called community, and favour a united opposition to imperialism. He was unable to subscribe to the idea of a composite elite formation either, disentangling himself from proprietorial social interests in every political form. He was beginning to harbour doubts about the claims of Muslim leaders who insisted they represented the interests of all Muslims, as well as of nationalist leaders from high-caste Hindu, property-owning backgrounds who claimed to represent all Indians. This position would be expanded to reject the social content and programmes of nationalist as well as communally exclusivist identities. Muzaffar's involvement in militant labour politics which heightened during 1920–21 in Calcutta and its suburbs, his simultaneous switch to radical journalism which increasingly made him write about the political movements of workers and peasants, and his growing interest in Marxian socialism and workers' power mediated by the Bolshevik Revolution of 1917, further weakened his attachment to a Bengali Muslim middle-class identity caught between sectional, ethno-linguistic and nationalist political considerations. City life had encouraged gravitation towards new structures of social interdependence absent in the village. In the complex web of urban struggles, perceptions of the self and society were changing. Communitarian values, imbibed through Islamic congregationist religious practice as well as heterodox socio-literary collectivities, were being reconfigured and transformed to arrive at a social understanding and political recognition of trans-communal oppressions. This meant going beyond the community. In 1919, Muzaffar Ahmad was on the verge of an ideological transition. The war years, by reshuffling the social components that went into the making of his political consciousness, prepared the ground for this shift. They opened the doors of future radicalism in more ways than one.

Notes and References

[1] Joya Chatterji, *Bengal Divided: Hindu communalism and partition, 1932–1947*, Delhi, 1995, pp. 8–12. Though Chatterji mainly concentrates on the Hindu landed gentry, the

social logic which propelled them toward colonial education and white-collar jobs could be extended to Muslim landed families also. For a detailed study on the search for jobs and education among the Bengali Muslim gentry, see Mohammad Shah, *In Search of an Identity: Bengali Muslims 1880–1940*, Calcutta, 1996.

[2] Rajkumar Chakrabarty and Anangomohan Das, *Sandwiper Itihas* (History of Sandwip), Calcutta, B 1330/1923–24, p. 7.

[3] *Final Report on the Survey and Settlement Operations in the District of Noakhali, 1914 to 1919*, Calcutta, 1920.

[4] For a treatment of the sense of community which preceded and was absorbed into nationalism, see Rajat Kanta Ray, *The Felt Community: Commonality and Mentality before the Emergence of Indian Nationalism*, Delhi, 2002.

[5] Amiya Kumar Bagchi, *The Political Economy of Underdevelopment*, Cambridge, 1993, p. 24. Irfan Habib, 'Colonization of the Indian Economy 1757–1900', in *Essays in Indian History: Towards a Marxist Perception*, reprint, Delhi, 1997, pp. 296–335.

[6] Sumit Sarkar, 'Rammohun Roy and the Break with the Past', in *A Critique of Colonial India*, Calcutta, 1985, pp. 12–13.

[7] *Noakhali*, 1, 1, B 1322/1916.

[8] *Eastern Bengal and Assam District Gazetteers, Noakhali*, Allahabad, 1911.

[9] Ibid.

[10] Gopal Haldar, *Rupnaraner Kule* (By the Shores of the Rupnaran River), Volume 1, Calcutta, 1963, republished 1992, p. 140.

[11] *Eastern Bengal and Assam District Gazetteers, Noakhali*.

[12] Chakrabarty and Das, *Sandwiper Itihas*, pp. 16–22, 219–22.

[13] *Imperial Gazetteer of India, Eastern Bengal and Assam*, Calcutta, 1909.

[14] *Eastern Bengal and Assam District Gazetteers, Noakhali*.

[15] Chakrabarty and Das, *Sandwiper Itihas*, pp. 210–12.

[16] Ibid., p. 201.

[17] *Imperial Gazetteer of India, Eastern Bengal and Assam*.

[18] Chakrabarty and Das, *Sandwiper Itihas*, p. 126.

[19] Ibid., pp. 163–96. *Final Report on the Survey and Settlement Operations in the District of Noakhali, 1914 to 1919*.

[20] Chakrabarty and Das, *Sandwiper Itihas* , pp. 215–16.

[21] *Noakhali District Gazetteer, Statistics 1901–02*, Calcutta, 1905.

[22] *Imperial Gazetteer of India, Eastern Bengal and Assam*.

[23] Chakrabarty and Das, *Sandwiper Itihas*, pp. 163–96. *Final Report on the Survey and Settlement Operations in the District of Noakhali, 1914 to 1919*.

[24] *Noakhali District Gazetteer, Statistics 1901–02*.

[25] *Eastern Bengal and Assam District Gazetteers, Noakhali*.

[26] Chakrabarty and Das, *Sandwiper Itihas*, pp. 11–12.

[27] Ibid., pp. 197–99, 201.

[28] Ibid., p. 126.

[29] Ibid., pp. 197–99, 201. For an analysis of Islamization in pre-colonial Bengal, see Richard M. Eaton, *The Rise of Islam and the Bengal Frontier, 1204–1760*, Berkeley, 1993.

[30] Studies in the structure of landownership in colonial Bengal, including the middle-peasant-dominated Chittagong–Tippera–Noakhali sub-region, can be found in Taj ul-Islam Hashmi, *Pakistan as a Peasant Utopia: The Communalization of Class Politics in East Bengal 1920–1947*, Oxford, 1992; Partha Chatterjee, *Bengal 1920–1947: The Land Question*, Calcutta, 1984; Nariaki Nakazato, *Agrarian System in Eastern Bengal, 1870–1910*, Calcutta, 1994.

[31] Hashmi, *Pakistan as a Peasant Utopia*, pp. 37, 39, 40.

[32] *Praja* politics emerged in Bengal as a movement upholding the interests of rich and middle peasants, mainly Muslim, against the permanently settled landlords who were overwhelmingly Hindu high-caste in composition. Though claiming to fight for the entire peasantry, the *praja* movement was primarily dominated by Muslim *jotedars* (rich tenant-farmers), a factor that made it ignore or downplay the interests of the *bargadars* (share-croppers) and the landless.

The *praja* movement led to the formation of a Praja Party in the 1920s, which changed its name to the Krishak Praja Party (KPP) in 1936. Its social base merged with the demand for Pakistan and contributed to the partition of Bengal in 1947. For a historical account, see Hashmi, *Pakistan as a Peasant Utopia*.

[33] Chakrabarty and Das, *Sandwiper Itihas*, pp. 101–05.

[34] Muzaffar Ahmad, *Samakaler Katha* (Story of My Times), 1963, fourth edition 1996, p. 8. Afifa Khatun, 'Abba Baro Gharer Sandhane Chilen Tai Choto Ghar Tanke Bandhte Pareni' (My Father Searched for a Larger Space), in Mazharul Islam (ed.), *Muzaffar Ahmad: Shango o Proshongo* (Muzaffar Ahmad: Reflections and Essays), Calcutta, 1989, pp. 15–16.

[35] Ahmad, *Samakaler Katha*, p. 6.

[36] *Noakhali District Gazetteer, Statistics 1901–02*. In remote Sandwip, colonial education with knowledge of English at its core was yet to make its mark. The process, in a very limited way, did not really take off before late nineteenth century. Only 66 people had any knowledge of English in 1901–02.

[37] Chakrabarty and Das, *Sandwiper Itihas*, pp. 148–49. Among the twenty *ukil*s and eleven *mokhtar*s (lawyers) who practised in the Sandwip Court, many were proficient only in Persian. Muslims were slightly in a majority over Hindus in the legal profession. Among the *ukil*s, eleven had Arabic names. Among the lesser legal practitioners, the *mokhtar*s, the percentage of men with Arabic names was still higher. There were seven Muslim and four Hindu *mokhtar*s. The continued use of Persian may have been an advantage to members of the local Muslim intelligentsia who otherwise lagged behind Hindus, especially in terms of access to English education.

[38] Ahmad, *Samakaler Katha*, p. 6. At the time of Muzaffar's birth in 1889, his family lived in Musapur. A Mansoor Ali is listed among the eleven *mokhtar*s who plied their trade in the Munsif's Court at Sandwip in 1883. Its difficult to say for certain whether he was Muzaffar's father. The list mentions Munshi Mansoor Ali's village as Rahmatpur. See Chakrabarty and Das, *Sandwiper Itihas*, p. 149.

[39] Ahmad, *Samakaler Katha*, p. 6. Muzaffar Ahmad, *Amar Jiban o Bharater Communist Party* (My Life and the Communist Party of India), Calcutta, 1969, fifth edition 1996, p. 23.

[40] Chakrabarty and Das, *Sandwiper Itihas*, pp. 121–23. The *Imperial Gazetteer of India, Eastern Bengal and Assam*, observed: 'The people are extremely litigious, but violent crime is rare.'

[41] Ahmad, *Samakaler Katha*, p. 6.

[42] Ibid., pp. 5–7.

[43] *Final Report on the Survey and Settlement Operations in the District of Noakhali, 1914 to 1919*. Half of the island's population had perished in the cyclone of 1876 and the epidemic that had followed. But the population in Sandwip was increasing at a faster rate than that of the other islands or the mainland. Between 1881 and 1911, the population density in Sandwip had risen by 73 per cent while the rest of the islands only registered a rise of 1 per cent and the mainland, of 61 per cent.

[44] Ahmad, *Samakaler Katha*, p. 7. Ahmad, *Amar Jiban o Bharater Communist Party*, p. 23.

[45] Ahmad, *Samakaler Katha*, p. 6.

[46] Chakrabarty and Das, *Sandwiper Itihas*, p. 211.

[47] Ahmad, *Samakaler Katha*, pp. 6–7.

[48] Ibid., pp. 6–8. Ahmad, *Amar Jiban o Bharater Communist Party*, p. 22.

[49] Ahmad, *Samakaler Katha*, pp. 6–7; *Amar Jiban o Bharater Communist Party*, p. 23.

[50] Ahmad, *Samakaler Katha*, p. 7.

[51] Ahmad, *Amar Jiban o Bharater Communist Party*, p. 24. For a treatment of the complexity which underlined Bankimchandra's communal representations, a feature which may have accounted for the simultaneous attraction and repulsion he generated among Muslim intellectuals of Bengal, see Tanika Sarkar, 'Imagining Hindu Rashtra: The Hindu and the Muslim in Bankimchandra's Writings', in *Hindu Wife, Hindu Nation: Community, Religion and Cultural Nationalism*, Delhi, 2001, pp. 163–90.

[52] The social aspirations underlining cultural engagements of the Bengal intelligentsia during the nineteenth century have been variously treated. See John McGuire, *The Making of a Colonial Mind: A Quantitative Study of the Bhadralok in Calcutta, 1857–1885*, Canberra, 1983. Sibaji Bandopadhyay, *Gopal–Rakhal Dwandasamas: Uponibeshbad o Bangla Shishu-Sahitya* (The Gopal–Rakhal Dialectic: Colonialism and Children's Literature in Bengal), Calcutta, 1991. Brian Hatcher, 'Indigent Brahmans, Industrious Pandits: Bourgeois Ideology and Sanskrit Pandits in Colonial Calcutta', *Comparative Studies of South Asia, Africa and the Middle East*, Special Issue: *Divergent Modernities*, 16, 1, 1996, pp. 15–26. Tithi Bhattacharya, *The Sentinels of Culture Class, Education, and the Colonial Intellectual in Bengal (1848–85)*, Oxford, 2005.

[53] Ahmad, *Samakaler Katha*, pp. 6–9.

[54] Muzaffar Ahmad, 'Sandwiper Punnal Briksha o Punnal Toila', *Prabasi*, 10, 4, B 1317/1910.

[55] Haldar, *Rupnaraner Kule*, Volume 1, p. 141.

[56] Muzaffar Ahmad, 'Kritabidya Musalman Chatra', *Prabasi*, 12, 2, B 1319/1912; 'A Successful Musalman Student', *Modern Review*, December 1912.

[57] Ahmad, *Amar Jiban o Bharater Communist Party*, p. 24; *Samakaler Katha*, pp. 7–8.

[58] Ahmad, *Amar Jiban o Bharater Communist Party*, pp. 24–25; *Samakaler Katha*, pp. 6–9.

[59] Ahmad, *Samakaler Katha*, pp. 8–9. Also Sumit Sarkar, *Swadeshi Movement in Bengal 1903–08*, Delhi, 1973.

[60] Ellen Meiksins Wood, 'Modernity, Postmodernity or Capitalism?', in Robert W. McChesney, Ellen Meiksins Wood and John Bellamy Foster (eds.), *Capitalism and the Information Age: The Political Economy of the Global Communication Revolution*, Kharagpur, 2001, p. 40. Meiksins Wood argues that a model of agrarian capitalism emerged in England which found expression in a distinctive ideology of improvement. For approaches on 'improvement ideology' among Muslim agrarian populations of East Bengal, see Pradip Kumar Datta, 'Muslim Peasant Improvement, Pir Abu Bakr and the Formation of Communalized Islam', in *Carving Blocs: Communal Ideology in Early Twentieth Century Bengal*, Delhi, 1999, pp. 64–108. Also Sumit Sarkar, 'Two Muslim Tracts for Peasants: Bengal 1909–1910', in *Beyond Nationalist Frames: Relocating Postmodernism, Hindutva, History*, Delhi, 2002, pp. 96–111. For an understanding of the socio-material changes that penetrated the world-view of rural Muslims, see Amit Dey, *The Image of The Prophet in Bengali Muslim Piety (1850–1947)*, Calcutta, 2006.

[61] Rafiuddin Ahmed, *The Bengal Muslims 1871–1906: A Quest for Identity*, Delhi, 1981, pp. 189–90.

[62] Abul Mansoor Ahmad, *Amar Dakha Rajnitir Panchash Bachar* (Fifty Years of Politics as I Saw It), Dhaka, 1968, p. 47.

[63] Amiya Kumar Bagchi, 'Wealth and Work in Calcutta 1860–1921', in Sukanta Chaudhuri (ed.), *Calcutta: The Living City*, Volume 1, Calcutta, 1995, p. 216.

[64] *Report on Municipal Administration of Calcutta*, 1912–13, Corporation of Calcutta. The social impact of nocturnal illumination on metropolitan existence is treated in Joachim Schlor, *Nights in the Big City: Paris, Berlin, London 1840–1930*, London, 1998, pp. 58–59.

[65] Suranjan Das, 'The Politics of Agitation: Calcutta 1912–1947', in Sukanta Chaudhuri (ed.), *Calcutta: The Living City*, Volume 2, Calcutta, 1995, p. 16.

[66] Rajat Ray, *Urban Roots of Indian Nationalism: Pressure Groups and Conflict of Interests in Calcutta City Politics, 1875–1939*, Delhi, 1979, pp. 4–6.

[67] *Report on Municipal Administration of Calcutta*, 1912–13.

[68] Ibid.

[69] *Report on Native Newspapers*, 1914.

[70] Ibid.

[71] *Report on Native Newspapers*, 1914–16. For a dissection of the apocalyptic mood which descended over major cities, such as New York, on the eve of the First World War, see Mike Davis, *Dead Cities and Other Tales*, New York, 2002, pp. 7, 9. The 'ruptured spleen' syndrome, a euphemism for the racist homicide of 'native' domestic servants, was also prevalent in other parts of the empire. For a survey of the African colonies, see Jock McCulloch,

'Empire and Violence, 1900–1939', in Philippa Levine (ed.), *Gender and Empire*, Oxford, 2004. Sumit Sarkar employs the phrase 'protectionist compassion' in his 'Vidyasagar and Brahmanical Society', in *Writing Social History*, Delhi, 1997, p. 280.

[72] Das, 'The Politics of Agitation', p. 17. J.H. Broomfield, *Elite Conflict in a Plural Society*, Berkeley, 1968, pp. 14, 62–65, 113–15, 117–22, 162–65. McPherson, *Muslim Microcosm*, pp. 1–19, 20–54. R.J. Popplewell, *Intelligence and Imperial Defence: British Intelligence and the Defence of the Indian Empire, 1904–1924*, London, 1995, p. 79.

[73] John Berwick, 'Chatra Samaj: The Social and Political Significance of the Student Community in Bengal *c.* 1870–1922', unpublished Ph.D. thesis, University of Sydney, 1986, p. 356. D.M. Laushey, *Bengal Terrorism and the Marxist Left: Aspects of Regional Nationalism in India, 1905–1942*, Calcutta, 1975, pp. 6–7.

[74] Ahmad, *Amar Jiban*, p. 24.

[75] Berwick, 'Chatra Samaj', pp. 305–06, 308–09, 352, 384. Ajitkumar Basu, *Kolikatar Rajpath, Samaje o Sanskritite* (Streets of Calcutta, In Society and Culture), Calcutta, 1996, pp. 339, 342, 346–47. Debasis Bose, 'College Street', in Sukanta Chaudhuri (ed.), *Calcutta: The Living City*, Volume 2, p. 219.

[76] *Report on Native Newspapers*, 1914–15. For a treatment of criminality in the city, see Debraj Bhattacharya, 'Kolkata "Underworld" in the Early 20th Century', *Economic and Political Weekly*, Vol. 38, No. 38, 2004.

[77] For a recent discussion on *Gemeinschaft, Gesellschaft* and Indian nationalism, see Rajat Kanta Ray, *Nationalism, Modernity and Civil Society: The Subalternist Critique and After*, Kolkata, 2007.

[78] The attachment of the first generation metropolitan Bengali Hindu migrant middle classes to their rural origins has been treated by historians. See Sumit Sarkar, 'The City Imagined', in *Writing Social History*, p. 170. Also Chatterji, *Bengal Divided*, p. 7.

[79] Berwick, 'Chatra Samaj', pp. 217, 246–53, 384. Chandiprasad Sarkar, *The Bengali Muslims, A Study in their Politicization (1912–1929)*, Calcutta, 1991, pp. 41–42. Muzaffar Ahmad, *Kazi Nazrul Islam: Smritikatha* (Kazi Nazrul Islam: Reminiscences), Calcutta, 1965, ninth edition 1998, pp. 1, 16. *Report on Native Newspapers*, 1916. McPherson, *Muslim Microcosm*, p. 4. *Census of India 1911*, Volume VI, Calcutta I. According to the Census of 1911, women constituted 15 per cent of the city's population. Among them, one-fourth engaged in various occupations. A quarter of these female workers were prostitutes.

[80] Berwick, 'Chatra Samaj', pp. 249, 253. Ahmad, *Samakaler Katha*, pp. 20–21.

[81] Berwick, 'Chatra Samaj', pp. 135, 242–43, 249. Ahmad, *Samakaler Katha*, p. 8.

[82] Berwick, 'Chatra Samaj', pp. 249–50.

[83] Ahmad, *Amar Jiban o Bharater Communist Party*, p. 36.

[84] *Abdullah* was serialized. See *Moslem Bharat*, 1, 1, B 1327/1920.

[85] Ahmad, *Amar Jiban o Bharater Communist Party*, p. 36.

[86] Ahmad, *Samakaler Katha*, pp. 20, 25–26. Basu, *Kolikatar Rajpath*, pp. 346–47.

[87] Berwick, 'Chatra Samaj', pp. 239–40, 305–06. Laushey, *Bengal Terrorism*, pp. 10–11. Ahmad, *Amar Jiban o Bharater Communist Party*, pp. 391–92.

[88] Muzaffar Ahmad, *Myself and the Communist Party of India 1920–1929*, Calcutta, 1970, p. 12. Ahmad, *Amar Jiban o Bharater Communist Party*, pp. 27–28. Italics mine. The political dimensions of the song are discussed in Sarkar, *Hindu Wife, Hindu Nation*, pp. 176–81. Also Sabyasachi Bhattacharya, *Bande Mataram: The Biography of a Song*, Delhi, 2003.

[89] This aspect is discussed later in the chapter.

[90] Ahmad, *Samakaler Katha*, pp. 19–23. Muzaffar Ahmad, *Kazi Nazrul Islam: Smritikatha*, (Kazi Nazrul Islam: Reminiscences), Calcutta 1965, ninth edition 1998, pp. 1–2. Ahmad, *Amar Jiban o Bharater Communist Party*, pp. 35–38.

[91] Ahmad, *Samakaler Katha*, pp. 19–23.

[92] A.K. Roy, 'A Short History of Calcutta', *Census of India, 1901*, Volume 7, Part 1.

[93] Ahmad, *Samakaler Katha*, pp. 19–23; *Kazi Nazrul Islam: Smritikatha*, pp. 1–2; *Amar Jiban o Bharater Communist Party*, pp. 35–38.

[94] *Census of India 1911*, Volume VI, Calcutta I.

[95] *Report on Native Newspapers*, 1914–16. McPherson, *Muslim Microcosm*, pp. 29, 30, 41.

[96] Ahmad, *Samakaler Katha*, pp. 23, 84; *Amar Jiban o Bharater Communist Party*, p. 30.

[97] Ahmad, *Samakaler Katha*, p. 23.

[98] 'Bir' (The Brave), based on a page from the Prophet's life, reflected religious piety but was of unremarkable literary merit. 'Bir', *Al-Eslam*, 1, 7, B 1322 /1916.

[99] Ahmad, *Kazi Nazrul Islam: Smritikatha*, pp. 22, 26, 232.

[100] 'Samiti Sangbad' (Society News), *Bangiya Musalman Sahitya Patrika*, 2, 3, B 1326/1919; 'Samiti Sangbad' (Society News), *Bangiya Musalman Sahitya Patrika*, 2, 4, B 1326/1919; 'Sangkalan' (Compilation), *Bangiya Musalman Sahitya Patrika*, 2, 3, B 1326/1919; 'Sangkalan' (Compilation), *Bangiya Musalman Sahitya Patrika*, 2, 4, B 1326/1919; 'Sangkalan' (Compilation), *Bangiya Musalman Sahitya Patrika*, 3, 1, B 1327/1920; 'Daktar Husayan' (Dr Husayan), *Bangiya Musalman Sahitya Patrika*, 3, 1, B 1327/1920.

[101] *Saogat*, 1, 5, B 1325/1919.

[102] *Bangiya Musalman Sahitya Patrika*, 1, 1, B 1325/1918. Also Anisuzzaman, *Muslim Banglar Samayik Patrika* (List of Bengali Muslim Periodicals), Dhaka, 1969, pp. 201–04.

[103] Anisuzzaman, *Muslim Banglar Samayik Patrika*, pp. 203–04. Muzaffar Ahmad, 'Urdu Bhasha o Bangiya Musalman', *Al-Eslam*, Sraban B 1324/1917. Sarkar, *The Bengali Muslims, A Study in their Politicization*, pp. 66–67. Amalendu De, 'The Social Thoughts and Consciousness of Bengali Muslims in the Colonial Period', *Social Scientist* , Vol. 23, Nos. 263–265, 1995.

[104] 'Banga Deshe Madrasa Shikhya', *Bangiya Musalman Sahitya Patrika*, 2, 3, B 1326/1919.

[105] 'Alochana' (Discussion), *Bangiya Musalman Sahitya Patrika*, 3, 1, B 1327/1920.

[106] 'Arab Itihaser Ak Pristha' (A Page from Arab History), *Bangiya Musalman Sahitya Patrika*, 2, 3, B 1326/1919. This article is significant only for being published under Muzaffar's *nom de plume*, 'Dwaipayan', which later became his *nom de guerre*. A deliberate pun, it referred to the mythical chronicler of the ancient Indian epic *Mahabharata*. Simultaneously it meant 'one who is from an island', a coded reference to his Sandwip origins. 'Arbi Bhasha' (Arabic Language), *Bangiya Musalman Sahitya Patrika*, 2, 3, B 1326/1919. 'Inayat Khan', *Bangiya Musalman Sahitya Patrika*, 2, 4, B 1326/1919. 'Ibne Tufail', *Bangiya Musalman Sahitya Patrika*, 2, 4, B 1326/1919.

[107] 'Premiker Pan', *Kohinoor*, 2, B 1322/1916.

[108] Anisuzzaman, *Muslim Banglar Samayik Patrika*, pp. 201–56.

[109] 'Patrer Uttar' (Reply to Sudhakanta Raychaudhuri), *Bangiya Musalman Sahitya Patrika*, 2, 4, B 1326/1919. 'Narir Mulya o Islam'er Jer-alochana' (The continuing discussion on the status of women and Islam), *Bangiya Musalman Sahitya Patrika*, 3, 1, B 1327/1920. Several years later Muzaffar again argued with Sudhakanta. By then a paradigm shift had taken place and the subject of the debate was middle-class values and communism.

[110] *Bangiya Musalman Sahitya Patrika*, 1, 2, B 1325/ 1918. *Bangiya Musalman Sahitya Patrika*, 2, 4, B 1326/1919. *Saogat*, 1, 1, B 1325/1919.

[111] *Al-Eslam*, 3 May 1915 – 5 May 1916. *Saogat*, 1, 1, B 1325/1919.

[112] *Moslem Bharat*, Asvin B 1327/1920.

[113] 'Imam Al-Ghazzali', *Bangiya Musalman Sahitya Patrika*, 1, 2, B 1325/1918.

[114] 'Alochana' (Discussion), *Bangiya Musalman Sahitya Patrika*, 3, 1, B 1327/1920.

[115] Tanzeen M. Murshid, *The Sacred and the Secular: Bengal Muslim Discourses 1871–1977*, Calcutta, 1995, pp. 130–31.

[116] Ahmad, *Kazi Nazrul Islam: Smritikatha*, pp. 1–2, 26–27, 105–10.

[117] Pabitra Gangopadhyay, *Chalaman Jiban* (Journey through Life), Calcutta, 1994, pp. 66–67, 93, 100, 205.

[118] *Modern Review*, Vol. 11, No. 3, March 1912.

[119] Satis Pakrasi, *Agnijuger Katha* (The Burning Times), Calcutta, third edition 1982, pp. 105, 109.

[120] 'Introduction', in Sipra Sarkar and Anamitra Das (eds.), *Bangalir Samyabad Charcha* (Communist Thinking in Bengal), Calcutta, 1998. Sarojnath Ghosh, *Rusiyar Pralay* (Apocalypse in Russia), Calcutta, 1920.

[121] Ahmad, *Kazi Nazrul Islam: Smritikatha*, p. 110.

[122] 'Introduction', in Sarkar and Das (eds.), *Bangalir Samyabad Charcha.*

[123] Hassan Mohammad, *Comrade Muzaffar Ahmad o Banglar Communist Andolan* (Comrade Muzaffar Ahmad and the Communist Movement in Bengal), Chattagram, 1989, p. 99.

[124] *Noakhali*, 1, 1, B 1322/1916. Ahmad, *Amar Jiban o Bharater Communist Party*, p. 83. Ahmad, *Kazi Nazrul Islam: Smritikatha*, p. 40.

[125] Mahendrakumar Ghosh, 'Katha o Karjyo' (Word and Deed), *Noakhali*, 1, 2, B 1323/1916.

[126] See 'The Bloomsbury Fraction', in Raymond Williams, *Problems in Materialism and Culture*, London, 1980. Williams describes avant-garde intellectuals of the Bloomsbury Circle as a 'fraction', isolated from the general directions of the upper classes.

[127] Ahmad, *Amar Jiban o Bharater Communist Party*, p. 83.

[128] IB 294 A/20 (133/1920). IB 294/20 (134/1920). Ray, *Urban Roots*, p. 96.

[129] IB 294 A/20 (133/1920). IB 294/20 (134/1920).

[130] *Census of India, 1921*, 4, 1.

[131] A.K. Roy, 'A Short History', p. 130. For a detailed study of the Calcutta Port's profitability and growth during the nineteenth century, see P. Banerjee, *Calcutta and Its Hinterland, 1833–1900*, Calcutta, 1975, pp. 24–69.

[132] E.P. Richards, 'C.I.T. Report on the Condition, Improvement and Town Planning of Calcutta and Contiguous Areas, Hertfordshire, 1914', pp. 10–11, quoted in Ray, *Urban Roots*, p. 5.

[133] *Report on Municipal Administration of Calcutta*, 1912–13.

[134] *Report on Municipal Administration of Calcutta*, 1918–19.

[135] *Report of the Committee on Industrial Unrest, 1921*, pp. 1194–1265.

[136] Ahmad, *Samakaler Katha*, p. 20; *Kazi Nazrul Islam: Smritikatha*, pp. 2, 47.

[137] McPherson, *Muslim Microcosm*, pp. 33, 37. The same author has pointed out that by early 1918, prices rose by 78 per cent. But wages had remained static since 1914 (p. 35).

[138] Broomfield, *Elite Conflict*, p. 122. Suranjan Das, *Communal Riots in Bengal 1905–1947*, Delhi, 1993, pp. 61, 67.

[139] Sumit Sarkar, *Modern India 1885–1947*, Hing Kong, 1989, p. 194.

[140] Ahmad, *Amar Jiban o Bharater Communist Party*, pp. 38, 83, 113–14, 263–66, 268, 292–93, 460.

CHAPTER TWO
Towards the Left

'And a vague, confused, search for a remedy,
A desire of revolt, prison, a desert where to flee.'
– Faiz Ahmad Faiz, 'As We Are'

It was in the years immediately following the First World War (1914–19) that Muzaffar Ahmad's politics was transformed. The change in direction was rooted in his encounter with left radicalism, a new political option emerging out of the complex interactions between class conflict, social location and political agency in a climate of mass post-war upsurge.

The history of Bengal in colonial times has often been read as a series of political initiatives spearheaded by the Bengal intelligentsia. Attempts to modify this trend have displayed a marked tendency to overemphasize either the autonomy of mass consciousness or the primacy of intellectual ideas over their social context, including popular movements. An investigation of the dialectical interplay between intellectual consciousness and mass action is called for. Those members of the intelligentsia who were unhappy with the ideological alternatives existing in the first quarter of the twentieth century in India were radicalized through this process.

City of Capital versus City of Labour

Guided by the changing fortunes of British colonialism, Calcutta emerged as the metropolis of the British empire, second only to London. The turn of the twentieth-century dream to 'raise it from its present fifth position among the chief cities of the old world to the fourth, if not third in rank'[1] died in the course of the next twenty years as Calcutta fell from imperial grace. What remained in the urban physiognomy were the social divisions inherited from a vanished past.

Their impact was felt on city life in the early 1920s, when 'a general spirit

City of workers

of unrest' staggered the colonial authorities.[2] From the ranks of workers engaged by industrial and non-industrial enterprises and institutions, conscious social militancy arose and assumed a scale never noticed before. Desperate economic conditions after the war, mounting resentment against the British empire among all sections of the colonized society, and the launching of the anti-colonial Khilafat and Non-Cooperation Movements motivated significant sections of the working class.[3] As labour joined forces with the anti-colonial political struggle, a whole new arena of urban radical action opened up.[4]

Wage Work and Post-War Upheavals
A vast variegated complex of exploitative labour relations emerged from the strategies adopted by colonial capital to optimize surplus extraction, using the city as its base. The growth of the Calcutta Port and allied enterprises in the late eighteenth century, the establishment of manufacturing units and the emergence of an industrial belt with jute as its core in the course of the nineteenth century, and the related development of a large service sector generated a sprawling labour market, encompassing both formal and informal labour.[5]

By the second decade of the twentieth century, Calcutta and its suburbs contained industries and manufacturing concerns where two-fifths of Bengal's factory labour were concentrated. Employment practices divided the wage workers according to skill, gender and age. Of the 78,890 workers, half were skilled. The unskilled workers (33,134) included 3,797 women and 2,638 children less than 14 years of age. A fifth of the managerial substratum engaged in supervision and clerical work were Europeans and Anglo-Indians.[6] Race played a major role in enforcing the work regime. Racial assaults by European foremen were not unknown in the work place.[7] At the very top of the industrial pyramid, in the realm of ownership and profits, white colonial interests towered. The leading industrial concerns were the jute mills, jute presses, printing presses, dockyards and port which included workshops under the Port Commissioner, gas and electric light works, oil mills and cotton mills. The jute industry dwarfed all the others. Before the First World War, European companies owned all the jute mills, all but one of the cotton mills, ten jute presses, and twelve machinery and engineering works. The port and docks were properties of the colonial government. The most profitable industries, whether private or public, were overwhelmingly controlled by British colonial capital.[8]

Repressive constraints built into the structure of work in the nineteenth century, especially coercive tactics at the disposal of employers, and the divisions along linguistic, religious and caste lines, have been cited in explaining the obstacles to labour unity and organized action.[9] Despite these impediments, workers showed signs of combination from the end of the nineteenth century. Changes in the scale of operation altered the structure of wage work. Many of the old, directly repressive methods that were at the disposal of employers could no longer be used.[10] Divisions into sub-communal groupings underlined the retention of rural ties.[11] Instead of acting as obstructions, these links, rooted in the shrinking material base in the villages, helped the worker to cope with the insecurity of the urban environment and boosted militant action in the industrial work place.[12]

Labour grievances snowballed into a massive labour upsurge in the late 1910s and early 1920s. It was preceded by distinct phases of working-class struggles to introduce coordinated action against capital. Though the root cause in all these phases was a decline in real wages, activism was also triggered by other, sometimes countrywide, mass movements.[13] Politicization of economic grievances through national and sectional movements was evident and proved to be persistent. These mobilizations accorded a hegemonic role to middle- and upper-class leaders who recognized in labour a support-base for their own socio-political programmes,[14] articulated through the ideologies of 'nation' and 'community'. There was also the realization, however, that economic problems had to be solved through politics and that these involved the entire society. This provided a radical space for the development of future self-conscious action of workers engaged in the formal sectors.

From the late nineteenth century onwards, racism, price rises and cyclical unemployment provoked repeated attempts by workers to bring about favourable changes in the work environment.[15] But it was in the aftermath of the First World War that the sporadic attempts to gain some rights through petitions, strikes and union formations in the preceding thirty years reached their boiling point. The deeply felt experience of social marginalization found its first organized expression on a mass scale. Though organized around the notion of liberal 'rights', the developing working-class activism was also influenced by more radical currents. Social dislocations and further impoverishment had ushered in an era of radical struggles against capitalism in the metropolitan countries, and against imperialism in the colonial world. India, where British war efforts had taken a heavy toll in terms of material and human resources,[16] readily responded to global popular protests. This phenomenon, related to the beginning of a wider trade union movement, found manifestation in the All India Trade Union Congress (AITUC), formed in Bombay in 1920.[17]

War-induced price rise of essential commodities had made conditions desperate, especially for the indigent. The intensity of material hardship remained unchanged in the immediate post-war years: while the real wage of workers declined, capital flourished as never before.[18] The situation was fraught with paradoxes. The workers retaliated against predatory profit-making with heightened drives for unionization and strike-action, especially targeting formal sectors of the economy, both industrial and non-industrial, owned by European capitalists and some Indians. The colonial government's facilities faced major disruptions. A large number of trade unions in Calcutta emerged between 1919 and 1920. They covered white- and blue-collar employees, government and non-government staff.[19] Many of these groups were active in previous periods of protest,[20] though the sheer scale and intensity of agitation marked out this period from the past. The *Report of the Committee on Industrial Unrest* (1921) shows that every industry in Bengal was affected by a strike-wave during 1920 and 1921. Waged in 137 European as well as Indian-owned concerns, the strikes immobilized all major industries over a considerable period of time. In Calcutta and its immediate vicinity, jute workers, tram workers, employees of tailoring firms, sweepers of the Calcutta Corporation, coachmen, motor workers, porters, press compositors, tobacco workers, taxi drivers, sailors, crewmen and workers of the Port Commissioner's workshops, all ceased work. Even coolies working for the Salvation Army and at the Victoria Memorial were on strike. Employers ranging from the Calcutta Corporation to the Indian newspaper house, *Amrita Bazaar Patrika*, were affected. Waiters and chefs in the city's leading European hotels also stopped work. The main demands of the working class centred on wage increase. Other issues which figured prominently were reduced working hours, paid and increased holidays, better working conditions, an end to managerial harassment, redressal of grievances and compensation in case of physical assault by supervisory staff. The right of

Muslim workers to pray during work hours and solidarity with other striking workers also provoked strikes.[21]

Of the 110 strikes conducted for higher pay in Bengal, 4 were totally successful, 48 were partially successful, 17 ended in extraction of promises to
settle grievances and 36 failed. The complementary damage to capital accumulation was not insignificant either. In the 137 strikes between July 1920
and March 1921, 244,180 workers were involved, and the total duration
of these strikes in terms of working days was 2,631,488. The significant
success rate of the strikes boosted a self-conscious spirit of resistance. The
issues raised demonstrated that the prime mover of strike-action was not
just economic. An awareness of labour dignity and confidence, expressed in
sectional, national or purely local terms, and largely dependent on the politics of middle-class organizers, was at work; this was reflected in the
enhanced ability of workers to counter management pressure which was
noticed with growing alarm by colonial administrators. The Committee on
Industrial Unrest quite correctly pinpointed the 'economic cause' as predominant in a period of 'genuine hardship of labouring classes', when an
'increase in cost of food stuffs, cloth and necessities of life' had not been
matched by wage rises. The committee made a deeper and more astute observation, that 'labour is developing a new consciousness of its own solidarity
and value' from 'the record of the numerous strikes due to comparatively
petty causes, which even a year ago would have created nothing more than
passing local excitement'. 'Trivial complaints which never have resulted in
strikes' were becoming central reasons to stop work.[22]

Muslim Workers in Troubled Times

A sizeable section, though not the majority, of women and men of Calcutta's
working class were officially classified as followers of Islam. Alongside working
populations from other religious and caste denominations, they had made
the city habitable through indispensable labour. Some of the Bengali-speaking Muslim workers who had settled in Calcutta before the 1850s worked
in the growing service sector as street hawkers, laundry workers, weavers,
domestic servants, market gardeners, tailors, coachmen and day labourers.
The overwhelmingly 'non-respectable' character of the Muslim population
was reflected in the naming of streets after some of the more prominent
male workers engaged as tailors (*ostagar*), book-binders (*duftari*), butlers
(*khanshama*), sailors (*serang*), constables (*thanadar*):

> The street names of Calcutta which owe their designation to Muhameddans
> are few and far between. Many of them belong to individuals of whom little
> or nothing is known. By far the greater number refers to persons who filled the
> lowest rung in the social ladder and rejoiced in the humble vocations . . .

when Calcutta was peopled mostly by men of their stamp, at least in the particular quarters where they resided.[23]

From the second half of the nineteenth century Urdu-speaking Muslims from Uttar Pradesh and Bihar arrived in Calcutta and its suburbs in search of work in the rising industrial complex.[24] The meagre presence of Muslims in education and representative politics was a reminder of their poverty. The majority in the city was illiterate. According to 'community based' calculations, Muslims continued to have the lowest literacy rate. The rate of literacy among men was 14.2 per cent in 1881, 16.7 per cent in 1891 and 16.5 per cent in 1901.[25] This picture remained unchanged even two decades later.[26] Though colonial capital continued to have the foremost say in the running of the Calcutta Corporation, a limited scheme of enfranchisement was introduced in 1876 to give a voice to indigenous landowning, professional and mercantile classes in municipal affairs. High property qualifications were attached to franchise – one of the defining principles of the colonial electoral system. These qualifications effectively excluded nineteen out of twenty people living in the city from voting.[27] Muslims were heavily concentrated among the urban working class. The Census of 1901 recorded that municipal wards with the largest industrial population had a significant Muslim presence. The Coolootala ward had a high percentage (39.7 per cent) of workers and their dependants. It was also where a large percentage of the city's Muslim population lived (12.7 per cent). In the Port area, where 61.2 per cent of the population were working class, Muslim workers were predominant. They were also the majority in the Suburban Municipality of Garden Reach where 64.6 per cent of the population were engaged in industrial occupations. Jute and tailoring were the largest industrial employers in the suburbs.[28] Around 1911, Muslims were almost as numerous as Hindu workers in the jute industry. Muslims monopolized the tailoring profession, and they were overwhelmingly in the majority as sailors, boatmen, carters, coachmen and stable boys. They supplied most of the bakers, nearly all the butchers, the majority of construction workers, and also those engaged in the tobacco trade. Muslim workers also had a sizeable presence in the printing presses. Half of the beggars in Calcutta proper were Muslims.[29]

The Census of 1901 had hoped 'better results' could be expected in the future. Yet, the Censuses of 1911 and 1921 showed that the status of Muslim workers, alongside the rest of the working class, had undergone little change. The Census of 1911 calculated that a third of the Muslim population depended on industrial occupations, a fifth on transport, one-eighth on domestic service and one-seventh on trade. Less than 6,000 belonged to civil professions; here they were outnumbered by Hindus in the proportion of seven to one, and also by the Christians. The Census of 1921 showed that the number of Muslims engaged in the jute trade declined during this period, and may have contributed to the decline in the number of Muslims (24.5 per cent) living in the city. Muslims continued to supply the majority of bakers, butchers, tailors, tobacco workers, masons, brick-layers, book-binders, carters, boatmen and sailors. A third of Calcutta's Muslim population continued to depend on industry and a seventh on trade. A sixth depended on transport and one-eleventh on domestic service. Only one-twentieth were engaged in public administration and liberal arts.[30] The vast majority of Calcutta residents, including the bulk of Muslims, continued to be concentrated at the very bottom of society.

Labour organizations among Muslims displayed a continuous interplay between sectional and wider considerations, between immediate and larger issues. Workers attempted to find channels of meaningful action through heterodox political currents. Some of the oldest trade unions in the city had been formed in the Calcutta Docks and quite a few of the city's leading Muslim trade unionists were involved in organizing the local population. The Indian Seamen's Club, formed in 1895, was one of the earliest attempts to create working-class organizations in the city.[31] The Indian Seamen's Anjuman, formed in 1908, underwent several name changes and finally emerged as the Indian Seamen's Union (ISU) in 1920. The transition from 'Anjuman' to 'Union' meant a shift in the organizational outlook. The stress was no longer on the religious solidarity of members; even if they continued to be communally homogenous their occupation was seen as the common bond uniting them.[32] The Inland Steamship and Flat Employees' Association formed in 1920 organized the crew of steamers and river vessels. In contrast, the Anjuman Zahazian was set up by shipping brokers during the same year to counter initiatives from below. A.H. Zahirula, a Kidderpore physician, and Sheikh Samir, shipping broker, owner of taxi-cabs, and alleg-edly a cocaine and opium smuggler, were the leading figures of this rival organization, created to undermine the ISU.[33] To emphasize its 'religious' character as opposed to the 'a-religious' ISU, the first meeting of this organization took place in the yard of a mosque. The leaflet advertising the launch added 'Sri' as a prefix to Sheikh Samir's name, showing that he was not averse to terms used among the Hindu *bhadralok* to confer social respect-ability. Samir was against internal democracy, making himself the sole decision maker,[34] as opposed to the structure of the ISU which provided for an elected committee to lead the organization.[35]

In the organization of seamen, the most important role was played by Mohammad Daud, a lawyer in Alipore Court who had revitalized the ISU. He also recorded the history of its origin and development between the years 1918 and 1924.[36] Though socially aware and active in labour politics, he was politically independent of both the Congress nationalists and the

Khilafatists who dominated the labour movement. His primary commit-ment was to the union, a role interpreted as 'syndicalist'.[37] Daud was also actively involved in the Calcutta Tramway Employee's Union and the Anju-mani Khanshamas (Association of Chefs and Butlers). Both these organiza-tions led long-drawn strikes during the early 1920s.[38] The Anjumani Khansha-mas shut down leading hotels of the city frequented by Europeans in the heart of the Chowringhee area. The strikers – led by a waiter, Sirajuddin, Secretary of the Association of Chefs and Butlers – protested against low pay and the racial arrogance of those they served every day in establish-ments such as the Grand and the Continental, landmarks in the turn-of-the-century hotel world in colonial Asia. The white patrons were so enraged by this act of direct anti-racist defiance that Sirajuddin was charged with sedition and sentenced to eighteen months' hard labour.[39] Even in prison he continued to resist the authorities by participating in a hunger strike.[40]

All militant strike-actions included Muslims. A perception of worsening conditions resulted in a huge response to labour protests in the dock areas and supporting facilities. Assisted by pan-Islamist, nationalist and indepen-dent labour leaders, stoppage of work centred round demands for pay increase. Eight of these strikes were partially successful. One yielded a little. Seven ended in failure, but only after the management was able to break the morale of the work force through non-negotiation, police deployment and the assistance of the *sardars* (foremen) who enforced labour discipline on a daily basis. At least one of the incidents involved violent scuffles between the strikers and the authorities.[41]

Scenes from Labour Protests

The College Street–College Square area, the locale of all Calcutta-based writers and intellectuals, also felt the tremors of working-class protests. Workers made themselves visible as an organized social force in an urban space so far chiefly associated with the concerns of the middle-class intelligentsia. The Mahabodhi Society, the Theosophical Society, the Indian Association Hall and the Albert Hall were regular venues for political meetings where anti-colonial moderation and militancy were in ample display. A confronta-tional mood descended on the immediate urban environment through open-air labour meetings; they uncovered a different political texture, shaped by growing desperation and confidence from below. During the government printers' strike of 1920, at an afternoon meeting in College Square where large numbers of strikers, supporters and interested onlookers had gathered, a printing-press worker declared that strike-breakers must be beaten up severely to ensure that they are too scared to return. Later he retracted his earlier militant utterances, apologized and announced that those who wished to rejoin work should be dissuaded by peaceful means, on 'bended knees'.

The president, who spoke after him, suggested that those present should convince colleagues still at work to join the strike. The meeting then broke up and printers were seen walking away in groups towards their work places.[42]

Though the printers' meeting, described by police agents, implied that militancy from below was subject to curbs from above, there were instances when the levers of proprietorial control were paralysed. When Calcutta tram workers demanded a wage increase and an eight-hour working day, the Calcutta Tram Company, a colonial enterprise, engaged Anglo-Indian strike-breakers as buffers against the 'native' work force at the Kidderpore Dock and the Wellesley area. When this strategy, with racial overtones, was about to be repeated at the Kalighat Tram Depot, clashes broke out between the strikers and the Anglo-Indian strike-breakers, backed by a largely Anglo-Indian police force. While escaping their attackers some strikers sought refuge in a Muslim slum nearby, and its inhabitants joined them to fight the police. All attempts by middle-class leaders to make the workers resist peacefully collapsed. Following the violence, a bullet was fired from a police van without any provocation, killing a passer-by. Enquiries revealed that the dead man was a domestic servant. The police sergeant responsible could not be traced as the entire force closed ranks and covered up for him.[43] The Kalighat Tram Depot incident of 1921 reflected instant forging of class solidarities against forces of authority, linking unionized workers with other segments of the urban working class. Without regular formations to sustain them, however, the spaces set ablaze by such impromptu flickers of resistance were subject to the dissolution of a wider unity and rapid restoration of the existing order. Still, the closing of ranks on the part of the workers could suddenly take on a life of its own at a given conjuncture, and involve violent protests without warning, during a time of heightened poverty and shared experiences of long-term structural deprivation in working-class neighbourhoods.

The tram workers' actions contributed directly to the widening of Calcutta's transport network. In response to the disruption of tram services, buses emerged as an alternative form of transport. The Municipal authorities observed:

> The strike [of tram workers] gave a great impetus to motor transport and several motor buses were improvised during the strike. Since the close of the year the Tramways Company have organized a motor bus service from Dalhousie Square to Ballygunge. Other transport companies are also in the field, and it is to be hoped that regular motor bus services will be organized before long to supplement the tramways.[44]

Ahindra Chaudhuri, a well-known actor, recalled:

Events followed one after another: Jalianwalabagh, Mahatmaji's movement etc. They were accompanied by continuous meetings and strikes. Strikes in the Tram Company were regular occurrences. Once, I cannot recall the exact year, the tram strike lasted for quite a long time. The office-going crowd were facing problems. The companies which owned lorries to carry goods, installed benches inside their vehicles and used them to transport their *baboo*s (clerks). . . . Soon [these] companies . . . secured the permission of the police commissioner and started plying the vehicles on a commercial basis. . . . Tickets had to be purchased [by passengers].[45]

These makeshift ventures soon gave way to a regular bus-service.[46] The size of workers engaged in the transport industry increased; new labour organizations emerged. During the strike-wave of 1920–21, the city was also brought to a near-standstill by the actions of workers of the Oriental Gas Company. Their strike plunged Calcutta into darkness since there were only 206 electric lights while gas lamps numbered 13,612 at the time.[47] Abdul Halim, who later turned to communism, observed people's fear of stepping outdoors after sunset. The threat of robbery hung in the air and streets wore a deserted look in the evenings.[48] The Calcutta Corporation sweepers, low-paid, socially despised lower-caste men and women, also stopped garbage collection for a few days, disrupting the maintenance of civic hygiene. Their strike was partially successful, though it had little impact on the Corporation authorities. A strike at the municipal workshops, lasting seven weeks, had greater impact and attracted much official attention. Net profit nose-dived, adversely affecting revenue margins, as was sourly recorded in the Corporation's annual report.[49]

Away from the public gaze, even the police agents sent to watch the crowds were demanding better working conditions. In a petition to the Deputy Commissioner of the Special Branch in 1921, they complained of insufficient rest and physical exhaustion associated with heightened surveillance. The sheer volume of political protests during the Khilafat and Non-Cooperation Movements required their presence at College Square between 4 and 6 each evening. They covered political meetings, then returned to the Elysium Row headquarters to write reports by candlelight and went home well after midnight. They demanded increased hours of rest and continued bargaining well into the 1920s.[50]

The transition from a curious bystander to a sympathetic onlooker, to a political activist, was not very unusual in such a climate. Workers disrupted routines of daily life, making other classes and class segments aware of labour struggles and politics. Working-class protests influenced anti-establishment thinking among sections of the intelligentsia. Multi-stranded reality momentarily fused into a framework of political opposition from below, and

image after image of social protests were stamped on the minds of some of
the observers. Sympathy towards working-class protests was very evident
among the circle of intellectuals who gathered at the Bengali Muslim Literary Society office at 32 College Street. Muzaffar wrote that there was a
general consensus in support of the ongoing steamer strike in East Bengal
during 1921.[51] From the balcony and windows of 32 College Street, sitting
at the Sango Valley tea-room and restaurant next door, or walking around
the neighbourhood streets, a spectacle of unfamiliar resistance could be witnessed: uncollected garbage piled on the streets, lamps unlit as darkness fell,
deserted tram-tracks, signs of resolution and energy on the faces of the anonymous crowd at the open-air labour meetings. An urge was building up to
make sense of these concerted actions by an invisible majority.

Middle-class Activists and 'the Cause of Labour'
That the involvement of 'Public men of all shades of opinion' had made
matters worse, was not doubted for a moment by the colonial authorities.
Among the men who 'devoted themselves to the cause of labour, often with
the highest motives, though sometimes with more zeal than knowledge',[52]
were lower-middle-class Bengali Muslim intellectuals such as Muzaffar
Ahmad. The distress years during and immediately after the war made them
victims of unemployment and price rise, and develop a marked interest in
anti-colonial activities. The participation of the middle classes, especially
members of the intelligentsia, in various protests was a feature not just confined to Bengal and India. From Egypt to China, close links were developing between a section of the radicalized intelligentsia and the emerging
communist movements. The middle-class participation in anti-imperialist
politics involved intellectuals and salaried professionals: students, writers,
clerks, school-teachers and journalists.[53] The Committee on Industrial Unrest made wider social connections when it reported that the 'strike fever' in
Bengal could not be isolated and was only one phase in 'the general unrest
which has prevailed since the close of the war in every country in the world'.
It related labour to larger anti-colonial movements and their convergence
with strike-actions.[54] The post-war international trend in the Indian context was documented by the colonial authorities to explain the readiness of
the middle-class intelligentsia to join and lead the masses during anti-colonial and anti-establishment protests of various kinds. They were seen as 'by
far the most bitter and enthusiastic elements in any anti-Government campaign'.[55]

The 'acute bread-problem' and unemployment that were making middle-
class young men 'desperate', leading to 'so-called political' and other crimes,
were recognized by middle-class Indian segments also.[56] Shrinking material
security, rising costs of living and deteriorating conditions of the middle

classes, particularly its lower echelons, were repeatedly highlighted through platforms old and new, making way for protest alliances across classes. A Muslim League petition sent to the secretary of the Calcutta Rent Committee in December 1919 pointed to the doubling of house rents in post-war Calcutta, hitting the middle classes hard. The 'abnormal increase' was blamed on speculation and profiteering, a 50 per cent increase in the expenses of building materials compared to pre-war costs, and acquisition of land by the Calcutta Improvement Trust.[57] A body created by the government and the Bengal Chamber of Commerce in 1911, the Trust was seen by 'Indian interest groups' in Calcutta as the bastion of European capitalist interests, and much resented.[58] The petition alleged that the Trust was involved in an 'indiscreet' acquisition drive, leading to widespread eviction and resale of surplus land at inflated prices. Profiteering landlords, taking advantage of the general increase in land value and house rents throughout Calcutta, also charged the tenants heavily, at extortion rates 'quite out of all proportion to previous and existing rents'.[59] The Rent Bill proposed by the government also provoked 'general dissatisfaction'. *Hitavadi* (The Utilitarian), the most widely circulating Bengali newspaper in 1920, felt that those who 'hired big houses, shops etc., will gain most'; there would be little difference for 'the middle-class tenants' living in small houses.[60]

The social uncertainty of lower-middle-class existence, the spectre of dispossession, and the widening gulf between the upper classes and low-paid, white-collar wage workers left their imprint on literature. Nabakrishna Ghosh's *Keranir Maskabar* (The Clerk's Month-End), a collection of stories published in 1921, treated the wretchedness of clerical workers. The opening story, 'Keranir Mashkabar', traces the disastrous visit of a rich, insensitive friend, pushing the clerk towards penury at the end of the month when wage workers generally run out of money. The story concludes with the departure of the parasitic friend and the appearance of a municipal tax assessment officer who harshly demands a steep sum for the crumbling residence. The ominous threat of future eviction hangs in the air as he leaves. One of the stories, 'Prayashchitta' (Penance), touches on a singularly unattractive, unenviable and monotonous routine:

> . . . a mess for clerks – one could call it an animal's den – in the morning by nine all would stuff their mouths and noses with half-cooked rice and lentil and run to the office and return home exhausted in the evening. After dinner [they] entered the world of sleep snoring loudly. This was their competition – who could fall asleep first.[61]

The harsh realities of lower-middle-class life, a prioritization of middle-class wants and the advocacy of anti-government alliances across classes shaped middle-class activism. Early meetings of the Employees' Association, a union of clerical staff, held in August 1920 highlighted the spiralling prices of essential commodities, bringing in their train 'diseases', 'bad and insufficient food', 'starvation', 'overcrowding' and 'attendant evils for the middle-class in general'. Demands were made for government schemes to protect the middle class and the 'masses', namely peasants with whom the middle classes supposedly had no conflict of interest. Yet, a fear of being reduced to the socio-material level of the very poor haunted these meetings. The government was criticized for neglecting the middle classes, 'the back-bone of society'. The members were promised a cooperative society to combat 'ruinous' prices, vocational training to set up small businesses for supplementing reduced real wages, and a reading room for leisure and instruction on trends in politics and culture. Evening classes offering training in book-keeping and export of gunny sacks were part of the organizational agenda. A cooperative society was indeed floated in the later half of 1920. It supplied clerks affected by scarcity with cloth (*dhuti*) and foodstuff.[62] The deliberations and resolutions emphasized self-help in hard times. They also actively expressed the desire to avoid loss of class and ameliorate the conditions of union members through routes created by capital; a 'partnership between labour and capital' was projected as the 'indigenous system prevailing in India from time immemorial'. In keeping with this ideological position and replete with dubious historical assertions, the Employees' Association, at this juncture, practised moderation vis-à-vis employers as a self-conscious white-collar trade union. A meeting held in October 1920 was anxious to avoid strikes.[63] Though the position of lower-middle-class unions on strikes, including that of the Employees' Association, changed after a few years,[64] radical confrontations with capital during the post-war economic and social crises were products of working-class initiative.[65]

Led by the proprietor classes, a strategy of monitored inclusion characterized the mass movements. Gandhi deeply distrusted mass initiatives which could spiral out of control.[66] This was equally true of non-Gandhians. Many Khilafatist and independent labour leaders who joined the broad anti-colonial struggles encouraged a protest mentality while suppressing the self-conscious agency of the workers.[67] As for the most militant among the nationalists, when it came to recruiting people from the lowest echelons of the social order, they displayed a deep political apathy. Jugantar participated in the Non-Cooperation and Khilafat Movements with the principal objective of swelling its ranks with young middle-class recruits. Suspension of terrorist activities confirmed their willingness to work within the framework of the larger anti-colonial struggle, a strategy opposed by Anushilan. 'Terrorist action' was not undertaken by any of the groups[68] in the era of unfolding mass struggles. Though the masses participated with immense enthusiasm, the militant nationalists continued to regard them as passive and rudderless, a lower-class multitude to be guided from above. Bhupendrakumar Datta, a leading figure of Jugantar, focused on the political contempt behind this attitude. The established view was that the peasants harboured a spirit of 'stoic submission' and that workers were a microscopic presence in the country; their struggles were motivated by economic demands only. That there could be an ideological leap from the movement for 'wage increase' to a political struggle was beyond 'thought'.[69] To Satis Pakrasi of Anushilan, who later became a communist, the concept of building a mass movement was external to his group's idea of 'armed revolution'.[70] Unlike Gandhian and other labour leaders, though occasionally celebrating the popular content of mass struggles, the militant nationalists desisted from engaging with labour issues. They endorsed the prevailing paternalistic strategy for mobilizing the masses, and subscribed to a wide class consensus on the need to establish hegemonic control over the poor and quell the search for self-aware activism from below. The role of the militant nationalists was 'passive' in this class project; they did not actively implement it. Active enforcement was left to other constituents of the anti-colonial leadership.

That middle-class caution was thrown to the winds and militant action resorted to at all, revealed the growing class confidence of the workers themselves. As they were drawn into strikes and wider mass movements, their actions reminded those above them of the divergent social interests embedded within mass politics. Muzaffar Ahmad was radicalized from his brush with this aspect of working-class activism, the tendency of workers to go beyond the hegemonic drives of the middle- and upper-class leadership. The positions adopted by nationalist leaders on most issues, including labour, alienated him. His distaste towards the loyalist position assumed by Congress leaders was clear during the First World War, when large numbers, mainly from Bengal, had been interned on charges of trying to subvert the British war efforts.[71] Post-war strategies of mainstream anti-colonialism also failed to impress, particularly the brakes Gandhi had applied on the popular upsurge in 1919. Gandhi had termed the first mass *satyagraha*, culminating in militant confrontations with the colonial state apparatus, a 'Himalayan blunder'. The nine Hindu and Muslim demonstrators gunned down in the Harrison Road–Chitpur–Burrabazar neighbourhood which had witnessed the anti-Marwari cloth riots a year before, was a show of defiant unity during this phase of the movement; this transition from sectionalism to anti-colonialism was ignored by the central anti-colonial leadership. The refusal of the Indian National Congress to officially congratulate Rabindranath Tagore after he had renounced his knighthood in protest against the Jallianwala Bagh massacre was also noticed.[72]

Social Pressures from Above and Below

Interaction with the urban poor in the late 1910s and early 1920s was instrumental in Muzaffar Ahmad's political transformation. The encounters between his intellectual milieu and popular upheavals propelled him towards left politics. The process was associated with the heightened interest in socialist ideas following the Bolshevik Revolution of 1917, and the post-war international mood of anti-capitalism and anti-colonialism. A focused analysis shows a political conjuncture for Muzaffar located within the shrinking material resources made acute by the post-war economic crisis; sympathetic exposure to the mass upsurge of the period; and increasing dissatisfaction with the existing political leadership at a time when leftist ideas were beginning to be disseminated.

Uncertain and Communitarian Locations

The 'educated unemployed' increasingly saw themselves as prisoners of social insecurities initiated by an imperialist war; they supplied the Non-Cooperation and Khilafat campaigns with 'volunteers'. Exposed to the degrading conditions that enveloped even white-collar 'mental' work, and with no control over their labour or the job market, many viewed themselves as plunging into an abyss. The curious case of Habibullah Khan, a 22-year-old 'suspected Bolshevik' briefly investigated by the secret police in 1920, reflected the desperations and dilemmas confronting fringe members of the intelligentsia. Like Muzaffar a migrant from Noakhali who had failed to qualify in the Matriculation examination, Habibullah was acquainted with prominent Khilafat leaders of the day: Akram Khan and Fazlul Haq. He also claimed to have visited and admired nationalist leaders such as Bipin Chandra Pal, C.R. Das, Byomkesh Chakrabarty and others. The Bengali Muslim undercover agent sent to watch over Habibullah returned with the impression that this was 'a man with cracked head'. According to the agent, Habibullah was in the habit of trying to convince his associates of the imminent triumph of Islam and Bolshevism. His 'discourses' resembled 'lectures'; he was extremely excitable while holding forth on the fallen state of Muslims. Fear of the police and of his own past, which he begged the police agent not to bring up, apparently gnawed at him. The house where he was engaged as a private tutor to the owner's son provided shelter and he seemed to lead an 'aimless life'. To the police, Habibullah was harmless, an emotionally disturbed and impoverished lower-middle-class youth suffering from a 'disordered' brain, which explained his 'extremism'.[73]

Not all of those placed in a similar material environment could be written off as insane. The social aimlessness of the young intelligentsia converged with a rising interest in political activism. Explanations behind daily experiences were being sought. Some were making connections between the success of the Bolshevik Revolution and the ongoing strikes, and reaching radical conclusions. In the immediate post-war period, an anti-authoritarian strain was gaining momentum among sections of the young city literati. This tendency formed an undercurrent during the First World War, becoming more pronounced in an atmosphere of political support for mass anti-colonialism, and of generational conflict with elders, leaders and patrons. Only a few broke away completely from the politics of the older generation. Those political views were reformulated and extended in keeping with changing political alignments and contexts. However, in times of widespread grievance and turbulence, many were dissatisfied with the available ideological options and political identities.

Muzaffar Ahmad's circle of literary acquaintances could be seen as a microcosm of these tendencies. A communitarian existence, a mode of survival for hard-pressed intellectuals such as Muzaffar from the pre-war period in the city, meant socialization into collective solidarities as well as going beyond their boundaries in difficult times. In the post-war years, as crises intensified and workers gained visibility as a social force, interactions between literary activists and workers produced new routes to political activism. Several members of de-rooted intellectual collectives embodied this process of transformation. At the end of the war, Muzaffar was a 'full-time worker' of the Bengal Muslim Literary Society (*Bangiya Musalman Sahitya Samiti*). During the war, he had been drawn to this organization as a migrant intellectual. In the post-war climate, the society acted as an incubator for his increased radical interests and to a very great extent facilitated connections that would eventually create the first socialist nucleus in the city.

From 1918, Muzaffar worked as the assistant general secretary of the Literary Society, and by January 1919, he was living in its premises at 32 College Street. The society office, a first floor apartment comprising two rooms, overlooked the road. From the balcony, the campus of the Medical College Hospital and a busy stretch of the street was visible. The office housed a library and reading room with a long table. Leading members of the Muslim and Hindu *bhadralok* intelligentsia contributed money, books and furniture to build the infrastructure. Apart from Muzaffar, the office welcomed and temporarily housed an unending flow of young Muslim intellectuals from the districts. Muzaffar Ahmad lived in the Bengal Muslim Literary Society office throughout 1919 and during the first half of 1920. Kazi Abdul Odud, Mohammed Shahidullah and Kazi Nazrul Islam, later to emerge as key cultural figures, also shared the premises.[74] Afzazul Haq, editor of a quality literary journal, *Moslem Bharat*, also stayed there. The social environment of the office alternated between the quiet of a reading room and the jovial, communitarian life of the mess. The office staff, library

32 College Street: the office of the *Bangiya Musalman Sahitya Samiti* was located on the first floor of this house

users, society members, residents, friends and visitors made it a lively centre of literary and political discourse; it was a literary *adda*[75] where middle-class writers, activists, demobilized soldiers and unemployed youth from diverse political and religious backgrounds participated. The public nature of the office generated a self-renewing, expanding, collective sphere; it was a topological space characterized by intersections and convergences of different circles and segments. Writers on the fringe were developing connections across the communal divide and interrogating the divide itself. Pabitra Gangopadhyay, well thought of in all the literary circles of the city for his open, friendly personality and ability to rise above different factions,[76] regarded the society office in 1919–20 as 'our meeting place', a 'den' visited 'at least once each day'. When Nazrul arrived in Calcutta and started staying with Muzaffar, Pabitra would go there at night and spend five to six hours with them.[77]

The shared weight of daily living meant becoming aware of the material hardships of those in the vicinity. Achintyakumar Sengupta called it an age of friendship. For him, Nazrul and Pabitra embodied this spirit of the times, where acts of practical solidarity sustained financially insecure writers. Publishers paid little, if at all, casually refusing or postponing payment of royalty.[78] Success was elusive. Sometimes suppression of identity opened the well-guarded doorways of established journals. Adoption of female pseudonyms increased the chances of being accepted, for, due to the shortage of women writers, editors were more willing to print their work. Writing was expen-

View from the balcony of the *Bangiya Musalman Sahitya Samiti* office at
32 College Street

sive. Authors normally used the cheapest available writing instrument and
material, the 'G-nib' and thick, hard-bound notebooks.[79] An official report
describing the general appearance of newspapers and journals in 1920 stated:
'The get-up and printing of the papers, showed no signs of recovery owing
to the high prices of paper and printing materials.'[80] Raising subscriptions
to help out friends and acquaintances was a way of tiding over hard times.
The circle of acquaintances at 32 College Street, ignoring communal divisions in the wider society, often deliberated on ways to take care of their
own. Fakirnath Bandopadhyay, who taught Philosophy at the Sanskrit
College located nearby, regarded Nazrul as a quasi-relation and offered financial help in 1921.[81]

For many of the intellectuals, a cheek-by-jowl existence with the lower
classes became unavoidable with the rise in rents, mentioned earlier. Often
forced to live near their patrons and employers, an experience that threatened to become oppressive whenever disagreements arose,[82] a struggling writer
could live independently in the semi-slum conditions of a lower-middle-
class mess or rented accommodation. During the second half of 1920, when
Muzaffar and Nazrul rented a single-storeyed house in a dark bylane where
Turner Street merged into a slum, the local slum dwellers became their friends
– not least because of Nazrul's 'winning personality'. Soon the house also
became the centre of a literary *adda*. Although they had moved away from
the centrally located Literary Society office, Nazrul's undiminished popu-

larity ensured a steady flow of visitors, reproducing a similar communitarian ambience.[83] Shailajananda Mukhopadhyay, writer and friend Achintyakumar, and Nazrul lived in a 'ramshackle, derelict mess'. Located on the upper floor of a two-storeyed house stretching from east to west, it gave an impression of imminent collapse, its narrow balcony with wooden railings dangerously dislocated in places. The ground floor housed a melange of working-class trades: a Hindustani washerman, a fuel depot selling coal and wood, a snack-bar specializing in roadside fried food, a nut-seller and an ice-candy man. Achintyakumar has implied that the appearance of *Sanhati*, a trade union journal published at the initiative of an impoverished lower-middle-class intellectual in 1923, was inspired by this close proximity between the impoverished intelligentsia and workers.[84]

The world of print and many engaged in it suffered from reduced circumstances while living through upheavals, investing Bengali literature with a new social aesthetic. Muzaffar and Nazrul's friend, fellow-writer Sibram Chakrabarty, who was jailed for editing *Jugantar* (Epochal Change), a short-lived 'extremist' journal, in 1923,[85] developed socialist sympathies in the course of the 1920s.[86] His *Jakhan Tara Katha Bolbe* (When They Speak Out) had roots in the expanding climate of social militancy visible in the immediate surroundings of the writer from the late 1910s and early 1920s onwards. The unlikely (anti-)hero of the play is an unemployed working-class Muslim youth-turned-petty criminal. Not knowing that he had picked the pocket of a swindler, an Indian financier-capitalist in the process of de-camping with their savings, he is viciously assaulted by the morally out-raged middle-class clientele who had assembled outside the bank. From police custody, he is sent as a prisoner to a hospital to recover from his injuries, and there he shares a room with two Hindu *bhadralok* youths: one, a writer chronically starved because of non-payment of royalties by his publisher, and the other, a romantic wanderer in anarchic revolt against every social institution. These two characters, deliberate caricatures of the playwright's own kind, namely atypical impoverished bohemian intellectuals from a Hindu *bhadralok* background, are treated somewhat sympathetically. Though their predicament is grounded in social reality, they are satirized for their unthinking attachment to the subjective, as alienated members of a parasitic stratum in its death throes. To Sibram, the inability of these characters to rise above deeply individualized expressions of social dissent renders them incapable of any meaningful resistance. In the end the writer dies, the romantic goes mad, and the Muslim working-class youth, with street-smart pragmatism, manages to escape. His flight symbolizes the possibility of his future resistance, his potential to survive till people of his social class speak out.[87]

From Political Journalism to 'Bolshevism'

As the organized voices of the oppressed became increasingly difficult to ignore during 1920–21, Muzaffar tried to make sense of the multilayered and contradictory political aspirations around him. He turned towards socially aware radical journalism. This shift from cultural activism to political journalism was to transform his ideological perspective.

In 1920, Muzaffar and Nazrul were approached with a proposal to take charge of an evening daily. Fazlul Haq, top legal practitioner of the Calcutta High Court, and leader of the Bengal Congress and the ongoing Khilafat Movement, was floating this paper. Nazrul and Muzaffar were already thinking of switching to political journalism. The multiple social possibilities of the times were expressed through the name they chose for the paper: *Nabajug* (New Age). Their aim, when they joined Haq's initiative in the middle of 1920, was to write on popular–democratic movements mounted by ordinary people, 'especially workers and peasants'. Though started as an organ openly sympathetic to the anti-colonial mass upsurge, Haq did not dictate the adoption of any definite political line. Muzaffar and Nazrul were happy with Haq's non-interference since they had no clear-cut position at the time, except for anti-imperialism and an interest in mass struggles. They wrote on the basis of their experiences and inspirations, drawing upon contemporary social and political upheavals.

While Muzaffar worked there, *Nabajug* proved to be an exceptionally popular paper. He was responsible in all but name during the first six months of its publication, having fulfilled a similar function in the Literary Society journal. Haq had wanted a 'Muslim' name for the daily. He was convinced that Bengali Hindus, having so many superior print organs at their disposal, would not buy it. Muzaffar's desire to ensure a steady readership, rather than a communally exclusivist position, influenced Haq's thinking. A second disagreement with Haq emerged over the selection of writers. Haq believed that Bengali Muslim writers were far inferior to Hindu *bhadralok* writers. Muzaffar and Nazrul regarded Panchkori Bandopadhyay, a former editor of *Nayak*, as a hack writer capable of adopting completely contradictory political positions for money. They successfully prevented Haq from hiring this man.[88] Bandopadhyay apparently spoke at rallies organized in North Bengal, attended by Hindu and Muslim tenants, where he emotionally spoke out against zamindari oppression[89] while glorifying Hindu revivalism as the social blueprint of an ideal society in his writings.[90]

Soon Haq had reason to be pleased with his recruits. Nazrul's eye-catching headlines, his imaginative use of quotations from Tagore and other writers, the involved and highly charged tone of many of the articles, and the discussion on topical events and news analysis, at the end of the day, proved to be an instant success with the middle-class reading public. *Nabajug* sub-scribed to the Associated Press for the latest news. For a while, the idea of subscribing to the British Labour organ, *Daily Herald*, was also entertained. In form and content, the paper stood out from most Bengali evening dailies which reproduced items from English-language morning newspapers. Haq was pleased by the attention *Nabajug's* militancy attracted. As far as he was concerned, notoriety ensured sales. Many of his Hindu friends congratu-lated him. A British judge of the Calcutta High Court, who was in the habit of reading Bengali newspapers, personally called Haq to his chamber and expressed displeasure over the paper's tone. The police issued warnings to the publication several times. These incidents, according to Muzaffar, con-vinced Haq of the paper's success. Though he was the editor-in-chief, Haq was quite happy to leave the actual running of the organ to Nazrul and Muzaffar, and was keen to retain them, as both regarded the work as an act of political commitment and did not press for wages.[91]

The government had some idea of the militant anti-colonial position likely to be adopted. A rather steep deposit was demanded for the right to publish *Nabajug*.[92] The paper had a small circulation (3,000), compared to Bengali organs like *Hitavadi* (The Utilitarian), which had the highest circu-lation (25,000) in 1920. When contrasted with older Bengali Muslim periodi-cals such as *Mohammadi* (4,000), it was not far behind. *Nabajug* managed to find a place among the fourteen most widely circulated print organs under Indian ownership listed by the Home Department of the Bengal gov-ernment during the second half of 1920.[93]

The Annual Report on Indian Papers Printed or Published (1920) classi-fied the political press as pro-government, moderate, extremist and inde-pendent. The first two categories were perceived as having a waning influ-ence: 'The general tone of the Indian Press seemed as distrustful as before, but except for the Muslim section, was on the whole less violent in expres-sion.' In keeping with the atmosphere of Hindu–Muslim rapprochement, the relationship between the Hindu and the Muslim press had become 'even more friendly than ever before'. The report recognized that the anger of the Muslim literati was clearly directed towards the British government:

> The Moslem Press maintained its improvement in literary quality, some of the journals equalling the more established ones of the Hindu press. The political tone of the whole Moslem press . . . however, became even more objection-able than the year before. . . . Indeed, the Moslem extremists far outstripped their Hindu peers in point of rugged outspokenness. The prejudice against the British, and, indeed the whole of Christendom in its attitude towards the Cres-cent continued.

Nabajug was produced by, and in turn reproduced, this mood, though it had a wider radical populist outlook:

> Written in a fine Bengali style of direct appeal like the *Mohammadi*, but with slightly less fire and finish, the *Nava Yuga*, started as an Extremist on 12th July under the proprietorship of Mr. Fazl-ul-Haq, also an Extremist then. It held the government responsible for the degradation of the country. It extended support for Khilafat, support for self-government which, it felt, could not be attained through Montford Reforms alone, support for peasants and workers. ('We will rouse a sense of self-respect amongst rayats, peasants, labourers, etc.') In pursuance of the last principle, it often advocated cause of Indian seamen and rayats. It used very violent language over the Muhajirin affair at Kanchagarhi and asked: 'Are we not to retaliate?'

In July 1920, *Nabajug* was reprimanded for publishing Nazrul Islam's 'Who is Responsible for the Death of the Muhajirs?',[94] in response to the Kacha Garhi incident when the British army fired at the *muhajir* (Indian Muslim emigrants) near the Afghan border.[95] None of Muzaffar's writings in *Nabajug* survive.[96] Nazrul's 'Dharmaghat' (Strike), reflecting an emotional support for the working class, welcomed the countrywide industrial upsurge. Described as the last resort of the 'oppressed, dying race' of workers rather than as rebellion, the article, at the same time, saw the strikes as a global democratic impulse spreading 'from the West to the East' like 'forest fire'. Nazrul started with the theme of peasant exploitation and focused on the 'hellish' working conditions shrinking the life-span of miners, arguing that their average longevity did not go beyond 30 to 40 years. He pointed out he was equipped to speak from personal experience as he came from a mining area (Burdwan district).[97] All the elements contributing to a radical redefinition of self and politics were present: the ability to connect the local with the global; support for the underprivileged, even if articulated from the position of a sympathetic intellectual 'outsider'; attempts to make political sense of one's own social experience in an era of mass protest; and an emerging 'language of class' rooted in this political landscape.[98]

Nabajug, however, was to deflect from its original route:

> The *Nava Yuga* came under the operation of the Press Act for publishing a notice by the Khilafat Committee, and its security was forfeited, owing to which it was suspended from the 3rd August to the 20th September. When it reappeared its language was less violent, but its pronounced extremism continued. Thus it accepted Mr. Gandhi's Non Cooperation as 'the remedy best suited for an unarmed people like the Indians.' . . . It was even prepared to 'accept the prospect of anarchy before we break the chain that binds us.' But

by the middle of November, the *Nava Yuga* was saying in self defence that 'we do not discuss higher politics' because 'being a dependent and subject people, we have not the right to do so. Now the task lying before us is not to abuse or indulge in tall talk, but to rouse Indians and to generate in them a sense of self-respect.' . . . This change towards sobriety has further developed on its renewal after a temporary suspension (due to private reasons) from eighteenth December last.

This shift towards quasi-loyalist positions was directly related to divisions within the Bengal Khilafat Committee. By aligning with the minority which was against rapprochement with Hindus and the politics of strengthening the anti-colonial coalition, Haq lost all influence here.[99]

According to Muzaffar, Haq's retreat from his previous support for mass anti-colonialism became apparent during the *puja* holidays in autumn – the harvest season when the Hindu goddess Durga is worshipped in Bengal – while they were enjoying a vacation at Haq's ancestral home in rural East Bengal. Abul Kashem, a prominent Muslim leader and scion of a wealthy family from Burdwan district who had already retreated from his anti-colonial past, visited Haq, his former schoolmate. Soon Haq was 'singing a different tune'[100] and by December 1920, distanced himself from the on-going mass movements. Haq met the arch-loyalist Nawab of Dhaka and reportedly told him that rapprochement would harm Muslim interests.[101] He 'formally denounced Congress and the Non-Cooperation programme at a conference' hosted by the Nawab. As a result, in January 1921, he was removed from the Presidency Muslim League alongside his close friend Abul Kashem.[102] The situation was not without irony. Haq had risen as a Muslim leader under the patronage of Salimulla, the former Nawab, and then led a successful coup against the loyalists during the war years in favour of rapprochement with the Hindu Congress leaders.[103]

While Haq was returning to the loyalist fold, his employees were expressing their opposition to imperialism. In September, Nazrul and Muzaffar covered the Special Congress Session in Calcutta, where Lala Lajpat Rai, 'recently returned from America' and temporarily sympathetic to socialist ideas, presided. This conference prepared the ground for the Nagpur Congress held in December, where all shades of anti-colonial forces buried their differences;[104] heightened mass movements followed. Muzaffar was nominated to the Bengal Provincial Khilafat Committee, but he did not accept the post.[105] The nomination may have been related to his proximity to leading figures such as Abdul Karim, Fazlul Haq and Akram Khan. Despite his refusal to formally join the existing political platforms, he continued to attend political meetings, including joint meetings of Khilafatists and Non-Cooperators.[106] In November, while touring East Bengal, Fazlur Rahman, a

Nabajug sub-editor, insulted the holders of the colonial title 'Rai Bahadur' as 'Bhut Bahadur'. He called for a boycott of colonial titles at Khilafat meetings, vehemently criticizing sections of the Indian elite who continued to be loyal to the Crown.[107] Rahman was repeating the decisions adopted at the special session of the Congress in Calcutta.[108] These events seem to confirm Muzaffar's contention that tension was brewing at the *Nabajug* office over Haq's retreat to moderation. His militant employees probably saw his conversion in a very poor light. Haq was also turning away from his former populism. By early February 1921, official reports observed that 'Moulvi A.K. Fazlul Haque, M.L.C has circulated 1,000 copies of a lengthy leaflet in Urdu containing fatwas of eminent maulanas contradicting the non-co-operation', and warned Muslims of the harm it would cause to their community. Fazlul Haq apparently proposed translating this into Bengali.[109] Muzaffar left the paper in December 1920, presumably in response to these political differences as his own position, in contrast, was becoming more radical.

Increasing grievances relating to work conditions, as he was forced to take on more responsibilities, made his exit easier. Some of the issues were the troublesome technical problems he had to straighten out; the sense of feeling abandoned by Literary Society friends and colleagues, who had initially agreed to work for *Nabajug*, as they got involved in College Square meetings, underground pan-Islamist activities and family problems; government warnings; police harassment for obscure reasons; and suspension of publication for over a month. Muzaffar had tried to avoid direct confrontation with censorship laws whenever possible to ensure public circulation of critical material. He had replaced the phrase 'Red Army' with 'Army of Mass Liberation' when printing Nazrul's 'Byathar Dan' (The Gift of Pain) in 1919. Despite the caution, certain situations were beyond his control. When Fazlul Haq's revolver, carelessly kept in an unlocked trunk, was stolen, an Intelligence Branch official arrived at the *Nabajug* office, located at Haq's residence in Turner Street. Instead of investigating the local Anglo-Indian smugglers who apparently conducted a flourishing arms trade in the neighbourhood, the police concentrated on Muzaffar and Nazrul for their political leanings. Nazrul was especially suspect since the police refused to believe that a 20-year-old ex-army man-turned-militant had nothing to do with gunrunning.[110] Though the revolver was never traced and papers were shuffled around in the Intelligence Branch office till the enquiry was finally abandoned,[111] in 1921, this incident made M. Yusuf a regular fixture at the *Nabajug* office.[112] When the paper was shut down temporarily by the government soon after being launched, Yusuf filed a report describing the 'sullen mood' that descended on the *Nabajug* office. A pamphlet by Akram Khan, on behalf of the Bengal Khilafat Committee, found officially objectionable and leading to the closure of the paper, had appeared in *Dainik Basumati* and *Mohammadi* also. The staff of *Nabajug* alleged that they had been singled out for censorship since they ran a 'popular paper'.[113] After the ban was lifted the paper restarted publication under Muzaffar's name, and, for the first time, his personal profile entered the Intelligence Branch records.[114] Prosecution prompted laborious editing; Muzaffar had to screen each article carefully to prevent the paper from being shut down. This task was apparently made even more difficult by militant colleagues, such as the Khilafatist preacher Shelbarshi, who tried to slip in openly 'seditious' material whenever Muzaffar was not looking.[115] Matters worsened for Muzaffar when even Nazrul left. In January 1921, Muzaffar suspected Haq was planning to sell his paper to Bux Ilahi, a prominent tobacco merchant who had supplied the deposit necessary to restart publication. Haq's evasion upon being confronted, and refusal to consult him and other staff members over the proposed transfer of ownership, made Muzaffar resign. *Nabajug* continued publication only for a short time after his exit.[116]

A period of uncertainty followed. Though the 'doors were open', Muzaffar could not return to the Literary Society. *Nabajug* had changed him. No longer primarily interested in literary activism, though engaged by literary issues, he had come to realize that political journalism was his forte. He continued to visit the Literary Society office at College Street every day but intellectually, he was in transit. The interplay between the intellectual environment and his rapid radicalization became pronounced as Muzaffar frequented his old neighbourhood. 'Moslem Publishing House', a printing establishment owned by his friend Afzazul Haq[117] at College Square, became his regular haunt. Visitors like him must have influenced the changing tone of *Moslem Bharat*: though the police initially thought 'nothing was known against him', by April 1921, Afzazul was officially warned to restrict his periodical to its 'literary' aims.[118]

In the unoccupied months that followed his exit from *Nabajug*, interactions with overlapping circles of activists, movements and thought, in the conjoined realms of culture and politics, deepened Muzaffar's growing interest in social radicalism. By July, he was beginning to regard communism as a plausible ideology, its hazy contours worth exploring in order to float an organization. Renewed attempts to launch a newspaper with the help of Kutubuddin Ahmad, a pan-Islamist and nationalist labour leader whom he met during the same month, was a step in this direction. Some *madrasa* students rented the ground floor of Kutubuddin's Moulavi Lane residence, where they ran a Khilafatist weaving centre in response to Gandhi's call for economic self-sufficiency. In their leisure hours, these boys frequented the Bengal Muslim Literary Society office located nearby. They mentioned Muzaffar and Nazrul's interest in floating a paper to their trade unionist

7 Moulavi Lane: the residence of Kutubuddin Ahmad

landlord, also a veteran Urdu journalist. Kutubuddin promptly got in touch and agreed to make initial investments. Though an Urdu-speaking activist, he identified with the aim to start a socially radical Bengali newspaper in the form of a joint-stock company.[119] Before he met Kutubuddin in 1921, Muzaffar had sought the advice of Kazi Abdul Odud on floating a paper. Odud was most encouraging, and also suggested that Bengali Muslim journalistic projects suffered from an overdose of sentimentality, and that this ought to be avoided in future publications. Clearly, Muzaffar's own writings such as 'Durjoger Pari', which he himself regarded as 'uncharacteristically sentimental', were no longer to be entertained.[120] A change in tone, as envisaged by Muzaffar, found an echo in his attempted collaboration with Kutubuddin.

The project was advertised with great fanfare in the pages of the *Bengal Muslim Literary Journal*: the launching and registration of 'National Journals Limited' to publish a daily newspaper that would not hesitate to criticize the Congress, the Muslim League, the great and the rich, and strive to uphold the dignity of 'labourers, coolies, seamen, peasants and rayats'.[121] Muzaffar felt that at this stage they had to be 'careful with words' since mainstream leaders had agreed to sponsor the venture. Kiransankar Ray and Maulana Abu Bakar were made directors to encourage 'Hindu and Muslim middle-classes' to buy shares. In the English-language document announcing the aims of the company, the word 'Proletariat' was consciously inserted for the first time in the history of Bengal, to describe those whom the daily wished to represent.

The plan came to nothing. Muzaffar's self-confessed 'lack of commercial judgement' resulted in financial loss for Kutubuddin. But their political co-operation assumed a new dimension and their close friendship continued till Kutubuddin's death in 1948.[122] Strikes by workers from diverse linguistic and religious groups prompted both to move to the left.[123] Muzaffar was increasingly conscious of the hazards of working with established leaders who had no clear commitment to the causes he had started to believe in. So he turned to Kutubuddin, a deeply involved grassroot-level activist. Their burgeoning political friendship in the later half of 1921 also indicated that certain fringe members of circles centring around influential political leaders such as Fazlul Haq and Abul Kalam Azad were moving away from the mainstream political positions held by their leaders. These men were trying to work out ways of subverting hierarchical relationships at a larger social, as well as immediate personal, level.

The connection with Kutubuddin through acquaintances in the Literary Society was followed by others. In late 1921, a colleague in the Bengal Muslim Literary Society and writer from a Hindu *bhadralok* background, Makhanlal Gangopadhyay, directed Muzaffar to a certain neighbourhood bookshop, at the junction of College Street and College Square, importing literature on socialism.[124] Muzaffar had noticed a book on socialism in Hindi as early as 1919;[125] during late 1921, when the Khilafat and Non-Cooperation Movements were at their height,[126] he started reading literature on socialist theory and organization. Smuggled books, if found, were immediately confiscated.[127] Chakrabarty, Chatterjee and Company had already attracted official attention and surveillance,[128] and when Muzaffar walked into the bookshop, his attire of '*dhuti*' and '*punjabi*', the standard dress of Bengali Hindu gentlemen and plainclothesmen alike, immediately aroused suspicion. The magic of the name Mozammel Haq, Muzaffar's friend from the Literary Society and a shareholder of the bookshop, finally opened doors. The staff took Muzaffar to the store-room and he returned home with ten rupees worth of books on socialism, 'quite a large sum in those days', which he had borrowed for this purpose. During this eventful trip, Muzaffar got hold of Lenin's *Leftwing Communism: An Infantile Disorder* and *How will Bolsheviks Retain Power?*, an abridged version of Marx's *Capital* entitled *People's Marx*, an anti-socialist catechist text written by a Christian priest, and other titles on socialism, some of them opposed to it.[129] Some of these books had just appeared on the market and reflected contemporary

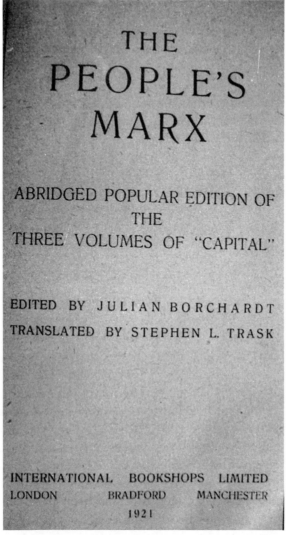

THE
PEOPLE'S
MARX

ABRIDGED POPULAR EDITION OF
THE
THREE VOLUMES OF "CAPITAL"

EDITED BY JULIAN BORCHARDT
TRANSLATED BY STEPHEN L. TRASK

INTERNATIONAL BOOKSHOPS LIMITED
LONDON   BRADFORD   MANCHESTER
1921

Title page of *The People's Marx*: a book Muzaffar
Ahmad read in late 1921, soon after it was published

approaches to Marxism. Julian Borchardt, author of *People's Marx*, printed
from London in 1921, belonged to the anti-Bolshevik socialist left in Germany.[130] Nevertheless, even the anti-Leninist and anti-communist works
bolstered the growing attraction to the Leninist current among intellectuals
such as Muzaffar Ahmad. The formation and continued existence of the
first socialist state gave Leninism a legitimacy no other socialist tendency
came to enjoy.

Soon Muzaffar developed links with the Book Company; this institution
started supplying Muzaffar and his early colleagues with Marxist literature,

often collected on credit in Kutubuddin's name. Established in 1914, the shop, located at College Square, was doing brisk business by the time the war ended. It soon outreached the European-owned Thacker–Spinck, so far recognized as one of the biggest concerns in the book-import trade. The Book Company was perceived as a centre of literary *adda* and alleged revolutionary intrigue. Though these associations led to repeated police searches, Girin Mitra, the owner, became a friend over the years, and never turned Muzaffar and other political activists away.[131] Girin was also interested in publishing leftist literature. The Book Company published Shaileshnath Bishi's *Bolshevikbad* (1924), a translation of Bertrand Russell's critical appraisal of the Soviet experiment, with a foreword written by Nareshchandra Sengupta,[132] barrister, famous novelist, and an independent socialist who worked closely with Muzaffar and other communists during the second half of the 1920s.[133]

The Generation Wars

The developing reservations toward the leading figures facilitated a turn to the left among fringe members of intellectual and activist circles. The scope and meaning of the politics of opposition were changing. Disagreements with elders ranged from the interpretation of events to practical action. Younger political activists, such as the revolutionary nationalist Bhupendrakumar Datta, displayed an interest in socialism despite the disapproval of some of the '*dadas*' (militant nationalist elders). A divergence in vision, marked by rejection of certain entrenched social strategies from above, was especially true of young cultural activists and writers. For some, the opposition extended to include the type of social order the leading figures represented. To Pabitra Gangopadhyay, Congress politics of the 1910s was marked by a predominance of the rich, especially landlords, a phenomenon increasingly intolerable to him. He also felt the need to organize democratic dissent from the marginalized ranks of the impoverished lower middle classes and the poor, who had no entry into the world of the Indian elite: a 'highly educated' upper class who treated people below as unfit to decide what was best for society.[134]

Prominent figures of the Bengali literary establishment exercised control over publishing houses, periodicals, newspapers, cultural foundations and academic institutions. Their hegemonic claims were advanced through investments in print and culture. The dependence of younger writers for material and intellectual support on such patriarchs generated both conformity and tension. A few on the margins were questioning the roots of social authority by opposing their elders and betters within institutions, and the way these organizations were run. Temporary victories for the younger crowd pointed to underlying power struggles. Pabitra Gangopadhyay led a coup against Sir Ashutosh Mukhopadhyay, influential Judge of the Calcutta High Court, Vice Chancellor of Calcutta University and a giant in the field of education. Ashutosh was trying to take over the functions of the *Bangiya Sahitya Parishat*, the federation of literary societies in Bengal which had been set up in the nineteenth century to promote and develop the Bengali language and different literary circles and trends, thereby facilitating an atmosphere of exchange among the Bengal intelligentsia as a whole. All major literary societies of Bengal, including the Bengal Muslim Literary Society, were linked to this institution. Ashutosh attempted to set up a rival body to undermine the older institution's status as the sole representative platform of Bengali letters. To thwart this attempt, Pabitra Gangopadhyay secured the support of Muzaffar and his colleagues. In April 1919, he visited 32 College Street for the first time, to meet and mobilize activists of the Bengal Muslim Literary Society. Among the three men present that day, he was most struck by the response of the youngest, Muzaffar Ahmad. After giving him a patient hearing, Muzaffar firmly declared that attempts by dictatorial individuals to take over organizations for personal gain were unacceptable. He assured Pabitra of full support. Following this meeting, they became lifelong friends, even though Muzaffar's increasing involvement in direct politics made it difficult for them to meet regularly in the later decades of their lives.[135]

Personal struggles against various kinds of authority, including the wealthy and influential segments of their own class and 'community', were intertwined with the larger political experiences of mass politics. Authority figures prominent in the anti-colonial struggles displayed an overwhelming willingness to regard the masses as a political constituency. This strategy encouraged many of the younger and materially impoverished intellectuals to concentrate on the popular content of contemporary formations, to pay closer attention to the social energies of workers and peasants. While learning from their elders to regard the masses as a support base, a few of them, with increasing exposure to mass politics, were simultaneously learning to reject the control exercised by the elders on them as well as the masses. This form of social thinking contained half-formulated traces of socialistic and social-democratic tendencies. It was the product of a fluid situation, a transitory phase of social interaction and widening solidarity networks, where many individuals from materially similar yet communally and politically diverse backgrounds came close and then drifted apart. Some relationships survived. They had been forged between individuals whose break with the dominant strains of thought and action were more convincing to themselves. Writers and journalists like Pabitra Gangopadhyay and Muzaffar Ahmad belonged to this stream.

Class was one way of explaining, in ideological terms, the experience of the times. A radical interventionist model was emerging, a process that un-veiled the weakness of the 'extremist' model which the Hindu *bhadralok* militants projected as 'revolutionary'. *Banglay Biplabbad* (Revolutionary Politics in Bengal), published in 1923 during a renewal of militant nation-alist activity, made a dubious case for intervention from above. The author, Nalinikishore Guha, who was imprisoned during the war, argued that a revolutionary should intervene if he witnesses abuses directed by Europeans against hapless plebeians, though he must not risk arrest and jeopardize his group. He should exercise restraint on his emotions, temporarily retreat if necessary and inflict revenge on the oppressive European later. Guha also argued for a wider base for the revolutionary terrorist movement through the recruitment of women.[136] Unlike the nationalist revolutionary main-stream, he belonged to the minority supporting the popular content of the Non-Cooperation Movement; he even pinpointed the participation of Mus-lims as a boon.[137] Yet, with the vanishing of mass politics, his ideas on revolution remained a middle-class programme where issues of wider social oppression were mentioned in passing and then firmly suppressed.

In contrast, at the core of the new model of intervention was a political belief in 'shifting the agency' for change: the idea that enduring, egalitarian transformations could be brought about only through self-conscious initia-tives from below. This model originated from but went far beyond mere protectionist sympathy, or even solidarity, with the poor. Practical experi-ences of solidarity were paving the way for a new ideological alternative focused on the self-conscious agency of the dispossessed rather than their 'traditional' leaders. Only a few in the early 1920s believed in such a struc-ture; yet their appearance suggested the emergence of a new and more radi-cal leadership which would influence the masses in future. Although these activists were of middle-class origin, they were undergoing a process of 'dis-affiliation' from the upper-class consensus vis-à-vis the poor. This minority radical fraction disagreed with the dominant sections of the anti-colonial leadership on the role of the poor in the anti-colonial struggle. The poor, they felt, were more than a 'constituency'. The image of 'passive' masses, unable to take action without paternalistic directives from above, was shat-tered repeatedly during moments of actual confrontation. These intellec-tuals were trying to make sense of such social experiences in ideological terms.

In early 1921, as already stated, Muzaffar left *Nabajug* following its retreat from 'extremism'.[138] Was he an 'extremist'? He was certainly not sympathetic to, and was indeed repelled by, Hindu revivalist politics, a cru-cial ingredient of *bhadralok* 'extremism'. Some of the younger members of these revolutionary circles and a few of their leaders were in dialogue with Muslim 'extremists', temporarily brushing aside communal differences. Many

were well-disposed towards Bolshevism for its anti-imperialist mass character. Both Akram Khan, editor of *Mohammadi*, and Shyamsundar Chakrabarty, editor of *Servant*, were regarded as 'extremists'.[139] However, these sections were neither able to reach a consensus on the social order in colonial
Bengal rooted in the land question, nor to dispense with the social politics
of hierarchical alignments. Radical ideas were entertained and gained credi-
bility during the heady days of the Khilafat and Non-Cooperation Movements, when the physical presence of workers and peasants ensured the success of a broad united front against colonial capital. The waning of these
movements also marked the end of joint campaigns. A contraction of wider
social solidarity followed, with proto-socialist thinking among 'extremists'
disintegrating into shards of narrower, exclusive identities.

Muzaffar's radicalism was somewhat different. During the late 1910s
and early 1920s, he shared the views of Hindu and Muslim 'extremist' leaders and their followers, who praised and displayed interest in Bolshevism.[140]
He parted from them over their primary attachment to their own class segments. The same recognition prompted several former nationalists from a
Muslim background to join Muzaffar.[141]

Roots of Secession

In a larger panorama of worldwide reactions to imperialism and the emergence of socialism as a systemic alternative to capitalism, pressures from
above and below, critical social components of the political conjuncture,
facilitated Muzaffar's secession from the more entrenched and readily available ideologies. The anti-imperialism of the mass movements provided the
political entry-point for many intellectuals and led them to grassroot politics. Deeper exposure convinced some that anti-colonialism, whether expressed through the prism of 'nation' or 'community', did not necessarily
involve a radical reordering of society. This stream of thought led Muzaffar
and others to communism.

Beyond 'Community'
Muzaffar's initial engagements with working-class mobilizations were guided
by anti-colonial and community-based movements. As mentioned earlier,
apart from 'syndicalist' activists, many Muslim politicians, influential in
the world of struggling writers from Bengali Muslim backgrounds, were
also active in labour movements through Non-Cooperation and Khilafat.
Since 'community' was a key category through which colonial institutional
politics operated, they primarily concentrated on Muslim workers. These
leaders encouraged middle-class intellectuals to engage in the creation of a
political constituency in labour.[142] This kind of 'constituency'-building was

not merely a product of instrumentalist attitudes to enable greater elitist leverage within limited access to governance; ideologies of weaving social hegemony came to be refined through such moves.

The close-knit relationship between the post-war strikes and the Khilafat and Non-Cooperation Movements, following the anti-Rowlatt agitation of 1919, set the context for greater interaction between the Muslim intelligentsia and Muslim workers. The ideology of pan-Islam, popularized among Muslim workers from the late nineteenth century, acted as the main prop of the Khilafat Movement, bringing diverse social sections and classes closer. It would be simplistic to argue that 'faith' or 'community consciousness' bound the middle-class Khilafat leaders with their working-class followers. A strong emphasis on material issues in a period of extreme hardship acted as a stimulus. An economic agenda was added to the Khilafat question from the second half of 1920 by Khilafatist organizers, to attract the indigent.[143] A police report dating back to May 1920 can be read as a prequel to such a strategy. It claimed: 'as such the Turkish peace treaty and the Khilafat question, including *Hijrat* (exodus from the land ruled by the infidel) had little or no impact in the mill-belt. Though some *sirdar*s (foremen) pretend to understand, most workers are indifferent.' To them, 'travelling to Afghanistan is not a practical idea' since it 'is not a paddy growing country' and 'has no jute mill'.[144] The material factor also crops up in the following report on the Association of Chefs and Butlers, where many of Muzaffar's acquaintances were present:

> A private meeting was held in September 1920 at the Bengal Khilafat Office where Abdul Karim (Retd. Inspector of Schools), Fazlul Haq, Shamsuddin, Maniruzzaman, Kabiruddin Ahmed (a pleader), Akram Khan and Nazimuddin were present. A proposal was made to draw Khansamas and Baburchis into the boycott movement in December and raise funds so that they can be provided for and start a business.[145]

During the 'Hindu–Muslim' rapprochements between upper-class politicians in the late 1910s and early 1920s, nationalist and Khilafatist leaders addressed working-class meetings together. United action was emphasized in industrial and political matters. The idea of working-class unity was strengthened even though its base was fragile; the broad agreement among mainstream politicians to manage working-class protests on the basis of 'national' and 'communal' considerations deepened the gulf between diverse labour segments. While some labour organizers promoted ideas of exclusive political constituencies, others, inspired by more radical currents, were moving away from such a position. Though all were keen, at this stage, to forge combinations and alignments within the larger movement, the second category of trade unionists expressed interest in long-term class and professional solidarities. This political tendency shaped some of the later struggles launched among the organized working class.

It was the more radical Muslim trade union leaders and activists who enabled Muzaffar to participate directly in politics through workers' organizations. Among Muzaffar's closest friends in 1921, Kutubuddin Ahmad was primarily active among Muslim workers, a plebian crowd, the 'body' of the Khilafat and Non-Cooperation Movements. As an Urdu-speaking intellectual and trade unionist, he led the *khanshama*s and was also active in the dock and jute workers' movements.[146] As an anti-imperialist and pan-Islamist labour leader, he had always advocated the participation of Muslims in nationalist politics. His close association with Abul Kalam Azad, who championed this position, dated back to the period of the First World War. Kutubuddin was the manager of the pan-Islamist organs *Al Hilal* and *Al Balagh* which Azad edited.[147] After the war, Azad and Kutubuddin became nationalist–Khilafatists. Like Azad, Kutubuddin hardly displayed any 'doctrinal commitment' to Gandhian non-violence,[148] despite allowing a 'Khilafat Cotton and Textile Weaving Centre' to function at his residence[149] in response to Gandhi's call for *swadeshi* enterprise. Furthermore, Kutubuddin began to collect Marxist and other radical literature on socialism, communism, labour politics and revolution.[150] He continued to associate with the Hindu *bhadralok* revolutionary set whom Azad had known in the 1910s; some of these figures reinvented themselves as 'terrorist-communists' during the 1920s. Muzaffar Ahmad believed his friend nurtured these links and even supplied financial help,[151] in keeping with his tendency to sponsor several aborted anti-imperialist causes. During 1921, the police suspected Kutubuddin of plotting to assassinate prominent Europeans in concert with nationalist revolutionaries through the Khanshama Association.[152] Kutubuddin followed the founder of the pan-Islamic movement, Jamal al-din Al-Afghani, in seeing no contradiction between pan-Islam and Indian nationalism, a view Al-Afghani expressed during his visit to Calcutta during the early 1880s.[153] To Al-Afghani, both were primarily motivated by anti-colonialism. By the early 1920s, with his growing activism among working-class Muslims, Kutubuddin's militant anti-imperialist perspective changed further, and his thoughts differed considerably from most Muslim activists and leaders within the anti-colonial movement. Hitherto, he had espoused a concoction of diverse though overlapping ideologies. After 1917, the success of the Russian Revolution added a new dimension to his thought and action. Like many intellectuals and activists, Kutubuddin was developing an interest in 'socialistic' thinking.

AITUC, formed in 1920 as a direct response to the all-India labour upsurge, also reflected this tendency. Lala Lajpat Rai, otherwise associated with Hindu nationalism, stressed workers' self-education as a means to overthrow class rule and take over the reins of state power in his presidential speech.[154] As strike-actions and popular anti-colonialism intensified, the intellectual curiosity towards Bolshevism increased in volume. While the city turned into a turbulent zone, intellectuals such as Muzaffar learnt to decipher the layered and contradictory social aspirations vested in the gigantic mass mobilizations. Their milieu embodied material insecurity, but not solitude. The spaces they frequented were turning into incubators of radical collectivism and social geographies of class dissent. Those who could not be coopted, appropriated or made to conform to mainstream middle-class aspirations and political views, were searching for new models of political action involving the poor.

While writing for *Nabajug* in 1920 and covering various movements, Muzaffar started to frequent workers' meetings. Since the workers laboured all day to earn a living, special meetings were held for them in the evenings. Muzaffar's association with intellectual and labour circles showing interest and support for Bolshevism generated a desire in him to learn more. After leaving *Nabajug*, his intertwined interest in labour and labour ideologies gained further momentum; the meeting with Kutubuddin encouraged direct political activism among workers. Muzaffar was no longer engaged with labour indirectly as a sympathetic political journalist, but participated in day-to-day organizational initiatives. By the end of 1921, he was convinced that 'class' was to be the basis of his political activity. With Nazrul's support, he gave serious thought to the idea of setting up a communist organization. The two were staying together again, in a rented flat at Taltala Lane, an impoverished, predominantly Muslim, working-class neighbourhood.[155] Muzaffar had not yet met the emissary of the Communist International who was to visit them there, and put him in touch with M.N. Roy and Moscow. But critical encounters with the comtemporary conjuncture made him arrive at the door of a new ideology.

Transitions

Muzaffar's journey as an activist in the city had begun at a street named after an obscure Muslim butler, indicating the crucial role of labour in the making of Calcutta. During the war, his existence was dominated by contemporary issues, by organizations and individuals who articulated the interests and concerns of his milieu. A continuous though marginal aspect of his life in the city was his interaction with sailors in the Calcutta docks, men who were not of his precariously respectable stamp, but migrants from the same region that had pushed him towards Calcutta. Their combined impact propelled him, and others like him, towards direct activism in the post-war period. As he became a habitué of urban spaces associated with poverty and heightened post-war protests, Muzaffar began examining his political intentions. His muted protest mentality found direct outlet through post-war social convulsions, and a persistent urge to think through the layers of large and small disappointments confronting radicalized middle-class segments: unfulfilled popular aspirations; the contradictory political directions underlying polyphonic anti-colonial resistance; the sudden, repeated assertions from below that went against hegemonies built through mass movements to advance proprietorial social interests; and, finally, class as a social force.

By late 1921, he had aligned himself with a left political course. None of his directly political writings from this period of transition survive. The articles that could be traced, appeared in the *Bangiya Musalman Sahitya Patrika*. They mirror his original aim of writing on culture, civilization and ideals of character-building in Islam. His new interests were revealed, however, in the small news-features composed for the *Bangiya Musalman Sahitya Patrika*. As early as 1919, he wrote a short sketch on the Boer War as a significant event in international politics.[156] An article published in *Moslem Bharat* in 1920, at Afzazul Haq's insistence, hinted at the ideological and personal turmoil Muzaffar was undergoing while becoming politically active. 'Durjoger Pari' (The Journey through Storm), written at a moment of personal frustration when *Nabajug* was temporarily shut down by the state, was a sentimental piece which later embarrassed its author. The confused search for a coherent perspective was expressed through the possibly deliberate, opaque and despairing language; repeated emphasis on the need to put one's trust in god and act according to one's convictions even when facing the severest of trials; the emerging identifications with a world on the move against established systems; and the possibilities of great societal change.[157]

Muzaffar's changing political focus was initially rooted in the critical social thinking of his milieu; several Bengali Muslim intellectuals voiced concern over the rule of property through their writings. The first part of Azizal Islam's article, 'Nabajuger Katha' (The Story of a New Age), in the first issue of *Moslem Bharat*,[158] appeared at a time when Muzaffar exercised great influence over the journal. The article combined socialist ideas with community development, nationalism and freedom of the individual. Though expressing a confused sympathy for Bolshevism, it did not really succeed in conveying any central ideological position. Abul Hussain's 'Banglar Bolshi' (The Bolsheviks of Bengal), published in the *Bengal Muslim Literary Journal*, was more focused. Hussain reiterated and expanded a theme emphasized by many nineteenth-century *bhadralok* critics of the colonial land revenue system (Permanent Settlement of 1793). The article argued that if the peasants continued to live in abject poverty, they would destroy the existing social order through violent revolution, emerging as rural 'Bolsheviks' of the future. The author pleaded for social reform to prevent such an

outcome: he argued that if society was to be saved, the feudal oppression at
the root of the peasants' squalid, 'hopeless' conditions, sapping the life-
blood of the Bengal villages, had to be crushed. If a violent climax proved
unavoidable, Hussain was willing to side with the agrarian 'Bolshies'.[159]
Similar sentiments on the Permanent Settlement and Bolshevism were being
voiced in public gatherings attended by the more radical and critical young
activists involved in the ongoing Khilafat–Non-Cooperation Movements, a
reflection of interest in social questions related to existing property relations
in the wake of the Bolshevik Revolution of 1917 and mass participation in
anti-colonial movements.[160] Hussain did not develop the more radical aspects of his anti-exploitation critique to reject all forms of private ownership. Instead he chose a middle path, a reformist position, linking him to
the Bengali Muslim intellectuals who identified with the middle-class *praja*
movement in the post Khilafat–Non-Cooperation Bengal countryside.[161]

For Muzaffar Ahmad, the social divisions prompted looking elsewhere.
Bolshevism and its association with mass upsurge from below led him to
conclusions which differed radically from those of writers such as Hussain.
The differences in the political evolution of Muzaffar and Hussain stemmed
not from their failure to acknowledge oppression, but in interpreting the
agency of social change. As Muzaffar moved closer to working-class politics, he increasingly saw the possibilities of social transformation by way of
proletarian uprising, represented by the Bolshevik Revolution. His urban
location and circumstances facilitated greater access to workers than to peasants; he was drawn to a world of active resistance represented by radical
figures such as Sirajuddin the waiter. Muzaffar's ideas on social revolution
were initially propagated among the familiar and easily accessible circles
and political networks, primarily working-class trade unions and intellectuals located in and around Calcutta. Still, his writings and activities throughout the 1920s showed that he continued to regard peasants as crucial agents
of social transformation. By the 1930s, he was paying even greater attention to the Bengal peasantry and making a detailed attempt to theorize
their conditions in Marxist terms.[162]

A change took place in Muzaffar's position between 1919 and 1921. In
1919, he was still torn between literary and political activism, between his
original aim to write on a Bengali–Islamic identity and the developing anti-
colonial mass movements. By the middle of 1920, he was determined to be
politically active through journalism. In early 1921, his experiences of political journalism made him wary of those who retreated from mass politics.
Communal identity, if it was used to move away from the ongoing mass
upsurge, was no longer acceptable to him. He was looking for alternatives
to sectional identity-thinking and one route was to explore socialist ideas.
At some point in this period, first-hand experiences of the labour move-

ment, circulation of Marxist texts in his milieu and rapid changes in his social identifications convinced Muzaffar of the need to start a communist organization. This turn towards the left also marked the beginning of attempts to relate to an internationalist current. By the end of 1921, he was actively exploring ways of giving his semi-coherent ideological intentions an organizational shape.

How symptomatic of the times was the beginning of a left tendency in Calcutta? As already noted, Calcutta in the late 1910s and early 1920s was not immune to a worldwide current sweeping across urban centres of the colonies and the colonizing countries. At its core were visions of social redistribution inspired by the success of the Bolshevik Revolution. The immediate post-war years were unique, in the sense that left-wing politics in Bengal was initiated at this juncture. An identifiable ideological tendency emerged, offering an alternative to those alienated by the mainstream. However, the late 1910s and early 1920s were not an enclosed time zone without past roots and future consequences. As political crisis and social dislocation recurred, members of the intelligentsia were again encouraged to turn leftward.

To intellectuals like Muzaffar Ahmad, in the process of disaffiliating from the general directions of their own class, the novelty of communism was in the social meaning of class politics, in working-class self-emancipation, divorced from an appeal to national origin or communal composition. This social perspective clashed sharply with the delimiting role played by nationalist and pan-Islamist ideologies during the actual process of labour mobilization in Calcutta. The gradual waning of the Khilafat and Non-Cooperation Movements, involving the loss of mass appeal, helped to vindicate Muzaffar's feelings of ambivalence about the leadership of these movements. His own poverty and marginal existence had attracted Muzaffar to the social demands of the masses. In the course of his interactions with the impoverished intelligentsia and the working class, he came to realize that the great majority of the colonized multitude was poor, though not in the same way; even semi-starved lower middle classes harboured hegemonic ambitions that ignored or suppressed the aspirations of workers and peasants. He represented a microscopic minority within the intelligentsia: a 'fraction' interpreting and supporting counter-claims to social hegemony by those at the bottom of the social hierarchy.

With the stabilization of prices from the second half of 1921, militant working-class protest gradually waned. But the workers had already created a political environment conducive to the emergence of broad platforms to coordinate the movements of the future. By late December 1921, Muzaffar was active in this sphere. He was working on his own, rejecting nationalist and Muslim ideological approaches to politics, and receiving help from Kazi

Nazrul Islam and Kutubuddin Ahmad who shared his concerns. A year
before, he was searching for political ideas to explain the role of labour in
society and to grasp the social meanings invested in the quotidian, the experiential. In 1921, he found a way which involved walking in an unfamiliar
direction, leading to a transformation of the self.

Notes and References

[1] A.K. Roy, 'A Short History of Calcutta', *Census of India, 1901,* Volume 7, Part 1, p. 86.
[2] *Resolution on the Report of the Committee on Industrial Unrest, 1921,* p. 1182.
[3] Sumit Sarkar, *Modern India 1885–1947,* Hong Kong, 1989, pp. 175–78, 189–210. Subho
   Basu, *Does Class Matter? Colonial Capital and Workers' Resistance in Bengal, 1890–1937,*
   Oxford, 2004, pp. 149–87.
[4] Rajat Ray, *Urban Roots of Indian Nationalism, Pressure Groups and Conflict of Interests in
   Calcutta City Politics, 1875–1939,* Delhi, 1979, pp. 84, 92, 98. Partho Datta, 'Strikes in the
   Greater Calcutta Region, 1918–1924', *Indian Economic and Social History Review,* Vol. 30,
   No. 1, 1993, pp. 57–84.
[5] S. N. Gourlay, 'Trade Unionism in Bengal before 1922: Historical Origins, Development and
   Characteristics', unpublished Ph.D. thesis, University of London, 1983, pp. 46–47. Subho
   Basu, 'Emergence of the Jute Mill Towns in Bengal 1880–1920: Migration Pattern and
   Survival Strategy of Industrial Workers', *Calcutta Historical Journal,* Vol. 18, No. 1, 1996,
   p. 97.
[6] *Census of India, 1911,* Volume 4, Calcutta, Part 1, p. 60.
[7] The theme of racial assault has been discussed in the previous chapter also. L.F. Rushbrook
   Williams, *India in 1920–21, A Report prepared for presentation to Parliament in accordance
   with the requirements of the 26th section of the Govt. of India Act (5 & 6 Geo. V, Chap. 61),*
   Calcutta, 1922, Appendix X, pp. 340–41. In the early 1920s, even Viceroy Lord Reading
   cautiously acknowledged 'race'-related abuse as a source of antipathy to colonial rule.
   During his 'Address to both Houses of Imperial Legislature', a defensive tone surfaced: 'The
   evidence of strong racial antagonism that to some extent prevails has caused me the greatest
   concern. At the same time I am far from asserting that the fault is all on one side. It seems to
   me that among the factors contributing to this unhappy racial tension, instances of violence
   and discourtesy by Europeans against Indians which occur from time to time, although in
   truth I believe infrequently, cannot be overlooked.'
[8] *Census of India, 1911,* Volume 4, Calcutta, Part 1, p. 61.
[9] Gourlay, 'Trade Unionism in Bengal', p. 69. Dipesh Chakrabarty, *Rethinking Working-Class
   History, Bengal 1890 to 1940,* Princeton, 2000, p. 220.
[10] Gourlay, 'Trade Unionism in Bengal', pp. 45, 69.
[11] Arjan De Haan, *Unsettled Settlers, Migrant Workers and Industrial Capitalism in Calcutta,*
   Calcutta, 1996, pp. 116–17. De Haan's study of Titagarh, a mill town in the Calcutta
   hinterland, suggests that the largely migrant labour force, particularly jute workers from
   Bihar, retained ties with their native villages. Retirement and unemployment prompted
   return to rural settings.
[12] Basu, 'Emergence of the Jute Mill Towns in Bengal', pp. 98, 120.
[13] Gourlay, 'Trade Unionism', pp. 218, 290.
[14] Ray, *Urban Roots,* pp. 92–93.
[15] Gourlay, 'Trade Unionism in Bengal', p. 72.
[16] For an extensive treatment, see D.C. Ellinwood and S.D. Pradhan, *India and World War I,*
   New Delhi, 1978. Also, Sarkar, *Modern India,* p. 168. Upendra Narayan Chakraborty,
   Indian Nationalism and the First World War (1914–1918), Calcutta, 1997, pp. 10–33, 125–
   51. Rozina Visram, *Asians in Britain: 400 Years of History,* London, 2002, pp. 169–79.

[17] Sukomal Sen, *Working Class of India, History of Emergence and Movement, 1830–1970*, Calcutta, 1977, pp. 161–83. Sarkar, *Modern India*, p. 200.

[18] Amiya Kumar Bagchi, *Private Investment in India, 1900–1939*, Delhi, 1980, pp. 275–76, 278–79. Sarkar, *Modern India*, p. 171.

[19] Ray, *Urban Roots*, pp. 83–89.

[20] Gourlay, 'Trade Unionism in Bengal', pp. 187–88.

[21] *Report of the Committee on Industrial Unrest*, 1921, pp. 1184–85, 1194–1265, 1185. IB 121/21 (118/1921).

[22] *Report of the Committee on Industrial Unrest*, 1921, pp. 1185–86.

[23] Roy, 'A Short History', p. 103. Sumanta Banerjee, 'The World of Ramjan Ostagar: The Common Man of Old Calcutta', in Sukanta Chaudhuri (ed.), *Calcutta: The Living City*, Volume 1, Calcutta, 1995, p. 77.

[24] Kenneth McPherson, *The Muslim Microcosm: Calcutta 1918 to 1935*, Wiesbaden, 1974, p. 9. Suranjan Das, *Communal Riots in Bengal 1905–1947*, Delhi, 1993, p. 21.

[25] *Census of India, 1901*, Volume 7, Calcutta Town and Suburbs, Part 4.

[26] *Census of India, 1921*, Volume 4, City of Calcutta, Part 1.

[27] McPherson, *Muslim Microcosm*, pp. 7–8.

[28] *Census of India, 1901*, Volume 7, Calcutta Town and Suburbs, Part 4.

[29] *Census of India, 1911*, Volume 4, City of Calcutta, Part 1.

[30] Ibid. *Census of India, 1921*, Volume 4, Part 1. Basu, *Does Class Matter?*, p. 160.

[31] Gourlay, 'Trade Unionism in Bengal', p. 77.

[32] IB 294 A/20 (133/1920); IB 294/20 (134/1920); IB 318/1921(51/1921).

[33] Ray, *Urban Roots*, pp. 91, 96–97.

[34] IB 294 A/20 (133/1920).

[35] IB 294/20 (134/1920).

[36] M. Daud, *The Indian Seamen's Union: History and Developments 1908–1924*, Calcutta, publication date unknown, as mentioned by Gourlay.

[37] F.J.A. Broeze, 'The Muscles of Empire: Indian Seamen and the Raj 1919–1939', *Indian Economic and Social History Review*, Vol. 18, No. 1, 1981, p. 52.

[38] Ray, *Urban Roots*, p. 96. IB 14/21 (4/1921).

[39] Abdul Halim, *Nabajibaner Pathe* (Towards a New Life), 1966, second edition 1990, Calcutta, pp. 61–62.

[40] IB file number suppressed.

[41] *Report of the Committee on Industrial Unrest*, 1921, pp. 1194–1265.

[42] IB 261/1920 (148/1920).

[43] Resolution on the Disturbance of the 18th February, 1921 at Kalighat Tram Depot, Govt. of Bengal, Police Dept., 1921, pp. 1167–71, *Supplement to the Calcutta Gazette*, January–June 1921.

[44] *Report on Municipal Administration of Calcutta*, 1920–21.

[45] Quoted in Radharaman Mitra, *Kolikata-Darpan* (A Mirror of Calcutta), Calcutta, 1997, pp. 188–89.

[46] Ibid.

[47] *Report on Municipal Administration of Calcutta*, 1920–21.

[48] Halim, *Nabajibaner Pathe*, p. 54.

[49] *Report on Municipal Administration of Calcutta*, 1920–21. Muzaffar became active among corporation sweepers during renewed strike-actions of 1928, having identified them as one of the worst victim-segments of devalued manual work.

[50] IB 65/22 (5/22).

[51] Muzaffar Ahmad, *Kazi Nazrul Islam: Smritikatha* (Kazi Nazrul Islam: Reminiscences), Calcutta, 1965, ninth edition 1998, p. 62.

[52] *Report on Municipal Administration of Calcutta*, 1920–21, pp. 1185–86.

[53] Joel Beinin and Zachary Lockman, *Workers on the Nile: Nationalism, Communism, Islam and the Egyptian Working Class*, Princeton, 1987. Arif Dirlik, *The Origins of Chinese Communism*, Oxford, 1989.

[54] *Report on Municipal Administration of Calcutta*, 1920–21, pp. 1185–86.

[55] Rushbrook Williams, *India in 1921–22*, pp. 200–01.

[56] IB 293/20 (136/1920).

[57] IB 136/20 (81/1920). IB 320/20 (310/1920). 6 Turner Street, rented by A.K. Fazlul Haq, where Muzaffar worked from the middle of 1920 to early 1921, was cited to support this claim. Other addresses in this petition were six located in Mirzapur Street, a familiar neighbourhood; the Bengal Muslim Literary Society office was briefly located here in 1918. 37 Harrison Road, the office of the Peasants and Workers Party, the first organization of Bengal socialists for a brief period later, was also mentioned. See Ahmad, *Kazi Nazrul Islam: Smritikatha*, p. 1. Muzaffar Ahmad, *Amar Jiban o Bharater Communist Party* (My Life and the Communist Party of India), Calcutta, 1969, fifth edition 1996, pp. 338, 343.

[58] Ray, *Urban Roots*, p. 71.

[59] IB 422/20 (2/1920).

[60] IB 275/21 (6/1921). *Annual Report on Indian Papers Printed or Published in the Bengal Presidency during the Year 1920*, Calcutta, 1921. Jogindranath Chattopadhyay, the editor of *Hitavadi*, sometimes attended the informal social gatherings at the Bengal Muslim Literary Society office. He belonged to Muzaffar's circle of acquaintances. See Ahmad, *Kazi Nazrul Islam: Smritikatha*, pp. 38–39.

[61] Nabakrishna Ghosh, *Keranir Maskabar*, Calcutta, 1921, p. 107. Mukundalal Sarkar, an ex-clerk and leading trade unionist of the period, was the chief organizer of the Employees' Association. Muzaffar came to work with him during 1922–23.

[62] IB 293/20 (136/1920).

[63] Ibid.

[64] *Amrita Bazar Patrika*, 11/8/1920, IB 293/20 (136/1920). For a treatment of Gandhian views on the labour movement, see Sanat Basu, 'Parties and Politics in Indian Trade Union Movement: Early Phase (1917–1924)', in *Essays on Indian Labour*, Calcutta, 1996, pp. 33–36. Sarkar, *Modern India*, p. 208.

[65] Resolution on the Disturbance of the 18th February, 1921 at Kalighat Tram Depot, pp. 1267–68.

[66] Sarkar, *Modern India*, p. 225.

[67] Sanat Basu, 'Industrial Unrest and Growth of Labour Unions in Bengal', in *Essays on Indian Labour*, p. 84.

[68] D.M. Laushey, *Bengal Terrorism and the Marxist Left*, Aspects of Regional Nationalism in India, 1905–1942, Calcutta, 1975, pp. 21–22.

[69] Bhupendrakumar Datta, *Biplaber Padachinha* (Footprints of Revolution), Calcutta, 1999, pp. 210–11.

[70] Satis Pakrasi, *Agnijuger Katha* (The Burning Times), Calcutta, third edition 1982, p. 111.

[71] Muzaffar Ahmad, *Samakaler Katha* (Story of My Times), 1963, fourth edition 1996, pp. 13–14.

[72] Ibid., pp. 17, 19. Muzaffar wrote (p.17): 'How can I say Gandhiji was not pained by the Punjab atrocities? Yet he termed Satyagraha a Himalayan blunder.' Also see Sarkar, *Modern India*, p. 194.

[73] IB 112/20 (80/1920).

[74] Ahmad, *Kazi Nazrul Islam: Smritikatha*, pp. 1–2, 16–17. Ahmad, *Amar Jiban o Bharater Communist Party*, p. 38. Subodh Chandra Sengupta and Anjali Basu (eds.), *Sansad Bangali Charitabhidhan* (Dictionary of Bengali Biography), Vol. 1, Calcutta, 1994, pp. 46, 518, 237–38. For a recent analysis, see Priti Kumar Mitra, *The Dissent of Nazrul Islam: poetry and history*, Delhi, 2007.

[75] Pratap Kumar Ray, 'The Calcutta Adda', in Sukanta Chaudhuri (ed.), *Calcutta: The Living City*, Volume 2, 1995, p. 247. 'It is a long talking session, commonly of a recurrent sort among friends or co-activists. It is not simply conversation or discussion, or debate, or gossip; and yet it is all these.'

[76] Achintyakumar Sengupta, *Kalloljug*, Calcutta, 1960, p. 37. Achintyakumar Sengupta, a close friend and contemporary of Pabitra Gangopadhyay and Nazrul Islam, described

intersecting literary circles, intellectual trends and writers prominent in Calcutta during the 1920s.

[77] Pabitra Gangopadhyay, 'Amar Bandhu Muzzaffar Ahmad' (My Friend Muzaffar Ahmad), in Mazharul Islam (ed.), *Muzaffar Ahmad: Sanga o Prasanga* (Muzaffar Ahmad: Reflections and Essays), Calcutta, 1989, p. 77.

[78] Sengupta, *Kalloljug*, pp. 37, 84, 93–94. Ahmad, *Kazi Nazrul Islam: Smritikatha*, pp. 175–81.

[79] Sengupta, *Kalloljug*, pp. 1, 4.

[80] *Annual Report on Indian Papers Printed and Published in the Bengal Presidency during the Year 1920.*

[81] Ahmad, *Kazi Nazrul Islam: Smritikatha*, p. 62.

[82] Ibid., p. 47. Pabitra Gangopadhyay, *Chalaman Jiban* (Journey through Life), Calcutta, 1994, pp. 67, 177.

[83] Ahmad, *Kazi Nazrul Islam: Smritikatha*, pp. 40, 47.

[84] Sengupta, *Kalloljug*, p. 36.

[85] IB 275/21 (6/1921). Sibram eventually became one of the most celebrated writers of comic fiction. His work concentrated on the pathetic world of social losers. Innovative use of puns was his unique stylistic contribution to humorous literature.

[86] Sibram Chakrabarty, *Moscow banam Pondicherry* (Moscow versus Pondicherry), Calcutta, 1929. This is a collection of articles promoting communism over nationalism. The book advocates materialism and internationalism over the idealist spirituality upheld by Indian nationalists. It was an energetic defence of communist ideology at a time when leading communists were being tried at Meerut.

[87] Sibram Chakrabarty, *Jakhan Tara Katha Bolbe*, Nabashakti, 1, 45, 1930. Gita Chattopadhyay, *Bangla Samayik Patrikapanji, 1915–1930* (List of Bengali Periodicals, 1915–1930), Calcutta, 1994, pp. 322–23.

[88] Ahmad, *Kazi Nazrul Islam: Smritikatha*, pp. 31, 33.

[89] IB 89/1920 (84/1920).

[90] IB 275/21(6/1921). *Annual Report on Indian Papers Printed or Published during the Year 1920.*

[91] Ahmad, *Kazi Nazrul Islam: Smritikatha*, pp. 31, 34, 43.

[92] Ibid., p. 43. IB 244/20 (85/1920).

[93] IB 275/21(6/1921). *Annual Report on Indian Papers Printed or Published during the Year 1920.*

[94] IB 266/20 (130/1920). Ahmad, *Kazi Nazrul Islam: Smritikatha*, p. 35.

[95] Rushbrook Williams, *India in 1920–21*, p. 52.

[96] Ahmad, *Kazi Nazrul Islam: Smritikatha*, pp. 31, 33.

[97] Ibid., pp. 37–38. Anjan Bera, *Srishti Sukher Ullase* (Joy of Creation), Calcutta, 1999, p. 28. Nazrul Islam, *Jugabani*, Calcutta, 1922.

[98] The 'language of class' is discussed in the next chapter.

[99] McPherson, *Muslim Microcosm*, pp. 63–64.

[100] Ahmad, *Kazi Nazrul Islam: Smritikatha*, pp. 44–45.

[101] IB 267 F/20 (155/1920).

[102] McPherson, *Muslim Microcosm*, p. 66. Chandiprasad Sarkar, *The Bengali Muslims: A Study in their Politicization (1912–1929)*, Calcutta, 1991, pp. 108–10.

[103] J.H. Broomfield, *Elite Conflict in a Plural Society*, Berkeley, 1968, pp. 65, 113–14. Sarkar, *Bengali Muslims*, pp. 38–40, 45, 50–51. Leonard A. Gordon, *Bengal: The Nationalist Movement 1876–1940*, New York, 1974, p. 159.

[104] Sarkar, *Modern India*, p. 197. Gordon, *Bengal: The Nationalist Movement*, pp. 172–73.

[105] Ahmad, *Amar Jiban o Bharater Communist Party*, p. 84.

[106] Ibid, p. 85.

[107] IB 267 F/20 (155/1920). 'Bhut Bahadur' was a conscious caricature. The word '*bhut*' in Bengali means 'ghost'.

[108] Sarkar, *Modern India*, p. 197.

[109] IB 428/1920 (6/1920).

[110] Ahmad, *Kazi Nazrul Islam: Smritikatha*, pp. 42–43, 105.

[111] IB 422/20 (2/1920).

[112] Ahmad, *Kazi Nazrul Islam: Smritikatha*, pp. 42, 35.

[113] IB 266/20 (130/1920).

[114] IB 244/20 (85/1920).

[115] Ahmad, *Kazi Nazrul Islam: Smritikatha*, pp. 45–46. Shelbarshi's militancy died in the course of the 1920s. He was a prosecution witness against Muzaffar Ahmad during the Meerut Communist Conspiracy Case (1929).

[116] IB 244/21(40/1921). Ahmad, *Kazi Nazrul Islam: Smritikatha*, p. 47.

[117] Ahmad, *Kazi Nazrul Islam: Smritikatha*, pp. 1, 31, 40, 46–47, 52.

[118] IB 244/21 (40/1921). IB 186/21 (40/1921).

[119] Ahmad, *Kazi Nazrul Islam: Smritikatha*, pp. 22, 34–35,153–55. Halim, *Nabajibaner Pathe*, p. 61.

[120] Ahmad, *Kazi Nazrul Islam: Smritikatha*, pp. 22, 34–35, 153–55.

[121] *Bangiya Musalman Sahitya Patrika*, Magh B 1328/1921.

[122] Ahmad, *Kazi Nazrul Islam: Smritikatha*, p. 155.

[123] Ibid., pp. 154–55.

[124] Ahmad, *Amar Jiban*, pp. 82–83, 85.

[125] Ahmad, *Smritikatha*, p. 110.

[126] Sarkar, *Modern India*, p. 219.

[127] IB 38/21 (130/1921).

[128] IB 58/17 (3/1917).

[129] Ahmad, *Amar Jiban o Bharater Communist Party*, pp. 83–84. Mozammel Haq served as a secretary of the Literary Society, and worked closely with Muzaffar when he was the assistant secretary. Mozammel also mediated in the initial talks Fazlul Haq held with Muzaffar and Nazrul during 1919 on the possibilities of launching a newspaper, though the project could not take off before the middle of 1920.

[130] Julian Borchardt (ed.), *The People's Marx: abridged popular edition of the three volumes of 'Capital'*, translated by Stephen L. Trask, London, 1921.

[131] IB 58/17 (3/1917). Ahmad, *Samakaler Katha*, pp. 25–26. Ajitkumar Basu, *Kolikatar Rajpath, Samaje o Sanskritite* (Streets of Calcutta, In Society and Culture), Calcutta, 1996, p. 346.

[132] Shaileshnath Bishi, *Bolshevikbad* (Bolshevism), Calcutta, 1924.

[133] Nareshchandra Sengupta, 'Atmakatha' (My Story), in *Jugoporikrama* (Survey of an Age), Vol. 1, Calcutta, 1981, p. 15.

[134] Gangopadhyay, *Chalaman Jiban*, p. 93.

[135] Gangopadhyay, 'Amar Bandhu', pp. 75, 77.

[136] Nalinikishore Guha, *Banglay Biplabbad*, Calcutta, 1923, republished 1924.

[137] Nalinikishore Guha, *Manushyattva* (Humanity), Calcutta, 1920–21.

[138] IB 275/21(6/1921). *Annual Report on Indian Papers Printed or Published in the Bengal Presidency*, 1920.

[139] Subodh Roy (ed.), *Communism in India, Unpublished Documents, 1919–1924*, Calcutta, 1997, p. 19. *Annual Report on Indian Papers Printed or Published in the Bengal Presidency*, 1920.

[140] The interest in 'Bolshevism' among pan-Islamists and Hindu *bhadralok* revolutionaries, classified in the official literature of the period as 'extremists', is treated in the next chapter.

[141] IB 67/24 (105/1924). IB 95/24 (97/1924). Ahmad, *Amar Jiban o Bharater Communist Party*, pp. 85, 113.

[142] Ray, *Urban Roots*, pp. 84, 92.

[143] IB 267F/1920 (155/1920).

[144] IB194/20 (105/1920).

[145] IB 318/20 (5/1920).

[146] Halim, *Nabajibaner Pathe*, pp. 61–62.

[147] Ahmad, *Kazi Nazrul Islam: Smritikatha*, p. 154.

[148] Rajat Ray, 'Revolutionaries, Pan-Islamists, Bolshevists: Maulana Abul Kalam Azad and the Political Underground of Calcutta', in Mushirul Hasan (ed.), *Communal and Pan-Islamic Trends in Colonial India*, Delhi, 1981, pp. 102–03.

[149] Halim, *Nabajibaner Pathe*, pp. 61–62. Ahmad, *Kazi Nazrul Islam: Smritikatha*, p. 153.

[150] Halim, *Nabajibaner Pathe*, p. 62.

[151] Ahmad, 'Amar Pointallish Bacharer Sathi' (My Friend for Forty-Five Years), in Halim, *Nabajibaner Pathe*, p. 9.

[152] Ray, 'Revolutionaries, Pan-Islamists, Bolshevists', p. 103.

[153] Sarkar, *Modern India*, p. 79.

[154] IB 354/20 (152/1920).

[155] Ahmad, *Kazi Nazrul Islam: Smritikatha*, pp. 78, 116, 153–54. Ahmad, *Amar Jiban o Bharater Communist Party*, p. 85.

[156] Ahmad, 'Buyor'er Juddha' (Boer War), *Bangiya Musalman Sahitya Patrika*, 2, 4, B 1326/ 1919.

[157] *Moslem Bharat, Asvin* B 1327/1920.

[158] *Moslem Bharat, Boisakh* B 1327/ 1920.

[159] *Bangiya Musalman Sahitya Patrika*, Sraban B 1328/1921; reprinted in Sipra Sarkar and Anamitra Das (eds.), *Bangalir Samyabad Charcha* (Communist Thinking in Bengal), Calcutta, 1998, pp. 42–45.

[160] IB 311/1920 (41/1920).

[161] Sengupta and Basu (eds.), *Sansad Bangali Charitabidhan*, Vol. 1, p. 51.

[162] Muzaffar Ahmad, 'Krishak Samasya', in *Prabandha Sangkalan* (Selection of Essays), Calcutta, 1970, pp. 159–202.

CHAPTER THREE

'Talking Bolshevism'

'Shadow of a shadow fearing a shadow.'
— Miroslav Holub, 'We Who Laughed'

The international anti-capitalist and anti-imperialist groundswell at the end of the First World War encouraged a group of urban intellectuals and political activists, predominantly Muslim, to initiate an early socialist nucleus in Calcutta, during 1922–24. The impact of the revolution in Russia (1917) with its emphasis on decolonization, and the hostility of the western colonial powers, especially Britain, to Bolshevism, stimulated an interest in socialism and communism among the intelligentsia worldwide. The failure of the Non-Cooperation and Khilafat Movements, and disillusionment with mainstream politics centred around ideologies of 'nation' and 'community', set the immediate local context for the popularization of a 'class'-based anti-colonial tendency. The emergence of a socialist nucleus with Muzaffar Ahmad as its leading figure and the social implications of this left turn will be examined against the backdrop of the city and beyond.

Roots of Socialism

As early as the late nineteenth century, an interest in socialism could be discerned among a section of the city intelligentsia. A correspondent, whose identity remains shrouded in mystery, wrote to the First Communist International in 1871, the year of the Paris Commune, 'asking for powers to start a section in India'. The minutes of the meeting held on 15 August 1871, and attended by Marx and Engels, recorded: 'The Secretary was instructed to write and advise the establishment of a branch, but he was to inform the writer that it must be self-supporting. He was also to urge the necessity of enrolling natives in the Association.'[1] By 1912, an article on

Karl Marx appeared in *Modern Review*, the sister publication of the popular Bengali literary journal *Prabasi*.[2] 'Karl Marx: A Modern Rishi' was a eulogistic biographical sketch by Lala Hardayal,[3] a leading figure of the nationalist–revolutionary Ghadr Party based in North America. But it was only at the end of the First World War, and during the Non-Cooperation and Khilafat Movements, that proto-socialist and socialistic ideas gained wider currency.[4]

Anti-Capitalist Polyphony

The nature of class divisions was a developing concern during the early 1920s, received and understood over a period of time by members of the left-leaning intelligentsia. All radical ideological currents rejecting capital and private ownership were initially perceived as the manifestations of an unknown ideology of social revolution. The Jugantar revolutionary Bhupendrakumar Datta, the pan-Islamist labour leader-turned-socialist Kutubuddin Ahmad and the early communist activist Abdul Halim initially read various strands of critical political literature without making clear-cut distinctions between the polyphonic streams. The *Student*, advocating self-rule or *swaraj*, expressed sympathy for socialism and nihilism alike.[5] 'Communism' was just beginning to be known as a radical ideological option; it was still an alien concept in the world of thought. Accompanying early attempts to explore Leninism as an alternative to the Gandhian ideology was an inability to distinguish between Anarchism, Syndicalism and Marxism. Often, socialist and social realist fiction from Europe supplemented the study of socialist theory and history. Pabitra Gangopadhyay, Muzaffar's friend and fellow-writer, came across *Nihilist Rahasya* (Mysteries of Nihilism) during the 1910s and later graduated to reading Gorky. He wrote that it was Gorky's fiction which gave him a clearer idea of class divisions and social oppression.[6] Halim, during his transition from nationalist to communist ideology in 1922, read widely and indiscriminately: 'extremist' periodicals, some influenced by socialist ideas; Russian novels such as Tolstoy's *Resurrection*, Chernishevsky's *What is to be Done?* and Dostoevsky's *Crime and Punishment*; theoretical works on private ownership, social oppression and class politics such as Kropotkin's *Field, Factory and Works*, Bakunin's *God and the State*, Lenin's *Leftwing Communism: An Infantile Disorder*, Marx's *Capital, A Critique of Political Economy* and *The Poverty of Philosophy*, Lafargue's *Evolution of Property*, Engels' *The Origin of the Family, Private Property and the State*, Bebel's *Women and Socialism*. He also received *Gandhi vs. Lenin* (1921) and *Socialist*, an early Bombay-based left paper, the one written and the other edited by S.A. Dange. Halim describes his response to all these works as 'enthusiastic' but 'unclear'.[7]

Internationalist Prism, Communist Critique

Critiquing of local property regimes, a current present among Bengali intellectuals and social activists from a much earlier period, sought redefinitions
and possible departures through left-leaning internationalist thinking. Sometimes the social meaning of '*swaraj*' (self-rule) was stretched and equated
with militancy from below. Hemantakumar Sarkar, a left–Swarajist and
C.R. Das's secretary during the Non-Cooperation Movement, displayed a
marked interest in mass revolutionary movements all over the globe, including communism, in the early 1920s.[8] After a stint in prison for his political role, he wrote *Biplaber Pancharishi* (Five Sages of Revolution), which
appeared in 1923. Co-authored with Vijaylal Chattopadhyay, who shared
his views, the book contained character sketches of Rousseau, Mazzini, Marx,
Bakunin and Tolstoy.[9] *Swadhinatar Saptasurja* (Seven Suns of Freedom), a
collection of biographical sketches published a year later, dealt with contemporary figures associated with international anti-imperialist struggles:
Sun Yat Sen, Kamal Pasha, Zaglul Pasha, Lenin, Michael Collins, Griffith
and De Valera. The section on Lenin attempted to relate biography with
ideology. It was supplemented by a separate article on 'Bolshevism' where
communist ideas on class and Bolshevik experiments on the basis of those
ideas came to be discussed. Sarkar's analysis came from secondary sources.[10]
Recycling of material was common enough, though they revealed shifts in
emphasis rather than mechanical repitition. Sarkar's article on Lenin was
based on Phanibhushan Ghosh's *Lenin* (1921). Ghosh's work, in turn, was
derived from Dange's *Gandhi vs. Lenin* and G.V. Krishna Rao's *Lenin*, a
biography. Following Dange, Ghosh attempted to compare Gandhi and
Lenin as two contrasting advocates of liberation from colonialism, capitalism, inequality and social oppression. He concluded with a plea to end
brahmanical caste oppression, showing greater preference for Gandhi than
Lenin.[11] The appearance of *Swadhinatar Saptasurja* coincided with the publication of Shaileshnath Bishi's *Bolshevikbad*[12] and Atul Sen's *Biplaber Pathe
Rusiyar Rupantar* (The Transformation of Russia through Revolution).[13]
Bishi's work was an abridged translation of Bertrand Russell's *Theory and
Practice of Bolshevism*. Russell disagreed with the Soviet experiment and
argued for a peaceful devolution of power from the capitalists to the workers. The translation was introduced by Nareshchandra Sengupta, a barrister
and writer who later became the president of the first socialist organization
in Bengal. Sengupta summed up the common impulse behind all these writings. He argued that parliamentary socialism, syndicalism, anarchism and
communism were all anti-capitalist theories deserving attention, and praised
Bishi for his efforts as well as similar attempts by 'others elsewhere'.[14]

The first attempt to offer a Marxist–Leninist critique of Indian society
and its anti-colonial movement came in the form of a leaflet by M.N. Roy

and Abani Mukherjee, 'Manifesto to the 36th Indian National Congress, Ahmedabad, 1921'. Smuggled into India, and printed and circulated by Roy's contacts in Ajmer, it projected 'complete independence' as the foremost demand, and argued for a transformation of the Congress into a platform for the majority of the population, namely the workers and the peasants, rather than upholding the aims of the propertied sections as 'the so-called national interest'. Roy was also carefully building a combined analysis of the Indian proletariat, of reformism in trade union circles, and of imperialist and anti-imperialist strategies. He criticized the nationalist ideology, including its 'extremist' variant, for its dependence on Hindu revivalist forms, and its subordination of the demands of the working class and the peasantry. By connecting these themes, Roy's articles in *Vanguard* such as 'The Collapse of Extremism', or polemical booklets such as *India in Transition, India's Problems and Its Solutions* and *What Do We Want?*, advanced a critique of the existing frameworks of anti-colonial struggle. Evelyn Roy, his comrade and wife, writing under the pseudonym Shanti Devi, offered a critical perspective on Gandhi. While paying tribute to his integrity, she examined the political implications of his ideology and his saintly image. This article was serialized in *Vanguard* in May 1922, and possibly inspired Muzaffar to start writing a multi-part, unauthorized biography of Gandhi in Nazrul Islam's *Dhumketu,* which started publication from August the same year.[15] While sections of the anti-colonial intelligentsia were often keen to project Marx as a '*rishi*' (prophet or sage), in keeping with the spiritual principles of ascetic self-sacrifice associated with nationalist ideas, the early communists were trying to trace the material foundations of Marx's saint-like rival in India. The focus on individuals and their ideas was being politically reconfigured to stress the concept of 'class'.

Languages of Class
The popularization of socialist ideas implied the growth of a political language to receive and express them. The writings of M.N. Roy and his associates were significant as the first initiatives to forge a communist vocabulary. The impact of Roy's interventions was being registered in militant political circles. Jibanlal Chatterjee, a Jugantar revolutionary, in a letter to *Amritabazar Patrika* and *Servant* in January 1923, claimed that his object was not to praise Roy, but 'to tell my countrymen that none of us may misunderstand that man and refuse to pay as much attention as is due'.[16] The 'attention' that was 'due' was rooted in the emergent 'language of class'[17] and terminology, consisting of words such as 'socialism', 'communism' and the 'proletariat'. The new language even penetrated police reports where an analysis of early socialist thinking was often made using phrases employed by the socialists themselves. By 1922, the police were pointing out the

increased attention being given to ideas of social egalitarianism in the pages of journals and newspapers informed by a 'language of class'. Phrases such as 'Masses and Classes' and 'interests of the Proletariat' were used in police reports as a 'touchstone for judging the value of political propaganda'. It was noted that 'poems, stories, sketches on the Proletariat', alongside demands for equality between men and women in every sphere, were appearing in large numbers.[18] Nazrul's *Dhumketu* (The Comet) published interventions by Muzaffar on behalf of workers and peasants, and early feminists writing under pseudonyms. Mahamaya Debi's 'Narir Mukti Kon Pathe?' (Which is the Road to Women's Emancipation?) argued for an ideological alternative to all patriarchal institutions based on a new theory of knowledge and praxis.[19] The fact that the repressive apparatus of the state was utilized to dissect this new literature proved that the authorities were alarmed by the social content of the 'language of class' and its political implications. The neo-idealist theoretical claim that normally accompanies the deployment of this phrase, holds linguistic expression as the starting-point of politics rather than the symptom of a political need. The production, circulation, reception and surveillance of the 'language of class', and the material processes and social acts related to its development, overturn this assumption. They indicate that a political tendency, rather than asocial, autonomous and self-generating formal linguistic structures, created this new language.

Talking Bolshevism

Accompanying the interpretations offered by the intelligentsia were stray, anti-establishment connotations invested in the word 'Bolshevism'. During the late 1910s and the early 1920s, a critique of local property regimes, a current present among Bengali intellectuals and social activists from a much earlier period, sought a redefinition and possible departure at the popular level through the circulation of this term. A survey of contemporary police reports reveals that this was happening all over India, Bengal being no exception.

Popular Images

A Home (Political) report dating back to 1920 stated: 'A Durani Pathan was recently found at Amritsar Station *talking Bolshevism* and praising the Bolsheviks.' The man, claiming to be a horse-dealer, had allegedly declared that if the Bolsheviks came to India 'all land would be divided' and no one will be poor any more.[20] An Intelligence Branch report from Eastern Bengal focused on a group of Muslims in the Khulna Railway Station in 1921. Travelling to Furfura Sharif, a centre of pilgrimage in Hooghly district, they had supposedly announced the coming of the Bolsheviks with considerable enthusiasm. They held that once these Bolsheviks arrived, they would be welcomed everywhere since they were friends of cultivators.[21] An anonymous letter, signed under the assumed nomenclature of 'Bolshevik Captain', was circulated among prominent, wealthy Hindus and Muslims in the rural community in Pabna district, threatening them with robbery. The police suspected the involvement of some local youth activists from both communities who were bent on reviving the cultural life of the village. They had apparently set up a school named after the poet Rajanikanta Sen who was born there, and the institution was suffering from paucity of funds. No robbery took place. This was generally the outcome of such threatening letters. The police routinely dismissed them as the handiwork of local *shaitan*s (evil-doers) intended to foment *golmal* (chaos).[22] A contemporary police report from Calcutta covered a meeting held at the Theosophical Society Hall in College Square, to discuss *Rayater Katha* (The Peasants' Story). Written by Pramatha Chaudhuri, editor of *Sabuj Patra* (The Green Leaf), a modernist journal on literature and society, the pamphlet strongly urged immediate abolition and dismantling of the Permanent Settlement, the colonial land revenue system in Bengal. At this meeting, several speakers voiced support for the peasants in a way that resembled the opinions expressed by Abul Hussain a year later, in 'Banglar Bolshi'. They included various constituents of the contemporary mass movement: Basanta Majumder, an 'ex-detenu' from the Jugantar circle; Saritulla, 'who attacked usurers as well as zaminders'; and a 'Muhammedan gentleman' from Khulna whose name the police agents 'could not ascertain'. These alleged 'Bolshevik sympathizers' congratulated each other on the similarity of their positions, much to the chagrin of an opponent who asked them to behave in an orderly manner befitting 'gentlemen'. 'Upon this the supporters of Bolshevism became incensed and the President apprehending' that 'they would come to blows', decided to quickly dissolve the meeting.[23] These incidents reflected how images of Bolshevism were becoming intertwined with social desire to overturn the existing power relations among different segments of society.

The Neighbourhood 'Bolshevik'
The climate of widespread social disenchantment generated an urgency to invest social activism and political identity with new meaning. The first socialists, termed 'Bolshevik Agents' in police parlance, emerged in this context. Far from being agents planted by Moscow, these individuals were mostly young activists no longer satisfied with the theoretical parameters of dominant anti-colonial ideologies and movements. They were unable to put their practical political trust in the existing leadership. Thus the early socialist network which emerged with Muzaffar Ahmad at its centre was peopled

with ex-nationalist and Khilafat activists, as well as politically unformed recruits. They had participated in the mass upsurge against imperialism in the early 1920s or taken sympathetic interest. The abrupt halting of the movement in early 1922 had created a sense of defeatism, disorientation and despondency. As the mass upsurge waned and the poor withdrew from the political arena, the world no longer seemed the same to them.

Abdur Rezzaq Khan (1900–1984) and Abdul Halim (1901–1966), two of the earliest communists who were to remain with the movement in all its complexities throughout their lives, represented this trend. A.R. Khan, cousin and son-in-law of the Congress leader and prominent Khilafatist, Akram Khan, came from a family where more than one member was suspected of being a 'Bolshevik'. His father-in-law's Urdu paper *Zamana* (The Times) praised the new Soviet state in the early 1920s. Another family member and a fellow-merchant of salted hides, Muhammad Yusha Khan, was the subject of colonial anti-Bolshevik surveillance:

> Some time ago it was reported that certain individuals in Calcutta had subscribed to and were receiving the *Workers Dreadnought* from England. . . . One of them only, Muhammad Yusha Khan, has been found to be receiving the paper. . . . Muhammad Yusha Khan is a member of a big firm in Calcutta dealing in salted hides, he is Wahabi and a cousin of Mohammad Akram Khan, Khilafat agitator and editor of the *Mohammadi*. Yusha Khan helped Akram Khan with money to start his paper and supports him generally in political matters. This paper describes itself as published by the C.P. (British section of the Third International) editor Sylvia Pankhurst. Miss Pankhurst of course receives money from the Soviet Government and attended the recent conference of the Third International at Moscow.[24]

The police regarded Abdur Rezzaq Khan as a prime example of the Khilafatist agitator sympathetic to 'Bolshevism'. A police report on a Khilafat/Non-Cooperation meeting in 1921 alleged that Khan had incited the assembled crowd, predominantly Muslim, with a substantial presence of *baburchi*s and *khanshama*s, stressing that the British would be 'annihilated' like the Russian czar if they tried to harm Turkey. Militant leaders of the Khanshama Union, Sirajuddin and Rahmatulla, who later led a strike in big European hotels of the city, were also present.[25] From this and other descriptions, it seems that Khan's anti-imperialism was initially motivated by pan-Islamism. In his own words, his family background, linked to anti-colonial Wahabi wars in the nineteenth century, played a formative role in shaping his political activism.[26]

Abdur Rezzaq Khan was known to Muzaffar Ahmad long before either of them considered communism as an ideological alternative. Akram Khan, a prominent Bengali Muslim intellectual, acted as a link between their overlapping circles. After Muzaffar became a permanent resident of Calcutta from 1913, he had begun frequenting the office of the weekly *Mohammadi*, Akram Khan's Bengali paper. Since Akram Khan was a member of the Bengal Muslim Literary Society, its meetings were often held at the *Mohammadi* office. It was in this connection that Muzaffar met Abdur Rezzaq Khan, then a teenage student of Arabic at the Calcutta Madrasa, some time in the 1910s.[27] Influenced during the war by Abul Kalam Azad's pan-Islamic revolutionary underground in Calcutta, Khan's attraction to this form of politics persisted in the early 1920s, till he gradually shifted to the left.[28] Aga Moizuddin, an exile from Persia who lived in the Park Circus area of Calcutta around 1920–21, first encouraged Khan to think of a different kind of revolution, pioneered by Bolsheviks and based on class-conscious action of the masses. It was at this stage that Muzaffar Ahmad approached Khan and asked him if he was interested in starting a socialist nucleus. In search of an alternative to the existing nationalist leadership, Khan was curious to know the extent to which M.N. Roy and the Comintern represented an alternative. Though 'Muzaffar Ahmad could give no clear cut reply and for the time being the matter ended there', he felt an attraction 'towards Soviet Russia and communism'. He was 'still a firm nationalist, with liberation of India' as his 'primary aim'. He was 'starting to look towards the communist movement as a dependable and good ally – nothing more than that as yet'.[29] Mutual acquaintance and exchange of views gradually brought Khan and Muzaffar to a shared position on the need to further the cause of communism. They were soon to be joined in their endeavours by Abdul Halim.

Halim had left his native village in Birbhum district and arrived in Calcutta around 1918–19, to make a living. While working as a shipping clerk at the docks in 1920, he was gradually drawn to the anti-colonial movement, having witnessed the oppression and exploitation of dock workers at close quarters. It was the post-war strike-wave and mass movements which transformed him into an activist. Beyond the daylight hours, he 'waded in darkness' during the gas workers strike and was disturbed by the police firing at the Kalighat Tram Depot to suppress working-class militancy. Like many who turned to left politics through the route of anti-colonial mass nationalism, contemporary realities pushed him to action.[30]

The year after, Halim left his job and joined the ongoing nationalist movement. He signed up as a Congress volunteer and was arrested for picketing at Burrabazar under the leadership of C.R. Das. During the six months of rigorous imprisonment at the Kidderpore Dock jail, he met Abdur Rezzaq Khan. Meanwhile his politics was undergoing radical changes. He was gradually moving away from the Congress and mainstream nationalism. The halting of the Non-Cooperation Movement in early 1922 by Gandhi dashed the hopes harboured by many ordinary activists. Halim no longer wished to

Abdul Halim

return to his old job, something he had come to abhor as a form of 'servitude'. Though determined 'to work for the country', he did not know how to go about it. He came to know some revolutionary nationalists during this period but their methods alienated him.

Months passed in a state of mental restlessness and fits of insecurity, typical of the unemployed. To avoid starvation, Halim began working as a private tutor. He soon lost that job and became a door-to-door bookseller. For a short while, he even looked for employment in the East India Railway. All his efforts to earn a living met with failure. Struck by the realization that he had 'nowhere to stay and nothing to eat', he left Calcutta for a short span and roamed the villages of Birbhum as a Congress volunteer. His ideological frustration continued. He returned to Calcutta in a state of political directionlessness in mid-1922, and began frequenting the library of the Bengal Muslim Literary Society, reading extremist publications such as *Servant*, *Bharatbarsha* (India) *Bijali* (Lightning) and *Atmasakti* (Will to Power).[31] At the time, M.N. Roy was in touch with the editors of most of these journals through Muzaffar, and the colonial authorities regarded them as 'Pro-Bol-shevik'.[32] Halim also read a host of other monthly and weekly magazines. These readings widened his political horizon, though he remained confused over the anti-colonial route to follow. Having lost faith in the Gandhian method of passive resistance as a way of 'liberating the mass of workers and peasants', he had ruled out the option of returning to the Congress. 'Lead-ing an aimless life', he regarded 'freedom' as a 'remote dream'. Material tra-vail and the desire to do something for the masses were his primary preoccu-pations at the time.[33] It was at this juncture that Halim met Muzaffar Ahmad. The meeting was crucial, and changed their political and personal lives. Halim has described the encounter in the following terms:

> I was at the cross-roads of my life and roaming around in a state of mental conflict. I had seen comrade Muzaffar Ahmad at the library of the Bengal Muslim Literary Society. One day he called me and started a conversation. We talked at length on my personal situation and politics. I was deeply im-pressed by Muzaffar and it was from this moment that my future political path was decided forever. Comrade Muzaffar had no fixed address or means of subsistence during this period. . . . He was physically weak and his health was fragile. I had no home either. I often stayed at my former residence at Nilmadhab Sen Lane and later at 110 Harrison Road where comrade Muzaffar would visit me. But I was unable to stay there for long. Finally, I joined the unknown path Muzaffar traversed. During the day we would roam here and there. We would visit friends and acquaintances, have discussions in rooming houses and private residences; eat at [cheap] hotels. We would put up for the night wherever convenient.[34]

The meeting with this 21-year-old, wearing a 'short sleeved shirt' in fash-ion among released political prisoners who led a vagabond existence,[35] was no less significant for Muzaffar. Halim was his first recruit to the socialist nucleus he was gradually hoping to build. Though Halim was convinced by Muzaffar's ideology, Muzaffar was still not confident of his own grasp over communist theory and practice. Nevertheless he was encouraged to talk to Halim by Abdur Rezzaq Khan, Halim's associate in prison. Khan gave Muzaf-far a favourable impression of Halim's potential as a recruit. Muzaffar wrote:

> The first floor of 32 College Street was my regular haunt. I went there every-day. Halim came almost daily to read at the literary society library. This was June–July 1922. I was not yet experienced in convincing others to join my politics. I was yet to acquire a firm grip over Marxism–Leninism. I still spoke to him.[36]

The fact that Halim came from a nationalist background he no longer found enticing may have motivated Muzaffar to discuss 'our path which

was completely new'. Muzaffar convinced Halim in the course of their conversation that they 'would have to work on the basis of the little that they
knew' and study further to understand more 'of communism'.[37] Muzaffar
and Halim were still unclear on the exact nature of socialist theory and
consciousness. Still, convinced by the Marxist critique of the nationalist
movement, they tried to make sense of their own political experiences and
concluded: 'The Congress did not seek the liberation of workers, peasants
and the oppressed. It did not represent [the interests of] 98% of the population and seek their swaraj.'[38]

Muzaffar's second recruit was Abani Chaudhuri, a 17-year-old *bhadralok*
youth from Bally, a small town in Howrah district. Though politically in-
experienced, he was sincerely interested. Muzaffar met him in July at a College Street cafe next to the Bengal Muslim Literary Society office, where
both of them took tea. Abani, like Halim, was impressed by Muzaffar's personality and was drawn to his ideology in a period of political vacuum. A
year later, Abani Chaudhuri recalled this meeting in police custody:

> I met Muzaffar Ahmad at the Sango Valley restaurant in July 1922 where I
> used to take tea. Muzaffar Ahmad took tea there as well. I used to come to
> Calcutta regularly from Bally to learn the *Pali* language at the Mahabodhi
> society. Through discussions with him, I realized that Muzaffar Ahmad was a
> socialist. I called Muzaffar Ahmad '*Darbeshda*' since he resembled a *Darbesh*
> (Dervish) whose picture I had seen in a Bengali periodical published from
> Benaras.[39]

Abani was an avid reader, 'interested in disseminating education among
the poor'. His discussions with Muzaffar ranged from literature to politics,
and he soon became friendly with Halim, another 'book lover'. Muzaffar
also introduced him to Abdur Rezzaq Khan and Nazrul Islam. Abani came
to regard Khan as a member of Muzaffar's 'party'. Muzaffar's influence on
Abani was apparent in the latter's statement before the Kanpur Trial Court
in 1924: 'I know Muzaffar Ahmad: he was an instructor of mine and a
friend and like a brother. . . . I knew Muzaffar Ahmad for one year before
his arrest. I don't know what his occupation was but he was wandering
about.'[40]

Another 'proletarianized intellectual' who joined this circle was Mahiuddin
Chaudhuri (1906–1975). Halim writes that Mahiuddin became Muzaffar
and Khan's 'fellow-traveller' in 1922–23. A young poet, described by Halim
as a 'bohemian anarchist type', he worked as a compositor and lived in the
slum on Colin Street with his countrymen from Dhaka who worked as
seafarers, waiters and chefs. Kutubuddin Ahmad, Muzaffar's friend and pan-
Islamist labour leader who was active among these workers, lived close by,

in Moulavi Lane, where meetings and discussions among young socialists were held regularly.[41]

The poet who occupied an important place in the circle was Kazi Nazrul Islam. He cut an iconic figure among the young intellectuals as much for his fiercely anti-colonial and anti-establishment prose and poetry, as his non-conformist appearance.[42] Muzaffar and Nazrul, by November 1921, had resolved to form a communist party.[43] For Nazrul, who regarded all brands of revolutionary movement with enthusiasm, the Russian Revolution had a special place. From his days as a soldier in the British Army during the war, he was an admirer of the Bolsheviks. He had an anarchic vision of social re-organization, as articulated in the poem 'Bidrohi' (Rebel), composed during the visit of M.N. Roy's emissary, Nalini Gupta.[44]

The process of forming a socialist network gained momentum after Nalini Gupta arrived. Probably having heard of Muzaffar and Nazrul's intentions, he met them during the last week of December 1921. It was Muzaffar's work in the Bengal Muslim Literary Society that brought Gupta to his doorstep. Abdul Hafiz Sharifabadi, an estate agent and former member of the Literary Society who had known Muzaffar from the 1910s, brought him to Muzaffar. After they met, Nalini Gupta decided Muzaffar was the best equipped to become the Comintern's contact in Calcutta.[45]

As mentioned, the first socialists congregated at 7 Moulavi Lane, Kutubuddin Ahmad's residence, viewed by their acquaintances as the 'Bolshevik headquarters'. It was here that Nalini Gupta, before his departure for Europe in early 1922, introduced Muzaffar Ahmad to Bhupendrakumar Datta, the young Jugantar revolutionary who briefly became a part of the early socialist nucleus, bringing with him some of his colleagues.[46] This was also where Muzaffar and Halim often lived in their homeless days, and read the Marxist, socialist and social-democratic literature their host collected.[47] Another address where the door was 'always open' to the socialist duo was 3 Gumghar Lane. Muzaffar's former employers, the family of the famous Urdu writer Munshi Alimuddin, lived there, and received them with 'unforgettable warmth and hospitality' whenever they needed a place to stay at night.[48] Some members of the literary circuit such as Shantipada Sinha, another *bhadralok* youth who called Muzaffar '*Darbeshda*', also helped Muzaffar. Nazrul and Muzaffar had met Shantipada through their acquaintance with his teacher, the well-known Bengali poet Mohitlal Majumdar, an early champion of Nazrul's work. Sinha became so close to them that he was inspired to become a literary, though not political, activist. He frequented the Bengal Muslim Literary Society office at 32 College Street and became the manager of Nazrul's journal *Dhumketu*. Muzaffar was often invited to dinner at his place since Shantipada's family had a great regard for him.[49]

Encouraging the fringe members of the circle to engage with Marxism was one of the ways to bring them politically closer. Muzaffar asked Shantipada to read socialist literature by inserting his name in Roy's mailing list.[50] Halim also tried to make Mohammad Walliullah, a teenage Khilafatist student, read socialist tracts, and enquired what he made of the ideas expressed in them.[51] Walliullah rented a portion of the ground floor in Kutubuddin's house, and ran the 'Khilafat Cotton and Textile Weaving Centre'. He was among those who had introduced Kutubuddin to Muzaffar and Nazrul in 1921, knew the group of young socialists as members of the 'Bolshevik Party', and regarded the other portion of the apartment as their headquarters.[52] Both Shantipada and Walliullah found socialist literature very difficult to understand. Walliullah questioned the ability of the 'communalized and fanatical' Indian proletariat to launch an all-out class war, and overthrow imperialist and other oppressors. Muzaffar apparently answered by suggesting that Walliullah was possibly underestimating the masses, capable of achieving what 'appeared impossible'.[53] Muzaffar also earned the friendship of T.N. Roy. Critical of Gandhian methods, the physician had developed left sympathies, having shared his late elder brother and nationalist J.N. Roy's concern for the peasants. He offered free medical advice to the early socialists despite routine police 'threats'.[54]

Muzaffar's political interactions with these individuals varied according to the level of their political engagement. Part of his immediate and wider milieu was being transformed into an early socialist nucleus. Advocating different shades of anti-colonial political opinion and critical of class exploitation, a loose network of activists was emerging. This segment of the alienated intelligentsia included journalists, writers, militant nationalists, pan-Islamists, former political prisoners, students, unemployed youth and labour activists who habituated the overlapping literary and political circles, associations, offices, neighbourhoods, streets and private addresses that had become spaces of formal and informal social convergence from the 1910s onwards. The spectrum covered hardened political workers and naïve beginners, poets and bomb experts, an Urdu-speaking trade unionist and a Bengali *bhadralok* doctor interested in agrarian socialism. As the central figure who had consciously activated the process of forming a nucleus that could mutate into a communist organization, Muzaffar worked very closely with certain seasoned activists. Like him, they were turning voluntarily to left politics, having traversed other routes. One of them was Bhupendrakumar Datta, his fellow-traveller during 1922–23. While in prison during the closing years of the First World War, Datta read radical literature and became an agnostic, an opponent of caste oppression and a sympathizer of radical ideas on social reconstruction. These included the reorganization of society as a part of the anti-colonial project, sexual freedom and women's liberation. Datta first met M.N. Roy's emissary Nalini Gupta on behalf of the Jugantar leadership during the latter's visit to Calcutta; he was then introduced by Datta to Muzaffar at Kutubuddin's house before his departure. This initial meeting resulted in a brief interaction between some nationalist revolutionaries and Muzaffar Ahmad. Datta writes that the leaders of his group established contact with Roy through Muzaffar. Among these were Bhupati Majumdar and Barin Ghosh, personal acquaintances of Roy who had been in their circle before his long exile. Through Datta, Muzaffar met Jibanlal Chatterjee, another Jugantar revolutionary, whose engagement with socialism went deeper than that of other militant nationalists.[55] Muzaffar later wrote:

> My first contact once I joined the communist movement was with Bhupendra-kumar Datta. However, he later returned to his old path.
>
> I had known Abdur Rezzaq Khan for many years. . . . After Bhupendrakumar Datta he was my second contact. This association matured into an intimate one. We worked closely.
>
> Abdul Halim was my third political associate. I worked with him for forty five years. His sudden death ended our journey together.
>
> In early 1922 . . . these political connections were made. They happened within a very short span. But I have still recorded the chronological sequence of these meetings. Someday someone may need this reference.[56]

As this extract shows, Muzaffar was later concerned to present these early encounters as the beginning of a socialist network. There seems no reason to doubt this interpretation, at least in regard to the consequences. It would seem that Muzaffar had set up a core group with the help of Bhupendra-kumar Datta, A.R. Khan, Kutubuddin Ahmad and Nazrul Islam. They were the most convinced section among those aware of the need to build a socialist formation. They were soon joined by Abdul Halim and Jibanlal Chatterjee. Bhupendrakumar and Jibanlal were aware of Muzaffar's links with the Comintern. While Bhupendrakumar possibly knew most, Jibanlal was the more ideologically convinced.

According to police reports, after Muzaffar's arrest in 1923, M.N. Roy tried to set up Jibanlal as Muzaffar's successor, as the leading figure of the early socialist network.[57] A pamphlet published by Jibanlal during his association with the left nucleus reveals that he too was at an ideological crossroads. *Udarer Chinta* (The Problem of Hunger), regarded by the police as advocating 'communist ideas', argued that the people were being deprived of their means of subsistence by foreign exploiters, capitalists, merchants and zamindars who were in connivance with the British government. The laws of the land upheld exploitation of the poor by a handful of rich people. Equality of wealth could only be achieved if the toiling masses were organized so that they seized power. The booklet also suggested that money should be collected to build such an organization.[58] Jibanlal was one of the anti-colonial activists faced with the choice of either continuing within 'a nationalist framework' and the 'struggle to win political independence', or going beyond that framework and seeking radical social change.[59]

In a sense, Muzaffar's situation was unique. He knew and worked with political figures and developed political opinions. No longer in his early youth, he turned to active politics through communism as a mature 31-year-old individual. His own emergence as a full-time political figure and the origins of the left in the city became inseparable. As the central figure of the socialist nucleus in 1922, he tried to convince others, some with greater practical political experience and ideological training, of a route he himself had adopted only recently and was in the process of exploring. However, his political inexperience was not a handicap: he was already an organizer when he turned to communism. Unable to settle into a secure middle-class existence, he became aware of the value of collective effort. By the time he turned to Marxism–Leninism, he was already a literary figure active in the civil society; a familiar face in certain circles dotting the colonized public sphere; an intellectual with writing and editorial skills that could be put to use in producing and disseminating political literature, and with experience of police harassment and censorship. While the slightly older or politically mature young activists became the leading figures of the early socialist nucleus and developed connections with the Comintern, an 'outer fringe' was created from teenagers who frequented 32 College Street, the Bengal Muslim Literary Society office, and later the *Dhumketu* office when it was shifted to the nearby 7 Pratap Chatterjee Lane. Abani Chaudhuri's primary function was to act as a 'post-box', a term used by revolutionaries and policemen alike to denote sympathizers who offered their address for secret correspondence. Moinuddin, a young writer and the editor of *Moslem Jagat*, also hid letters to Muzaffar from abroad. Sympathetic to political radicalism, he had spent six months in jail for writing an anti-colonial editorial, 'Bidrohi' (Rebel), in mid-1922. Though many of them never joined the early socialists, a relationship of mutual regard, personal fondness, social solidarity and concern continued to exist between these young men and Muzaffar. They displayed different degrees of support for socialistic views. Walliullah wrote that they were on such informal and familiar terms that after hours of tiring and intense revolutionary discussions at Moulavi Lane, Nazrul and Muzaffar would often visit their section of the rented apartment and flop down on their beds after summarily ejecting the occupants. Shantipada stayed with Muzaffar at the *Dhumketu* office whenever he wished to avoid a scene with his family for returning late. Sometimes he suspected that

Muzaffar was reading banned literature, the nature of which was never divulged, possibly to ensure Shantipada's safety.[60]

A wider network of support also developed with organizations and working-class individuals, which ensured political survival. Nazrul was threatened with eviction when the 'revolutionary' *adda* attracted police attention, and the landlords objected to the publication of *Dhumketu* from the office of the Bengal Muslim Literary Society at 32 College Street. A poor Hindu street-hawker called Dubey helped them to find an apartment in the nearby Pratap Chatterjee Lane. He was on very friendly terms with Nazrul and Muzaffar from their days with the evening daily *Nabajug*.[61] A postman warned Muzaffar in late 1922 that the police were opening his mail regularly.[62] In the face of social marginalization and official persecution, these unexpected overtures and assistance from ordinary people indicated that the advocacy of mass radical action could evoke popular sympathy, even if there was no identifiable left political organization or movement at that time.

Dislodging the 'Spectre of Authority'

A major reason for working-class as well as white-collar middle-class participation in the anti-colonial struggles of the late 1910s and the early 1920s was little or no control over work and employment; this stimulated literary production and labour journalism in the city. An echo of the mass movements could be felt in the concern and concentration of a section of the intelligentsia on issues of 'labour' and 'poverty', even if organized protests waned from 1922. The rise of 'Swarajism' guided the main directions of contemporary politics; this nationalist political formation had seceded from the Gandhian strategies of non-participation in the colonial constitutional process, while learning from the Gandhian techniques of controlled mass movements. The Swarajists, led by C.R. Das, bargained for greater political power with the colonial rulers through the limited 'self-government' institutionalized by the Montagu–Chelmsford reforms; this earned them support from wide segments of middle-class activists engaged with labour and peasant issues. Many trade unions, formed during the post-war strike-wave, politically aligned with the social-democratic agenda of 'Swaraj for the masses' stressed by Das. Following the anti-colonial upsurge of the early 1920s, this populist vision came to the forefront as a viable political programme in Bengal. Das's rival J.N. Roy, another barrister and a Bengal Congress leader who supported entry into constitutional politics, also represented this view, demonstrating a broad consensus in favour of populism.[63]

Labour Represented

Labour journals that were floated during the early 1920s upheld Swarajism, advocating friendship between labour and capital: *Karmi* (Activist) appeared in 1921, followed by *Sanhati* (Unity) and *Sramik* (Worker) during 1923–24. These organs also stressed the need for workers as a class to organize, to make their presence felt in society and to fight for better living conditions. Attempts to appropriate and subordinate labour to Indian capital, recognition of workers as a political constituency and an irrepressible search for dignity among workers from below posed a dilemma for the middle-class activists engaged in trade unionism, even as the hegemony of the Indian proprietor classes was being established in the name of the 'nation'. [64]

Literary representations of poverty characterized modernism in Bengal, touching on themes of devalued manual labour, the relationships between gender and class, destitution, the lives of labourers and the impoverished lower middle classes. Socialism and Swarajism influenced young writers of the *Kallol* circle, since they were part of the same social and political complex enveloping large sections of the politicized intelligentsia. *Kallol* (Wave), a modernist literary journal, appeared on the literary scene in 1923. It emerged from the short-lived 'Four Arts Club' (1921–22), a cultural forum promoting the development of literature, painting, music and drama, founded by Gokulchandra Nag and other young writers. Nazrul Islam, his best friend Shailajananda Mukhopadhyay, Sibram Chakrabarty, Premendra Mitra, Pabitra Gangopadhyay and Achintyakumar Sengupta were prolific in its pages. The writers associated with *Kallol* introduced social realism into literature, with a focus on class, alienation, sexuality, oppressive gender relations and marginalization. Shalajananda's novel on working-class existence, *Bangali Bhaiya* (Bengali Brother), was serialized in *Sanhati*, which started publication in the same month (April 1923) as *Kallol*. To Achintyakumar Sengupta, *Kallol* complemented *Sanhati*; both attempted to deal with social crisis from their respective standpoints of 'rebellion' and 'collective solidarity'. From his descriptions it seems that though *Sanhati* was officially jointly edited by the trade unionists Muralidhar Basu, a 'downwardly mobile' schoolteacher, and Jnananjan Pal, son of 'extremist' Congress leader Bipin Chandra Pal, there was an unsung figure behind the scenes: Jitendranath Gupta, a middle-aged press worker who had started the paper, 'undeterred' either by ill-health or poverty. To Achintyakumar, Jitendranath embodied the convergence of socially aware literary themes and labour activism: his 'disease-wracked body' and 'lungs poisoned by lead', common maladies of press workers, pointed towards continuous exposure to unhealthy working conditions from an early age. His living quarters were a study in claustrophobic scarcity: a tiny, dark, airless apartment with 'a broken almirah' and a sparse bed without even a cloth cover, which he shared with his young son. He was well known for his commitment to *Sanhati*, his 'hospitality', 'enthusiastic initiative' and 'dream of a better future' for workers. His death from lung disease in early 1924 was followed by a rapid decline of the paper.[65]

The younger group of writers represented the generation of intellectuals whose world-view had been significantly altered by the war.[66] Their novels, short stories and poems broke away from nineteenth-century Bengali literary conventions in style and content. They were virulently criticized on those grounds by conservatives such as Nazrul's erstwhile champion and mentor, Mohitlal Majumdar. *Shanibarer Chithi* (Mail on Saturday), started by cultural conservatives in 1924, represented this negative reception.[67] In a spirited defence of 'modern writing' in the face of mounting attacks, Premendra Mitra prepared a 'statement' which could be interpreted as a 'manifesto'. He argued that their 'great crime' as writers was that 'they did not subscribe to literary elitism'. They dared to focus on 'manual workers', 'sailors', 'poverty', 'slums' and other 'disturbing truths' which their detractors regarded as unpleasant invasions into 'the self-indulgent world of dreamy literature'.[68] The new writers were appreciated by literary stalwarts: Rabindranath Tagore engaged with them even though *Kallol* had stylistically broken with him; Pramatha Chaudhuri encouraged them; Nareshchandra Sengupta was supportive.[69] By the early 1920s the journal was known, even in official circles, for its discussion of 'social topics' and articles on politics, sometimes in a 'light' but 'cynical' tone.[70]

It seems that a dialectical relationship evolved between the new and original modern literary styles pioneered by these writers, and the early socialist prose initiated among others by writer and journalist-turned-political activist, Muzaffar Ahmad. This could be related to the pull in contrary social directions experienced by the new writers; a culture of 'antinomian' individualism was pitted against the 'irresistible urge' to identify with the dispossessed masses, 'to fuse one's individuality with the people'.[71] The reception to the new writers varied among the early socialists also. Abdul Halim conceded that there were 'one or two exceptions', but regarded the *Kallol* circle in general as a den of middle-class, self-indulgent individualists whose vacillations ultimately made them side with the cultural values of the proprietorial class in writing and social practice.[72] Nazrul inspired and identified with the *Kallol* circle. The association with 'seditious' elements had a price: the police searched the *Kallol* premises, and the writers were subjected to official surveillance for their association with Nazrul and other political troublemakers.[73] Shailajananda writes that Muzaffar appreciated his writings on 'coolies and labourers'. Sibram Chakrabarty, an ex-political prisoner, also knew and admired Muzaffar. Sibram's support for communism, as opposed to nationalism, became pronounced as the decade progressed.[74]

People's Power Imagined

Early socialist activity was focused on the connected spheres of print and trade unions, spaces already familiar to Muzaffar and his colleagues. Dissemination of socialist literature and ideas was one of Muzaffar's principal aims. This implied the declaration of an ideological war against the dominant politics of the young intelligentsia, a contestation of the 'spectre of authority' haunting them. Reception and distribution of M.N. Roy's *Vanguard*, a newspaper started from Berlin in 1922, was one way of propagating Bolshevik ideas. The paper and other literature arrived in packages to individual and organizational addresses supplied to Roy by Muzaffar. Muzaffar then collected the material and redistributed them by post or by hand. Sometimes he sent the literature to unknown members of revolutionary nationalist groups in Calcutta and outside, whom M.N. Roy and Bhupendrakumar Datta had identified as potential recruits or sympathizers. A police report on the interception of 'Bolshevik' literature between September and December 1922 reveals organized attempts to circulate communist literature in the districts. Large quantities of newspapapers and booklets were confiscated from post offices in Noakhali, Bakhargunj, Chittagong, Barishal, Dhaka, Tripura, as well the mining towns of Asansol and Raniganj and Diamond Harbour in 24 Parganas,[75] the family home of Akram and Abdur Rezzaq Khan. To evade police censorship, M.N. Roy's paper changed its name first to *Advanceguard*, and was known in its final incarnation as *Masses of India*.[76]

Since Muzaffar was part of the anti-colonial literary circle in Calcutta, and had access to periodicals and journalists, he also managed to influence some radical anti-imperialist Muslim vernacular organs. During his correspondence with Roy in 1922–23, he was encouraged to take over and transform *Moslem Jagat* (Moslem World) into a communist newspaper.[77] The paper enjoyed only a brief life and Muzaffar's stint there as the de facto editor was even shorter, lasting only a few months.[78] Nevertheless, his efforts among Muslim anti-colonial activists and Roy's correspondence with the *bhadralok* revolutionaries yielded results. British Intelligence reports complained that 'extremist' newspapers such as *Bijali*, *Atmasakti* and *Shankha* (The Bugle), mostly published by Bengal revolutionaries of the Jugantar group, paraphrased and published news items appearing in banned Bolshevik literature.[79] Under the radical subheading 'Masses and Classes', a police report noted:

> . . . the association of the masses with politics was encouraged . . . either in the true interest of the masses or in the interest of the success of present-day political agitation under the dominance of the classes. And this brings us to the noteworthy fact that this increased interest in the masses, when it came to

- SWARAJ FOR THE 98 PER CENT -

THE MASSES
OF INDIA

PUBLISHED MONTHLY

Vol. II. – No 8 PARIS *August 1926*

POINT OF VIEW
OF THE MASSES

Faith in the Masses

One turns with relief from the usual articles in the nationalist press, filled as they mostly are with empty sentiment or communal bitterness, to two recent leading articles published in the Forward (June 6 and June 8.) They are devoted to the question of the way out from the present blind alley of religious rivalry and petty political intrigue, and they point out clearly and correctly. 1) that the strength of the non-co-operation movement " lay in the success which it attained in harnessing mass energy to the cause of Indian freedom ", 2) that " the fate of India will not be decided by the votes of a few representatives of the middle class ", 3) that " there is an unfortunate tendency to limit our activities to capturing the legislatures ", and 4) that it is time to take up that portion of the programme of C. R. Das wich has been left unfulfilled, viz. Work among the masses. All this is undeniably true and its enunciation in the columns of the leading Swarajist organ is evidence of the growth of a realistic point of view. But it is important to note that there are dangers in the method of presentation and statement adopted in the articles quoted. They indicate a tendency still remaining to look upon the masses as something separate and apart on whose behalf charitable exertions should be made and who should be induced to " co-operate in the national struggle for freedom ". The writer says that Das's object was " the uplift of the masses whose power of resistance had been practically crushed by age long oppression ", he speaks of " work among the lowly and the down trodden ", and he harks back to the time a few years ago when " Congress workers strained every nerve to bring the masses of the people under the influence of the national institution ". There are at least two dangers in this kind of expression. In the first place it resembles the usual philanthropic sentiment which the liberals can produce at least equally easily. Note, for instance, the strong expressions on behalf of the " welfare of the masses " and the " uplift of the working classes " used at the Bombay Non-Brahmin Conference last May. The President claimed that they were " inspired by the desire to secure the welfare of the masses " and again that their " movement aims at the elevation of the masses ". This is traditional liberal hypocrisy. In the second place the idea of drawing the masses into the national struggle conveys the impression that they are to be used as weapons in a fight which is not primarily waged on their behalf. That this is the intention and practice of the middle class is shown by all historical experience. It is characteristic of the liberal bourgeoisie that it arrogates to itself position of protector, representative and governor of the toiling masses and utilises them to further its own interests. In the struggle against imperial domination and exploitation this attitude can lead only to betrayal and defeat. Success can only be achieved when it is realised that the struggle of the masses is the essence and real meaning of the national struggle and when all revolutionary nationalists join in fighting with them and for them in the battle for the overthrow of exploitation.

Will Bengal Lead ?

The clearest call for work among the masses comes now from Bengal. The rank and file of Congress workers, all the vigorous elements in the national movement there are demanding that less attention shall be given to the puppet council and more to the real work among the people. The signatories to the manifesto on the present situation, published above the names of Mr. T. Goswami and others, declare that they long ago pointed out the need for constructive work in the villages but that they found that things were drifting, and that the office of the B. P. C. C. and of the Swarajya Party were

The Masses of India, a successor of *Vanguard*: this was published by M.N. Roy from Paris and secretly despatched to India

translating it into practice, were found deprecating steps which would conflict with the interests of the classes, especially the middle classes. A more outspoken school was that represented by the Atmasakti, the Bijali, the Dhumketu, also the Banglar Katha, which were frankly for upholding the interests of the masses if necessary by the deliberate sacrifice of those of the classes. . . . In short, these papers championed the view that the interests of the proletariat afforded the only touchstone of political policies and creeds.

Atmasakti, started under the editorship of Jugantar veteran Upendranath Bandopadhyay from March 1922 , was singled out for its 'socialistic' outlook:

(*Atmasakti*) showed independence in its own line of supplementary criticism of the Congress programme. . . . It recognized the 'painful truth' that the non-cooperation agitation 'had not proved a popular success', ascribing this to its failure to enlist the sympathy of the masses. 'The Congress propaganda', it said 'has not been accepted by labourers, cultivators, etc.'

The police were also struck by the fact that *Atmasakti* did not distinguish between the Gandhians and the Swarajists; it professed little 'faith in the classes who wanted to achieve the salvation of India by joining the Councils', and regarded the 'present quarrel' between those who advocated council entry and the British government as 'simply a love-quarrel which will end in union before long'. In fact it regarded the controversy surrounding council entry as 'nonsense'. For the paper, 'Real work' remained 'outside the councils and amongst coolies, peasants etc.', who had to be made aware that 'it is not God's law but purely man's law that they should work all day long and die starving; and they can alter this law if they try to do so unitedly'. The paper felt that the masses 'must be made to taste . . . power. That is the only road to make India free.'[80]

Bhupendrakumar Datta echoed this view in his memoirs. He wrote that the Jugantar leader Upendranath Bandopadhyay publicized 'Bolshevism' through *Atmasakti* as well as *Amritabazar Patrika*, which he joined as a paid editor and had to leave for this reason.[81] Editors of leading print organs, Shyamsundar Chakrabarty (*The Servant*), Akram Khan (*Mohammadi* and *Zamana*), Barin Ghosh (*Bijali*) and Upendranath Bandopadhyay (*Atmasakti*), were all regarded by the British as 'extremists' for their militant opposition to colonial rule, and their association with Hindu *bhadralok* and pan-Islamist revolutionary circles.[82] The connections between Azad's pan-Islamist group and the Jugantar revolutionaries during the war, Kutubuddin's links with revolutionary circles, and A.R. Khan's involvement in revolutionary politics testified to these interconnections. These sections had operated through the Congress-led mass movement. Withdrawal of the movement made them critical of mainstream nationalism and its methods of resisting colonialism. The tone and content of many of the 'extremist' organs were therefore very similar at this juncture.

Among the papers published in 1922, the police also regarded *Hitavadi*, *Zamana* and *Nayak* as upholders of 'Bolshevism'. *Nayak* paid tribute to Lenin as an 'incomparable savant and philosopher'. *Zamana* felt that Muslims should be grateful to the Bolsheviks for all the help extended to the Islamic peoples by the Soviets. All three were opposed to the official British versions of Bolshevism. Nazrul Islam's *Dhumketu* was perceived as the most 'Bolshevist' among these organs. It was seen as 'advocating a subversion of the existing order of things, social, economic etc., in order, apparently, that the masses might come into their own'. Its radicalism lay in its 'clear-cut enunciation of its political creed' which was 'full freedom' for India; in its 'peculiarity . . . not only in its hostile attitude vis-à-vis the Government, but also and even more in its rampant preaching of revolt and destruction in respect of settled authority in all other spheres – social, economic or religious'; and in its defiance to all dominant institutions, asking readers not to obey 'religion, society, the King, God, anybody'.[83] *Dhumketu* was so popular among contemporary youth that police agents reported reprints of some editions to meet the frenzied demand. The paper, they felt, clearly represented a 'Bolshevist' tendency in printing 'seditious' articles.[84]

People's Power Polemicized

Muzaffar did not think so. He had severe problems with the 'middle-class' character of *Dhumketu*'s radicalism. He felt the journal was becoming the ideological expression of *bhadralok* revolutionary nationalism, rather than mass action with a socialist agenda. He made these views known through a series of sharply critical 'letters to the editor' in 1922, which Nazrul dutifully published. They were the earliest examples of his socialist prose and vigorously argued for attention to class.[85]

Despite its professed sympathy for the workers and the peasants, Muzaffar argued, the paper had remained tied to middle-class roots and interests; the challenge was to go beyond middle-class radical traditions linked with the nationalist ideology and its class project to dominate the poor; and 'sympathy' for the poor, evident in the pages of *Dhumketu*, was not enough. Muzaffar felt that middle-class activists interested in freeing the country from 'servitude' needed to realize that the 'oppressed people' of 'our land' were not the middle classes, but the peasants and the workers; the middle classes were guilty of exploiting them alongside the landlords and the capitalists; the middle-class press and writers shed 'bitter tears' for their own class, though their 'intellectual bankruptcy' was apparent from the complete denial of their own survival as social 'parasites'. Muzaffar pointed out that Bengali words for the labouring classes of society, such as '*chasha*' (peasant) and '*majur*' (worker), were used as terms of abuse and derision by the so-called '*bhadralok*' (respectable folk). The opposite of '*bhadralok*' was '*chotolok*' (the plebian lesser folk/low-life), a clear example, according to Muzaffar, of promoting class divisions through language. This in itself indicated that the poor were subjected to continuous disrespect and indignity. By degrading the poor, those who lived on their labour made the process of exploitation invisible.[86] The third and final letter pieced together Muzaffar's arguments against a middle-class anti-colonial leadership. He stressed the communist position: the *bhadralok* were incapable of liberating the country from imperialist rule; it was mere folly to ignore the 'life force' (*pran-sakti*) of the country, suppressed and marginalized by middle-class leaders; the Congress '*babus*' treated coolies with contempt, and strikes and strikers were refused help by 'our countrymen', that is, the respectable public. As a concrete example, he cited the case of the East India Railway strikers who were forced to retreat due to lack of funds at a time when the Congress spent '17 Lakhs of Rupees on Khadi'. He ended the polemics by appealing to those who ran the paper to think over these arguments a little by dislodging 'the spectre of authority' they carried on their shoulders.[87]

Though Bhupendrakumar Datta later wrote that *Dhumketu* was the centre of Bolshevik activity with Muzaffar at the helm of affairs,[88] contemporary and later criticisms from Muzaffar as well as the content of the paper do not confirm such a view. Police reports, though concluding that it was 'Bolshevist', pointed at an anarchic and emotive romanticism, the culture-staple of militant nationalism that mutated through the new prose of Nazrul and others to attract middle-class recruits from the younger generation:

> . . . sentiments . . . were expressed with remarkable literary effect . . . its blustering diction offended against all classic traditions of repose, but inspite of all these, and, perhaps, because of all these . . . the whirlwind energy of the style and inflammatory character of the language had a great unsettling effect on premature and unbalanced minds, with whom the paper was immensely popular.[89]

Besides, revolutionary leaders like Bhupati Majumder and Barin Ghosh were regular associates of Nazrul. Amaresh Kanjilal, a member of Jugantar, even became the editor of *Dhumketu* for a brief period in 1923 following Nazrul's arrest and conviction on charges of sedition.[90] These men participated in the lively literary and political *adda* at the *Dhumketu* office, alongside writers and intellectuals such as Pabitra Gangopadhyay, Sibram Chakra-varty and Achintyakumar Sengupta, among others. A young economics lecturer, Satkari Mitra, whose house shared a common boundary wall with 7 Pratap Chatterjee Lane, also became an integral member of the circle. His sister, an 11-year-old, contributed poems to the periodical. Nazrul's poem 'Bidrohi' (Rebel) influenced others to write in a similar vein, and this child was motivated to produce a piece entitled 'Bidrohir Koifiyat' (A Rebel's Defence). It appeared after Nazrul's politically inflammatory poem, 'Anando-moyeer Agamane' (Arrival of the Goddess), in the autumn of 1922. The edition was immediately banned by the government for these 'objectionable' items and a criminal case was launched against Nazrul.[91]

Towards Unions

Socialist ideas and activity had a degree of impact on literary and trade union circles of the period, and trade unionists displaying socialistic tenden-

cies possibly had an impact on the wage earners they organized. An exasperated police report from Mymensingh complained that Roy's *Advanceguard*
was making its way to one Amulyacharan Sarbadhikari since the local post
master was refusing to cooperate with attempts to intercept such mail.[92] The
postal workers' union probably influenced this attitude, as well as the solidarity offered by a postal worker towards Muzaffar when his mail attracted
colonial surveillance. At a trade union meeting hosted by the Employees'
Association in late 1922, Tarapada Mukherjee of the Postal Employees' Association and Mohammad Daud of the Indian Seamen's Union emphasized
the need to destroy not just imperialism, but capitalism itself. The Employees' Association argued for 'emancipation of Indian workers from colonial
and Indian capitalist oppression'. This confrontational spirit was a departure; only two years before, the leadership of this union, catering to impoverished lower-middle-class clerical workers, had emphasized cooperation with
employers and the need to avoid strikes.[93] Each of these speakers, as well as
the Employees' Association led by Mukundalal Sarkar, were receiving *Vanguard*[94] at Muzaffar's initiative. For a while Muzaffar succeeded in transforming the common office of the 'Employees' Association' and 'Bengal
Trade Union Federation', also established by Mukundalal Sarkar, into his
'post-box', where 'red literature' addressed to him arrived from Europe.[95]
Mohammad Daud, Samad Khan and Aftab Ali, the leadership of the ISU,
belonged to sailors' circles known to Muzaffar. Nalini Gupta and Muzaffar
Ahmad had approached Daud to arrange Nalini's return to Europe by sea.
Later in 1923, Muzaffar approached Samad Khan to request a secret pas-
sage to Europe.[96] His connections with the contemporary labour circles earned
Muzaffar a 'special invitation' to the Lahore session of the AITUC in March
1923, alongside leaders such as Daud and Sarkar.[97]

Though most trade unionists increasingly became attached to the Swarajist
agenda of reform rather than to revolutionary change, recognition of more
radical positions pushed them further left. Some, including Kutubuddin
Ahmad, who remained connected with mainstream anti-colonial platforms
even after turning to socialism, constituted the left-wing of the Swarajist
movement and worked towards a more radical position.[98] Muzaffar's political relationship with Kutubuddin, a veteran of Urdu journalism and a
leader of the ongoing waiters' strike in the leading European hotels, may
have influenced the Anjumani Khanshamas, the association of chefs and
butlers, to bring out an Urdu mouthpiece, *Mazdoor* (The Worker), in 1925.
It was the first labour journal in Bengal professing socialist sympathies.[99]

Nowhere was the exposure to early socialist activity more evident, however, than in the naming and self-description of a contemporary journal.
The editor of *Samyabadi*, Wazid Ali, was Muzaffar's old acquaintance from
his days as a key figure of the Bengal Muslim Literary Society; the periodical's

office was located at Maharani Swarnomoyee Road where Muzaffar's comrade, A.R. Khan, also resided. And among its contributors was Muzaffar's young friend Shantipada Sinha. Primarily concerned with class and caste differences among the Bengal Muslims, *Samyabadi* argued for community consolidation. Yet its semi-digested links to the early socialist outlook could be discerned in a letter written to S.A. Dange. Requesting copies of *Socialist*, the correspondent on behalf of *Samyabadi*, instead of deploying conventional rhetoric of self-improvement, claimed to represent 'a quarterly journal preaching social equality and equitable treatment to labouring classes.' That the journal was named '*Samyabadi*' (The Egalitarian) was itself significant.[100] The word would eventually denote 'communist' in the Bengali language.

The 'Bolshevik Menace'

Muzaffar Ahmad moved independently towards Marxist and Leninist ideology; no links with the Third International existed for him before late 1921. Yet an anti-Bolshevik surveillance network was already in place by this time, and its origins could be traced back to the closing years of the First World War. The popularity of socialist ideas inspired by the Russian Revolution became a source of anxiety, real and imagined, for the British state from 1917 onwards.

Between Fear and Loathing

The crisis of liberal imperialism during and after the war culminated in systematic vigilance against the 'Bolshevist tendency' from 1919. The Bolsheviks themselves, confronted by a violent civil war aided by western powers such as Britain, could not take up concerted anti-imperialist activity in the immediate aftermath of the revolution. It was not before 1921 that they clearly attempted to send ex-*muhajir*s (Muslim religious exiles who left India in protest against British rule) and other emissaries into India. The aim of those returning was to organize the masses and connect with networks that were emerging independently. The government response preceded these weak and negligible initiatives; it was a combination of the worldwide fear of the ruling classes following the Bolshevik Revolution[101] and a well thought-out pre-emptive strike to prevent the 'red contagion' from spreading. The official imagination, haunted by a spectre of all the enemies of the empire joining forces, interpreted interconnections and pronouncements of solidarity among anti-colonial revolutionary circles and socialists as an international conspiracy of Irish Sinn-Feiners, Ghadr revolutionaries comprising Indian residents in North America, pan-Islamists and Bolsheviks. Colonial officials were encouraged to believe that the empire's demons were merging, combining, dissolving their differences to mutate into a fear-some opposition.[102] To prevent Bolshevism from spreading, an intelligence network with a global reach emerged. Watch over Persia, Afghanistan, Chinese Turkestan, the Far East, North America and Europe created a defensive barrier around India.[103] The colonial system of surveillance was also the primary stumbling block erected to prevent early communists from creating a viable organizational network inside India. Surveillance worked at various levels to combat and destroy what was known in official rhetoric as the 'Bolshevik Menace'. Prevention of inflow of socialist literature was one method; counter-propaganda was another. The 'language of class', gaining popularity among trade unionists and rural activists, uncorked popular images of the Russian Revolution and radical social aspirations. Perceived as direct threats to the established order of society, they had to be challenged. The propaganda war against the 'Bolshevik Menace' was carried out through official and non-official channels. A high-powered interdepartmental committee formed by the British government in the immediate aftermath of the First World War assessed the extent to which the 'threat' of Bolshevism loomed over the empire. This committee included senior bureaucrats and statesmen with knowledge of colonial administration. Among its advisors were former Viceroy Lord Curzon and the Secretary of State for India, Edwin Montagu.[104] Conservatives as a whole, and Churchill in particular, played a key role in channelling significant financial resources in order to combat the 'Bolshevik Menace' from spreading in the British empire.[105]

In the Calcutta offices of the Intelligence Branch, 'Weekly Bolshevik Reports' were maintained during the late 1910s and the early 1920s.[106] A special post was created; the 'Anti-Bolshevik Officer' was authorized to detect and monitor signs of Bolshevik activities at the provincial level. Considerable pressure was mounted from Bengal to retain this post when the Central Intelligence attempted to do away with it in 1921, possibly due to a reduction in the secret service grant as post-war bureaucratic austerity measures set in. The central circular insisted that though the Bengal government did not regard the threat to be over, the post was to be abolished unless requested since ordinary intelligence officers were equipped to perform this specific duty. At the same time, the document hastened to emphasize that the abolition of a 'separate post' would not weaken anti-Bolshevik surveillance or make it any less stringent in the future.[107]

P.C. Bamford of the Bengal Police, as the officer in charge of countering Bolshevism, paid particular attention to the 'menace'. In November 1922, he turned to the industrial suburbs of Calcutta 'in view of the activity in Bengal of persons in touch with the Communist Party in Europe and also of Labour agitators'. His query on methods of keeping watch was circulated in the districts of Hooghly, Howrah and 24-Parganas. All three District Intelligence Branches reported there were no special provisions for this purpose. Only Colson from 24-Parganas went further and added that this was indeed a deficiency since Bolshevik agents were capable of influencing the labour movement including Khilafatist and Congress-led trade unionists. Colson felt an urgent need to assess the extent to which these organizers had used methods invented by Bolsheviks and of official guidelines on ways of watching Bolshevik inroads in the labour front.[108] Bamford must have taken these suggestions seriously. His zeal in Bengal made him an experienced officer in the eyes of his superiors, accounting for a speedy promotion. When the government was preparing to launch a major operation against 'Bolshevism' in 1923, he was 'placed on special duty under the Director, Intelligence Bureau, to tour through India . . . in connection with recent active attempts at Bolshevik penetration'. He was graded Deputy Inspector General of the Bengal Intelligence Branch for this purpose. Bamford's travel itinerary from March to May, indicating the geographic reach of the anti-Bolshevik surveillance network being put in place, included all the major centres of the British Indian empire: Calcutta, Patna, Allahabad, Lucknow, Delhi, Peshawar, Quetta, Karachi, Bombay, Nagpur, Poona, Madras, Rangoon and Shillong. His efforts were acknowledged. In May 1924, Colonel Cecil Kaye, Director of the Central Intelligence Bureau, specially congratulated him for his efforts in bringing the 'Kanpur Bolshevik Conspiracy Case' to 'a satisfactory conclusion'. Two of the four accused, Nalini Gupta and Muzaffar Ahmad, were from Bengal, and statements of policemen as prosecution witnesses played a principal role in determining their quick conviction. This fact alone earned the operatives of the Intelligence Branch of the Bengal Police and of the Special Branch of the Calcutta Police praise from the Director. However the praise did not translate into material benefits. Requests for financial rewards from lower-grade Indian policemen associated with the case were not entertained.[109]

The curiosity of the already alert Central Intelligence Bureau was stirred in 1920, when letters expressing distaste over hostile reports on Bolshevism generated a brief but forceful debate in the pages of *The Englishman*. European-owned English-language newspapers echoed official views by carrying blood-curdling stories of atrocities and outrages in revolutionary Russia. This was a field of contestations. Though the rejoinder primarily came from anti-colonial Indian newspapers and public opinion, there were rare instances of protest letters being sent to European newspapers from anonymous sources. The controversy in *The Englishman* began when a long letter from a reader, signing as 'Chicot', appeared in early January. 'Chicot' suggested that the press desist from anti-Bolshevik propaganda and report 'impartially' so that the public can form ideas for themselves. The writer felt the

'Western Empires' were wrong to encourage counter-revolutionaries; it was a mistake to intervene in the quagmire that was Russia; and, quoting from Victor Hugo, he stressed, 'the armed forces of every Empire' could not suppress 'ideas' whose time had come. The letter successfully predicted that the Russian and British governments would soon come to an agreement since 'necessity demands it and wisdom encourages it'. The Central Intelligence Bureau immediately ordered F.D. Bartley, Deputy Commissioner of the Port Police, to uncover Chicot's identity.[110] An anonymous writer, who further provoked the authorities by using 'Bolshevik' as his *nom de plume*, created a minor upheaval. This correspondence followed closely on the heels of the 'Chicot' episode. The 'Bolshevik' letter launched an attack on *The Englishman* for its hostile perception of Bolshevism as a 'Menace'. It projected Bolshevism as 'a menace only to the government of those countries where the masses of the people were enslaved for the benefit of the selfish few. . . . For countries where these conditions do not exist, where by considerable administrative and wise legislation such conditions are being changed, the danger does not exist.' Though the letter stood for 'popular cause' and 'welfare of the masses', which the writer felt could also be achieved through non-revolutionary means, it concluded on a militant and rather threatening note:

> Is it too much to ask of you that you should desist from the course you have been following of accepting as true everything to the discredit of Bolshevism in a hostile and prejudiced form, and turn to some of those fair-minded journals both English and American, which give the other side of the shield? For it is only by studying both sides of the shield yourself and by presenting them to your readers that a just judgement can be formed. The time for judgement is nigh at hand, and it may not be well for you that the records of your journals show that you have misdirected it.

The 'Bolshevik' letter generated a sarcastic response from another reader who signed as 'CIVBRITSUM' (loyal subject of the British empire). A stern critic of Bolshevism, this letter stressed the need for a 'genuine representative government' to correct the wrongs of the existing system and not the rule of the 'rabble' Bolshevism necessarily represented, concluding that the 'correspondent Bolshevik' should have named himself 'Armchair Bolshevik'. A more troubled response came from the authorities. Central Intelligence felt that it was 'worse, even than the "Chicot" production', and instructed Bartley to pressurize *The Englishman* to divulge the identity of the correspondents. Upon learning that Sandbrook of *The Englishman* had refused, the Central Intelligence suggested that the Special Branch be mobilized: 'These newspaper people will hardly ever give up voluntarily the names of their correspondents. . . . A great deal comes out of newspaper offices in roundabout ways and it may be there are channels of communication which either Bird or Kidd could tap.'[111]

Apart from reluctant newspapermen, internal bureaucratic mix-ups often created unforeseen hindrances. Attempts to open private mail 'discreetly' could undermine the confidence of the general public in the postal services. To prevent such mishaps and the ensuing panic, controversy and scandal, a government circular secretly pressurized postal employees to 'avail' themselves of police assistance while sorting mail. A letter from the Deputy Inspector General, Intelligence Branch, complained to Cecil Kaye that upon returning from holiday, he was dismayed to find that the circular had been destroyed while a written memorandum on the destruction had been preserved. The letter bemoaned that without the circular, any hope of cooperation from postal authorities in matters of intercepting seditious material was 'remote'.[112]

Alien Biology

The nature of British counter-propaganda to deal with Bolshevik 'sedition' was a combination of racial prejudice and attempts to win over the 'respectable' classes of Indians. Several attempts were made to counter the Bolshevik ideology. Edmund Candler C.B.E was appointed by the Home Department to write *Bolshevism, the Dream and the Fact*. Printed and distributed through Oxford University Press, it was primarily aimed at the intelligentsia. The work offered a 'sober and reasoned' opposition to Bolshevism.[113] Members of the target audience recycled the information contained within it to project Bolshevism as an emancipatory movement. The early socialist Hemantakumar Sarkar's *Swadhinatar Saptosurya* (Seven Suns of Freedom) included an article on Bolshevism based on the facts supplied by Candler, but without Candler's interpretations.[114] More populist and less highbrow versions were also circulated. A collection of documents entitled 'The Bolshevik Menace to India', sent from Britain for circulation of propaganda in official and non-official circles, was forwarded by the office of the Director of Central Intelligence to regional headquarters, including the Bengal Intelligence Branch. The following observation was made in this collection:

> So we arrive at the curious fact that the majority of Bolshevik leaders are not Russians but Russian Jews who have been living far from Russia for years, who have been all the time nursing their grievances and vowing 'Revenge' on Russia, while turning their undoubtedly clever brains to the study of the Extremist forms of socialist experiments and just waiting for the opportunity. What did they care if Russia was ruined by attempts to put their wonderful theories into practice. The Jews who were ringleaders cared no more for Russia than any other country. But unfortunately Russia was undoubtedly the best field for

their efforts. They knew they were in the minority, they knew their party was mainly supported and led by Jews but they also knew this; they had a programme, destructive though it was , they were well organized and they had no scruples in making rash promises to the poor peasant masses which would give them their temporary support and they were sure to be believed for long enough for them to carry through their ruthless destruction of whatever civilization existed, which would then enable them to rebuild Russia on a purely imaginary basis.[115]

This racist perception was reflected in the policy-thinking behind the actual practice of keeping watch on 'suspected Bolsheviks'. The practical uses of this distorted vision lay in tarring forms of anti-colonial dissent and resistance drawing inspiration from internationalist and diffusionary currents with the brush of 'unnatural' and 'alien' ideologies, namely Bolshevism and pan-Islam. While racial stereotyping of political opposition enjoys an older and developed history, what was novel about this period was the systematic emphasis of colonial surveillance to conjoin pan-Islam with Bolshevism. They were perceived as twin ideologies produced and upheld by 'savage' races to undermine and assault the superior ideological–racial complex of 'civilized' colonizers. The colonial officialdom in their central headquarters in London, as well as in key outposts like Calcutta, fostered and laboured under the belief that Bolsheviks and pan-Islamists were barbarians at the gates; 'hordes' about to enter in waves of toxic migration; products of ungovernable geographical spaces where different currents met. The fear of 'barbarians' overrunning the empire, particularly India, reflected grand imperialist self-perceptions intertwined with a more prosaic and realistic fear of an imminent material debacle. If they could not be repulsed, all civilizing values represented by a liberal imperialism would vanish, the mechanisms of colonial surplus extraction which sustained metropolitan capitalism would collapse, and the rule of the colonizing bourgeoisie would crumble at home and abroad. A war had to be waged against them if the empire was to be saved.

In the official imagination, Bolshevism embodied racialized physicality. Repugnant, dangerous and difficult to control, the Bolshevik had a Jewish brain and an Islamic body, representing the return of the repressed. Often the language describing contemporary epidemics and diseases, familiarized during the influenza onslaught, was deployed to represent Bolshevism as an alien biological threat committed to corroding a healthy empire. Around 1920–21, central circulars would direct the Calcutta intelligence officials to observe individuals with 'semitic features' or of a 'somewhat Jewish appearance', allegedly acting as 'Bolshevik Agents'. The ceaseless arrival and departure of casual visitors of European origin through Calcutta port, especially those matching certain racialized descriptions, were a source of official un-ease. During this period, shops owned by Jewish jewellers in the city were zealously watched. They were seen as potential buyers of Russian crown jewels confiscated and sold by the newly formed, acutely cash-strapped Soviet state. Other diasporas in the city were also subjected to surveillance. Business establishments run by people of Central, East and North European origin were often suspected as fronts for Bolshevik operations in India [116]

The Asian counterpart of the cosmopolitan, slippery and destructive 'Jew-ish Bolshevist' was the comparatively unsophisticated, dangerously fanati-cal 'Moslem Bolshevist agitator'. This stereotype, a mutant of older colo-nial constructions and racial representations of Islam, was launched in the context of the developing connections between pan-Islam and Bolshevism in post-1917 Central Asia. The Bolsheviks were keen to win over Muslim populations of the Russian empire who were concentrated in this region. This was evident from the Second Congress of the Comintern in July–August 1920 and the 'Baku Congress of the Peoples of the East' in Septem-ber 1920. The latter was specifically aimed at dealing with the colonial question.[117] During the same year, a communist party was formed in Tashkent by ex-*muhajir*s from India who had made their way through the North West Frontier Province to Afghanistan, and from there to Soviet Asia. The process of *hijrat*, or religious exodus from the land ruled by the infidel, was an anti-colonial impulse expressed in pan-Islamist terms. It gained popular-ity among a section of Indian Muslims during the closing years and in the immediate aftermath of the First World War. The Khilafat Movement and the freedom of Afghanistan from British control in 1919 bolstered this move-ment. Some of these *muhajir*s travelled beyond Afghanistan, their original destination, ended up in Bolshevik territories and underwent an ideological transformation. Mohammad Shafiq, a former *muhajir*, was elected secretary of the party thus formed in Tashkent. Among the first members were M.N. Roy and his friend Abani Mukherjee, who later became his bitter rival.[118] At its first meeting on 17 October 1920, it was decided that the organization was to be formally called 'The Indian Communist Party' (ICP). After a pre-liminary discussion on membership procedure, the need to draft a programme and affiliation to the Comintern, the meeting adjourned with the singing of 'The International'.[119] During this period, Muzaffar Ahmad and Nazrul Islam were working for *Nabajug* (the newspaper warned by the government for publishing a 'seditious' article by Nazrul in July 1920), which scathingly condemned the shooting of unarmed *muhajir*s by the British military police near the Afghan border.[120] They had no idea at the time that a communist party was about to emerge from the ranks of these emigrants within three months.

The former *muhajir*s attempted to return to India from 1921 onwards through the northwestern frontier, and to form a communist organization inside India. The state came down heavily on them. From 1921 to 1924, they were tried in four 'conspiracy cases' and sentenced to imprisonment.[121] The series of conspiracy cases at Peshawar and the millenarian pronouncements of Islamic preachers at various public forums were held up as examples of Bolshevik infiltration into India through the ideology of pan-Islamism.[122] Though these early communists had already moved away or were in the process of moving away from pan-Islam, little distinction was made in the official reports between communists from a pan-Islamic background and pan-Islamists displaying interest in communism. By 1925, the Intelligence Branch had drawn up detailed reports on suspected Bolshevik sympathizers in Calcutta and the districts. Once again, the tendency to collapse different strands of opposition into a single, uniform category can be noticed. The reports included a diverse range of the government's political opponents who had formed, or were close to, the anti-colonial coalition of forces: Congress activists, Khilafatists, trade unionists and early communists. The reports recorded the tendency among Wahabis, Khilafatists and pan-Islamists to display a positive interest in Bolshevism.[123]

In the early 1920s, apart from Akram Khan's family, the Ispahanis, a prominent Persian Shia merchant family, also active in the hide trade, was suspected of being 'Moslem–Bolshevists'. A young member of another Shia Persian merchant family, who worked briefly for the Ispahanis, apparently also received *Workers Dreadnought*. His brother had lectured on Khilafat in 1921, at 'The Four Arts Club' discussion forum set up by young Hindu *bhadralok* intellectuals. Though his speech was not found to be 'extravagantly objectionable', the Khasani brothers were discreetly watched for a while.[124] Aga Moizuddin, Abdur Rezzaq's early mentor, was obviously not the only individual of Persian origin domiciled in Calcutta who attracted police attention. The police regarded Moizuddin, a political exile, as a Bolshevik who was trying to create a radical political cell in the city.[125] Lower-class Muslim seamen returning from England were also suspects and faced interrogation in Calcutta for their alleged links with S. Saklatvala of the Communist Party of Great Britain.[126] The geographically mobile nature ascribed to the Bengali Muslim seamen, alongside pan-Islamists and Jewish travellers, further bolstered the image of an itinerant danger in official perceptions, and influenced the texture of the propaganda. Images of the peripatetic Bolshevik 'agent', necessarily an outsider, were circulated widely. These accompanied and supplemented British accounts of atrocities committed by Bolsheviks, particularly against those owning property.[127] The diversity in the demographic composition of the city was seen as conducive to Bolshevik penetration. Though some religious or ethno-linguistic groups were given priority as potential carriers of the 'Bolshevik Menace', the multilay-

ered urban space itself was perceived as the ideal incubator of an enemy
with ever-changing, multiple racial features. To British officialdom, the supposedly flexible transmutation of its physical form made Bolshevism dangerously equipped to penetrate ethnic, national and linguistic barriers existing
in the city. Colonial urbanism unsettled the colonial authorities themselves,
exposing the deep parochialism and xenophobia that underlined liberal colonial responses to contemporary challenges. The empire, as thesis, was being
forced to grapple with its antithesis in a treacherous terrain of its own creation. A self-laudatory celebration of colonial cosmopolitanism prevalent in
the imperial circles, in a moment of extraordinary crisis, was therefore inseparable from the fear of a veritable nemesis: the anti-colonial 'urban chaos'
instigated by forces that could not be completely controlled.

Reception

The responses to Bolshevism and its propaganda were mixed. Precisely because the British were attacking them, many among the local intelligentsia
thought well of Bolshevik Russia and socialism. The poor quality of the
anti-Bolshevik material disseminated on behalf of the state further discredi-
ted the government's position. An official secret letter circulated within the
Home Department in 1919 felt that the outdated material on Bolshevism
required immediate 'updating'.[128] Anti-Soviet reports in the loyalist, predominantly English-language newspapers failed to provoke strong antipathy.
Satis Pakrasi, Anushilan revolutionary-turned-communist, was to recall that
while imprisoned during the late 1910s, his chief source of news on Russia
was European-owned dailies such as *The Statesman*, seen as running 'a campaign against the Russian Revolution'. Despite the negative versions in these
reports, many of the political prisoners trying to understand the event through
its pages enthusiastically greeted the revolution as the harbinger of 'happi-
ness, peace and liberty'.[129]

Interest in the Russian Revolution of 1917 was related to the growing
engagement among cultural and political activists with contemporary upheavals. Shombhu Roy, a Hindu *bhadralok* youth close to Nazrul from his
days in the Bengal Battalion in Peshawar, recalled congregating to mark the
victory of the Red Army against the Whites in Nazrul's room in the army
barracks. For them, the Russian Revolution represented a victory of oppressed people over their oppressors; this sense was carried into the *adda* at College Street following demobilization.[130] Peshawar was the focal point of the
geographic zone identified by British officialdom as the target of ideological penetration from Bolshevized Central Asia.[131] In Calcutta too, a city far
removed from the possibility of any direct influence, the events in Russia
were followed with avid interest. The exact nature of the distant events in

Russia was unclear to most. According to Pabitra Gangopadhyay, the state was making concerted attempts to project the Bolsheviks as villains.[132] Sometimes this effort tended to have the opposite effect among members of the general public.[133]

The reaction among a sizeable section of the intelligentsia to the events in Russia was confused but positive. The 'Hindu–Muslim rapprochement' of the immediate post-war years played a curious role in bringing together 'extremist' leaders of the anti-colonial movement, who also praised Bolshevism as an anti-imperialist creed. The Secretary of State for India, Edwin Montagu, while defending the Rowlatt Act of 1919, claimed in a speech before the Commons that repressive legislation was necessary to protect British India from Bolshevism, and that the empire was being menaced by 'that dark and murderous doctrine which fattens upon unrest, feeds on discontent, spreads disorder where-ever it shows its head – Bolshevism, and the Bolshevist emissaries of Russia.'[134] In contrast, the following year, Lala Lajpat Rai, in his presidential address before the foundation conference of the AITUC, remarked:

> While the Anglo-Indian Press is engaged day and night in disseminating palpable lies about Soviet Russia, the Government of India steps in, to prevent the people from knowing the other side of the story. . . . My own experience of Europe and America leads me to think that socialistic, even Bolshevik truth is any day better, than the capitalist and imperialist truth.[135]

Lajpat Rai's contact with Indian revolutionary circles abroad that had greater exposure to socialist ideas influenced his thinking during this period.[136] Fellow extremist leader Bipin Chandra Pal was also held responsible for making 'a violently pro-Bolshevik speech at Calcutta' after sharing platforms in England with pro-Bolshevik elements.[137] The police agent who was keeping an eye on a 'suspected Bolshevik' in Calcutta, Habibullah Khan, mentioned the youth's admiration for Bipin Pal and other leading figures of the anti-colonial movement. He reported that Habibullah was trying to persuade these leaders to accept the correctness of the Bolshevik method.[138] From the pronouncements of some of these leaders, it seems that sympathy for Bolshevism was already a part of their initial response. Fringe activists during the mass upsurge of the late 1910s and the early 1920s, and some of its leaders could therefore often arrive at the same conclusion.

But some sections, including opponents of the colonial regime, were persuaded by colonial views since their ideology and social location made them hostile to a 'classless society'. The official and demi-official versions did exercise some impact on them. According to the nationalist revolutionary terrorist leader Bhupendrakumar Datta, most leaders of Jugantar and all the leaders of Anushilan, the principal nationalist revolutionary organizations, harboured deep reservations about communism despite their personal regard for M.N. Roy. Many chose to believe the official accounts of Bolshevism promoted by the colonial government.[139] While the Hindu *bhadralok* revolutionary leaders identified it as an ideological challenge, the majority of the Muslim intelligentsia stayed away from socialist politics. By perceiving 'educated Muhammadans' as 'naturally sympathetic to this [Bolshevik] movement', British intelligence characteristically overstated the case. Their reports indiscriminately linked all shades of anti-colonial Muslim opinion with Bolshevism. In reality, most were outside the first socialist network and continued to remain so.[140]

A New Category of Local Opponents

A close watch on the movements of Muzaffar Ahmad and other activists of the first socialist nucleus became the most effective method of pre-emptive action in the city. Muzaffar's association with M.N. Roy, which started and developed during 1922, first brought him to the attention of the anti-Bolshevik network. The colonial authorities, keen to intercept every secret communication from the Comintern to individuals residing in British India, uncovered Muzaffar's correspondence with Roy. A low-level surveillance began immediately. Links with the Third International made the police identify Muzaffar as a 'Bolshevik Agent' and they began opening his letters. Police agents would keep a watch on the post offices, open and copy all the mail coming from Roy, and then carefully re-seal and send them to Muzaffar, to keep track of future plans. Muzaffar was unaware of this process before he was warned by a sympathetic postal worker. The maze-like streets, the lanes and bylanes of central and north Calcutta attained a new significance for Muzaffar after this discovery. They became the shadowy realms through which he tried, repeatedly and fruitlessly, to evade those who kept pursuing him. The aim of the police vigilance was to prevent the early socialist network from becoming politically effective. In its initial stages, surveillance was arbitrary and random. The net was deliberately wide and covered diverse groups and individuals who were seen as potential upholders of Bolshevism. Once the potential was realized in the form of identifiable suspects, it contracted and tightened around the subject of its concentrated focus. The outcome of surveillance generally resulted in the transformation of the suspect into a captive. The principal figures of the early socialist network were discreetly but closely monitored, followed by open surveillance culminating in arrest on charges of sedition.[141] Data collected on the individual at each level prior to his arrest were cited in court to secure conviction, and to project the state as the custodian of not just British but also Indian propertied interests under threat from a communist deluge.[142] Monitoring and police surveillance, arrest and court actions were self-legitimizing expressions of bureaucratic power from the nineteenth century onwards, enabling the colonial state to project itself as the custodian of public interests.[143] Despite these strategies, the official construction of a 'Bolshevik Menace' facilitated its counter-construction. Saturated with racial stereotypes designed to uphold the supremacy of the colonizers and harnessed to defeat Bolshevism, the colonial imagination failed to grasp what lay beyond its racialized prism. By criminalizing early socialist politics and projecting it as a potent tool of anti-colonial action, the state ironically brought about what it had tried to curb and destroy; a new category of opponents, aware of the mechanisms of colonial surveillance, emerged as a result of this exercise. The conditions that had made Muzaffar Ahmad turn to socialism remained in place despite the repression directed at him. The state had paid attention to him as an individual activist as well as his associates. What it had singularly failed to control was the deeper political compulsions that propelled Muzaffar in this direction. His first colleagues, though in a state of disarray after his arrest, gradually came together again while Muzaffar was still in jail. Despite the creation of an elaborate surveillance network based on the myth of the 'outsider', the government failed to eradicate interest in socialist ideas and politics. It had not bargained for the persistent reappearance of dissident 'insiders'; activists of a new type impossible to control were transforming their existing social and political circles into minute bastions of what the state defined as the 'Bolshevist' tendency.

Constraints, Contradictions

Though colonial surveillance could not wipe out the early socialists, its operation revealed the fragility of the early socialist network. From contemporary police records and memoirs of some of the actors themselves, it would seem that this was a major impediment in the path of its expansion. Certain other difficulties also riddled activism.

Differences

Factionalism among the Indian revolutionaries abroad who were in touch with the Comintern,[144] divisions among the revolutionary terrorists interested primarily in arms supply and funds from Moscow, and ideological disagreements between their lines of thinking and that of Muzaffar created certain internal constraints. Despite broad agreement and coordination, differences and disjunctions created ruptures at various levels between Roy and Muzaffar. The problems of communication were often heightened by differences over organizational decisions.

Following Nalini Gupta's visit, a direct link was established between M.N. Roy, based in Berlin, and Muzaffar Ahmad. Letters exchanged between the two reflect attempts to evolve an effective socialist organization and strategy. The Roy–Muzaffar correspondence began when Muzaffar Ahmad was able to send a letter to the Comintern, successfully evading the police. He was politically unknown at the time and was not under surveillance. This letter, written in March 1922, was addressed to 'The Secretary, Communist International, Moscow, Russia' from '10/1 Bright Street, Ballygunge, Calcutta'. The letter indicated that this was the 'Head Office' of 'Bharat Samyatantra Samiti' (Indian Socialist Association). Muzaffar Ahmad signed as the 'Secretary' of this organization. The letter mentioned 'Comrade Nalini Gupta' who 'came here and kindly paid a visit'. It requested funds to facilitate socialist activity in a country where 'the suffering of the people is great'.[145] Muzaffar Ahmad had moved to Bright Street immediately after Nalini's departure and had probably decided to utilize his new address as the centre of the first socialist nucleus. According to him, Roy first heard of him and obtained his address in April 1922 through the Comintern. Their correspondence began when Roy wrote to him on behalf of the Indian section of the Third International.[146]

The house at 10/1 Bright Street where Muzaffar Ahmad lived in early 1922; in a letter to the Comintern in March 1922, he gave this as the address of the 'Bharatiya Samyatantra Samiti' office

The focus of their correspondence, mostly carried on during 1922, was on the need to propagate 'class identity' through the dissemination of socialist literature, and the creation of a network of members and sympathizers in Bengal. Muzaffar was instrumental in carrying out these decisions. Roy and Muzaffar were keen to work together. There were repeated overtures from Roy inviting Muzaffar to visit him in Europe, so that they could discuss theory and practical action face to face.[147] The latter's illness and police surveillance on his movements followed by swift arrest prevented such a meeting. Roy mainly concentrated on advising Muzaffar to send able recruits for training in Europe, receive and distribute literature sent to India, send reports on political movements and individuals Roy was in touch with. Muzaffar in turn sent prompt progress reports and suggestions, often critical of Roy's strategies.

Muzaffar was particularly sceptical of Roy's initiatives to rope in *bhadralok* nationalists to the nascent communist movement. He was disconcerted by the links between class and communalism that underlined this form of politics: the refusal of this section to review the Hindu high-caste revivalist aspects of their ideology; the embedded secret agenda of elite domination; the methods of political recruitment, a source of alienation and irritation to Muzaffar and others from a Muslim background. Despite professed solidarity with the masses, which some nationalist revolutionaries did recognize as important at this stage, they effectively stayed away from working-class and peasant movements. The familiar practice of forming secret societies composed exclusively of middle-class youth was still acceptable to them, but very unacceptable to Muzaffar. Mass-based organizations were external to their mode of creating political formations. In an exasperated letter to Roy, Muzaffar expressed deep reservations regarding *Atmasakti* and highlighted the limits of the middle-class radicalism it advocated. He implied that it was extremely difficult for him to work with those who were still tied to the *bhadralok* nationalist ethos. Roy displayed an unwillingness to sever ties with his former colleagues from his Jugantar days. He empathized with Muzaffar and identified with his distaste for their political culture. Yet he simultaneously felt that *Atmasakti* did publish some 'good articles' from time to time, and that Muzaffar should make an effort to maintain communication unless and until all dialogue became impossible.

Muzaffar urged greater caution; he felt Roy should be more careful and take certain concrete steps to evade British censorship and interception of Comintern literature. On one occasion he bitterly chastised Roy for his naivety and lack of practical sense, particularly regarding police informers who were penetrating the pan-Islamic underground and the *bhadralok* revolutionary circles. Some of Muzaffar's suggestions, initially dismissed by Roy, were later accepted. One of these was changing the name of *Vanguard*. Differences between Roy and Muzaffar over potential recruits, disagreements with revolutionary nationalists and constant surveillance made Muzaffar's attempts to establish the Comintern's influence among various shades of radicals quite difficult.[148] The minute size of the organization and dearth of able activists made matters worse.

There was also some ideological competition. Anonymous sources circulated anarchist literature originating from Europe in Calcutta. In 1923, the 'International Workingmen's Association', an Anarcho–Syndicalist group based in Berlin, was disseminating material denouncing the Third Communist International.[149] Though this stream failed to have any noticeable political impact, the arrival of Abani Mukherjee most certainly did. Mukherjee, Roy's former colleague who had since become his sworn enemy, succeeded in creating considerable confusion in the revolutionary nationalist circles interested in establishing links with the Comintern. In a letter to the Comintern he accused Roy of associating with 'swindlers' such as Muzaffar Ahmad, Nalini Gupta, Dr T.N. Roy and Mohammad Daud, among others. This letter, intercepted by the police, was later used as evidence against the early communists.[150] After Muzaffar's arrest in May 1923, Bhupendranath Datta, followed by Jibanlal Chatterjee, severed links with the early socialist nucleus. From Datta's narrative, it seems he was never fully convinced of a doctrine which propagated replacement of middle-class leaders by those of working-class and peasant origins. He still saw peasants as 'passive' elements of society and workers as politically 'ineffective', and could not at the time visualize a revolution from below. His friend Jibanlal's return to revolutionary nationalist methods was apparently more reluctant. The top leaders of their militant nationalist circle were intent on persecuting him for his allegedly 'anti-nationalist' role in encouraging young recruits to read Bolshevik literature.[151] Though he was to identify himself with socialist politics in the 1940s,[152] the pull of militant nationalism was still strong and managed to reclaim Jibanlal Chatterjee during the 1920s. Though *Udarer Chinta* reveals a tone decidedly influenced by socialist ideas, in his letter to *Servant* and *Amrita Bazar Patrika* in January 1923, Jibanlal articulated his ideological doubts and confusion. While stressing that M.N. Roy should be well received, he also indicated that Roy was someone 'whose views I cannot accept in full'.[153]

Jibanlal's return to revolutionary nationalism also revealed the weakness of socialist protest at this stage. Despite the novelty of socialist ideas and their radical potential, socialist politics and Muzaffar's role in upholding it had a marginal impact on the larger political scenario. Muzaffar's efforts to build a network which could be distinguished from the type of anti-colonialism associated with the Congress and Khilafat could not take off. The network failed to crystallize into a regular organization capable of systematically pursuing its radical aims. Instead, reformist agenda of the Swarajist variety made greater progress, and influenced middle-class Bengali Muslim and Hindu *bhadralok* intellectuals interested in social change. Muzaffar could only influence a tiny section among his circle of literary and political acquaintances. Despite Muzaffar's initiatives, Moinuddin Hussain, a politically promising acquaintance and erudite intellectual, remained a nationalist.[154] The same was true of other prominent Bengali Muslim intellectuals such as Kazi Abdul Odud who belonged to Muzaffar's wider circle. Odud was a critical admirer of Gandhi.[155] The new generation of writers, including Nazrul, were impressed by and supported mass participation in politics. However, the social character of this participation was still unclear to them and found manifestation in their connection with syndicalist labour journals such as *Sanhati*. Neither could Muzaffar win over labour leaders such as Mohammad Daud or Mukundalal Sarkar. Though not unsympathetic to left ideas, most labour leaders displayed a syndicalist and reformist tendency, emphasising class-conscious unionization; they discouraged workers to step beyond these formations to launch a revolutionary collective.

A Precarious Existence

Muzaffar's precarious existence restricted activism. Life centred round constant shortage of money, attempts to counter the influence of nationalists in his milieu, and playing hide and seek with the police. An irregular and unstable network was created through stray political conversations at cafes, meetings with contacts and recruits at offices of periodicals and trade unions, and at city parks and street-corners. This 'irregularity' made it vulnerable, particularly to surveillance. The state's knowledge of all his political contacts and 'post-boxes' restricted Muzaffar. His every move was watched. An intelligence report filed on the eve of the AITUC Conference at Lahore in March 1923 suggested that since Muzaffar had received a special invitation to attend and 'is evidently going', it would 'be worthwhile to warn the Lahore police to watch over him and someone who knows him should shadow him up to Lahore'. The report stressed: 'This is important in view of the fact that he is anxious to smuggle out of India.' Consequently, the Intelligence Branch of the Bengal Police decided to approach the Special Branch of the Calcutta Police, and declared they would be 'glad to know' if they could supply 'such a man' since Muzaffar was being watched by them.[156] The police were successful in planting informers who infiltrated his milieu. Hafiz Masud Ahmad, a friend of Kutubuddin and a regular visitor to 7 Moulavi Lane, was spying on the entire circle. Muzaffar's suspicion was confirmed in February 1923 during the visit of Shaukat Usmani, an ex-*muhajir* sent to Calcutta as Roy's second emissary. Another police agent, Sisirkumar Ghosh, befriended A.R. Khan for a short while. Muzaffar became alert to his activities after being warned by Bhupendrakumar Datta.[157] He could hardly undertake concerted activity under such conditions.[158] Since he could not afford rent, there were only contact addresses. The proto-organization he tried to create had no fixed location, even if the Moulavi Lane–Gumghar Lane–College Street–Pratap Chatterjee Street addresses supported his work. As he moved from place to place, during much of this period, the routine of roaming was often interrupted by news of arrests in his circle and visits to friends in prison. He was about to join their ranks. One early morning, at Kutubuddin's house, the sound of heavy boots on the stairs would wake him.[159]

The arrest and internment of Muzaffar Ahmad in May 1923 acted as a temporary blow to the early socialist network in Calcutta. As described above, the police had made him ineffective through constant surveillance even before his arrest. As the central figure of the Calcutta socialist network, Muzaffar had initiated activism informed by Marxist thought, was Roy's trusted correspondent, and was on the verge of creating an organizational network involving labour activists, other political and cultural activists, and fresh recruits new to any kind of politics. He was also linking this circle with the Comintern, socialist networks in other parts of India, local trade unions and radical journalism. M.N. Roy expressed concern for Muzaffar and the desire to 'rescue' him after his arrest. He also tried to keep the network going in Muzaffar's absence by getting in touch with other members of the circle such as Jibanlal Chatterjee and Kutubuddin Ahmad.[160] These attempts were unsuccessful, partially because of police interference. Besides, Jibanlal's arrest and decision to sever links with communism symbolized the exit of revolutionary terrorists from the network.[161]

However Kutubuddin and Nazrul, along with Abdul Halim and Abdur Rezzaq Khan, revived the socialist circle with the help of left Swarajist activists such as Hemantakumar Sarkar and Shamsuddin Hussain, the elder brother of Abdul Halim. No longer satisfied with the Swarajist agenda, its crisis made acute by the death of C.R. Das and the end of the populist coalition he headed, this left-wing fraction was joined by radical lawyers interested in securing land rights for peasants, Atulchandra Gupta and Nareshchandra Sengupta. There were temporary setbacks. For a while, especially during the year 1924, Kutubuddin, A.R. Khan and Nazrul abandoned the independent nucleus started by Muzaffar. In his absence, virtually cut off from the wider Comintern and socialist connections, they returned to the familiar nationalist organizational structure with which Kutubuddin and A.R. Khan had been previously associated. Though working under C.R. Das's leadership, they constituted a radical fringe and encouraged others to join the left current. By 1925, they were again confident enough to form an organization of their own with the help of like-minded individuals they had met through the Swarajist network. In marked similarity with the earlier network, this group also emerged from local conditions; though not subordinate to the Comintern, a relationship of mutual support was soon established. The government had failed in its aim of weeding out a left connected with the international communist movement. When Muzaffar was released and joined his colleagues again in 1926, preliminary work was already under way. With his return, the efforts would assume wider dimensions. A socialist political identity in Bengal was still novel and obscure; yet it offered an ideological alternative to the mainstream anti-colonial options and related to a non-hierarchical vision of a future society in India.

Notes and References

[1] Gautam Chattopadhyay, *Communism and Bengal's Freedom Movement*, Bombay, 1970, pp. 9–10. Amar Datta, 'Paris Commune o Prothom Antarjatiker Samakalin Banglar Samajtantrik Bhabna' (Paris Commune, the First International and Contemporary Socialist Thought in Bengal), in *Amritabazar Patrika o Ananya* (Amritabazar Patrika and Other Essays), Calcutta, 1997, pp. 43–44.

[2] Subodh Chandra Sengupta and Anjali Basu (eds.), *Sansad Bangali Charitabhidhan* (Dictionary of Bengali Biography), Vol. 1, Calcutta, 1994, pp. 489–90.

[3] *Modern Review*, Vol. 11, No. 3, March 1912. In December 1912, Muzaffar Ahmad's article, 'A Successful Musalman Student', had appeared in *Modern Review*. Its Bengali version was printed in *Prabasi*. This has been treated in Chapter One.

[4] Sipra Sarkar and Anamitra Das (eds.), *Bangalir Samyabad Charcha* (Communist Thinking in Bengal), Calcutta, 1998, Introduction.

[5] IB 275/21 (6/1921).

[6] Pabitra Gangopadhyay, *Chalaman Jiban* (Journey through Life), Calcutta, 1994, pp. 63–64.

[7] Abdul Halim, 'Nabajibaner Pathe' (Towards a New Life), in *Nabajibaner Pathe*, Calcutta, 1966, second edition 1990, pp. 57, 62–63. Halim also recalled reading *Town Labour*, on the British working-class movement. He may have been referring to J.L. Hammond and Barbara Hammond's *The Town Labourer, 1760–1832: the new civilization*, published from London in 1917.

[8] IB 93/26 (1/1926). IB 320/26 (310/1926).

[9] Hemantakumar Sarkar, *Biplaber Pancharishi* (Five Sages of Revolution), Calcutta, 1923.

[10] Hemantakumar Sarkar, *Swadhinatar Saptasurja* (Seven Suns of Freedom), Calcutta, 1924.

[11] Phanibhushan Ghosh, *Lenin*, Calcutta, 1921.

[12] Shaileshnath Bishi, *Bolshevikbad* (Bolshevism), Calcutta, 1924.

[13] P.C. Joshi, 'Lenin: Contemporary Indian Image', in P.C. Joshi, Gautam Chattopadhyay, Devendra Kaushik (eds.), *Lenin in Contemporary Indian Press*, Delhi, 1970, pp. 34–35.

[14] Nareshchandra Sengupta, 'Introduction', in Bishi, *Bolshevikbad*.

[15] G. Adhikary (ed.), *Documents of the History of the Communist Party of India*, Volume 1: 1917–1922, Delhi, 1971, pp. 339, 341–45, 359–60, 412, 437–44, 450–59, 489–94. Mushirul Hasan, 'Religion and Politics in India: The Ulama and the Khilafat Movement', in Mushirul Hasan (ed.), *Communal and Pan-Islamic Trends in Colonial India*, Delhi, 1981, pp. 16-17. *Gandhi-Charita* (The Persona of Gandhi), *Dhumketu*, 1, 19, B 1329/1922.

[16] IB 1041/16 (69/1916).

[17] The phrase 'language of class' appears in Gareth Stedman Jones, *Languages of Class, Studies in English Working Class History 1832–1982*, Cambridge, 1983. For a contestation of this paradigm, see John Foster, 'The Declassing of Language', *New Left Review*, 150, March/April 1985.

[18] IB 275/21 (6/1921).

[19] *Dhumketu*, 1, 18, B 1329/1922. The third and final part of a polemical letter from Muzaffar criticizing middle-class nationalists appeared in this issue. It also contained the first instalment of Mahamaya Debi's article.

[20] Subodh Roy (ed.), *Communism in India, Unpublished Documents, 1917–1924*, Calcutta, 1997, p. 13. Italics mine.

[21] IB 20/1921 (66/1921).

[22] IB 61/1920 (52/1920).

[23] IB 311/1920 (41/1920). Abul Hussain's 'Banglar Bolshi', written in 1921, has been discussed in Chapter Two.

[24] Roy (ed.), *Communism in India*, p.19.

[25] IB 95/24 (41/1924).

[26] Appendix A, Interview (29 May 1970, Calcutta), in Chattopadhyay, *Communism and Bengal's Freedom Movement*, p. 152.

[27] Muzaffar Ahmad, *Amar Jiban o Bharater Communist Party* (My Life and the Communist Party of India), Calcutta, 1969, fifth edition 1996, p. 97. IB 95/24 (41/1924).

[28] Appendix A, Interview (29 May 1970, Calcutta), in Chattopadhyay, *Communism and Bengal's Freedom Movement*, pp. 153–54.

[29] Ibid.

[30] Halim, *Nabajibaner Pathe*, pp. 53–57. The actions of the gas and tram workers have been treated in Chapter Two.

[31] Ibid.

[32] IB 275/21 (6/1921). IB 340/22 (26/1922). IB 109/23 (131/1923). IB 95/24 (41/1924).

[33] Halim, *Nabajibaner Pathe*, pp. 55–59. IB 210/27 (23/1927).

[34] Halim, *Nabajibaner Pathe*, p. 60.

[35] Ahmad, *Amar Jiban o Bharater Communist Party*, p. 112.

[36] Muzaffar Ahmad, 'Amar Pointallish Bacharer Shathi' (My Companion for Forty-Five Years), in Halim, *Nabajibaner Pathe*, pp. 6–7.

[37] Ahmad, *Amar Jiban o Bharater Communist Party*, p. 113. IB 67/24 (105/1924). IB 210/27 (23/ 1927).

[38] Halim, *Nabajibaner Pathe*, p. 59.

[39] Statement of Abani Chowdhury, PW 18, S/O Manindra, Bengali, 19, Service, Bally, Howrah, *Kanpur Communist Conspiracy Case (1924) Papers*.

[40] Ibid. IB 67/24 (105/1924).

[41] Halim, *Nabajibaner Pathe*, pp. 64–65.

[42] Bhupendrakumar Datta, *Biplaber Padachinha* (Footprints of Revolution), Calcutta, 1999, p. 208. Halim, 'Bidrohi Banglar Kobi: Kazi Nazrul Islam' (Poet of Rebel Bengal: Kazi Nazrul Islam), in *Nabajibaner Pathe*, p. 208. Achintyakumar Sengupta, *Kalloljug* (Age of Kallol), Calcutta, 1960, p. 84.

[43] Ahmad, *Kazi Nazrul Islam: Smritikatha* (Kazi Nazrul Islam: Reminiscences), Calcutta, 1965, ninth edition 1998, p. 164.

[44] Ibid., p. 122.

[45] IB 168/20 (110/1920). IB 67/24 (105/1924). Ahmad, *Amar Jiban o Bharater Communist Party*, pp. 85–87, 101.

[46] Chattopadhyay, *Communism and Bengal's Freedom Movement*, p. 154.

[47] Halim, *Nabajibaner Pathe*, pp. 61–62.

[48] Muzaffar Ahmad, *Samakaler Katha* (Story of My Times), 1963, fourth edition 1996, p. 21. Halim, *Nabajibaner Pathe*, p. 60.

[49] Shantipada Sinha, 'Amader Darbeshda' (Our Darbeshda), in Mazharul Islam (ed.), *Muzaffar Ahmad: Shango o Prashango* (Muzaffar Ahmad: Reflections and Essays), Calcutta, 1989, pp. 101–02. Ahmad, *Kazi Nazrul Islam: Smritikatha*, p. 41.

[50] Sinha, 'Amader Darbeshda', in Islam (ed.), *Muzaffar Ahmad: Shango o Prashango*, pp. 108–09.

[51] Mohammad Walliullah, 'Comrade Muzaffar Ahmad', in Islam (ed.), *Muzaffar Ahmad: Shango o Prashango*, pp. 152–53.

[52] Ibid. Halim, *Nabajibaner Pathe*, p. 61.

[53] Sinha, 'Amader Darbeshda', in Islam (ed.), *Muzaffar Ahmad: Shango o Prashango*, pp. 108–09. Walliullah, 'Comrade Muzaffar Ahmad', in Islam (ed.), *Muzaffar Ahmad: Shango o Prashango*, pp. 152–53.

[54] Ahmad, *Amar Jiban o Bharater Communist Party*, pp. 188, 266. Muzaffar Ahmad, 'Doctor T.N. Roy (Obituary)', *Ganabani*, 1, 16, B 1334/1927.

[55] IB 1041/16 (69/16). Datta, *Biplaber Padachinha*, pp. 99–105, 209.

[56] Ahmad, *Amar Jiban o Bharater Communist Party*, pp. 113–14.

[57] Datta, *Biplaber Padachinha*, pp. 207–08. IB 1041/16 (69/16). Ahmad, *Amar Jiban o Bharater Communist Party*, p. 161.

[58] IB 1041/16 (196/1916).

[59] B.G. Gafurov and G.F. Kim (eds.), *Lenin and National Liberation in the East*, Moscow, 1978, p. 361.

[60] Sinha, 'Amader Darbeshda', in Islam (ed.), *Muzaffar Ahmad: Shango o Prashango*, p. 102. Walliullah, 'Comrade Muzaffar Ahmad', in Islam (ed.), *Muzaffar Ahmad: Shango o Prashango*, pp. 152–53. Moinuddin, 'Ekti Sangrami Jiban: Ekti Adarsho' (A Life of Struggle), in Islam (ed.), *Muzaffar Ahmad: Shango o Prashango*, pp. 80–81. IB 275/21 (6/ 1921).

[61] Ahmad, *Kazi Nazrul Islam: Smritikatha*, pp. 163–64.

[62] IB 67/24 (105/1924).

[63] IB 267F/20 (155/1920).

[64] Sanat Bose, 'Labour Journalism in Bengal in the Early 1920s: A Case Study of Two Bengali Labour Journals', in *Essays on Indian Labour*, Calcutta, 1996, pp. 98–99, 104. Gita Chatto-padhyay, *Bangla Samayik Patrikapanji* (List of Bengali Periodicals), 1915–1930, Calcutta, 1994, p. 188.

[65] Sengupta, *Kalloljug*, pp. 30–35, 82–83, 201. Gautam Chattopadhyay (ed.), *Sanhati–Langal–Ganavani*, Calcutta, 1992, pp. xii–xiv, 62–65.

[66] Tapobroto Ghosh, 'Literature and Literary Life in Calcutta: The Age of Rabindranath', in Sukanta Chaudhury (ed.), *Calcutta: The Living City*, Volume 2, Calcutta, 1995, p. 230.

[67] Halim, 'Bidrohi Banglar Kobi', in *Nabajibaner Pathe*, p. 137. Sengupta, *Kalloljug*, pp. 83, 205–07. Ghosh, 'Literature and Literary Life in Calcutta', pp. 224, 226, 228–30. For a discussion on modernist currents and the break with nineteenth-century culture in the European context, see Arnold Hauser, *The Social History of Art*, Volume 4, London, 1983, pp. 218–19.

[68] Sengupta, *Kalloljug*, pp. 270–71.

[69] Ghosh, 'Literature and Literary Life in Calcutta', p. 227. Alokeranjan Dasgupta, 'The Social and Cultural World of the Men of Literature in Calcutta', in Surajit Sinha (ed.), *Cultural Profile of Calcutta*, 1972, p. 163.

[70] *Statement of Newspapers and Periodicals Published or Printed in Bengal (Revised up to 31st December 1923)*, IB 275/21 (6/1921).

[71] Dasgupta, 'The Social and Cultural World of the Men of Literature in Calcutta', in Sinha (ed.), *Cultural Profile of Calcutta*, p. 163. For a culturalist critique, see Rajarshi Dasgupta, 'Marxism and the middle class intelligentsia: culture and politics in Bengal, 1920s–1950s', unpublished Ph.D. thesis, University of Oxford, 2003. For a discussion on the relationships between dissident writers and radical politics, see Eric Hobsbawm, 'Socialism and the Avant-Garde, 1880–1914', in *Uncommon People: Resistance, Rebellion and Jazz*, London, 1999, pp. 171–72, 180.

[72] Halim, 'Bangla Sahitye Marxbadi Bhabdharar Suchana' (The Beginning of Marxist Themes in Bengali Literature), in *Nabajibaner Pathe*, pp. 120–22. Despite Halim's reservations, a certain exchange of ideas and spirit of solidarity existed. While many undoubtedly surrendered to strands of middle-class culture, some, such as Pabitra Gangopadhyay, Sibram Chakrabarty and Premendra Mitra, remained committed radical writers. For a biographical sketch of Premendra Mitra, see Subodh Chandra Sengupta and Anjali Basu (eds.), *Sansad Bangali*

Charitabhidhan (Dictionary of Bengali Biography), Vol. 2, Calcutta, 1996, pp. 89–90.

73 Sengupta, *Kalloljug*, p. 80. Sibram Chakrabarty's play on the limits of middle-class intellectual anarchy and resistance has been treated in Chapter Two.

74 Shailajananda Mukhopadhyay, 'Janab Muzaffar Ahmad', in Islam (ed.), *Muzaffar Ahmad: Shango o Prashango*, pp. 73–74. Sibram Chakrabarty, 'Bangla Sahityer Bishista Gadya Bhangir Sroshta: Muzaffar Ahmad' (The Creator of a Distinctive Bengali Prose: Muzaffar Ahmad), in Islam (ed.), *Muzaffar Ahmad: Shango o Prashango*, p. 130.

75 IB 273/21(2/1921). Ahmad, *Amar Jiban o Bharater Communist Party*, p. 65.

76 IB 273/21(2/1921). IB 95/24 (41/1924). Ahmad, *Amar Jiban o Bharater Communist Party*, pp. 64–67, 213.

77 IB 95/24 (41/1924).

78 Moinuddin, 'Ekti Sangrami Jiban: Ekti Adarsho', in Islam (ed.), *Muzaffar Ahmad: Shango o Prashango*, pp.80–81.

79 IB 273/21(2/1921). IB 275/21(6/1921). IB 340/22(26/1922).IB 109/23 (131/1923). IB 95/24 (41/1924).

80 *Annual Report on Indian Papers Printed or Published in the Bengal Presidency during the Year 1922*, Calcutta, 1923. IB 275/21 (6/1921).

81 Datta, *Biplaber Padachinha*, pp. 208–09.

82 IB 275/21 (6/1921).

83 *Annual Report on Indian Papers Printed or Published in the Bengal Presidency during the Year 1922*.

84 IB 273/21 (21/1921).

85 'Dwaipayaner Patra' (Letter from Dwaipayan), *Dhumketu*, 1, 13, B 1329/1922. 'Dwaipayaner Patra' (Letter from Dwaipayan), *Dhumketu*, 1, 16, B 1329/1922. 'Dwaipayaner Patra' (Letter from Dwaipayan), *Dhumketu*, 1, 18, B 1329/1922.

86 'Dwaipayaner Patra' (Letter from Dwaipayan), *Dhumketu*, 1, 13, B 1329/1922. Reprinted in Sarkar and Das (eds.), *Bangalir Samyabad Charcha*, pp. 48–49.

87 'Dwaipayaner Patra' (Letter from Dwaipayan), *Dhumketu*, 1, 18, B 1329/1922. Muzaffar must have borrowed the phrase 'spectre of authority' (*'kartar bhut'*) from Rabindranath Tagore's short story/prose poem of the same name.

88 Datta, *Biplaber Padachinha*, p. 208.

89 *Annual Report on Indian Papers Printed or Published in the Bengal Presidency during the Year 1922*.

90 Halim, *Nabajibaner Pathe*, p. 130. Ahmad, *Kazi Nazrul Islam: Smritikatha*, pp. 91, 160, 163–64. IB 196/25 (44/1925), cited in Ladlimohon Raychaudhury (ed.), *The Seed-Time of Communist Movement in Bengal*, Calcutta, 2000, p. 137. This is a collection of official surveillance reports dating back to the late 1910s and the 1920s.

91 IB 275/21 (6/1921). IB 273/21 (21/1921). Ahmad, *Kazi Nazrul Islam: Smritikatha*, pp. 163–67.

92 IB 212/23 (111/1923).

93 IB 293/20 (136/1920).

94 IB 263/20 (83/1920). IB 273/21 (21/1921).

95 IB 235/22 (1/1922).

96 Halim, *Nabajibaner Pathe*, p. 65. Ahmad, *Amar Jiban o Bharater Communist Party*, pp. 95, 99, 191, 267.

97 IB 369/22 (28/1922).

98 IB 93/26 (1/ 1926). IB 320/26 (310/1926). Ahmad, *Amar Jiban o Bharater Communist Party*, pp. 337–38.

99 IB 273/21 (21/1921). Ahmad, 'Amar Pointallish Bacharer Sathi', in Halim, *Nabajibaner Pathe*, pp. 11–12. Ahmad, *Samakaler Katha*, p. 54. Anjan Bera, *Sangbadik Nazrul* (Nazrul as a Journalist), Calcutta, 1998, p. 13.

100 IB 95/24 (41/1924). *Samyabadi*, B 1329/1923. Anisuzzaman, *Muslim Banglar Samayik Patrika* (List of Bengali Muslim Periodicals), Dhaka, 1969, pp. 379–80.

101 Sarkar, *Modern India*, p. 249.

[102] IB 68/22 (73/22).

[103] R.J. Popplewell, *Intelligence and Imperial Defence: British Intelligence and the Defence of the Indian Empire, 1904–1924*, London, 1995, p. 309.

[104] John Fisher, 'The Interdepartmental Committee on Eastern Unrest and British Responses to Bolshevik and Other Intrigues against the Empire during the 1920s', *Journal of Asian History*, Vol. 34, No. 1, 2000.

[105] IB 353/20 (30/1920).

[106] IB 273/21 (2/1921).

[107] IB 20/21 (66/1921).

[108] IB 369/22 (28/1922). Colson's vigilance also meant promotion. By 1928 he was Deputy Inspector General of the Bengal Intelligence Branch, in charge of preparing detailed reports on communist activity, particularly in the industrial belt. The dossier prepared by his office in July 1928 is discussed in Chapter Five.

[109] IB 109/1923 (131/1923), IB 273/1921 (2/1921), IB 67/1924 (105/1924).

[110] IB 112/20 (80/1920). It seems 'Chicot' was well versed in French literature. The pseudonym was probably borrowed, with a touch of subversive humour, from 'Chicot the Jester' by Alexandre Dumas. The quotation from Hugo was taken from 'The History of a Crime', a republican polemical tract written in 1852, and directed against Louis Bonaparte's dictatorship.

[111] *The Englishman*, January 1920. IB 112/20 (80/1920).

[112] IB 212/23 (111/1923).

[113] Adhikary (ed.), *Documents*, Vol. 1, pp. 69–70.

[114] Hemantakumar Sarkar, *Swadhinatar Saptasurja*, Calcutta, 1924.

[115] IB 126/20 (161/1920), cited in Raychaudhury (ed.), *The Seed-Time of Communist Movement in Bengal*, p. 33.

[116] IB 112/20 (80/1920).

[117] Ahmad, *Amar Jiban o Bharater Communist Party*, p. 45. Helene Carrare d'Encausse and Stuart R. Schram, *Marxism and Asia*, London, 1969, pp. 31–38.

[118] Ahmad, *Amar Jiban o Bharater Communist Party*, pp. 45–76. K.H. Ansari, 'Pan-Islam and the Making of the Early Indian Muslim Socialists', *Modern Asian Studies*, 20, 3, 1986, pp. 509–37. K.H. Ansari, *The Emergence of Socialist Thought among North Indian Muslims (1917–1947)*, Lahore, 1990, pp. 15–42.

[119] Ahmad, *Amar Jiban o Bharater Communist Party*, p. 53. Purabi Roy, Sobhanlal Datta Gupta and Hari Vasudevan (eds.), *Indo-Russian Relations 1917–1947, Select Documents from the Archives of the Russian Federation, Part I: 1917–1928*, Calcutta, 1999, pp. 38–39.

[120] IB 266/1920 (130/1920). Ahmad, *Kazi Nazrul Islam: Smritikatha*, p. 35.

[121] Ahmad, *Amar Jiban o Bharater Communist Party*, p. 133.

[122] Roy, *Communism in India*, p. 13. Ahmad, *Amar Jiban o Bharater Communist Party*, pp. 133–34. Ansari, *Emergence of Socialist Thought among North Indian Muslims*, pp. 23–42.

[123] Raychaudhury, *The Seed-Time of Communist Movement in Bengal*, pp. 135–44.

[124] IB 49/21 (431/1921). Sengupta, *Kalloljug*, pp. 6–7.

[125] IB 95/24 (41/1924).

[126] IB 352/22 (12/22).

[127] IB 126/20 (161/1920). IB 311/20 (41/1920).

[128] IB 311/20 (41/1920).

[129] Pakrasi, *Agnijuger Katha*, p. 109.

[130] Ahmad, *Kazi Narul Islam: Smritikatha*, pp. 35, 106.

[131] L.F. Rushbrook Williams, *India in 1920*, Calcutta, 1921, pp. 1–50.

[132] Pabitra Gangopadhyay, *Chalaman Jiban*, Calcutta, 1994, p. 100.

[133] Ahmad, *Amar Jiban o Bharater Communist Party*, p. 31.

[134] D.M. Laushey, *Bengal Terrorism and the Marxist Left, Aspects of Regional Nationalism in India, 1905–1942*, Calcutta, 1975, pp. 17–18.

[135] IB 354/20 (152/1920).

[136] On Indian revolutionaries and left connections, see A.K. Basu, *Indian Revolutionaries Abroad, 1905–1922: In the Background of International Developments*, Patna, 1971. Janice R.

MacKinnon and Stephen R. MacKinnon, *Agnes Smedley: The life and times of an American Radical*, London, 1988. Agnes Smedley, journalist, feminist and socialist activist, was connected with anti-imperialist movements in India and China. She met Lala Lajpat Rai through Indian revolutionaries in the United States during the late 1910s.

[137] IB 126/20 (161/1920), in Raychaudhury (ed.), *The Seed-Time of Communist Movement in Bengal*, p. 114.

[138] IB 112/20 (80/1920).

[139] Datta, *Biplaber Padachinha*, pp. 209–11.

[140] IB 196/25 (44/1925), in Raychaudhury (ed.), *The Seed-Time of Communist Movement in Bengal*, pp. 135–44.

[141] IB 67/24 (105/1924).

[142] Statement of Cecil Kaye, PW1, *Kanpur Communist Conspiracy Case (1924) Papers*.

[143] Peter Robb, 'The ordering of rural India: the policing of nineteenth century Bengal and Bihar', in David M. Anderson and David Killingray (eds.), *Policing the Empire, Government, Authority and Control, 1830–1940*, Manchester, 1991, p. 126.

[144] Bhupendranath Datta, *Aprakashita Rajnitik Itihas* (Unpublished Political History), Calcutta, 1984, pp. 1–68. Ahmad, *Amar Jiban o Bharater Communist Party*, pp. 62–64.

[145] Collected by Subodh Roy from the Archive of the Russian Federation, Moscow; a copy of this letter is available at the CPI(M) Archives, Calcutta.

[146] Ahmad, *Amar Jiban o Bharater Communist Party*, pp. 95, 405.

[147] IB 95/24 (41/1924). IB 273/21 (2/1921). Ahmad, *Amar Jiban o Bharater Communist Party*, pp. 266–67.

[148] IB 67/24 (105/1924).

[149] IB 107/23 (72/1923).

[150] IB 95/24 (41/1924). IB 67/24 (105/1924). Datta, *Biplaber Padachinha*, p. 208. Ahmad, *Amar Jiban o Bharater Communist Party*, pp. 184–201. Datta, *Aprakashita Rajnitik Itihas*, p. 43.

[151] Datta, *Biplaber Padachinha*, pp. 209–11.

[152] IB 1041Y/16 (120/1916). IB 1041Z/16 (120/1916).

[153] IB 1041/16 (69/1916).

[154] Ahmad, *Kazi Narul Islam: Smritikatha*, p. 19.

[155] Zahirul Hasan, *Kazi Abdul Wadud*, New Delhi, 1997, pp. 75–84.

[156] IB 369/22 (28/1922).

[157] Ahmad, *Amar Jiban o Bharater Communist Party*, pp. 244, 114–17.

[158] IB 95/24 (41/1924). IB 67/24 (105/1924). Ahmad, *Amar Jiban o Bharater Communist Party*, pp. 265–67.

[159] Ahmad, *Kazi Nazrul Islam: Smritikatha*, pp. 96–97, 170. Ahmad, *Amar Jiban o Bharater Communist Party*, pp. 214, 267–68.

[160] IB 1041/16 (69/16). Ahmad, *Amar Jiban o Bharater Communist Party*, pp. 161, 256–57.

[161] Ahmad, *Amar Jiban o Bharater Communist Party*, pp. 162–63.

CHAPTER FOUR

Organization

'In the house of cards in this desperate city
the breeze is a sigh
of many voices, many notes, high and low . . .'
— Bishnu De, 'Kankalitala'

Some time in the second half of the 1920s, Atulya Ghosh, subsequently a towering figure in the post-independence Bengal Congress, while making his way through European Asylum Lane, noticed the signboard of a political organization named after peasants (*krishak*) and workers (*sramik*). Unfamiliar with any organization in Bengal which included the peasantry in its agenda at the time, Ghosh was intrigued. He climbed the stairs leading to the group's office where he met a man named Muzaffar Ahmad and was struck by the latter's 'integrity' and 'commitment'.[1] Despite Muzaffar's trial and conviction alongside S.A. Dange, Nalini Gupta and Shaukat Usmani in 1924,[2] the state had failed to wipe out the communist left from the city. Muzaffar had successfully initiated a socialist network; a group of activists and an organization had emerged. A product of convergence, this first socialist organization was peopled with left Swarajists, radical writers, agrarian socialists and early communists in a state of disarray after the suppression of their network in 1923. After Muzaffar's release and return to Calcutta, the communists came to lead this group.

During the second half of the 1920s, significant transformations in the realm of politics were registered in Bengal. Most historians have overwhelmingly focused on the impact of the changes introduced by colonial constitutional reforms on intensified communal polarization, and the concomitant making of segmented 'constituencies'. Only a few have treated the demands for redistributive justice that came from below, expressed through new approaches to political identity and movements. The role of Muzaffar Ahmad and his colleagues in systematically developing a left perspective on contemporary social conflicts through the prism of 'class' started in this period. This ideological orientation also made them look beyond the urban metropolitan boundaries, even if Calcutta was the centre of activism. The first socialist organization thus signalled the appearance of a new political formation in the history of modern Bengal; its structure and expansion also created a political space for a wider reception of communist ideas and practice in the region.

Swarajist Politics Rejected

The first socialist organization was related to a wider current: similar groups emerged in Bombay, Madras, Uttar Pradesh and Punjab.[3] These were local left formations inspired by the October Revolution of 1917, regarded by the colonial state as open units of the banned Communist Party of India (CPI) and sponsored by Moscow.[4] The official interpretation was inspired by the Comintern's suggestion to create a 'Peasants and Workers Party' through circulars sent to India.[5] Though founders of the 'Labour-Swaraj Party of the Indian National Congress' may have read M.N. Roy's articles urging organization, Muzaffar thought Roy's direct influence was negligible. Muzaffar held that the distinctly non-Marxist origins and nationalist connections of the Bengal group were evident in the name of the organization. Liberal quotations in the first party programme from the nationalist revolutionary-turned-sage, Aurobindo Ghosh, were further proof.[6] Muzaffar's observations were rooted in the curious fusion characterizing the group's inception: it brought together left-leaning nationalists who were gradually rejecting the social orientation of nationalism, and socialists who had already traversed that field and left it behind.

Differences over 'Swaraj'

After Muzaffar's imprisonment, his colleagues in the early socialist network became active in the Swarajist movement, closely aligned with those in favour of council entry among the Congress leadership. Even Abdul Halim, who was a confirmed communist by this time, attended the annual conference of the Bengal Congress at Faridpur in 1925.[7] Though maintaining ties with mainstream anti-colonialism in the hope of spreading their ideas through existing platforms, their chief interest was in forming an organization of their own. An indication of this was Kutubuddin Ahmad's candidacy in a by-election to the Legislative Council as an 'Independent Communist'.[8] Nazrul Islam and Halim canvassed on his behalf.[9] The defection of a section of the middle-class *bhadralok* intelligentsia from the Swarajist fold boosted their efforts. When Hemantakumar Sarkar argued in favour of land rights for actual cultivators at a Congress meeting in Jessore, Swarajist leader Biren

Sasmal labelled him an 'upstart', and he was vilified as a 'police agent' in the Congress circles championing landlord interests.[10]

Like many others, Hemantakumar Sarkar had started distancing himself from the social content of *bhadralok* nationalism from the early 1920s. A lecturer in Linguistics at Calcutta University and engaged in doctoral research, he gave up a promising academic career to become active in the Non-Cooperation Movement[11] and was jailed.[12] As a trained linguist and a participant in a mass upsurge, he argued that Bengalis were non-Aryans; and that the so-called upper castes, from where the Bengali intelligentsia originated, were a tiny minority. Therefore this intelligentsia could not claim to represent the ordinary people of the region and their culture.[13] On the waning of the anti-colonial mass upsurge, he observed that Non-Cooperation had been directed against the colonial 'administrative machinery' (*shasanjantra*) and that future movements required a struggle against the 'exploitation machinery' (*shoshanjantra*). In an article titled 'Non-Cooperation o Socialist Andolan' (Non-Cooperation and the Socialist Movement) which cited the Paris Commune of 1871, the Bolshevik Revolution of 1917, and the socialist uprisings in Germany (1918), Austria (1918) and Hungary (1919), he praised Karl Marx's *Capital* as a 'visionary' work.[14] In 1923, Sarkar, still a nationalist, entered the Bengal Legislative Council as a Swarajist representative.[15] As the Swarajists rapidly abandoned their original promise of 'Swaraj for the 98 per cent' he rejected them, even parting ways with his close friend Subhash Chandra Bose.[16]

Sarkar's alienation from nationalist politics of the Swarajist variety was set in motion by the contraction of the Swarajist platform into a vehicle of *bhadralok* social interests; he had learnt to oppose these interests during the mass upsurge of the early 1920s. Led by the Bengal Congress leader, C.R. Das, the Swarajya Party was the joint constitutional platform of middle- and upper-class leaders from the districts and urban centres. During 1923, its candidates won in constituencies formed around the cardinal principles of separate electorates, as well as property and educational qualifications. The Bengal/Hindu–Muslim Pact of 1923, popularly known as the C.R. Das Pact, promised the Muslim proprietor class a favourable share of administrative posts and political representation. It dissolved soon after Das's death in 1925. The collapse of the coalition was followed by communal fragmentation of the Swarajist support-base. Henceforth, a steady slide into violent communalism, interrupted by occasional joint campaigns and coalition formations, would become the order of the day in colonial Bengal.[17]

This was evident in the debate (1923–28) over the 'Bengal Tenancy Act Amendment Bill'. At the very beginning of the Tenancy Bill controversy, joint opposition from Hindu and Muslim landed proprietors forced the government to drop proposals to extend occupancy rights to the *bargadars* (share-croppers). The predominantly Muslim rich and middle peasants (*jotedars/talukdars*) united with large landowners (zamindars) from a Hindu high-caste background to remove this clause curtailing their collective social interests as owners of large tracts of land. After this, the Hindu and Muslim landed gentry concentrated fire on each other. All the Hindu representatives, bar one, sided with the permanently settled landlords, while the Muslim representatives championed *jotedar* interests. This development, along with the annulment of the Das Pact, dissolved the Swarajist following among the Muslim electorate.[18]

Criticisms from the Right and the Left

The configuration of class and community interests in shaping the political agenda of the Swarajist leadership triggered a range of reactions. An elite critique of Swarajist populism emerged during the mid-1920s. Pramathanath Bishi, a close associate of Tagore and son of a nationalist zamindar who later attained fame as a prominent intellectual,[19] exposed the fear and contempt a section of the intelligentsia harboured towards the city's proletariat and its emergence as a political constituency in the course of the anti-colonial mass upsurge. His *Desher Shatru* (Enemy of the Country), described by the author as an 'essay-novel' (*probondhoponyash*), set in the context of the Non-Cooperation Movement and Swarajist politics, condemned the entry of the masses into the public arena. While criticizing the colonial state for demonizing the masses as 'thieves, robbers, thugs, rowdies, Bolsheviks, seditious elements', the narrative repeatedly refers to them as ignorant plebians. Swarajists are projected as contemptible for turning to 'illiterate persons of the coach-man class' (*kochowan srenir nirakkhar lok*) for support. The villain 'Hridaybabu' and his corrupt followers have no intention of changing the condition of the masses, but make use of populist demagoguery to attain political power.[20] Since '*hriday*' and '*chitta*' are synonymous in Bengali, meaning the 'heart', it is obvious that 'Hridaybabu' is none other than C. (Chitta) R. Das. As an alternative to Hridaybabu/Das, the author introduces an imaginary upper-class intellectual who is viciously persecuted as an 'enemy of the country' by the rabble-rousers, the yellow press they control, and Hridaybabu's conniving wife who bribes the Muslim under-class support-base. In the face of this combined attack, the cultured hero is more convinced than ever of the need to exclude the masses from politics. Though not clearly stated in the novel, the much-maligned protagonist, projected as the tragic voice of conscientious intellectual elitism, is strikingly similar to Plato's conception of the 'Philosopher-King'.[21] As the literary embodiment of benevolent despotism, he regards aristocracy of the mind rather than embourgeoisement as the route to liberty. Labelling capitalism as '*kaler jug*' (the machine age), the hero concludes that Indians should not accumulate capital for such a process necessarily involves the 'enslavement' of society; the colonizers, already masters of the 'machine age', would not allow it; and the fate of slaves from Africa should serve as a warning to all colonized people who aspire to become like their masters. While trying to imitate the master, the colonized can only cast themselves in the images of slaves. Only the wise intellectual who knows the real nature of capitalism-induced servitude and the dangers of investing power in the masses can steer society towards a meaningful transformation that ensures freedom for all.[22] By combining anti-capitalism and anti-imperialism with anti-populism, the novel advocates an elite, anti-democratic vision of change from above as salvation for the colonial world.

The Labour-Swaraj Party, representing a rejection of contemporary Swarajist politics from the left, emerged in November 1925.[23] Earlier, Hemantakumar Sarkar, Nareshchandra Sengupta, Atulchandra Gupta, Kutubuddin Ahmad, Nazrul Islam, A.R. Khan and Abdul Halim had attended the first All Bengal Peasants Conference held at Bogra on 7–8 February 1925. Dominated by *jotedar*/middle-peasant interests with virtually no agenda for the share-croppers and the landless,[24] the radical members of the Bengal intelligentsia active among the impoverished and the destitute were attracted by its demand for abolition of the zamindari system. Interactions among these radicals paved the way for the first socialist organization. Nareshchandra Sengupta, a successful barrister, novelist and a staunch champion of the poor peasantry, already saw himself as an 'independent socialist'[25] and was keen to join. The dismantling of private estates, redistribution of land and formation of rural cooperatives were advocated in his novel *Rajagi* (1926), centred on the scion of a rich zamindar family who leads a hedonistic existence until he comes across, wrestles with and is finally won over by these radical ideas. The novel also connects the social base of the *bhadralok* intelligentsia with landed property, calling for an ideological rejection of the existing property relations and the transfer of social leadership to the dispossessed.[26]

The Labour-Swaraj Party, formed and supported by activists such as Sarkar and Sengupta, expanded the political idea of social equality when it defined *swaraj* as 'complete Independence of India based on social and economic emancipation and political freedom for men and women'. The policy and programme of the party put forward a charter of immediate goals: minimum wages, eight-hour working day, free and compulsory education, introduction of cooperatives, legalization of trade unions, public ownership of industries and collective ownership of land by the autonomous village community.[27] These demands could be interpreted as socially redistributive and proto-socialist, rather than as a distinctly identifiable Marxist programme. The dissatisfaction expressed by Muzaffar and other communists soon afterwards was related to their reading of the programme as limited in its social radicalism.

Further Left

The communists led by Muzaffar attempted to influence and change the organization in stages. The first attempt of the communist bloc within it to introduce Marxist theoretical formulations, and thereby alter the organization's political programme, was seen when the Labour-Swaraj Party convened the second All Bengal Praja Conference at Krishnanagar, Nadia, in February 1926.[28] It was inaugurated with Nazrul's 'Sramiker Gan' (Song of the Worker) and Muzaffar, who had just returned to Bengal, was supported by his early socialist colleagues in an attempt to change the name of the organization to 'Workers and Peasants Party', in keeping with the Marxist principle of proletarian dictatorship. Well aware that the majority did not share their politics and were likely to remain unconvinced,[29] the communists advanced a poor technical argument, proposing that 'Workers and Peasants Party of Bengal' was more suitable since it was shorter than 'Labour-Swaraj Party of the Indian National Congress'. But the preponderance of non-communist rural delegates and activists meant that they had to compromise. Apart from being outnumbered, the communists were also keen not to wreck their alliance with the agrarian socialists.[30] The session of the conference accepted a resolution to rename the organization 'Peasants and Workers Party of Bengal' (PWP).[31] The communists did not oppose this move[32] and the change was unanimously adopted. A new executive committee elected at Krishnanagar affirmed the unity between the CPI and the independent socialists. Nareshchandra Sengupta was elected president; Atulchandra Gupta became vice-president; Muzaffar, Nazrul and Soumendranath Tagore were executive members, and Kutubuddin was joint secretary along with Hemantakumar Sarkar.[33]

The communist strategy to ideologically dominate the left bloc created through the PWP was a partial success. On 23 February 1926, Muzaffar wrote to K.N. Joglekar, a leading communist in Bombay, that the Labour-Swaraj Party was a 'provisional organization' which had undergone a name change.[34] For the time being, the communists were unable to establish the hegemony of the proletariat. Work among the turbulent working class during 1927–28 and the relative lack of activity on the peasant front created a situation where the name changed for a second time to 'Workers and Peasants Party' in 1928. By then, shifts in the organizational base and Muzaffar's elevation to the rank of secretary precluded the necessity of a flimsy pretext.

For the moment it was decided that the party would try to influence the Congress and engage in joint anti-colonial actions. The thinking behind this move was to form a 'bloc within', in keeping with the underlying aim of winning over and bringing the nationalist mass-base under the left influence. Consequently, Muzaffar Ahmad became a member of the Bengal Provincial Committee of the Congress in 1926.[35] Members of the PWP sought election at various levels of the Congress organization, to give 'a real shape to the rights and demands of the masses of India'.[36] However, by dropping 'Swaraj' and 'INC', and replacing the words with 'Peasants and Workers', the renamed party signalled an ideological break with mainstream nationalism. By erasing the quotation from Aurobindo Ghosh in the new programme, by attaching new conditions to individual membership and by asking organizations to affiliate themselves to it, the PWP consciously distanced itself from the nationalists.[37] Individuals and societies were still welcome so long as they subscribed to the aims and ideas of the party. Individual members could be a part of other organizations if the objects and programmes of these organizations were not hostile to the PWP. This meant alignment to and taking advantage of the INC policy, which theoretically encouraged formation of separate bodies for those who did not subscribe to the line adopted by its leadership.

Forging the Communist Influence

Early communist politics in India was facilitated by travel. Indians had joined this internationalist current during their journeys through Europe and the Americas; activist visitors from the imperialist countries joined or contributed to the efforts of the local organizers. The aim was to forge an ideological perspective on the workings of capital and class, directed against regimes of complex and varied exploitation at local and national levels, as links in a chain binding the world.

The Kanpur Communist Conference, organized by Satyabhakta in December 1925, which Muzaffar attended after his release from prison, was the first open effort to develop a communist network all over the country. This first communist conference decided to establish the headquarters of the CPI in Bombay, which later shifted to Delhi, with metropolitan branches at Lahore, Kanpur, Madras and Calcutta. Muzaffar, despite his uneasiness regarding the ill-defined politics of the conference and its leading organizers,[38] agreed to being entrusted with the Bengal section with Calcutta as its centre.[39]

Members
While a communist party had been formed in 1920, this was the formal launching of the party in India. Muzaffar remarked in a letter to M.N. Roy in early 1927 that the communists were forced to 'capture' the conference. Many 'masquerading' as communists were actually linked with Hindu and

Muslim communal organizations. This 'insult' to the communist ideology forced the 'real' communists to corner reactionary elements and prevent the launching of a fake organization.[40] Inspector S. Bhattacharjee of the Bengal Intelligence Branch, who had managed to enlist himself as a delegate, reported on the divisions that appeared over the connection with the Comintern between S.V. Ghate, Joglekar and Muzaffar, on the one hand, and Hasrat Mohani, Arjanlal Sethi and Satyabhakta, on the other. With the ascendancy of the former group, Satyabhakta and his friends 'retired'.[41] Opposing affiliation to the Comintern, they wished to form a non-Marxist, 'national' communist party.[42] From the very beginning, the relationship between the communists and the Congress took a certain turn. About 400 delegates, mostly peasants from Ajmer and some districts of Uttar Pradesh, attended the communist conference, which was held outside the compound where the annual Congress session was taking place. When the peasant delegates tried to enter the Congress pavilion, they were stopped. A 'free fight' ensued in which several Congress volunteers, including Jawaharlal Nehru, and the communist delegates Arjanlal Sethi, Hasrat Mohani and his wife, were slightly injured.[43]

The immediate political gains for the communists from the conference were limited. The party could claim only 200–300 members. Till 1927, when a programme and a constitution were adopted, it was felt that the party had no clear Marxist programme, even though the communists had wrested the organization from Satyabhakta. A central committee of the Communist Party of India was formed in 1925 at the Kanpur Conference, with S.V. Ghate and J. Bagerhatta as joint secretaries. Bagerhatta resigned in 1927, but Ghate remained general secretary till the Meerut arrests of March 1929.[44] Though the CPI headquarters were in Bombay, and later in Delhi, Muzaffar was regularly consulted for major decisions. In the absence of Dange and Usmani, who were still in prison, he played a crucial role in managing the party's affairs. The initial activities of the CPI were not vigorous as no clear direction was given at Kanpur; Muzaffar complained to Joglekar in February 1926 that the party centre was inactive, making work difficult. He suggested a meeting of the CPI Central Executive in Bombay, in order to start regular functioning of the party.[45] Over the years, his dissatisfaction continued. In February 1929, Muzaffar wrote to Ghate: 'We are extremely anxious to hear about your activities in connection with the Bombay riots. . . . Please let us know all detailed news. Manifestos in different languages must be issued by the Girni Kamgar Union. We must interpret the situation from our viewpoint.' A surveillance report observed: 'Muzaffar is far from satisfied with the manner in which the Bombay Branch of the Party is dealing with the . . . riots . . . he has issued definite instructions that the situation must be interpreted from their point of view.'[46]

The CPI, like other communist parties in the colonial world, drew guidance until 1928 from the 'Colonial Thesis' adopted at the Second Congress of the Communist International (1920), advising the communists in colonized countries to work with nationalists through a broad anti-imperialist front and, at the same time, establish their own organization.[47] Differences between M.N. Roy and Lenin resulted in the adoption of this middle path. Roy had argued for independent development of the communist forces, while Lenin, sensing the virtual non-existence of communists in India at the time, emphasized the need to maintain links with the anti-colonial mainstream. Communists soon emerged as a small but organized group in India. Their appearance brought to light the differences between the communist and the nationalist social agendas. By 1928, the communists were advocating the need to devise a role independent of the nationalists. The changed context brought about by the emergence of communism inexorably led towards the formulation of a new strategy.

The connection between the CPI and the international communist movement was mediated through contacts in London, Paris, Berlin and Moscow. Though officially affiliated to the Comintern since 1930, alongside the Communist Party of Vietnam, the CPI was first unofficially recognized as a section of the Comintern. The Comintern sent communists, mainly from the Communist Party of Great Britain (CPGB), to assist the work in India. The visits of George Allison, Philip Spratt and Ben Bradley were a part of this drive.[48] From 1924, the task of directly assisting Indian communists was assigned to the CPGB. A colonial committee of the CPGB started functioning in order to extend help to the anti-colonial struggle in India. A 'Foreign Bureau' of the CPI, set up at the initiative of exiled Indian and British communists at Paris in 1925, acted as an intermediary between the Comintern and the CPI. M.N. Roy, C.P. Dutt and Mohammad Ali, an ex-*muhajir* known by his pseudonym 'Sepassi', worked through this bureau. Banned from entering British India, Ali led the life of a political emigré and was put in charge of the bureau office located in Paris. Even after the Foreign Bureau ceased to function he remained active, and was executed when the city fell to the Nazis in 1940.[49]

Foreign, especially British, communists started arriving at Bombay and Calcutta from 1925. These visits were often terminated by deportations, arrests and imprisonments. Percy Gladding, sent by the CPGB in 1925, was unsuccessful in establishing an effective contact. Following his departure, in November 1926, George Allison arrived at Calcutta, travelling under the assumed name of Donald Campbell. There he met Muzaffar who introduced him to Shibnath Banerjee, the secretary of the Bengal Jute Worker's Association. Allison also associated with Kishorilal Ghosh. Staying at the Continental Hotel initially, he later moved to a boarding house at Sudder

Street, a haunt of European visitors, probably to gain a degree of anony-
mity. His attempts to hide in Europeanized spaces while negotiating with
trade unionists was cut short in January 1927, when he was arrested, convicted, imprisoned and then summarily deported. In December 1926, Philip
Spratt, a Cambridge graduate, reached Bombay. Though charged with sedition for writing an anti-imperialist pamphlet, 'India and China', he was
discharged by a sympathetic Indian jury. The arrival of Ben Bradley to work
in Bombay in September 1927 prompted the CPI to send Spratt to Calcutta
in March 1928, where he was active in the Bengal WPP till his arrest in
March 1929.[50] Spratt lived at European Asylum Lane and quickly adapted
to the reduced circumstances. Apparently he came to resemble his Indian
comrades in every sense except his clothes, which remained 'half European'.[51]
A police dossier described Spratt as 'an emissary of the British Communist
Party' who provided a 'distinct impetus' to the 'machinations' of the Bengal PWP/WPP through his 'energy and experience'.[52]

Apart from the CPGB, the Comintern sent emissaries on specific mis-
sions: Spratt and Muzaffar met a visitor of Russian-Jewish origin travelling
in India disguised as an American tourist of German extraction, at the Continental Hotel in Calcutta and later at the YMCA in Bombay;[53] Spratt accompanied Bradley to hold a discussion with the unknown visitor at the top of
one of the columns of the Taj;[54] J.W. Johnstone, the US Communist Party's
representative to the Comintern, came to Calcutta during 1928, addressed
striking workers at Bauria and attended the All India WPP Conference in
December 1929. From Calcutta Johnstone travelled to Jharia, where an
AITUC conference was taking place. After having successfully persuaded
the AITUC to recognize the 'League against Imperialism', he was arrested
and swiftly deported.[55] Jack Ryan, an Australian communist who arrived
with the declared mission to persuade the AITUC to recognize the Pan-
Pacific Trade Union Secretariat (PPTUS), also set up by the Comintern, was
unsuccessful at Jharia. The police regarded him as a seasoned anti-colonial
and anti-capitalist activist. His speech at the WPP conference confirmed
this view: he urged the establishment of a 'workers' swaraj', and expressed
solidarity on behalf of the PPTU with the struggle against British imperialists, landlords and capitalists.[56] Apart from foreign delegates representing
different branches of the Comintern, Indian communists returning from
Europe also attended the All India WPP conference and the CPI meeting
which were held at Calcutta in late December 1928.[57]

Efforts to strengthen the communist party gained momentum in 1927. A
'Party Constitution' was adopted in May 1927 at a CPI Conference.[58] Membership was restricted to those who agreed to subscribe to the programme of
the Communist International. A five-member presidium was formed which
included Muzaffar. It was decided that 'fractions' comprising party mem-

bers controlled by the presidium would be organized in all working-class and anti-colonial political organizations. Comrades unable to return to India were to work through the Foreign Bureau of the party. No member of the party could be part of a communal organization.[59]

The first 'Programme' of the CPI, adopted in May 1927, stated that the Indian bourgeoisie were betraying the anti-colonial movement; their demand for 'Dominion Status', as opposed to complete independence, revealed their bargaining mentality with regard to colonial rule. In terms of immediate strategy, the CPI retained the principle of working with other classes within the nationalist movement in order to secure full freedom while it attempted to give the anti-colonial struggle a mass revolutionary content. However, in the course of that year, there was a shift from a critical attitude towards the nationalists to a firm rejection of nationalist strategies. Muzaffar, an architect of this transition, in his report to the Bhatpara conference of the Bengal WPP in March–April 1928, argued that unity with other forces could not be 'based on abandonment of principles'. The Bhatpara resolution, 'A Call to Action', stressed the subordination of the national movement to a people's democratic movement. The programme, which deviated from the Comintern's position as it stood at the time, could be regarded as a predecessor of the strategy adopted at the Sixth Congress of the Comintern later that year.[60] A handbill advertising 'A Call to Action' indicated the changing attitude of the communists towards the nationalists:

> After years of agitation and organization, India is still a slave-nation, is farther from freedom than ever. Why is this? . . . Why do your leaders invariably say one thing and do another? For a clear, consistent, Marxist analysis and explanation of these disturbing phenomena, for a clear, practical lead as to what to do to remedy this state of things, see, "A Call to Action".[61]

A police review of 'A Call to Action' suggested that a new militancy could be observed in the drive to mobilize workers, peasants and youth.[62]

The number of communists active through the PWP increased with the arrival of Indians who had visited Moscow or who were sent by the Comintern. Gopen Chakraborty, a former Anushilan member, had reached Moscow via Berlin with Nalini Gupta's help. Upon his return in 1925, he wished to establish a communist party in Bengal when the Comintern asked him to get in touch with Muzaffar.[63] Shamsul Huda was an impoverished dock worker from East Bengal who had left Calcutta in the early 1920s as a sailor, gone to the United States, joined the US Communist Party (CPUSA), and studied English and engineering there. He then travelled to Moscow where he studied Marxism at the 'University of the Toilers of the East', and returned to Bengal to assist CPI members working with the PWP. Huda reached Calcutta from Moscow in 1928, having taken a long route to mislead the colonial authorities. Immediately after his arrival, a picture was circulated in the Intelligence Branch office in Calcutta to make operatives aware of the presence of a new 'Moscow-returned youth' in the city. The photograph reveals a chubby 'oriental gentleman' impeccably turned out in a suit and hat, and elegantly sporting a cane. The image gave little idea of Huda's origins.[64] These arrivants were to play a crucial role on behalf of the WPP during its most intense phase of activism in 1928.

The strength of the communists in Calcutta was also supplemented by the periodic presence of activists from other provinces. Ayodhyaprasad, a former Non-Cooperator from Jhansi who joined the CPI during the Communist Conference at Kanpur,[65] came to Calcutta in 1926 and stayed at the PWP office. He returned to Jhansi to rejoin his former profession as a government schoolteacher. Yet, in December 1928, he came back to Calcutta to stay with Muzaffar, Halim, Spratt and Huda at 2/1 European Asylum Lane, 'working as a party propagandist'.[66]

Former Congress activists and revolutionary nationalists from the city and the districts swelled the ranks of communists in the PWP. Soumendranath Tagore, a grandnephew of Rabindranath, became very active in the PWP and was soon incorporated into the communist bloc. The suspension of the mass movement by Gandhi had 'disheartened' him. At this stage he began reading books on socialism. Like Muzaffar, he came across anti-socialist texts, which increased his interest. One day he noticed a hawker selling Langal (The Plough), the mouthpiece of the PWP, and took a liking to the 'unusual' name of the paper. Shamsuddin Hussain, whom he knew a little, replied on behalf of the group when he wrote to them. He met Shamsuddin, Muzaffar, Halim and Nalini Gupta at 37 Harrison Road, attended the Krishnanagàr Conference in February 1926, and was made secretary of the PWP in 1927.[67] Shortly afterwards he left for Berlin to pursue higher studies and was a participant in the Sixth Congress of the Comintern in 1928.[68]

In February 1927, a group of former Anushilan activists, Dharani Goswami, Nirad Chakraborty and Pyarimohan Das, joined the PWP, alongside their old colleague Gopen Chakraborty. Nirad Chakraborty worked as a book-keeper at the Book Company in College Square, which supplied leftists with political literature.[69] He came to know Muzaffar, read the PWP journal Langal, and started visiting the party office at 37 Harrison Road and later at 2/1 European Asylum Lane where the office shifted. In the autumn of 1928, he gave up his job and started living at the European Asylum Lane office, working with Spratt and other residents.[70] Dharani Goswami was introduced to Halim through common acquaintances in the revolutionary nationalist circles.[71]

The connections of these former Anushilan activists with the districts of Bengal led to further recruitment. Manindranath Sinha, or Mani Singh as he later came to be known, was persuaded by Gopen Chakraborty, when they met in December 1925, that revolutionary nationalism excluded the poor from Muslim, low-caste and *adivasi* backgrounds. Singh met Muzaffar at 37 Harrison Road [72] through Dharani Goswami. Muzaffar was struck by the lack of any 'Brahmanical attitudes' in Singh, who came from an aristocratic brahmin family in Mymensingh. It seems Singh was trying his hand at business when he turned to left politics. He opened an office in Clive Street to run commercial ventures and attempted dealing in wild animals, including tigers and snakes. When these endeavours proved abortive, he turned to full-time trade union activity where his initiatives met with greater success.[73] A meeting with Faizuddin, an agrarian socialist, facilitated his entry into rural politics in his native district, where he became a major peasant organizer in later life.[74] Gopal Basak, 'of poor physique and a studious disposition', was a bookseller from Dhaka. While assisting his father in the family business, he became involved in the 'production and dissemination' of political literature, in work among Dhaka's scavengers and mill workers, and in organizing peasants in Mymensingh.[75] Kali Sen was inspired by the working-class upsurge in the late 1920s to join left politics.[76] Though not a formal member of the CPI during the 1920s, he was among those activists who regarded themselves 'communists by conviction'.[77]

Allies, Contacts

Very few in Bengal were communist party members in the 1920s. Yet communism as an ideology won adherents among the left-leaning intelligentsia. The PWP became the rallying point for activists who came to see themselves as communists or as close sympathizers, and who shared an active distrust of the Gandhian and Swarajist leadership. Having consciously abandoned formal education and the civil professions that might have enabled them to rejoin the social mainstream, many of them displayed a political distaste for a social order that was based on property and propriety. In this sense, they were guided by experiences of social alienation similar to those that had led Muzaffar and his early colleagues turn leftwards in the early 1920s.

Following the Kanpur communist conference, Muzaffar returned to Calcutta and moved into 37 Harrison Road, the office of the Labour-Swaraj Party and its mouthpiece *Langal*. Under his leadership, the first socialist organization in Bengal made a concerted attempt to disseminate Marxist ideas from early 1926 on wards. As the most important link between the CPI and the PWP/WPP, Muzaffar was instrumental in bringing the two organizations closer and in touch with the Third International.

Among the earliest activists of the PWP were Muzaffar's associates from the first socialist nucleus, Kutubuddin Ahmed and Nazrul Islam. Hemantakumar Sarkar, Nareshchandra Sengupta, Atulchandra Gupta and Faizuddin

37 Harrison Road: the Peasants and Workers Party (PWP) started functioning from here in 1926

were also close to Muzaffar, and identified with the aims of the CPI. Halim's elder brother Shamsuddin Hussein was about to join the communist party when a sudden illness cut short his life in October 1926.[78]

A varied crowd of organizers and former activists remained outside the CPI but came under the influence of communists. Disenchanted Non-Co-operators from the eastern districts of Bengal, with persistent belief in mass action, became sympathetic to the communist ideas put forward by Muzaffar and Halim, and interested in working with the PWP/WPP. The state regard-ed some of these young correspondents in their early 20s as mostly inactive individuals without any social prospect or inclination to become absorbed into the middle-class *bhadralok* mainstream, and worth monitoring politi-cally as they had little respect for political or social authority. Bhabaniprasad Roy, Halim's contact in Jessore and the son of a rich man, had given up school to become a Congress volunteer and a district organizer during the Non-Cooperation movement. His father, according to police reports, 'had no control over him'. He had inherited his father's jute business only to incur 'considerable' losses, and eventually shut it down. Unemployed and unoccupied, spending most of his time at home, Roy displayed an interest in the activities of the PWP, asked for subscription books so that he could raise funds for the organization in his locality, and requested pamphlets for distribution. Prabhat Sarkar, the son of a doctor, was another recluse who corresponded with Halim from Natore. Derisively described in the police reports as 'a vagabond' who depended solely on his father for material sustenance, Sarkar was also a former Non-Cooperator and Congress organizer. In 1927 he joined the PWP, and started regularly receiving the party journal and literature. Though he had no friends and seldom went out, he wrote to Halim of his past 'experience' of working with peasants and being 'well acquainted' with them. He promised to make the rural folk realize the need to be free from the 'grip' of 'moneylenders' and 'capitalists', and to struggle for liberation from the 'misery' they were in. He also promised to send an annual subscription to the party, and wished the WPP members 'victory in struggle'.[79] Political withdrawal and disillusionment, it seems, had taken the form of social withdrawal in young men like Roy and Sarkar. Attempts to reach out and reactivate them in their milieu met with limited success.

Muzaffar corresponded with Muslim anti-colonial youths in the districts who had participated in the Non-Cooperation Movement and were getting increasingly alienated by the Hindu communal content of Swarajist politics. He also exchanged letters with dissatisfied Noakhali Congressmen. Serajur Rahman, teacher, rural organizer, Non-Cooperator and journalist, had given up his studies to join the mass upsurge in the early 1920s. By the late 1920s, he was seeking direction from Muzaffar and the PWP on ways to organize peasants.[80] This circle also included Abanimohan Chakraborty, a Non-Cooperator and Swarajist; Kalikeshab Ghosh, a former political prisoner working as a *kobiraj* in Muzaffar's native island, Sandwip; and Khitish Raychaudhuri, secretary of the local Congress committee in Noakhali and a former detenu. Raychaudhuri, a contemporary of Muzaffar from Sandwip, had contributed to his defence during the Kanpur trial. He requested regular communication during 1928, and later joined the CPI. Didarul Alam, a 22-year-old radical from Chittagong who had edited the pro-left journals *Juger Alo* (Light of the Age) and *Sammilani* (Communitarian Gathering) while in Rangoon, wrote to Muzaffar stressing the need to draw the Muslim youth towards social revolution. Police enquiries revealed that Didarul had attacked the policies pursued by the management of Steamship Company, a local capitalist concern, and incurred the displeasure of Abdul Bari Chaudhuri, the local agent of the company and president of the Burma Labour Association.[81] Abdul Kader and Nurul Islam, young activists in touch with Muzaffar, Halim and Nazrul, became active in the Dhaka branch of the WPP during 1928–29. Mahiuddin, a member of the first socialist nucleus which had emerged in Calcutta during the early 1920s,[82] introduced himself to Gopal Basak as an old friend of Muzaffar and suggested ways to begin work in the villages of East Bengal.[83]

A section of trade unionists in Calcutta and its suburbs became connected with the PWP/WPP and the communists active in its fold. Aftab Ali, a leading figure of the Indian Seamen's Union (ISU), joined the organization and associated closely with the communists, especially Muzaffar. At first a saloon-boy and later a steward in outgoing vessels,[84] he was repeatedly labelled a 'communist' in police records; like other socialists active in the PWP who were sympathetic to communism, he never joined the CPI.[85] Kalidas Bhattacharya, an organizer of jute workers, also joined the group. Among the independent leftist trade unionists who worked with PWP/WPP members and affiliated labour organizations were Prabhabati Dasgupta, Bankim Mukherjee, who later joined the CPI, and Radharaman Mitra.[86]

A fluid mass of young activists without any formed political position were drawn towards the PWP/WPP during specific strike actions. Godbole, a young Marathi office worker living and working in Calcutta, was neither a PWP activist nor a communist, but joined their efforts to organize port workers during a strike in 1927. Shachinandan Chattopadhyay, a very young anti-colonial activist, also established contact with the left through his friend Abani Chaudhuri; working closely with Muzaffar and other leaders, Shachinandan was active in the WPP efforts during the scavengers' strike of 1928. Hailed by the nationalist press as a 'boy-wonder', he had become a seasoned orator during the Non-Cooperation Movement after having left school in protest. Batukeswar Datta, a 20-year-old apprentice tailor who later joined forces with Bhagat Singh, also worked with the PWP to organize the scavengers' strike in Howrah. Datta grew up in Kanpur, received schooling in Hindi, lived in a Howrah lodging house and was attending a tailoring school in Burrabazar when he became acquainted with Muzaffar, prior to the strike. Datta's knowledge of Hindi proved useful during the strike; he addressed workers' meetings and wrote a pamphlet for the union in Hindi. Chiranjilal Sroff, whom the communists had come to know through industrial action in Asansol, helped organize the long-drawn strike led by the PWP at Bauria.[87]

The geographic locations and backgrounds of recruits to and sympathizers of the PWP/WPP indicated attempts to create a multi-lingual, multi-ethnic, translocal organization with its headquarters in Calcutta, and branches in the towns and districts of Bengal. The members and supporters were subject to overlapping influences exercised on them by the CPI and the PWP/WPP, a process in which Muzaffar played a crucial role. Though the levels of political activism among members and sympathizers varied widely, they collectively comprised a small yet visible bloc of dissenters, unable to reconcile themselves to the political trends gaining predominance over the region and the country. The socialist nucleus, which had emerged in 1922, recorded their presence. By 1926 the nucleus had mutated from a radical tendency into an organizational structure. This provided a political platform to the expanding socialist bloc and to the communist 'fraction' within it.

The Socialist Press

Muzaffar's expertise as a former editor and journalist was central to the functioning of a socialist press. *Langal*, later renamed *Ganabani*, became the principal vehicle of expressing communist ideas and socialist views in Bengal. Prior to the expansion of organizational activities in 1928, the PWP/WPP was identified with its journal.

Genesis

The genealogy of the socialist press can be traced back to the mid-1920s. *Mazdoor* (Worker), a short-lived Urdu weekly started by Kutubuddin in 1925, was the first socialist newspaper to be published from Bengal.[88] Kutubuddin and Nazrul, long associated with radical journalism, soon turned their attention to a Bengali weekly. Since the government prevented Nazrul from reviving *Dhumketu*,[89] a fresh beginning was made in the form of *Langal* (Plough). Kutubuddin, who had consistently supported and even lost money in such initiatives, financially assisted in starting the paper and in its later attempts to stand on its own feet.[90] The first socialist paper in Bengali, *Langal* appeared as the organ of the Labour-Swaraj Party in December 1925.[91] Nazrul called himself the 'editor-in-chief', while his friend Manimohan Mukherjee was the 'editor'. The police felt Mukherjee 'has nothing to do with "Langal"!! His name had been put in the paper as he expressed his willingness to go to jail, if necessary, for any objectionable or seditious article appearing in it.'[92]

The links developed with Swarajism by Muzaffar's socialist colleagues and founders of the Labour-Swaraj Party were evident in the early issues of *Langal*. Muzaffar thought Hemantakumar's earlier association with Subhash Chandra Bose was responsible for the publication of such material, though by this time, Hemantakumar was distancing himself from all Swarajists.[93] Eulogistic features on Bose, including his horoscope, earned the ridicule of Soumendranath. An early reader who was soon motivated by the changing tone of the paper, he was to join the PWP and the CPI.[94]

Swarajist Link Severed

The return of Muzaffar Ahmad to Calcutta and the formation of a communist fraction within the first socialist organization signalled a shift in the political direction of the paper also. The special edition on Bose also carried Muzaffar Ahmad's 'Abedan' (Appeal), requesting those interested to come forward and join the CPI in Bengal.[95] The alliance between Muzaffar's socialist colleagues and ex-Swarajists was further cemented after this, even though the communists ensured that *Langal* would clearly distance itself from Swarajist politics and its leaders. Under Muzaffar's editorship, *Langal* became extremely critical of all nationalist tendencies, including those of the Swarajists and Subhash Bose, highlighting their ties with propertied elements and communal identity politics. When Nazrul moved from Calcutta to Krishnanagar in early 1926, Muzaffar found himself in charge of running the paper.[96] He discontinued Nazrul's attempts to fuse the contradictory ideological influences of communism, revolutionary terrorism and Swarajist populism in the pages of *Langal*. He also systematically directed socialist journalism towards enlargement of the PWP/WPP support-base and the recruitment of communists. His first article, 'Bharat Kano Swadhin Noy?' (Why is India not Free?), appearing in the fourth issue of *Langal*, argued that the politically committed middle-class youth and the radical intelligentsia should support the struggle of the masses for self-emancipation, and labelled community identity as one of the primary obstacles to the development of class consciousness.[97] After the second Praja Conference where the organization changed its name and became independent of the INC, Muzaffar's articles in *Langal* even more vigorously emphasized Marxist–Leninist ideas in order to understand and organize political and social struggles. Renaming the paper was a step in this direction. The last issue of *Langal* appeared on 15 April 1926;[98] it was revived as *Ganabani* (Voice of the People) on 12 August 1926.[99] By changing the name of the organ, the communists attempted to give the PWP a wider left dimension so that working-class and other issues could be incorporated.[100] The first issue of *Ganabani* declared that the paper would uphold the interest of the masses as opposed to certain classes, and that it stood by the slogan 'Victory to the People's India'.[101]

Langal, followed by *Ganabani*, became the focal point of spreading left politics and culture. The Calcutta-based printing and distribution network created through the PWP journal enabled communist and socialist authors to be published, and literature originating from outside Calcutta to be circulated. 'Cosmopolitan Printing Works', a press started by Kutubuddin at his 7 Moulavi Lane residence, temporarily boosted the publication of left literature.[102] Muzaffar and Halim arranged the publication[103] of Dange's *Hell Found* and Shaukat Usmani's *Peshawar to Moscow*.[104] Having discovered the existence of a receptive market for back issues of *The Socialist*, Muzaffar also wrote to Bombay requesting more publications for distribution in Bengal.[105] The police read these moves as an advancement of the Comintern's strategy to influence the 'lower strata of the intelligentsia' with an avalanche of left literature, and routinely intercepted writings by international

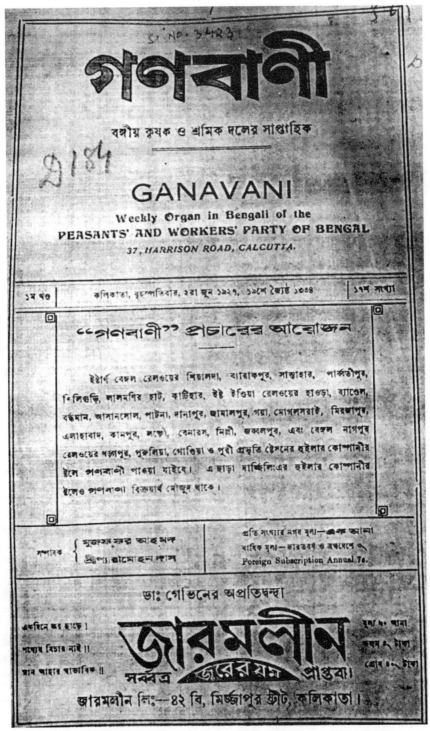

Front page of an issue of *Ganabani*, 'weekly organ in Bengali of the Peasants' and Workers' Party of Bengal'

An article by Muzaffar Ahmad in *Ganabani*

১৬ গণবাণী Reg. No. C 4140

BOOKS ON SOCIALISM.

1. The Coming of Socialism.
by
LUCIEN.
Price—Ans. 6/- only.

2. Scientific Socialism.
Its Aims and Ideals.
BY
WM. PAUL
Price—As. 4/- only.

3. The Religion of Capital
BY
PAUL LAFARGUE.
Price—As. 6/- only.

4. Manifesto of the Communist Party
BY
KARL MARX & FREDERICK ENGELS.
Price—As. 6/- only.

To be had of
The Book Company Ltd.
4/4A, College Square, Calcutta.

Sources of Law and Society in Ancient India.
Evolution of Law.
Published by the Calcutta University.

Printed by Muzaffar Ahmad at the Sree Saraswati Press at 1, Ramanath Mazumdar Street, Calcutta, and published by the same at 37, Harrison Road, Calcutta.

Advertisement for The Book Company in *Ganabani*

communist figures such as C.P. Dutt from London and Paris, Agnes Smedley from Berlin, and M.N. Roy from Moscow, Zurich and Berlin. Apart from the European and Comintern connection, pamphlets and other literature printed locally by the Bengal WPP for 'propaganda purposes' were a source of growing alarm. Among these were *Hell Found* by Dange; *What the Students of Other Countries Have Done* and *What our Students Should Do*, describing the role of revolutionary students and youth in Russia in the overthrow of the czarist government as an example before Indian students; *A Manifesto to Our Countrymen*, urging mass mobilization to fight for the emancipation of workers and peasants; *A Call to Action*, drafted by Spratt to develop WPP into a 'fighting organization'; and *Krishaker Katha*, an appeal to impoverished and landless peasants to mobilize along 'Bolshevik' lines for their own emancipation.[106]

Wider Literary Connections

Langal and *Ganabani* benefited from the links of their editor and regular contributors with sympathetic and wider literary circles; indeed they were a part of these links. The same urban environment that had made the emergence of a left tendency possible in the early 1920s also enabled the paper to function. Advertisements that partially financed the journal came from publishing houses, bookshops and other commercial concerns, mostly located around the Harrison Road–College Street area. The items on offer in these ranged from Marxist tracts and works by writers associated with the organization, to sports equipment, medicine, tea and office stationery.[107] Since the Bengal Muslim Literary Society had acted as an incubator of early left politics to a great extent, Muzaffar retained his connection with this body, publishing news of the society's activities. The literary avant-garde, who were under attack from conservative and pro-establishment critics, continued to receive praise and solidarity from Muzaffar, Nareshchandra Sengupta and Hemantakumar Sarkar. The solidarity between socialists and avant-garde writers reflected an overlapping and shared concern on issues related to sexual and political liberty. *Kali-Kalam* (Pen and Ink), edited by Premendra Mitra, Sailajananda Mukhopadhyay and Muralidhar Basu of the *Kallol* circle, and containing sections on literary criticism, painting and poetry, faced an immediate conservative backlash when it appeared in 1926. Writings on sexual themes such as Nazrul's poem 'Madhabi-Pralap', which appeared in the first issue, were considered immoral. The police instituted a case against the publisher and the editors for printing 'obscene' material. In court, however, the magistrate dismissed the case, 'unimpressed' by the public prosecutor's interpretations of literature and social science.[108] Soumendranath Tagore survived severe criticism from the 'moralist brigade', led by *Shanibarer Chithi* (Mail on Saturday), for his 'Nara-Nari' (Man and Woman), an article on sex education, published in *Kali-Kalam*.[109] Sajanikanta Das, the neo-conservative editor of *Shanibarer Chithi*, who detested both communism and new writing, made Nazrul his chief target of attack.[110] Despite Halim's later evaluation of the *Kallol* circle as representative of 'petit-bourgeois anarchy, individualism and despair',[111] the physical proximity of the two circles, due to their offices being situated in neighbouring areas, ensured that they continued to share mutual goodwill and activists frequented both circles.[112] Members of the *Kallol* circle also defended communists and their ideas during lean periods. Sibram Chakraborty's *Moscow banam Pondicherry* (Moscow vs. Pondicherry), published in 1929, strongly opposed the 'spiritual nationalism' which dominated anti-colonial politics and defended the materialist philosophy of the communists.[113]

Langal and *Ganabani* consciously promoted creative literature along left lines. Fiction and non-fiction, prose and poetry dealt with the social expression of oppressions, and the institutional mechanisms that perpetuated and enforced them. Alongside articles on political and social issues, literary works against caste, gender and class exploitation appeared. Writer Jagadish Basu and poets Jibanananda Das and Jasimuddin published their early works in *Ganabani*. Music and poetry became important tools to popularize the left ideology. Nazrul's poem *Samyabadi* (Communist) upheld visions of radical social transformation in the pages of *Langal*. A month before the Second All Bengal Praja Conference, Nazrul's *Krishaker Gan* (Song of the Peasant) was printed, displaying a similar mood. The communist anthem 'International' reached Bengal in 1926, when Nazrul translated its lyrics at Muzaffar's request. In 1927, Soumendranath also sent his translated version from Berlin.[114] Though intercepted, it was not held up on the grounds that even if the song was 'objectionable', a copy could be 'easily obtained from elsewhere'.[115] Though these versions appeared in *Ganabani*, the opportunity to sing them never arose. Spratt was preparing to remedy the situation in 1929 by setting it to tune, when the Meerut arrests aborted all plans in this direction.[116]

Radical Content

More generally, the socialist journal contained articles on international and local political issues, the working class and the peasantry, students and youth, Marxist theory, anti-fascism and colonial oppression. A focus on anti-imperialist and class struggles in other parts of Asia, such as communist-led uprisings in rural Indonesia in 1926 and urban China in 1927, could be discerned. Victims of varied forms of social exploitation in Bengal and activists highlighting their conditions, including those who did not clearly identify with class politics, were given space. Rezaul Karim, Mohinimohan Das and Sailendranath Guha Roy were among those who offered critiques of caste and class hierarchies in the pages of *Ganabani*.[117] Muzaffar and other leftists had emerged as communists and socialists in an intellectual and political milieu that drew on, and contributed to, older critiques exposing the oppression of women, *adivasi*s and lower-caste populations of Bengal. These were now fused with a left opposition to the existing property relations and social control based on private ownership.

Upper-caste Hindu proprietor interests advocated in the nationalist press were contested by communist and socialist writers. The *bhadralok* nationalist press and the socialist press clashed over class. In the first issue of *Langal*, a 'Special Edition' appearing on 16 December 1925, Nazrul's editorial observed: 'If 'Swaraj' is realized who will inherit its gains? Those who will, already have a restricted access to power. Are they distributing this [power] equally among all?'[118] *Prabasi, Atmasakti, Forward, Amritabazar* and *Anandabazar* were among the periodicals and newspapers criticized for their proprietorial and communal alignments. *Prabasi*, according to Halim, displayed contempt for mass movements and the journals that supported them, particularly *Langal* and *Ganabani*.[119] During 1926, Taranath Ray, an *Atmasakti* journalist (pen-name 'Tarara'), attacked Muzaffar and his paper for professing socialist views. In response, Nazrul invited 'Tarara' to visit 37 Harrison Road to meet the image of 'half-starved' political activism as personified by Muzaffar, his 'emaciated' friend. Nazrul insisted that *Ganabani* stood for the dispossessed peasants, coolies and labourers, and he wondered if this was the reason behind Ray's contempt for *Ganabani* and its editor.[120] Nazrul himself faced similar attacks. Saratchandra Chatterjee's *Pather Dabi* (The Right of the Road), a novel celebrating the idea of a *bhadralok*-led revolution from above, was an instant hit when it appeared in 1926. An official ban made it even more wildly sought after among educated *bhadralok* youth.[121] Dismissive of politics from below, the novel ridiculed Nazrul by introducing as one of its characters a promising poet who had deluded himself into thinking that illiterate workers and peasants could become agents of revolutionary transformation.[122] When 'Tarara' sarcastically focused on Nazrul as depicted in *Pather Dabi*, playwright Shachindranath Sengupta wrote a rejoinder in *Ganabani*, condemning it as a personal attack. Italian fascism sharpened the rift. Muzaffar condemned 'Tarara' for writing a biography of Mussolini.[123] He also criticized the revolutionary leader Upendranath Bandopadhyay for hailing Mussolini as a true 'patriot' in his introduction to Ray's monograph, and considered Mrinalkanti Bose and Kishorilal Ghosh more than irresponsible for allowing a positive review of the book to appear in their paper, *Amritabazar*.[124]

Despite ideological opposition to the social content of nationalism, opposition to the colonial state created the practical need for an issue-based solidarity among the communists and the nationalists. While condemning

Forward's advocacy of landlord and capitalist interests, Muzaffar defended it against censorship. He also defended revolutionary terrorists and other political prisoners in the pages of the *Ganabani*, and campaigned against police brutality and surveillance.[125] By 1928, some nationalist organs started carrying news of communist and socialist activism. Mrinalkanti Bose and Kishorilal Ghosh, active trade unionists who worked closely with members of the CPI and WPP in 1928, played a role in this. The 14 August 1928 issue of *Forward* published news of the Comintern's drive to mobilize the masses from China to America, Bukharin's message of solidarity to the international working class, and Kuusinen's emphasis on the participation of landless peasants in revolution.[126] *Amritabazar* printed a notice circulated by organizers of the All India WPP Conference in late 1928, to publicize the event.[127] Colonial legislation also generated solidarity. While *The Statesman*, the voice of colonial capital, supported the Public Safety Bill (26 August 1928) aimed at the removal of foreign communists, and the Trade Dispute Bill (16 August 1928) which sought to curb militant trade unionism, *Forward* and *Amritabazar* opposed these. On 10 August 1928, *Forward* depicted the Trade Dispute Bill as a 'reactionary and retrograde piece of legislation', and *Amritabazar* thought it was 'an attempt to destroy trade unionism' through 'the most unabashed instance of encouragement' to strike-breaking.[128]

Other Left Initiatives
Local journals set up by left activists replicated the positions adopted by the organization and promoted through *Ganabani*. Hemantakumar's *Jagaran* (Awakening), published from Kushthea to motivate rural folk, upheld the WPP programme and was viewed as an organ partial to 'Bolshevik' articles. Muzaffar contributed to it.[129] *Lilooah ka Halchal*, a Hindi leaflet on the conditions of labour at the Lilooah railway workshop, and *Lal Paltan* (Red Army), a short-lived weekly that called itself 'Sramik Andolaner Saptahik Mukhopatra' (Weekly Mouthpiece of the Labour Movement), indicated efforts to build an awareness of communism on the industrial front. Carrying an image of the hammer and sickle, the second issue of *Lal Paltan*, on 6 October 1928, declared Bolshevism to be the worldwide choice of the working class and advocated the overthrow of capitalism as the only path to emancipation of the working class. It argued that ideas of meritocracy and religion had paved the way for upward mobility of the few and had left the mass of people behind, creating channels of 'professional' exploitation of the lower orders by men who had risen through these systems. Since every person in the world could not become a 'big man' in the existing society, it was best to overthrow it and establish equality. The period also witnessed the beginning of socialist cartoon-art in left journals to attract and amuse

workers, many of whom were illiterate. The second issue of *Lal Paltan* (Red Army) depicted a worker in rags gleefully blowing up a capitalist caught unawares with cannon-fire. The image, regarded as significant, was presented by the prosecution during the Meerut Conspiracy Case as 'a communist production'.[130] The appearance of these publications showed that the socialist ideas conveyed through *Langal* and *Ganabani* were gaining, in the Calcutta suburbs and districts, a wider audience among workers and peasants increasingly compelled to adopt militant means to defend their livelihoods.

Communalism versus Communism

1926 witnessed the high-point of communal rioting in Calcutta, followed by violent clashes in the districts during 1926, 1927 and 1931. The Calcutta riot of 1926 occurred in three phases between April and July, leaving 138 people dead and numerous wounded. Mixed commercial neighbourhoods in north-central Calcutta witnessed conflagrations with significant participation of the urban poor.[131] The structure of class formation under colonial rule had contributed to deep-rooted communal divisions. The concentration of landed property in the hands of Bengali Hindu high-caste landowners meant that an environment of class conflict could easily assume communal dimensions in rural areas where the majority of the oppressed cultivators were Bengali Muslims. In the metropolitan environment, looting and extensive damage to private property demonstrated the frustrations of the dispossessed. Communalism from below was a volatile mix of sectional and class hatred. In Calcutta, apart from attacking and killing each other, the Hindus and Muslims also jointly attacked mercantile establishments and shared the booty.[132]

The campaign against communal violence during the riots was the first significant political intervention by the PWP. Since the printed word had become a tool of communal propaganda, the PWP activists, numerically too weak to check communal violence, responded through a systemic interpretation of communalism by relating its origin to class. With their limited strength, they took on a highly communalized press. *Mohammadi, Doinik Soltan, Ananda Bazar Patrika* and *Matwala* offered direct incitement, with the editors of *Soltan* and *Matwala* later being prosecuted for their role.[133] *Ananda Bazar* became a 'widely circulated daily',[134] according to Muzaffar, during these clashes by projecting itself as a custodian of Hindu interests.[135] Since circulation of concocted news reports and anonymous leaflets intensified communal mobilization and violence,[136] a communist leaflet was printed and distributed that ideologically challenged communalism and explained its social roots in Marxist terms; this was the first such attempt in the city.

Muzaffar faced considerable obstruction before the leaflet was published. When he approached the Sri Gouranga Press, the social antipathy of the communalized literati was apparent in the cynical derision of Sureshchandra Majumdar, who owned this enterprise as well as *Ananda Bazar Patrika*.[137] Five years later, Muzaffar remarked: 'The Sri Gouranga Press detained the Manifesto of the Hindu Muslim problem for several days, got it examined by lawyers and then composed and printed it.'[138] Despite the hurdles posed by a hostile political climate, English, Bengali and Urdu versions of the leaflet were printed and circulated in Calcutta and surrounding areas.[139] The radical content of the leaflet was originally drafted by either Evelyn or M.N. Roy in the mid-1920s, as the spectre of communal violence overshadowed the anti-colonial unity forged during the late 1910s and early 1920s. A Marxist interpretation of the medieval Islamic civilization, absent in the earlier version, was inserted by Kutubuddin as the text was revised at Muzaffar's initiative.[140] The result of this collective effort was a unique document probing issues so far unexplored or ignored even by keen commentators like M.N. Roy. *The Manifesto of the Communist Party of India: Hindu–Moslem Problem*, published on 15 May 1926, appealed to working-class people to fight for socio-economic emancipation rather than engage in the politics of religious hatred. It identified Hindu and Muslim communalism as vehicles of 'civil war'; as generators of an artificial cross-class unity through 'Shuddhi', 'Sangathan', 'Tanzeem' and 'Tabliq'; as tools to deflect the people from the sufferings caused 'under the yoke of the most advanced capitalist system which holds India not to please God in heaven, but to make huge profits by exploiting the labour of starving millions in India'. The pamphlet, offering one of the earliest class analysis of Islam, claimed that material discontent within medieval Islam and under the Khilafat had created contradictions characterized by 'changing conditions of production', the 'rule of property' and the 'storm and stress of class warfare'. The *mujahidin* (religious warriors) had been mobilized for battle not just on the basis of religious slogans, but on the promise of material redistribution and rewards in the form of 'booties and concubines'. The pamphlet argued that a return to the Vedic age or to the Khilafat was not an option since they represented historically outmoded ideas and institutions. They obstructed a demystified understanding of the material interests of the masses irrespective of religion. A classical Marxist indictment of religious politics was stated:

> Have the Hindus and Musalman masses nothing in common in India? . . . Are they not economically ruined by the foreign and Indian capitalists and landlords? . . . You are taught to obey God, His apostles, obey parents, obey masters, obey your landlord, obey your king, and obey even those blessed souls, the rich people. . . . Fatalism, fanaticism, submission, superstition, obedience

and faith, the offspring of religion, are the offensive weapons in the hands of the oppressors.[141]

Identifying communalism as a betrayal of the people by their leaders, the need to side with the 'interests of 98%' rather than 'the remaining 2%' was emphasized:

> The problem of national freedom cannot be solved unless a new programme is adopted and new tactics employed. . . . Let us take a lesson from the failure of the gigantic movements of Non-cooperation. The Indian masses were in a fighting mood because they believed that the coming of Swaraj will make an end to their misery and starvation. . . . Let us not repeat that past mistake. [142]

Despite the militant note of resistance to religious identity politics struck in this pamphlet, the isolation of the anti-communal campaigners was evident in social and political terms. Other voices in Calcutta that attempted to counter communalism were Pramathanath Sanyal's tract *Mandir o Masjid* (Temple and Mosque),[143] and a short-lived Bengali periodical *Hindu–Musalman*, edited by Pannalal De and Syed Mohammad Ziaul Haq, and published on 11 July 1926 from Kidderpore. Its original circulation of 5,000 soon dwindled to 1,000.[144] Clearly, the market for non-communal publications was low among the literate readership at the time. Muzaffar saw 'a city in the grips of a collective insanity'. Beyond the known faces at 37 Harrison Road, everyone had become 'ultra-Hindu' or 'ultra-Muslim' aliens.[145] He felt that the *bhadralok* revolutionary nationalist leaders Upendranath Bandopadhyay, Amarendranath Chattopadhyay and Makhan Sen were acting as organizers of Hindu communal forces during the annual conference of the Bengal Congress at Krishnanagar in May 1926, where a 'viciously communal' Hindu-chauvinist pamphlet was circulated.[146] Soumendranath recalled watching communal mobs in action from the balcony of 37 Harrison Road. Once, the PWP activists unsuccessfully tried preventing a Hindu crowd from proceeding on its way to slaughter Muslims.[147] When some working-class Muslims who lived in the Jorasanko neighbourhood were given shelter, the Tagore mansion was attacked.[148] Soumendranath fired at the Hindu raiders and dispersed them. He also arranged for the safe passage of the trapped Muslims though he was slandered in the Muslim communal press as a hostage-taker who had deliberately locked up helpless victims of Hindu violence. Soumendranath led a delegation to meet the Bengal governor, and demanded that immediate intervention be made to protect the ordinary people and stop the rioting.[149]

Though non-believers, the PWP/WPP members did not launch an aggressive anti-religious propaganda; rather, their ideological strategy highlighted the a-religiosity of social relations that formed the basis of religious identity politics. Occasional displays of anti-religious views landed individual members in trouble. PWP/WPP activist Abdul Kader generated controversy as an undergraduate student at Dhaka University when lawyer and author Abul Hussain accused him of writing an article offensive to Muslim sentiments. He was warned not to do so in the future.[150] At the level of the internal organization, CPI and PWP/WPP members distanced themselves from religion. During the Kanpur trial of 1924, the accused declared that they had no religion.[151] The declaration form to be signed by CPI members in 1926 included 'non-association with any communal organization'.[152] Hasrat Mohani was expelled from the CPI in December 1928 for retaining membership of the Muslim League.[153]

Expansion of the organizational support-base of the PWP/WPP paved the way for physical interventions. In July 1928, the WPP campaigned against communalism among the predominantly Urdu-speaking Muslim workers of Keshoram Cotton Mill. The workers were urged to be wary of Arya Samajists hired by the mill management to foment riots and destroy labour unity.[154] Class rather than sectional solidarities were emphasized through unions under the control or influence of the left.

Agrarian Socialism

Though directly emerging from the anti-landlord *praja* movement linked with Swarajist populism, the first socialist organization could not make significant inroads among the peasantry. The dearth of rural activists and formidable competition from middle-class *praja* leaders serving *jotedar* interests impeded expansion in rural areas. It is often argued that privileging the worker over the peasant in theoretical terms by mechanically imitating a European communist model occluded the ideas and practice of the Indian communists in the 1920s, and postponed the opening of a peasant front by a decade. Yet, evidence shows that efforts in this direction were continuous. Muzaffar and Halim, having migrated from the countryside, regularly corresponded with contacts in rural areas, encouraging them to organize the local peasantry. In March 1926, A.R. Khan attempted to organize a *rayats*' conference at Berhampore.[155] Hemantakumar and Faizuddin opened branches of the organization in the districts.[156] While Faizuddin promoted the programme of the PWP/WPP in rural Mymensingh during 1927,[157] Hemantakumar tried to organize a fisherfolk's conference and to expand the WPP in Nadia and Bagura.[158]

These organized drives paved the way for a militant programme to mobilize the peasantry from 1928. The Bhatpara Conference of the WPP adopted 'A Call to Action', which included a recipe for radical action in the countryside. Muzaffar encouraged links with ongoing peasant struggles in East Bengal. When Gopal Basak suggested to Muzaffar, in August 1928, a visit to Dhaka to meet Nurul Huq, a lawyer defending the peasants of Bhawal, Muzaffar, Goswami and Spratt travelled from Calcutta to Dhaka to meet Basak and made their way to Mymensingh to stay with Faizuddin.[159] Muzaffar also actively campaigned on behalf of the Atia agriculturalists threatened with eviction. He was informed of this struggle in September 1928 by a contact, Pyar Mohammed, who was taking legal action against local officials and landowners on behalf of these peasants. His 'case' proved to be a difficult one as, fearing further victimization, the peasants hesitated in speaking out against their oppressors. Although Muzaffar's proposed visit to the area in October 1928 did not materialize as more responsibilities piled up in Calcutta, in his correspondence with Faizuddin, Muzaffar chastised the rural organizers 'for being blind' to the adverse role of the 'rural petit-bourgeoisie' in peasants' struggles. He probably had the *praja* leadership in mind when he urged a more systematic class mobilization of the pauperized peasants.[160]

By December 1928, the Comintern's new colonial thesis adopted at the Sixth Comintern Congress reached the communists in India. Its focus on the formation of a strong communist party with a mass peasant base influenced a cultivators' conference organized by Hemantakumar at Kusthea in Nadia district, in late February 1929. Spratt, Halim and Muzaffar attended the Kusthea conference with the aim of creating a 'Peasant League'.[161] The police noted: 'So large an exodus of Calcutta communists to rural areas is unprecedented in the history of communism in Bengal.'[162] At the conference, Faizuddin declared that the peasants of Mymensingh were eager to launch a no-rent campaign against the zamindars even though they could not act in isolation and were waiting for the launch of a wider movement. A militant peasant uprising in Mymensingh during 1930 was to confirm Faizuddin's observation on peasant 'readiness'. 'First Session of the All-Bengal Peasants' Conference', a policy report by Hemantakumar and Mohammed Rejoan Ali Khan Chaudhuri, advocated removal of zamindars without compensation, the end of usury, the abolition of indirect taxation, the introduction of compulsory primary education and universal adult franchise. They defined peasants as labourers working in the fields, village craftsmen, rural domestic servants and fisherfolk, and stressed the need to organize labour and rent strikes among the rural dispossessed.[163] After the conference a 'Bengal Peasants League' was formed in Kusthea. In a letter to Muzaffar on 10 March 1929, Hemantakumar was optimistic about opening district branches at Noakhali, Tripura and 24-Parganas. He suggested holding a working committee meeting in Calcutta soon. Twenty days later, arrests for the Meerut trial halted such a possibility.[164] The shift in the strategic thinking on the agrarian front was cited by the prosecution as yet another instance of the 'seditious' political character of the accused.[165]

Militant Trade Unionism

It was on the industrial front that the first socialist organization made significant inroads. Spearheaded by communist, socialist, radical and left-leaning trade union organizers, the left initiative struck a chord, chiefly among those engaged in formal wage work. In Calcutta and its suburbs during 1928, a surge in working-class militancy propelled the CPI, non-communist WPP members and their allies into playing an active role in organizing several strikes.[166] From 1927, working-class activism was again on the rise in many parts of India. The spectre of deteriorating living conditions triggered a confrontation between labour and capital. From the mid-1920s, increasing economic competition between Indian capitalists and colonial capital was evident from the tensions between the Marwari businessmen based in Calcutta and the British jute magnates of Bengal. However, the Indian capitalists were as dependent on the colonial state apparatus to curb working-class protests as their European rivals; hence, the competition was punctuated by cooperation.[167] Rising foodgrain prices, unemployment and the attendant impoverishment of a section of primarily North Indian migrant workers in Calcutta and its suburbs contributed to their participation in the communal violence of 1926.[168] Textile, jute and railways were particularly affected when British and Indian capitalists attempted to tide over economic stagnation through well-worn anti-labour strategies of wage reduction and retrenchment.[169] It is of little surprise that these sectors became sites of the greatest working-class militancy. The active role of the PWP/WPP and CPI in all these strikes resulted in a second, large-scale crackdown on Indian communists in 1929.

Early Days
Though they did not have any visible impact before 1928, attempts to establish communist and PWP/WPP hegemony over industrial workers began in 1926. Initial efforts were fragmentary. After shifting to Krishnanagar in 1926, Nazrul started an evening school in a working-class neighbourhood with Hemantakumar's help.[170] A Special Branch officer reported in July 1926 that Kutubuddin, Muzaffar and Shamsuddin had met at Kutubuddin's residence to discuss strike-action at Lansdowne Jute Mills in 24-Parganas.[171] From 1927, the left interventions became more systematic. The process involved a search for allies among the already existing union organizers, conflict with trade unionists opposed to a left political programme and

mobilization of workers who were not yet organized. Halim participated in the work of the Seamen's Union and the Bengal Trade Union Federation during late 1926 and early 1927.[172] When the PWP/WPP helped organize strikers at the Kashipur jute press in Calcutta, *The Statesman* noticed them and their future as 'troublemakers' was predicted.[173] In November 1927, Dange, Mirajkar, Halim and Muzaffar attended a conference convened by Mukundalal Sarkar at Kharagpur, the focal point of the all-India railwaymen's strike at the time. The police felt that communist participation in the Kharagpur conference proved that they were 'anxious' to incite a general strike, and that Dange's 'abuse' of C.F. Andrews, who had suggested a settlement, proved that a 'communistic flavour is being given to the question'.[174] Muzaffar and others also attended the Kanpur Conference of the AITUC in late 1927.[175] In December, communists, socialists and other trade unionists were involved in a strike by transit porters at the Port Commissioner's jetties. Muzaffar, Spratt, Goswami, Halim, Aftab Ali and Kishorilal took an 'active interest' in the newly formed Dock Worker's Union. Godbole, secretary of the union, was viewed as the man in 'charge of the strikers'. Despite attempts by the authorities to break the strike, only 70 out of 1,500 strikers initially returned to work.[176]

A Second Strike-Wave

By 1928, conditions were ripe for a second strike-wave. 'A Call to Action', the programme adopted by WPP at the Bhatpara Conference, reflected growing support for confrontation.[177] The railway workshops and the jute industry became the focus, in Bengal, of militant working-class resistance,[178] and a combination of different political forces active on the labour front. The long-drawn strike at the railway workshops in Lilooah (March–July 1928) was led by the trade union maverick Kiran Chandra Mitra (also known as '*jatadhari baba*'), the independent socialist Shibnath Banerjee, and communists Gopen Chakraborty, Dharani Goswami and Philip Spratt. When poverty and exhaustion finally broke the spirit of the workers, the strike collapsed. Despite attempts by the communists to spread the strike to related facilities at Asansol and Ondal, the management won the war of attrition.[179]

The strike of Keshoram Cotton Mill workers in Metiabruz, a primarily Muslim working-class suburb of Calcutta, helped the CPI to gain entry into this area. The workers had stopped work on their own but soon approached the organizers of ongoing strikes. Gopen Chakraborty, Abdul Halim, Muzaffar Ahmad, Philip Spratt and Mani Singh joined their efforts on behalf of the WPP. A union was formed and Mani Singh was made its secretary. According to Muzaffar, the strikers had initially approached Kiran Mitra with their grievances. Mitra was hesitant since the new owners of Keshoram, the Birlas, had promised to supply rice to the Lilooah strikers. The communists thwarted Mitra's attempts to make the 1,200 strikers return to work. Ultimately, the management had to negotiate and the main demands were achieved.[180] The WPP campaigned to strengthen this union by propagating class solidarity. Prabhabati Dasgupta, Philip Spratt and Radharaman Mitra accused G.D. Birla of resorting to communal tactics at public meetings, in order to divide the workers. The campaign against communalism and left trade unionism became linked. In July 1928, Muzaffar, Halim, Goswami, Singh and Amritalal Chandra, a dismissed worker from Asansol, warned workers at a public meeting that they must remain united irrespective of religious belief; otherwise, the capitalists would not offer any concessions.[181] Mukundalal Sarkar also requested Muzaffar to address the workers at local meetings in Kharagpur during 1928, on the need to counteract attempts by the management to drive a wedge between workers on communal lines.[182] Strengthening the unions also meant challenging the authority of those who acted on behalf of the management to enforce a disciplinary regime that regulated and curbed opposition to capital on the shop-floor. During the WPP-led strikes at the Kashipur and Chitpur jute presses in Calcutta in May 1928, the workers were told that the *sardars* were also petty exploiters; Spratt, among others, advised them to persist despite interference by 'police *badmashes*' who represented the interests of the management. On strike were 9,000 sorting coolies, including 1,000 women. Despite attempts by the *sardars* to make the work force return to work, most stayed away.[183]

Ideological differences with nationalist unions soon surfaced in a climate of increased working-class militancy. The communists accused the AITUC leaders of restricting workers' initiatives. During the 1928 PWP/WPP Conference in Bhatpara, Atulchandra Gupta criticized the reformist character of the AITUC leadership, including its links with the Labour leadership of the British Trade Union Congress. When Soumendranath wrote from Berlin in 1928 that he wished to publicize ongoing strikes in Bengal led by the WPP in the trade union circles of Europe,[184] Muzaffar's reply was that he had no objections though he regarded the German social-democratic unions to be a bit 'yellow'. He asked Soumendranath to emphasize that 'we belong to a more radical school of thought'.[185]

Scavenging and Class Struggle
The contradiction between a nationalist agenda and a socialist agenda came to the fore during the scavengers' strikes in Calcutta and Howrah. They pitted the WPP against the twin municipalities, highlighting the break between a proprietorial, proto-state perspective and a radical one. The strike-actions, which were started by the workers themselves and which disrupted civic life, forced the middle and upper classes to take notice of those below, and contributed to an eruption of class hostility. The social expression of

this hostility contributed to violence directed at the workers and their criminalization through the use of colonial law. In November 1927, the PWP started organizing one of the lowest paid and socially ostracized segments of urban workers, the sewage cleaners (*mathor*) and sweepers (*jharudar*) of Calcutta. A 'Scavengers' Union' was formed. Trade union activist Prabhabati Dasgupta, though not a member of the PWP, was made the president. Muzaffar became vice-president, with Dharani Goswami as secretary. Initial contact was made through modest efforts such as the publication of a Hindi leaflet and small-scale local meetings.[186] The police misread the situation. They thought the communists' endeavour to form a union by 'visiting the bustis where these men live and pointing out their grievances to them' yielded 'little interest in the proposal' among the scavengers. This perception was to be dramatically altered. The local gatherings soon culminated in a large meeting at the base of the Ochterlony monument at the city centre, with Muzaffar, Goswami, Halim and others present. A pamphlet was distributed, and the scavengers asked to strike and hold out against the Calcutta Corporation till it was compelled to give in to their demands.[187] On 4 March 1928, some scavengers arrived at the PWP/WPP office declaring that they were on strike. Within two days, the strike spread to all the areas covered by the Calcutta Corporation. Though the Swarajist Mayor, J.M. Sengupta, personally requested the workers to return to work, the strike continued until, after six days, the deteriorating conditions of the city forced the Mayor to speak to their union. A negotiated settlement was reached through the mediation of lawyers Kishorilal Ghosh and Mrinalkanti Bose, editors of *Amritabazar Patrika*, and the nationalist Bengal Trade Union Federation leaders. But the agreement had no legal basis as no document was signed, and Muzaffar later accused the two nationalist labour activists, who were trained lawyers, of carelessness. Though the Mayor promised a pay rise, at the meeting of Corporation Councillors held on 13 March, a majority of the Councillors, consisting of both Congressmen and their opponents, voted against any increase in wages. After this experience the organizers and workers started preparing for a second round of action.

A month later, the Scavengers' Union served a notice to the Corporation demanding higher pay and threatened to go on strike if their claims were ignored. Meanwhile, the anti-Swarajist bloc had gained a majority in the Calcutta Corporation elections. The new Mayor from the 'Coalition Party', Bijoykumar Basu, was determined not to cede an inch. The strike and a policy of suppression began almost simultaneously. On 25 June, the second day of the strike, Muzaffar and Prabhabati were arrested. Released on bail the next day, they were heartened to find that the entire organizational strength of the PWP had been mobilized to support the striking workers. The defeated mayoral candidate, Subhash Bose, and the Swarajist press also came out in support of the workers. Meanwhile, the municipal authorities, the city police force and the local *bhadralok* launched a campaign of physical intimidation. Though many of these *bhadralok* were economically impoverished and lived in close proximity to the strikers, they displayed overwhelming loyalty towards their social identity as 'respectable folk' through violence and contempt.[188] Halim wrote to Dange and Ghate in Bombay that the workers were holding out despite the systematic ferocity of the Calcutta Corporation, the deployment of police and military personnel, merciless beatings, the taking of 200 workers into custody under false charges, and the arrests of Muzaffar and Prabhabati.[189]

Continued resistance by the workers ultimately forced the new Mayor to negotiate. He agreed to a pay-rise, even promising that the scavengers would be paid for the days lost due to the strike. Emboldened by this retreat, the workers threatened to continue with the strike unless the promises were ratified at the Corporation Councillors' meeting. In response, Mayor Bejoy-kumar Basu, the former Swarajist Mayor J.M. Sengupta, Kishorilal Ghosh and Mrinalkanti Bose assured that this time the municipality would not go back on its word. The union agreed to end the strike. But on 16 July, at the Councillors' meeting, the Coalition Councillors and two Congress Councillors voted against paying the workers for the days they were on strike. No one paid any attention to the claim that the workers were being deprived of their legitimate pay since they had cleaned up the city by putting in extra work after withdrawing the strike.[190] Muzaffar saw the scavengers' strike at Howrah as one more instance of class consensus among the upper levels of Indian society. The Calcutta Corporation continued to dismiss and deny not just the legitimacy, but even the impact of the strike: 'The conservancy service went on smoothly as usual except with a slight interruption in June 1928 due to a partial strike of the coolies. This was however tided over without much difficulty and this District was not at all affected by it.'[191] This defensive and derisive version clashed sharply with the account provided by the colonial police, who noted that the 'scavengers' strike in the months of May and June' created 'serious dislocation of the conservancy arrangements in the city'.[192]

Class hostility towards devalued labour could be erected at a moment's notice and shatter the politics of 'compassionate protectionism' if segments of the proprietor class felt threatened by the actions of those below. During the scavengers' strike in Howrah, the vacillation and hostility of the nationalists demonstrated this. A branch of the Scavengers' Union, established at Shachinandan Chattopadhyay's initiative in the town of Howrah, had initially enlisted the help of three Congress nationalists, Jibankrishna Maiti, Agam Datta and Pramod Basu. The network paved the way for rallies among the sewage cleaners, who were sizeable in number since none of the municipal wards in Howrah had covered drains. The charter of demands included pay-rise, paid leave, an end to corruption and a month's notice for dismissal. The strike in Howrah started on 6 April with the scavengers suddenly stopping work at a municipal ward, and soon 3,000 workers were on strike. On 8 April, Anglo-Indian police sergeants attacked the slums inhabited by the scavengers, but retreated quickly when women workers emptied pails of garbage on them. Congressman Pramod Basu, who had earlier displayed great enthusiasm, made it clear that the Congress Municipality of Howrah had 'big plans' which the strikers had jeopardized. On 10 April, the municipal authorities met the union leaders and refused to concede any of their demands. The strikers had assembled outside to hear the outcome of the meeting. Jogesh Dasgupta, who was the secretary of Howrah Municipality, a member of the Provincial Congress Committee and the chief negotiator, threatened Jiban Maiti and Agam Datta with disciplinary action if they did not address the assembled workers and ask them to return to work. Datta and Maiti complied with extreme reluctance.[193]

Despite these efforts to break the strike, the scavengers held on. The workers faced physical harassment from gangs of Hindu *bhadralok* youth. Realizing that an increase in the workers' wages would mean a rise in the municipal taxes imposed on them as rate-payers, the middle classes advocated force to make the scavengers to return to work. The violence took a serious turn, revealing trans-communal proprietor hostility towards the strikers. When Muzaffar and other organizers tried to convince the residents of a Muslim neighbourhood to desist from assaulting the workers, he was told by a 'drunk but coherent' local businessman that 'otherwise . . . the little children' of their families would 'die from cholera and other diseases'. In the face of repeated threats and brutality, the strikers asked the union leadership to negotiate. On 16 April, after protracted negotiations with Prabhabati Dasgupta, the municipality agreed to a meagre salary increase and pay for the days of the strike. Though a board was formed for future negotiations by the municipality which included Prabhabati and Muzaffar as union representatives, Muzaffar noted that the 'bhadraloks of the Howrah Corporation' ensured that no meeting ever took place.[194]

Partial success for the scavengers in Calcutta and Howrah encouraged the PWP/WPP to open branches of the scavengers' union in Dhaka and Mymensingh. The scavengers of Mymensingh town went on strike in June 1928 and successfully gained a wage increase. Basak requested Muzaffar in August 1928 to send an expert trade unionist from the ranks of the Calcutta scavengers to help organize the union in Dhaka.[195] Didarul Alam wrote to Muzaffar on the abysmal conditions of municipal sweepers in Rangoon. R.S. Nimbker felt that work could be started among municipal workers in Bombay and an all-India federation could be set up. After reading Nimbker's intercepted letter, S.H.H. Mills, a senior official, dryly observed, 'I thought this was coming.'[196]

Other Actions

WPP activists helped organize historic strikes by jute workers in the industrial outskirts of Calcutta. Militant strikes at the Ludlow Jute Mills in Chengail and the Fort Gloster Jute Mills in Bauria during 1928 involved a brutal managerial counter-offensive, including police firing on the Bauria strikers. Though the strikers did not achieve anything in material terms, the unions came to stay and ensured the entry of communists in the Hooghly jute belt.[197] The last activity of the Bengal WPP was to lead the strikers of the Clive Jute Mill in Metiabruz, where the left already had a presence. In January 1929, Muzaffar, Halim, Kalikumar Sen, Shamsul Huda, Spratt, Pyarimohan Das, Goswami, Akhil Banerjee, Shachindranath Sinha and Mani Singh actively organized the mill-hands; clashes broke out during the strike and some workers were arrested for 'rioting'. Despite attempted suppression, the strike was successful.[198]

The Bengal communists and socialists were inspired by contemporary communist-led strike-actions in Bombay, especially the remarkable initiative taken by the textile workers.[199] Attempts to organize their counterparts in Bengal resulted in a cotton-mill workers' strike in Dhaka during September 1928. Assault by the managerial staff and extremely low wages motivated them. Gopal Basak described his role as that of an isolated organizer, comparable to the 'father of the bride as it were', since the Congress activists were determined to betray the strikers. As in Calcutta and Howrah, middle-class citizens attacked the strikers; a hunger march was pelted with stones by *bhadralok* youth. Ultimately, this strike for higher pay and labour dignity failed when the semi-starved workers could no longer hold on.[200]

Gopen Chakraborty later held that developing working-class consciousness was a multi-layered process; the workers displayed attachment to both sectional perceptions and the power of class solidarity.[201] This can be read as a reflection on the complexities that characterized the workers' attempts to become politicized. Ingredients of class consciousness were visible not just in the ideological orientation of some radical trade union leaders, but also in aspects of working-class culture such as the readiness to form more confrontational unions, the display of their own initiative during strike-actions, and the fact that they responded to political and not just economic slogans. At the same time, their socialization as members of distinct identity formations could contradict this consciousness, especially when non-communal unions built through strike-actions collapsed from repression, and became unavailable as a conduit of mobilization in the work place and the neighbourhood.[202]

To Bring Back the Workers

Campaigns for trade union rights reflected a concerted attempt by the WPP
to bring back the workers to the political arena. The WPP was gearing up to
launch a vigorous campaign against the Trade Disputes Bill. At a meeting
held at Albert Hall on 2 September 1928 where nationalists, independent
trade unionists and communists spoke against the Bill, union organizers
representing seamen, jute workers, railway workers, corporation teachers,
clerks and scavengers were visible. In October 1928, the Bengal WPP sent a
circular pointing to the party's intention to 'conduct as wide and intense a
campaign as possible against the Bill'.[203] The Bill posed a threat to organized
trade union-building at a time when the WPP was making its presence felt
as a political force among workers. By late 1928, WPP members were active
among scavengers, postmen, paper-mill hands, and jute, cotton, glass, metal
and shell factory workers.[204] Labour unions affiliated to the Bengal WPP in
1928 numbered seven in Calcutta, four in Howrah, three in Hooghly, ten in
24-Parganas, two in Dhaka and in Mymensingh.[205] In 1928, Sikh workers
in Calcutta formed a branch of the Punjab Kirti Dal, the sister organization
of the Bengal WPP, and merged with the Bengal WPP on the eve of the First
All-India WPP Conference. Activities among dock workers and sailors were
intensified. In November, a 'Transport Workers' Union' of *khalasis* and *lascars*
emerged.[206] The police had already noted in July 1928 that communists and
other organizers were circulating copies of *Ganabani* among members of
the ISU, the Bengal Mariners' Union and the Indian Quarter Masters' Union.[207]

Huda's report to the Comintern in October 1928 offered a detailed description of the strides made on the industrial front. Huda, himself an ex-sailor,
mentioned the WPP's engagements with seamen, work among the Port Trust
workers and winning control over the Gardenreach Workshop Workers'
Union. Among the unions affiliated to the WPP, he highlighted the Scavengers' Union of Bengal, with its central office in Calcutta and branches in
Howrah, Mymensingh and Dhaka. While the Calcutta branch had 1,000
registered and 9,000 unregistered members, Howrah had 200, Dhaka 300
and Mymensingh 200 members. Huda's list included the Bengal Textile
Workers' Union based in Calcutta with branches in Metiabruz and Dhaka;
the Bengal Glass Workers' Union based in Calcutta with a branch at Dum
Dum Cantonment, and formed in April 1928 with a total strength of 250
members; the Angus Engineering Workers' Union formed in January 1928
with 576 members; the Ichapur Ordnance Workers' Union that had emerged
in April 1928 with 247 members; and the Bengal Jute Workers' Union formed
in 1925 with its central office in Bhatpara. With branches at Bhatpara (2,500
members), Hajinagar (300 members), Rishra (450 members), Alambazar
(300 members), Titagarh (550 members), Angus (200 members), Metiabruz
(600 members) and Budge Budge (350 members), the total strength of the

Bengal Jute Workers' Union was 5,250. It ran a day school, a night school and a recreation club for workers. Huda reported that it was fighting against 'the strongest capitalist group of the province' and, by 1928, had conducted twenty-one strikes involving 128,125 workers for 198 days.[208]

Towards a Self-Aware Militancy

The WPP also tried to influence trade unions not affiliated to it. During the railway workers' strike in 1927, the decision to go on a general strike was a WPP initiative. During the East India Railway Workers' Strike in 1928, the WPP took the lead in trying to spread the strike from Lilooah to Ondal and Asansol. The workers of Lilooah marched to Hooghly and Kanchrapara under communist leadership to seek support in the industrial belt. WPP activists also gained entry into the Tramway Workers' Union.

Communists mounted a campaign to build labour solidarity against imperialism and capitalism. In 1928, Spratt and Muzaffar, while addressing sailors, stressed the need to boycott the Royal Commission on Labour.[209] The WPP, inspired by the CPI, held processions and meetings to introduce a culture of proletarian internationalism in Calcutta. On May Day of 1928, 1,000 workers led by Spratt, Muzaffar, Kishorilal and others marched from Mirzapur Street to the Calcutta Maidan, where workers from other unions joined them. A large trade union meeting was held.[210] A workers' meeting to mark Lenin's fifth death anniversary was held on 20 January 1929. Presided over by Dharani Goswami, Muzaffar, Spratt and Radharaman Mitra spoke on communism at this meeting. Red banners ac the venue displaying the slogan 'Workers of the World Unite!' alarmed the colonial authorities.[211] The WPP also aimed to connect the local with the international through repeated attempts to affiliate the AITUC to the Red International of Labour Unions (RILU), despite 'reactionary' opposition.[212]

These attempts to give contemporary labour movements a leftist form and content were also evident in the methods introduced to encourage self-aware working-class action. A weekly intelligence report filed on 10 October 1928 observed that communists were forming committees to conduct union affairs with an emphasis on workers' initiative. The report feared these could be changed into strike committees and pinpointed another WPP strategy to stimulate self-organization:

> An interesting feature of the week's activities has been the training of strikers in public speaking and the conduct of meetings. Each day one or two of the strikers addressed large audiences composed both of their fellow-strikers and the public and on each occasion a striker presided, while the so-called leaders were content to take a back seat.

The police also noticed a 'recent development' of 'lantern lectures', designed to attract 'the toilers'.[213] They noted the growing popularity of Marxist slogans even among lower-middle-class wage earners, citing the 'Annual Report' of the Calcutta Corporation Teachers' Union, which urged members during April 1928 'to realize the strength of combination and solidarity and to respond to the cry now ringing through the world – Workers of the World Unite!'[214]

Workers Return

The strikes and unions were seen by the WPP as a way of bringing the working class back into the anti-colonial struggle with greater recognition of their own political role as a class. The WPP and socialist trade unionists took advantage of the mobilization to mount pressure on the nationalist leaders. Workers in their thousands, under WPP leadership, marched into the annual session of the INC in December 1928 at Park Circus in Calcutta,[215] occupied the venue for two hours, and demanded the adoption of '*Purna Swaraj*' (complete independence) as immediate policy. The representative of the 'Congress Left', Subhash Chandra Bose, who was in charge of the volunteers, reportedly wanted to remove them with police help.[216] Satis Pakrasi, Ranen Sen and Saroj Mukherjee, who later joined the communist movement, have separately noted in their memoirs, the thrill and excitement they felt when the workers entered the Congress tent under the leadership of Muzaffar, Halim, Chakraborty, Goswami, Spratt, Huda and others.[217] A section of the nationalist youth who later became communists was perturbed by the insincerity of the nationalist leadership towards the demands of the workers. When Bankim Mukherjee spoke, in Hindi, on behalf of the workers, asking the nationalist leaders to pay attention to their demands, Gandhi responded very briefly, promised to 'consider' their claims and quickly withdrew.[218] The event was regarded as a high-point in class militancy by police agents as well. They recorded that 10,000 workers led by the WPP and other militant trade union leaders 'invaded' the Congress tent between 3 and 4 pm on 30 December 1928 with red flags, mostly shouting: '*Mazdoor Hukumat ki Jai*' (Long Live the Worker's State).[219] This pressure from below has been read as one of the major factors contributing to the adoption of 'complete independence' as Congress policy a year later.[220]

As part of its anti-imperialist drive, the Bengal WPP also mobilized thousands of workers to march against the Simon Commission on 19 February 1929. Apart from Congress and WPP activists, many working-class people joined the march and the militant communist slogan, 'Long Live the Revolution!' (*Inquilab Zindabad!*) was prominently displayed for the first time in India. The police objected and Aftab Ali was one of two people arrested for carrying such placards.[221] The route of the procession represented an urban geography of mass protest which remains unaltered to this day in

Calcutta: the convergence of large numbers of demonstrators on the centre of political power, physically embodied by huge colonial buildings housing the state administration. A Special Branch operative reported that the procession started at 3 pm and advanced through Harrison Road, College Street, Wellington Street, Dharmatala Street, Esplanade and Government Place East to the Ochterlony monument on the Maidan (open ground). At the junction of Esplanade and Central Avenue, the demonstrators were reinforced by 1,500 workers from Howrah led by Kiran Mitra, Radharaman Mitra and Bankim Mukherjee, as well as about 200 members of the Jute Mill unions of Kidderpore and Metiabruz led by Huda, Spratt and Goswami. 'There was some excitement' at Government Place East triggered 'by a basin of water . . . thrown from one of the upper flats of Esplanade Mansion on the processionists below'.[222]

Just a month later, the apparent forward march of labour was halted. Principal trade union leaders, communists and non-communists, were arrested on 20 March and brought to trial at Meerut. Nevertheless, by concentrating on workers, the WPP created the conditions for the emergence of a left political culture in the city and its suburbs. The methods introduced by the organization paved the way for future class-based movements.

Youth Activism

The average age of activists and organizers on the left, as well as those belonging to other political persuasions, placed them in the ranks of the young intelligentsia. Attempts were made to attract and mobilize youth through the formation of the Young Comrades League.[223] The aim was to launch a mass organization which would bring existing youth movements under the socialist and communist influence. Social reform movements and various branches of nationalism had tapped the energy and resources of students who had emerged as a distinct political constituency.[224] The PWP/WPP and the CPI added a class dimension to this formation by stressing the recruitment of young workers. The left alternative, even if its reach and visibility were restricted, generated a new kind of youth activism.

Since the Non-Cooperation Movement, many middle-class revolutionaries had vacillated between militant nationalist secret societies and movements guided by left thinking. Radicalism among middle-class youth came to be invested with contested ideological meanings, as was first evident in the early 1920s when some Jugantar revolutionaries temporarily joined the first socialist nucleus. The early activists continued to show an interest and this was evident in writings for anti-colonial youth during the late 1920s. Priyonath Ganguly, associated with Jugantar,[225] thought that highlighting student participation in revolutionary politics,[226] Irish nationalism[227] and

Bolshevism could motivate the middle-class youth. His *Lenin o Soviet* projected Lenin as a revolutionary thinker whose ideas and actions guided the mass uprising of the working class and peasants. The book was based on the US journalist Albert Rhys Williams' account,[228] *Through the Russian Revolution,* in circulation throughout the 1920s.[229] The intellectual tendency to study and write on the revolutionary changes in Russia further increased in the early 1930s. Pulakesh De, a nationalist activist and journalist, paid tribute to the 'Soviet Five Year Plan' in his *Bolsheviki Sankalpo* (The Bolshevik Project), a tract banned by the government.[230] The communists, through the PWP/ WPP, tried to win over those attracted by socially radical political programmes. The presence of young men from *bhadralok* revolutionary nationalist backgrounds at WPP events, conferences, meetings, processions and strikes was noted.[231] An informer reported in June 1927 that 37 Harrison Road drew 'Sentimental and impulsive young men, who are eager to get freedom for their country' and were 'attracted to this place to find out if they could free their country with Bolshevik help.'[232] At the WPP conference in Bhatpara and the peasant conference at Kusthea, young activists and students were 'allowed' to 'roam' freely.[233]

In order to consolidate these sections systematically and involve them in its activities, the WPP floated a separate youth front, the Young Comrades League (YCL), on 11 August 1928. Participation in the anti-colonial struggle, promoting the cause of workers and their unions, fighting for grievances specific to young people, particularly the unemployed, and recruitment of students and workers to the communist movement were the chief aims of the organization.[234] Ashutosh Roy, a chemist and PWP member from Dhaka, was made the secretary, and Nalindra Sengupta, a law student temporarily living in the WPP office at 2/1 European Asylum Lane, became the working secretary. Sudhirkumar Raha, who initially visited Calcutta in 1928 as a delegate of the Maldah District Congress Committee, while staying with Spratt, Muzaffar, Dharani, Huda and Halim at the WPP office, met Bankim Mukherjee, Radharaman Mitra and Gopen Chakraborty, and was inspired to sever links with the nationalist ideology and to devote himself to the YCL. Twenty members took part in the first meeting where a certain 'Young Comrade', Ratanbhushan Hazra, read a paper on 'Imperialism'. Halim, Spratt and Muzaffar were also present.[235] In early 1929, the former PWP office premises at 37 Harrison Road were hired by Nalindra Sen, Ashutosh Roy, Spratt, Goswami and others, and a separate office of the YCL was established. Raha lived on the premises; Goswami, Chakraborty, Spratt, Radharaman Mitra and Nalindra Sen were regular visitors. Although no one was allowed to join unless certified as responsible and reliable by an existing member, around fifty people were recruited. Spratt played a crucial role in publicizing the YCL through the columns of *Amritabazar*. He reiterated the communist position that the activists should abandon nationalist strategies and join mass struggles on a class agenda.[236]

The efforts of the YCL to win over young nationalists were assisted by former Jugantar revolutionary-turned-communist, Bhupendrakumar Datta. He had started a Marxist study circle in Calcutta in the second half of the 1920s, after leaving behind the life of a political emigré in Berlin. Saroj Mukherjee, a witness to the pressure on the nationalist leadership mounted by working-class people at the Congress session of 1928, consulted Datta to make sense of the incident, and was told of 'class interest' and 'class conflict' as social forces which shaped political action. Datta advised Mukherjee to read Marxist–Leninist literature, and encouraged him to attend the WPP conference in December 1928 and get in touch with Abdul Halim in 1931.[237] Ranen Sen, who had joined Jugantar in 1924–25, was convinced by the WPP-led strikes among jute workers of Bauria and Chengail, the workers' march to the Congress tent in December 1928, and the anti-Simon Commission march in February 1929, that communism was the only viable political option. His friend Akhil Banerjee introduced Ranen Sen to Halim. After meeting Halim, Sen joined Spratt's political classes.[238] These developments made the police agents observe with a degree of alarm: 'The members of the YCL . . . have begun to hold meetings in Calcutta to attract young men to their fold for the purposes of starting the practical work of conversion.'[239]

The launching of a communist youth mobilization programme reflected the first organized attempt to curb the nationalist influence over younger members of the intelligentsia, and to introduce them to the Marxist and Leninist alternative. The first socialist nucleus under Muzaffar's leadership had aimed to achieve this in a climate of waning mass protests; the resurgence of strikes in 1928 made the task of arguing for a socialist agenda easier.

Possibilities of a Communist Base in Bengal

As the WPP gained entry into labour politics, floated a youth front and showed signs of undertaking concerted activity on the peasant front, the confidence to build a large communist party was boosted. The work done by Muzaffar, Halim and others through the PWP/WPP generated the possibilities of creating a communist base in Bengal. In 1922, Muzaffar had typified a rejection of nationalist and sectional politics, playing a central role in the formation of a socialist nucleus. The political perceptions which made Muzaffar and his earliest associates shift to the left encouraged others to do the same during the second half of the 1920s. This radical 'fraction' chiefly comprised members of the middle-class intelligentsia disenchanted with mainstream anti-colonial and communal politics. As its size increased, the first socialist organization emerged and expanded. It was a coalition between communists and independent socialists sympathetic to but outside the CPI. However, the role of Muzaffar as the central figure of this organization meant a growing influence for communists within the organizational structure. The emphasis of the first socialist organization on mobilization of workers, peasants and youth reflected an attempt to win over social segments and classes which had emerged as political constituencies through their participation in nationalist and sectional political movements. The Comintern's encouragement in this direction also acted as a major stimulus. 'A Call to Action', adopted at the Bhatpara Conference of the WPP, was the first indication of the communist intention to adopt a systematic and militant strategy of influencing these constituencies through the prism of class politics.

The contrast between two reports sent to the Comintern, highlighting the growth of the PWP/WPP between 1926–27 and 1927–28, revealed the changes in outlook and strategy of the Bengal WPP and the CPI. The first report, written by an unknown Indian communist in Europe, described the activities of the organization up to its second conference in 1927. One can safely assume that the anonymous author was Soumendranath Tagore since he had been a participant in the activities mentioned. The report stated that the first conference of the organization was attended by a number of local peasants from Nadia, Rajshahi and Mymensingh; and that a fishermen's union was set up at the initiative of Kutubuddin, Hemantakumar and the author himself. Activities began among jute workers, paper-mill workers and seamen; and Aftab Ali and Kalidas Bhattacharya joined the PWP. The second conference of the WPP held in Calcutta in March 1927 registered a sizeable working-class presence. The report asserted that comrades were organizing peasant unions on a 'large and better basis'. The Scavengers' Union carried out a 'successful strike' despite 'intervention and repressive methods' adopted by the 'Swarajist Municipality'. This was the only activity of the group in 1928 about which the author knew in some detail.[240]

Shamsul Huda's detailed report to the Comintern reflected the widening of the organization's activities during 1928. Huda, who had returned from Europe that year, stated the central office of the party was in Calcutta, with branches in the district towns of Mymensingh, Dhaka and Bhatpara in 24-Parganas, and in villages such as Atia in Mymensingh, Narsinghdi in Dhaka and Ghuni in 24-Parganas. He described the unit in Atia as a fighting branch representing 1,00,000 peasants who were under threat of eviction from landlords and the Government Forest Department. Huda also mentioned preparations for an All India WPP Conference in Calcutta to coincide with the annual Congress session in the city.[241]

The emergence of the All India Workers and Peasants Party in Calcutta in

December 1928 represented the coming together of communist-dominated socialist organizations from Bombay, Bengal, Punjab and Uttar Pradesh, and continuation of the programme adopted at Bhatpara to create a radical mass-base for future action.[242] Although it has been argued that a change in the Comintern 'line' compelled the Indian communists to abruptly abandon the open organization through which they had so far operated,[243] WPP activities under Muzaffar's leadership during 1928–29 suggest that the aim of building a strong communist party was voiced even before any formal directive arrived from Moscow. The new directions from the Comintern were interpreted as a signal to build a party of the proletariat and to work with agrarian socialists to forge a militant front of the peasants; despite being targeted as a constituency of the first socialist organization from the very beginning, the peasantry remained outside its reach.[244] The preparations to launch a communist mass campaign encouraged Muzaffar to draft a new CPI constitution in early 1929. Muzaffar stated in 1931 that the new draft was an attempt to overcome the shortcomings of the constitution adopted in 1927 when the CPI was extremely weak in terms of both membership and organization. Though the CPI aspired to be a part of the Comintern in 1927, it was numerically strong enough to call itself a 'section of the Communist International' only in 1929 when its membership had sufficiently increased. Muzaffar's draft was informed by this development.[245] The Meerut trial, which began in 1929, contributed to the dissolution of the WPP and checked the activities of the CPI. Nevertheless, the growth of Bengal PWP/WPP between 1926 and 1928 indicated that the inter-connections between the regional and the international communist forces were making way for greater radicalization of politics, an expansion of support for socialism in Bengal, and the emergence of a left political space in Calcutta and its suburbs.

Notes and References

[1] Atulya Ghosh, *Kashto-Kolpito* (Difficult Imaginings), Calcutta, 1980, p. 65. Saroj Mukhopadhyay, *Bharater Communist Party o Amra* (The Communist Party of India and Ourselves), Vol. 1, Calcutta, 1993, p. 18. The encounter did not have any ideological impact on Ghosh. But he borrowed Marxist texts from younger Congress colleagues and argued against the premises of communism, decisively putting forward a nationalist position.

[2] IB 67/24 (105/1924).

[3] IB 320/1926 (310/26). Muzaffar Ahmad, *Kazi Nazrul Islam: Smritikatha* (Kazi Nazrul Islam: Reminiscences), Calcutta, 1965, ninth edition 1998, p. 196.

[4] Horace Williamson, *India and Communism*, edited by Mahadevprasad Saha, Calcutta, 1976, p. 132. Ahmad, *Kazi Nazrul Islam: Smritikatha*, p. 196. Though the Comintern had floated and supported the idea of launching such groups, their origins were rooted in the initiatives taken by local activists responding to socialist ideas that had become increasingly popular in the wake of the Bolshevik Revolution of 1917.

[5] IB 1041/ 1916 (69/16). Pramita Ghose, *Meerut Conspiracy Case and the Left-Wing in India*, Calcutta, 1978, p. 20.

[6] Muzaffar Ahmad, *Amar Jiban o Bharater Communist Party* (My Life and the Communist Party of India), Calcutta, 1969, fifth edition 1996, p. 339.

[7] Abdul Halim, 'Bidrohi Banglar Kobi: Kazi Nazrul Islam' (Rebel Poet of Bengal: Kazi Nazrul Islam), in *Nabajibaner Pathe*, Calcutta, 1966, second edition 1990, p. 136.

[8] David Petrie, *Communism in India (1924–1927)*, Calcutta, 1972, p. 128.

[9] IB 320/1926 (310/26). Ahmad, *Kazi Nazrul Islam: Smritikatha*, pp. 189–91. Halim, 'Bidrohi Banglar Kobi', in *Nabajibaner Pathe*, p. 136.

[10] Ahmad, *Kazi Nazrul Islam: Smritikatha*, p. 222.

[11] Ahmad, *Amar Jiban o Bharater Communist Party*, p. 338.

[12] Subodh Chandra Sengupta and Anjali Basu (eds.), *Sansad Bangali Charitabhidhan* (Dictionary of Bengali Biography), Vol. 1, Calcutta, 1994, p. 638. Ahmad, 'Amar Pointallish Bacharer Sathi', in Halim, *Nabajibaner Pathe*, pp. 6–7. Hemantakumar Sarkar, *Bandir Diary* (A Prisoner's Diary), Calcutta, 1922.

[13] Hemantakumar Sarkar, *Bhashatattva o Bangla Bhashar Itihas* (Linguistics and the History of the Bengali Language), Calcutta, 1922.

[14] Hemantakumar Sarkar, 'Non-Cooperation o Socialist Andolan' (Non-Cooperation and the Socialist Movement), in *Swaraj Kon Pathe?* (Whither Self-Rule?), Calcutta, 1922, pp. 33–39.

[15] Ahmad, *Kazi Nazrul Islam: Smritikatha*, p. 192.

[16] Leonard A. Gordon, *Brothers Against the Raj: A Biography of Sarat and Subhash Chandra Bose*, Delhi, 1990, pp. 36, 98, 101.

[17] For analyses of Swarajist politics in Bengal during the 1920s, see J.H.Broomfield, *Elite Conflict in a Plural Society*, Berkeley, 1968, pp. 204–81; Leonard A. Gordon, *Bengal: The Nationalist Movement 1876–1940*, New York, 1974, pp. 165–245; Rajat Ray, *Urban Roots of Indian Nationalism, Pressure Groups and Conflict of Interests in Calcutta City Politics, 1875–1939*, Delhi, 1979, pp. 106–32; Kenneth McPherson, *The Muslim Microcosm: Calcutta 1918 to 1935*, Wiesbaden, 1974, pp. 76–97; Tanika Sarkar, *Bengal 1928–1934: The Politics of Protest*, Delhi, 1987, pp. 11–75, Sumit Sarkar, *Modern India*, Hong Kong, 1989, pp. 231–33, 235.

[18] For discussions on Hindu *bhadralok* intransigence in relation to the structure of land tenure and alienation of Muslim proprietor interests, see Partha Chatterjee, 'Agrarian Relations and Politics in Bengal: Some Considerations on the Making of the Tenancy Act Amendment', Occasional Paper No. 30, Centre for Studies in Social Sciences, Calcutta, 1980; subsequently published as *Bengal 1920–1947: The Land Question*, Calcutta, 1984. Also Taj ul-Islam Hashmi, *Pakistan as a Peasant Utopia: The Communalization of Class Politics in East Bengal, 1920–1947*, Oxford, 1992, pp. 83–173. Joya Chatterji, *Bengal Divided: Hindu communalism and partition, 1932–1947*, Delhi, 1995, pp. 1–17, 55–102. Mohammad Shah, *In Search of an Identity: Bengali Muslims 1880–1940*, Calcutta, 1996. For a detailed survey of the varied attitudes and differences among Bengali intellectuals and activists on the colonial land revenue system, see Amalendu De, 'Bengali Intelligentsia's Attitudes to the Permanent Settlement', *Social Scientist*, Vol. 5, No. 56, 1977.

[19] Sengupta and Basu (eds.), *Charitabhidhan*, Vol. 1, p. 308.

[20] Pramathanath Bishi, *Desher Shatru* (Enemy of the Country), Santiniketan, 1925.

[21] Benjamin Jowett (transl.), 'Republic', in Irwin Edman (ed.), *The Works of Plato*, New York, 1956, p. 431. 'I said: *Until philosophers are kings, or the kings and princes of this world have the spirit and power of philosophy, and political greatness and wisdom meet in one, and those commoner natures who pursue either to the exclusion of the other are compelled to stand aside, cities will never have rest from their evils – nor the human race, as I believe, – and then only will this our State have a possibility of life and behold the light of day.*'

[22] Bishi, *Desher Shatru*.

[23] Mortuza Khaled, *A Study in Leadership: Muzaffar Ahmad and the Communist Movement in Bengal*, Calcutta, 2001, p. 21.

24 IB 320/1926 (310/26).

25 Nareshchandra Sengupta, 'Atmakatha' (My Story), in *Jugoporikrama* (Survey of an Age), Vol. 1, Calcutta, 1981, p. 15.

26 Nareshchandra Sengupta, *Rajagi* (Royal Estate), Calcutta, 1926.

27 Khaled, *Muzaffar Ahmad*, pp. 18–19.

28 Ahmad, *Kazi Nazrul Islam: Smritikatha*, pp. 194–95. Khaled, *Muzaffar Ahmad*, p. 21.

29 Ahmad, *Kazi Nazrul Islam: Smritikatha*, p. 195.

30 Ahmad, *Amar Jiban o Bharater Communist Party*, p. 340.

31 Khaled, *Muzaffar Ahmad*, p. 21. IB 320/1926 (310/26). Mani Sinha, *Jiban Sangram* (Life Struggle), Dhaka, 1986, p. 52. Elsewhere in Asia, communists and leftists in Japan, facing similar compulsions, were active through a Labour-Farmer Party in the 1920s. See Gail Lee Bernstein, *Japanese Marxist: A Portrait of Kawakami Hajime 1879–1946*, Cambridge (Massachusetts) and London, 1990, pp. 147–53.

32 Ahmad, *Amar Jiban o Bharater Communist Party*, p. 340.

33 Khaled, *Muzaffar Ahmad*, p. 21.

34 IB 93/26 (1/1926).

35 Ahmad, *Kazi Nazrul Islam: Smritikatha*, p. 196.

36 IB 95/24 (41/1924).

37 IB 320/26 (310/1926), in Ladlimohon Raychaudhury (ed.), *The Seed-Time of Communist Movement in Bengal*, Calcutta, 2000, pp. 157–60, 165.

38 Statement of Muzaffar Ahmad, in *Meerut Communist Conspiracy Case (1929) Papers*. Ahmad, *Amar Jiban o Bharater Communist Party*, pp. 332–36.

39 IB 320/26 (310/1926), in Raychaudhury (ed.), *The Seed-Time of Communist Movement in Bengal*, p. 148.

40 A copy of this letter is available at the CPI (M) Archives, Calcutta. The original is in Moscow.

41 Statement of Muzaffar Ahmad, *Meerut Communist Conspiracy Case (1929) Papers*.

42 Petrie, *Communism in India*, pp. 165–66. G. Adhikary (ed.), *Documents of the History of the Communist Party of India*, Volume III C, 1927, Delhi, 1979, p. 203. Williamson, *India and Communism*, edited by Saha, p. 132. Ahmad, *Amar Jiban*, pp. 332–36.

43 IB 320/26 (310/1926), in Raychaudhury (ed.), *The Seed-Time of Communist Movement in Bengal*, pp. 180–82.

44 Muzaffar Ahmad, *Bharater Communist Party Garar Prothom Jug* (The First Phase of the Communist Party of India), Calcutta, 1959, fourteenth edition 1997, pp. 12–15.

45 IB 210/27 (23/1927). IB 93/26 (1/1926).

46 IB file number censored.

47 Ghose, *Meerut Conspiracy Case and the Left-Wing in India*, p. 9.

48 Ahmad, *Bharater Communist Party Garar Prothom Jug*, pp. 16–19.

49 Purabi Roy, Sobhanlal Datta Gupta and Hari Vasudevan (eds.), *Indo-Russian Relations 1917–1947: Select Documents from the Archives of the Russian Federation, Part I: 1917–1928*, Calcutta, 1999 , pp. 22, 200–02. For a detailed study of the CPGB's efforts in this direction, see Jean Jones, 'The Anti-Colonial Politics and Policies of the Communist Party of Great Britain: 1920–1951', unpublished Ph.D. thesis, University of Wolverhampton, 1997. Ahmad, *Amar Jiban o Bharater Communist Party*, pp. 136–37.

50 Ahmad, *Amar Jiban o Bharater Communist Party*, pp. 368–72, 372–74. IB 320/26 (310/1926). IB 93/26 (1/1926).

51 See Philip Spratt, *Blowing up India: Reminiscences and Reflections of A Former Comintern Emissary*, Calcutta, 1955.

52 IB 320/26 (310/1926), in Raychaudhury (ed.), *The Seed-Time of Communist Movement in Bengal*, pp. 150–51.

53 Ahmad, *Amar Jiban o Bharater Communist Party*, pp. 374–75.

54 Spratt, *Blowing up India*, pp. 40–41. Perhaps he meant the Taj Mahal Hotel, Bombay.

55 Ahmad, *Amar Jiban o Bharater Communist Party*, p. 460. Spratt, *Blowing up India*, p. 41. Roy (ed.), *Communism in India*, pp. 57–58.

[56] Ahmad, *Amar Jiban o Bharater Communist Party*, p. 457. Roy (ed.), *Communism in India*, pp. 56–57.

[57] Ahmad, *Amar Jiban o Bharater Communist Party*, pp. 457, 459–60.

[58] Ibid., p. 355.

[59] Adhikary (ed.), *Documents*, Volume III C, 1927, pp. 206–15.

[60] Ahmad, *Amar Jiban o Bharater Communist Party*, pp. 368–72, 372–74. G.K. Leiten, *Colonialism, Class and Nation: The Confrontation in Bombay around 1930*, Calcutta, 1984, pp. 102–03. The history of Bhatpara, a large mill-town, has been extensively treated by Subho Basu, *Does Class Matter? Colonial Capital and Workers' Resistance in Bengal, 1890 – 1937*, Oxford, 2004, pp. 74–112.

[61] IB 320/26 (310/1926).

[62] Subodh Roy (ed.), *Communism in India, Unpublished Documents, 1925–1934*, Calcutta, 1998, pp. 42–48.

[63] IB 320/1926(310/26). Ahmad, *Amar Jiban o Bharater Communist Party*, pp. 344–346, 372, 374.

[64] IB file number censored. This file, opened in 1928, concentrated exclusively on Huda.

[65] Ahmad, *Amar Jiban o Bharater Communist Party*, pp. 251, 510–12.

[66] IB 210/27 (23/1927).

[67] Soumendranath Tagore, *Jatri* (Voyager), Calcutta, 1975, pp. 70, 77–78, 80–83, 85–88.

[68] Ahmad, *Amar Jiban o Bharater Communist Party*, pp. 346–47.

[69] Ibid, p. 346.

[70] IB 95/24 (41/1924).

[71] IB 320/1926 (310/26). Ahmad, *Amar Jiban o Bharater Communist Party*, pp. 341, 343.

[72] Sinha, *Jiban Sangram*, pp. 15–16, 18–20.

[73] Ahmad, *Amar Jiban o Bharater Communist Party*, p. 469.

[74] Sinha, *Jiban Sangram*, p. 52.

[75] Williamson, *India and Communism*, edited by Saha, p. 122.

[76] Kali Sen, 'Dharmaghater Smriti' (Memories of Lilooah Strike), *Ganabani*, 27 September 1928.

[77] Ahmad, *Bharater Communist Party Garar Prothom Jug*, pp. 18–19.

[78] Ahmad, 'Amar Pointallish Bacharer Sathi', in Halim, *Nabajibaner Pathe*, pp. 9–10.

[79] IB 210/27 (23/1927).

[80] IB file number censored.

[81] IB file number censored. IB 210/27 (23/1927). Sengupta and Basu (eds.), *Charitabhidhan*, Vol. 1, p. 117.

[82] IB file number censored. IB 210/27 (23/1927). 'Dhakar Narasinghdi Sakha' (Narasinghdi Branch of Dhaka), *Ganabani*, 13 September 1928, reprinted in *Communist Partyr Ardhashatak Purti Smarak Patra* (Fiftieth Anniversary of the Communist Party), A CPI Publication), Calcutta, 1975, pp. 24–25.

[83] IB file number censored.

[84] IB 93/26 (1/1926).

[85] IB 75/27 (34/1927).

[86] Ahmad, *Amar Jiban o Bharater Communist Party*, p. 349.

[87] Sengupta and Basu (eds.), *Charitabhidhan*, Vol. 1, pp. 327–28. Ahmad, *Amar Jiban o Bharater Communist Party*, pp. 463, 479, 481, 491. Shachinandan Chattopadhyay, *Muzaffar Ahmad Smriti* (Memories of Muzaffar Ahmad), Calcutta, 1988, pp. 1–14, 58–73.

[88] Muzaffar Ahmad, *Samakaler Katha* (Story of My Times), 1963, fourth edition 1996, p. 58. Anjan Bera, *Sangbadik Nazrul* (Journalist Nazrul), Calcutta, 1998, p. 13.

[89] Halim, 'Bidrohi Banglar Kobi', in *Nabajibaner Pathe*, p. 136.

[90] IB 93/26 (1/1926).

[91] Ahmad, *Kazi Nazrul Islam: Smritikatha*, p. 190.

[92] IB 93/26 (1/1926).

[93] Ahmad, *Samakaler Katha*, p. 55.

[94] Tagore, *Jatri*, p. 87.

[95] Bera, *Sangbadik Nazrul*, p. 29.

[96] Ahmad, 'Amar Pointallish Bacharer Sathi', in Halim, *Nabajibaner Pathe*, p. 12.

[97] Khaled, *Muzaffar Ahmad*, pp. 19–20, 22.

[98] Anisuzzaman, *Muslim Banglar Samayik Patrika* (List of Bengali Muslim Periodicals), Dhaka, 1969, pp. 398–99.

[99] Ahmad, *Samakaler Katha*, p. 56.

[100] Ahmad, *Bharater Communist Party Garar Prothom Jug*, p. 15.

[101] Anisuzzaman, *Samayik Patrika*, pp. 460–63. Gita Chattopadhyay, *Bangla Samayik Patrikapanji, 1915–1930* (List of Bengali Periodicals), Calcutta, 1994, pp. 240–41.

[102] Anisuzzaman, *Samayik Patrika*, pp. 460–63. Chattopadhyay, *Bangla Samayik Patrikapanji*, pp. 240–41.

[103] IB 210/27 (23/1927). IB file number censored.

[104] Adhikary (ed.), *Documents*, Volume IⅡI C, 1927, pp. 218, 223.

[105] IB 93/26 (1/1926).

[106] IB 320/26 (310/1926).

[107] *Langal* and *Ganabani* (selected years).

[108] Achintyakumar Sengupta, *Kalloljug* (Age of Kallol), Calcutta, first edition 1960, pp. 201–04, 211, 261–63, 265, 268.

[109] Tagore, *Jatri*, p. 99.

[110] Ahmad, *Kazi Nazrul Islam: Smritikatha*, p. 138. Halim, 'Bangla Sahitye Marxbadi Bhabdharar Suchana', in *Nabajibaner Pathe*, p. 121.

[111] Halim, 'Bangla Sahitye Marxbadi Bhabdharar Suchana', in *Nabajibaner Pathe*, pp. 120–21.

[112] IB 320/1926 (310/26).

[113] Sibram Chakraborty, *Moscow banam Pondicherry* (Moscow versus Pondicherry), Calcutta, 1929.

[114] Anisuzzaman, *Samayik Patrika*, pp. 460–63. IB file number censored. Ahmad, *Kazi Nazrul Islam: Smritikatha*, pp. 98–99, 190.

[115] IB file number censored.

[116] Ahmad, *Kazi Nazrul Islam: Smritikatha*, pp. 98–99, 190.

[117] See Anisuzzaman, *Samayik Patrika*, pp. 460–63. Chattopadhyay, *Bangla Samayik Patrikapanji*, pp. 240–41. Gautam Chattopadhyay (ed.), *Sanhati–Langal–Ganabani*, Calcutta, 1992. Muzaffar Ahmad, *Probondho Sangkalan* (Selected Essays), Calcutta, 1970. Muzaffar Ahmad, *Nirbachito Rachana Sangkalan* (Selected Writings), Calcutta, 1976, third edition 1990. Halim, *Nabajibaner Pathe*. Rezaul Karim, 'Jatyabhiman' (Caste Pride), *Ganabani*, 1, 10, B 1334/ 1927. Muzaffar Ahmad, 'Japane Chatroder Biplab Andolan' (Revolutionary Students' Movement in Japan), *Ganabani*, 19 May 1927, reprinted in *Nirbachito Rachana Sangkalan*, pp. 43–44. Abdul Halim, 'Javar Swadhinata Andolan' (Freedom Struggle in Java), *Ganabani*, 1, 21, B 1334 / 1927. Soumendranath Tagore, 'Fascist Italyte Krishakder Abastha' (Condition of Peasants in Fascist Italy), *Ganabani*, 1, 26, B 1334/1927. Mohinimohan Das, 'Dhakar Jubak Samproday' (Youth of Dhaka), *Ganabani*, 1, 27, B 1334/1927.

[118] Anisuzzaman, *Samayik Patrika*, pp. 398–99.

[119] Halim, 'Bidrohi Banglar Kobi', in *Nabajibaner Pathe*, p. 137.

[120] Bera, *Sangbadik Nazrul*, p. 32–34.

[121] Sarkar, *Modern India*, p. 251.

[122] Saratchandra Chatterjee, *Sarat Rachanabali* (Complete Works of Sarat), Vol. 5, Calcutta. 2002, pp. 159–60. Ahmad, *Kazi Nazrul Islam: Smritikatha*, p. 222. IB 320/1926 (310/26).

[123] Ahmad, *Kazi Nazrul Islam: Smritikatha*, pp. 222–23.

[124] Muzaffar Ahmad, 'Bhadrasrenir Manabikata' (Humanity of the Bhadralok), *Ganabani*, 16 June 1927, reprinted in *Probondho Sangkalan* (Selected Essays), pp. 93–95. The political tendency among a section of the Hindu *bhadralok* intelligentsia to promote fascism as an ideal revolutionary experiment from above, found other expressions as well. Translated by Pramathanath Roy and published by Chakraborty, Chatterjee and Co., Paolo Orano's *Mussolini* appeared in 1929. Orano, a fascist academic from Perugia University, championed

Mussolini as a true 'patriot' and condemned Bolshevism. The translator stated in his introduction that it was 'too early' to write off the fascist experiment, though he was aware of the controversy surrounding it. See Pramathanath Roy, *Mussolini*, Calcutta, 1929.

125 'Protikriyashil Forward' (Reactionary Forward), *Ganabani*, 1, 27, B 1334/ 1927. 'Protikriyashil Forward' (Reactionary Forward), *Ganabani*, 1, 30, B 1334/ 1927. 'Forward o Amra' (Forward and Us), *Ganabani*, 1, 28, B 1334/ 1927. 'Rajkumar Aka Noi' (He is not Alone), *Ganabani*, 1, 15, B 1334/ 19 May 1927. 'Bolshevik Atanko' (The Bolshevik Menace), *Ganabani*, 2, 11, B 1335/ 23 August 1928. 'Pulish Julum' (Police Excesses), *Ganabani*, 2, 4, B 1335/1928.

126 IB 320/26 (310/1926).

127 IB file number censored.

128 IB 320/26 (310/1926).

129 Roy (ed.), *Communism in India*, p. 47. IB 320/1926 (310/26). IB file number censored.

130 IB file number censored. Also see Roy (ed.), *Communism in India*, p. 28. Subho Basu, *Does Class Matter? Colonial Capital and Workers' Resistance in Bengal, 1890–1937*, pp. 204–05.

131 For analyses of contemporary communal mobilizations and riots in Calcutta, Bengal districts and India, see Suranjan Das, *Communal Riots in Bengal 1905–1947*, Delhi, 1993, pp. 75–141; Sarkar, *Modern India*, p. 233.

132 Das, *Communal Riots*, pp. 80, 101–02.

133 Ahmad, *Kazi Nazrul Islam: Smritikatha*, p. 197.

134 Das, *Communal Riots*, p. 79.

135 Ahmad, *Kazi Nazrul Islam: Smritikatha*, p. 197.

136 Das, *Communal Riots*, pp. 80, 101–02.

137 Ahmad, *Kazi Nazrul Islam: Smritikatha*, p. 197.

138 Statement of Muzaffar Ahmad, *Meerut Communist Conspiracy Case (1929) Papers*.

139 Ahmad, *Samakaler Katha*, pp. 63–64.

140 Ahmad, *Amar Jiban o Bharater Communist Party*, p. 353.

141 IB 35/26 (2/1926), in Raychaudhury (ed.), *The Seed-Time of Communist Movement in Bengal*, pp. 160–70, 172.

142 Ibid, pp. 172–73.

143 Pramathanath Sanyal, *Mandir o Masjid* (Temple and Mosque), Calcutta, 1926.

144 Anisuzzaman, *Samayik Patrika*, p. 460.

145 Ahmad, *Kazi Nazrul Islam: Smritikatha*, p. 197.

146 Ibid., pp. 201–02. For an account of the contemporary militant nationalist strategy on communalism, including a prominent role played in the final dissolution of the C.R. Das Pact, see D.M. Laushey, *Bengal Terrorism and the Marxist Left, Aspects of Regional Nationalism in India, 1905–1942*, Calcutta, 1975, pp. 41, 45–47.

147 Tagore, *Jatri*, pp. 93–97.

148 Das, *Communal Riots*, p. 88.

149 Tagore, *Jatri*, pp. 93–97. Ahmad, *Kazi Nazrul Islam: Smritikatha*, p. 197.

150 IB 320/26 (310/1926).

151 *Kanpur Communist Conspiracy Case (1924) Papers*.

152 IB file number censored.

153 Ahmad, *Amar Jiban o Bharater Communist Party*, p. 461.

154 IB 210/27 (23/1927).

155 IB 210/27 (23/1927).

156 IB 320/1926 (310/26). Sinha, *Jiban Sangram*, p. 52.

157 IB 320/1926 (310/26).

158 IB file number censored.

159 IB 320/26 (310/1926).

160 IB file number censored.

161 Ahmad, *Kazi Nazrul Islam: Smritikatha*, p. 201.

162 IB 210/27(23/1927).

163 IB file number censored.

[164] IB 210/27(23/1927). IB file number censored.

[165] Ahmad, *Kazi Nazrul Islam: Smritikatha*, p. 201.

[166] Ahmad, *Bharater Communist Party Garar Prothom Jug*, p. 17.

[167] Amiya Kumar Bagchi, *Private Investment in India 1900–1939*, Delhi, 1980, pp. 199, 208, 278–79. Sarkar, *Modern India*, pp. 238–39, 279–81.

[168] Das, *Communal Riots*, pp. 75–76.

[169] Sarkar, *Bengal 1928–1934*, p. 49. Sarkar , *Modern India*, p. 239.

[170] Ahmad, *Kazi Nazrul Islam: Smritikatha*, pp. 206–07.

[171] IB 320/26 (310/1926).

[172] IB 210/27 (23/1927).

[173] Ahmad, *Amar Jiban o Bharater Communist Party*, p. 463.

[174] IB 210/27 (23/1927).

[175] Ahmad, *Amar Jiban*, pp. 463–64, 471.

[176] IB 210/27 (23/1927).

[177] Roy (ed.), *Communism in India*, pp. 42–48.

[178] Sukomal Sen, *Working Class of India, History of Emergence and Movement, 1830–1970*, Calcutta, 1977, pp. 232–78. Sarkar, *Modern India*, pp. 269–70.

[179] Ahmad, *Amar Jiban o Bharater Communist Party*, pp. 465–66. For an organizer's account of the railway workers' strike, see Appendix A:1, Interview with Gopen Chakraborty, in Gautam Chattopadhyay, *Communism and Bengal's Freedom Movement*, Bombay, 1970, pp. 136–41.

[180] Ahmad, *Amar Jiban o Bharater Communist Party*, pp. 469–70.

[181] IB 210/27 (23/1927).

[182] IB file number censored.

[183] IB 210/27 (23/1927).

[184] Ibid.

[185] IB file number censored.

[186] Ahmad, *Amar Jiban o Bharater Communist Party*, pp. 471–79.

[187] IB file number censored.

[188] Ahmad, *Amar Jiban o Bharater Communist Party*, pp. 471–79. IB 320/26 (310/1926).

[189] IB 210/27 (23/1927).

[190] Ahmad, *Amar Jiban o Bharater Communist Party*, pp. 471–79. IB 210/27 (23/1927).

[191] *Report on Municipal Administration of Calcutta*, 1928–29.

[192] 'Annual Report of the Police Administration of the Town of Calcutta and its Suburbs. For the year 1928 by Sir Charles Tegart, Commissioner of Police, Calcutta.'

[193] Ahmad, *Amar Jiban o Bharater Communist Party*, pp. 471–84. Chattopadhyay, *Muzaffar Ahmad Smriti*, pp. 58–73.

[194] Ahmad, *Amar Jiban o Bharater Communist Party*, pp. 471–84.

[195] IB 320/26 (310/1926).

[196] IB file number censored.

[197] Ahmad, *Amar Jiban o Bharater Communist Party*, pp. 485–96. For oral testimonies of class militancy, see Sanat Bose, 'Two Old Jute Strikers of Bauria and Chengile (1928–29)', in *Essays on Indian Labour*, Calcutta, 1996, pp. 89–97; Subho Basu, *Does Class Matter? Colonial Capital and Workers' Resistance in Bengal, 1890–1937*, pp. 199–208; Mrinal Kanti Bose, *Smritikatha* (Recollections), Calcutta, 1949, pp. 209–10.

[198] IB 210/27 (23/1927). Ahmad, *Bharater Communist Party Garar Prothom Jug*, p. 18.

[199] Ahmad, *Amar Jiban o Bharater Communist Party*, pp. 493–96. For historical treatments of Bombay workers, see Richard Newman, *Workers and Unions in Bombay 1918–1929: A study of organization in the cotton mills*, Canberra, 1981; G.K. Leiten, *Colonialism, Class and Nation: The Confrontation in Bombay around 1930*, Calcutta, 1984; Rajnarayan Chandavarkar, *The origins of industrial capitalism in India: business strategies and the working classes in Bombay, 1900–1940*, Cambridge, 1992.

[200] IB 320/26 (310/1926).

[201] Interview with Gopen Chakraborty, in Chattopadhyay, *Communism and Bengal's Freedom Movement*, p. 139.

[202] For a reading of working-class consciousness as essentially sectional, see Dipesh Chakraborty, *Rethinking Working-Class History, Bengal 1890 to 1940*, Princeton, 2000. The most recent contestation of this position has been offered by Subho Basu in *Does Class Matter?*. For a critique of the historigraphic tendency which emphasizes the sectional identities of workers, rather than the dualism of 'class-for-itself' and 'class-in-itself' as manifested through the contradictions evident in developing solidarities on the basis of class consciousness, see Sumit Sarkar, 'From Class-Struggle to Identity Politics: Problematizing a Transition', *Calcutta Historical Journal*, Vols. 19–20, 1997–98. For an analytical framework to restore class as a key concept in understanding 'the biography of labour', see Amiya Kumar Bagchi, 'Workers and the Historians' Burden', in K.N. Panikkar, Terence J. Byres and Utsa Patnaik (eds.), *The Making of History: Essays Presented to Irfan Habib*, Delhi, 2000, pp. 276–327.

[203] IB file number censored.

[204] IB 320/26 (310/1926) in Raychaudhury (ed.), *The Seed-Time of Communist Movement in Bengal*, pp. 150–51.

[205] IB 320/26 (310/1926).

[206] Roy (ed.), *Communism in India*, pp. 52, 55.

[207] IB 210/27 (23/1927).

[208] Roy, Datta Gupta and Vasudevan (eds.), *Indo-Russian Relations 1917–1947, Part I: 1917–1928*, pp. 342–46. IB 75/27 (34/1927).

[209] IB 75/27 (34/1927).

[210] Statement of PW 249, *Meerut Communist Conspiracy Case (1929) Papers*.

[211] Statement of PW 233, *Meerut Communist Conspiracy Case (1929) Papers*.

[212] Roy, Datta Gupta and Vasudevan (eds.), *Indo-Russian Relations 1917–1947, Part I: 1917–1928*, pp. 342–46.

[213] IB 320/26 (310/1926).

[214] *Meerut Communist Conspiracy Case (1929) Papers*.

[215] Ahmad, *Amar Jiban o Bharater Communist Party*, pp. 350–51.

[216] Sarkar, *Modern India*, p. 269–70.

[217] The experiences of these activists have been treated in Chapter Five.

[218] Mukhopadhyay, *Bharater Communist Party o Amra*, pp. 17–18. Satis Pakrasi, *Agnijuger Katha* (The Burning Times), Calcutta, third edition 1982, p. 129. Naresh Bannerjee, 'Prokhyato Communist Neta Comrade Bankim Mukherjeer Janmoshatobarsho Upolokhye Sradhargho' (My Respects to Comrade Bankim Mukherjee at the Centenary of his Birth), in Chittabroto Majumder *et al.* (eds.), *Biplabi Nayak Bankim Mukherjee* (The Revolutionary Hero Bankim Mukherjee), Calcutta, 1998, pp. 89–91.

[219] Statement of PW 233, *Meerut Communist Conspiracy Case (1929) Papers*.

[220] Sarkar, *Modern India*, pp. 269–70, 283–84.

[221] Ahmad, *Amar Jiban o Bharater Communist Party*, pp. 520–21.

[222] IB 210/27 (23/1927).

[223] Khaled, *Muzaffar Ahmad*, pp. 36–38. For a brief account of the YCL, focusing on the activities of its members during 1929–31, see Amitabha Chandra, *Abibhakta Banglay Communist Andolan: Suchana Parbo* (Communist Movement in Undivided Bengal: The First Phase), Calcutta, 1992, pp. 8, 89–110.

[224] John Berwick, 'Chatra Samaj: The Social and Political Significance of the Student Community in Bengal *c.* 1870–1922', unpublished Ph.D. thesis, University of Sydney, 1986.

[225] Sengupta and Basu (eds.), *Charitabhidhan*, Vol. 1, p. 530.

[226] Priyonath Ganguly's *Lenin o Soviet* (1929) contained a bold advertisement of his book, *Biplab o Chatrasamaj* (Revolution and Students).

[227] Priyonath Ganguly, *Estar Bidroho o Gorila Juddho* (Easter Rising and Guerrilla War), Calcutta, 1929.

[228] Priyonath Ganguly, *Lenin o Soviet* (Lenin and the Soviet), Calcutta, 1929.

[229] Anjan Bera, *Banglay Marxbadi Prokashonar Prothom Parbo* (First Phase of Marxist Publications in Bengal), Calcutta, 2000, p. 10.

[230] Sengupta and Basu (eds.), *Charitabhidhan*, Vol. 1, p. 78.

[231] IB 210/27 (23/1927).

[232] IB 320/26 (310/1926).

[233] IB 95/24 (41/1924).

[234] Roy (ed.), *Communism in India*, pp. 42–48.

[235] IB 210/27 (23/1927). IB 320/26 (310/1926).

[236] IB 210/27 (23/1927).

[237] Mukhopadhyay, *Bharater Communist Party o Amra*, pp. 11, 16, 18, 28–29, 46.

[238] IB 320/1926 (310/26). Ranen Sen, *Bharater Communist Partyr Itibritta* (An Account of the Indian Communist Party), Calcutta, 1996, pp. 18–23, 215.

[239] IB 320/26 (310/1926).

[240] Roy, Datta Gupta and Vasudevan (eds.), *Indo-Russian Relations 1917–1947*, pp. 298–301.

[241] Ibid. pp. 342–346.

[242] IB file number censored.

[243] Aditya Mukherjee, 'The Workers' and Peasants' Parties, 1926–30: An Aspect of Communism in India' in Bipan Chandra (ed.), *The Indian Left: Critical Appraisals*, New Delhi, 1983.

[244] These aspects have been discussed in the next chapter.

[245] Statement of Muzaffar Ahmad, *Meerut Communist Conspiracy Case (1929) Papers*.

CHAPTER FIVE

Constraints

'we'll still laugh at the jokes being told,
we'll look out the window to see if its raining,
or still wait anxiously

. . .

about the outcome of the war, which could last years.'
                                    – Nazim Hikmet, 'On Living'

The constraints exercised on early left politics in Bengal, as shaped by Muzaffar Ahmad and his colleagues, suggest that multilayered contradictions existed both within and outside the 'subjective' arena of the movement. What were the identifiable tendencies, despite the potential, that hindered the growth of the first socialist organization and the nascent communist party from the mid-1920s to early 1929? Were the ideological understanding of society and approach to politics the chief impediments? An analysis of the principal defects points towards a restricted practical reach, a limitation that could be partially explained by occlusions in theory and practice; internal differences and ever-present financial worries; opposition from competing and more entrenched political formations based on ideologies of 'nation' and 'community'; and the renewed repression unleashed by the colonial state after a brief interval. Communists and socialists were late entrants in a political sphere where other currents already existed. Since they offered opposition to different facets of colonialism and social relations, the task of establishing political hegemony over different political constituencies and class segments proved difficult. Too weak to overturn the organized influences exercised by the Bengal Congress, the middle-class revolutionary groups, and agrarian movements dominated by proprietor interests and communalism, the left faced hostility and competition; it was also persecuted by the state as the most extreme form of opposition to the rule of private property and colonial capital.

Rural Base

The defection of early members from the districts to *praja* politics significantly weakened the early promise of the development of an agrarian base.
The Executive Committee of the PWP formed in 1926 was reconstituted in
1927, and again in 1928. Its changing composition led the police officials
in charge of surveillance to wonder: 'What happened to all these Muslim
members. . . . Did they drop out? If so,why?'[1] By 1927 Moulavi Shamsuddin
Ahmad, former Congress leader, and his brother Afsaruddin Ahmad, were
advancing the interests of *jotedar*s and lower-middle-class Muslims in
Kusthea; their campaign was directed against zamindars, *mahajan*s and
Marwari traders, identifying them as Hindu interests. Shamsuddin, along
with Azizur Rahman and Shah Abdul Hamid, the other early members,
dropped out, and emerged as prominent spokesmen of the lower-middle-
class faction of the *praja* movement in their subsequent careers.[2]

The PWP was unable to convince these Muslim activists, alienated by
Swarajism following the collapse of the C.R. Das Pact, to abandon proprietor interests and advance the cause of the share-croppers and the landless.
They had been attracted to a formation like the Labour-Swaraj Party of the
Indian National Congress since it represented a populist coalition. Forged
in the wake of the anti-colonial mass movement of the late 1910s and the
early 1920s, it was directed against the entrenched high-caste Hindu rural
proprietors represented by the Swarajists. But the transition to a 'Peasants
and Workers Party' led by the communists alienated them. Though the communists were in a minority at the conference where the new name was adopted, within the PWP, with its headquarters in Calcutta, a leftist perspective
rather than proprietorial populism was on the ascendant. When Pyar Mohammad of Mymensingh sent *Ganabani* a list of potential Bengali Muslim readers, he suggested that the 'prices of jute and other things' should be included
to make the paper popular.[3] Probably keeping such demands in mind, Muzaffar told his younger friend Moinuddin that the print-organ was not for
those who wished to profit from the rise and fall in jute prices.[4] Hemantakumar wrote to Muzaffar on the eve of the Peasant Conference organized
by WPP members and held at Kusthea in February 1929: 'I am getting no
help from the Hindus here . . . a section of the Muhammedans is against us
. . . Congress Party is carrying on propaganda against us.' The Swarajist
Forward, upholding the Congress position to support Hindu landlords and
proprietors in the countryside, also refused to publish the notice of the conference, and Afsaruddin displayed an open hostility through his local paper
Azad. At the Nadia Branch of the Bengal Rayat Conference floated by ex-
members Afsaruddin, Shamsuddin and Rajibuddin Tarafdar, speeches were
directed against the leftist peasant conference organized by Hemantakumar.[5]

The low turnout of peasants at the Kusthea Conference was, according to the police, due to deliberate abstention of Afsaruddin's party: 'Consequently the attendance of real cultivators . . . was very few.'[6]

Among the already existing hurdles in the path of agrarian socialism was the contradictory political consciousness of confused activists drawn from the middle classes. 'Habi', Muzaffar's correspondent from Dinajpur and recipient of *Ganabani,* wrote in August 1926 that his attempts to organize peasants were not successful; the reason, he felt, was that they were 'illiterate', and 'cannot distinguish between good and bad'. This reveals Habi's own confusion more than any problem of illiteracy. A dearth of activists crippled growth. During the Bhatpara Conference of WPP in March–April 1928, Faizuddin moved the resolution on peasants. Though this was unanimously accepted, no one could be elected 'Secretary of the Peasant's Group'.[7] Muzaffar's correspondence with Faizuddin towards the end of 1928 revealed persistent concern over the absence of a peasant front. The failure to secure a firm foothold in the countryside meant the peasantry, the bulk of the toilers, would remain outside the reach of the organization. In late 1928 and early 1929, Muzaffar and Hemantakumar were aiming to alter this situation; they were concentrating on building a rural organization in the form of a 'Peasant League', when the Meerut arrests in March 1929 abruptly halted their efforts.

Missing Members

As Muzaffar himself admitted, the inability to build a party of the masses was underlined by low recruitment from the ranks of the most exploited class segments and victims of social hierarchy. Though women workers displayed initiative and militancy during the scavengers' strike and other struggles led by the WPP, recruitment of women was never made a priority. While making a speedy exit after the retaliation by female scavengers of Howrah, the police sergeants sent to drag them back to work were heard muttering that they would not return to those slums unless they were authorized to shoot. During his trip to Bombay in 1928, Muzaffar noted the confidence of women workers on the picket-line.[8] In one of his early essays on decolonization, he argued that the country and the society cannot be regarded as 'monopoly possessions' of men; for long, men had deprived women of what belongs to them.[9] The communists were guided by the theoretical conviction that forms of social exploitation were not synonymous with class contradictions, even though these were integral to the working of class society and had to be part of the struggle of the dispossessed for self-emancipation. Yet they could only come up with a short critique of patriarchal institutions in their 'joint statement' at Meerut. In answer to the charge of the prosecu-

tion that communism opposed god, family and morality, they were to respond: '. . . under Socialism only will the use of the family for the exploitation of women and children cease. . . . And generally we consider that the
tendency towards the loosening of the ties of the family is a desirable thing
for the cultural future of society.'

On the existing 'position of women' they argued:

> [The] status of women has been traditionally one of inferiority to men, and at
> times of actual slavery. Under Capitalism there is a certain tendency towards
> restricted equality and communists oppose 'traditional bars' on women such
> as inequality in wage-rates, relative deprivation of education and institutions
> like the 'Purdah'. But complete emancipation of women is tied up with the
> emancipation of the great majority of those under subjection and exploita-
> tion.

The solution had to be on class lines, involving 'the establishment of complete equality between the sexes within the working class movement, and
the abolition of prejudices in the matter among the working class', 'the recognition of housewives as a category of workers of the highest importance,
and the encouragement of struggle by them for the improvement of their
position', 'the drawing of working women into the active working class
fight against Capitalism'. The communists rejected 'bourgeois morality'
which, they stressed, was 'an ideological means for waging . . . struggle
against the proletariat'.[10]

This reading, though seminal, was incomplete, indicating occlusion in
theory and practice. The analysis highlighted the general relationship between neo-traditional social practices and institutions; aspects of patriarchy
and sexism that were crucial to the functioning of existing society; and the
active confinement of women to subordinate and oppressive roles. Crucial-
ly missing were a nuanced understanding and a matching social politics.
There is also little evidence to suggest that any concrete strategy of mobilizing women on the basis of these insights was undertaken at this stage.
Despite social interactions with women in the families of PWP/WPP members, and political connections with women activists and workers in the
course of industrial strikes, the first socialists built an all-male organization.
Prabhabati Dasgupta, the sole female organizer working with WPP members, never joined; she remained a 'progressive nationalist'.[11]

Muzaffar held that the possibility of 'mass recruitment' of workers into
the WPP and CPI emerged for the first time during the strike-wave of 1928,
and 'political demands' on behalf of the working class were raised through
labour activism.[12] The WPP considered opening branches of the Scavengers'
Union in every town and gaining entry into local politics through them.
Despite an enthusiastic response from below, the aim of expanding this

union was thwarted by lack of funds and full-time organizers, as well as surveillance and police harassment.[13] Muzaffar observed in a Meerut court-room in 1931 that the task of drawing members to the CPI through 'the Trade Union Movement' was also made difficult by 'bourgeois reformists who had been preaching class collaboration'. Through the WPP, CPI members concentrated on the working-class movement and gave it 'a militant shape'. Consequently, by 1929, the possibility of recruiting members from almost every trade union arose, and a 'very powerful Communist Party' could emerge 'in the near future'.[14] Major repression on the labour front, including arrests of the principal organizers, prevented immediate realization of this optimistic plan.

The Irrepressible Attraction of Firearms

Nor did attempts to recruit the young intelligentsia evoke a favourable response. Muzaffar criticized the Young Comrades League (YCL) in his statement before the court during the Meerut trial. Though formed under the auspices of the WPP and meant to be 'a combined organization' of young workers and young intellectuals, he felt it started as and remained an organization of the 'young petty bourgeois'. It could not serve the purpose the WPP wanted.[15] Besides, the nationalist ideology still exercised a firm political hold, even over those who had a tendency to stray from its social programmes. After the suppression of militant nationalist organizations through large-scale detention of principal figures in 1924, the veteran leaders of Anushilan and Jugantar increasingly asserted themselves through mutual recrimination over strategy, competition over recruitment, support for different Congress factions, and Hindu *bhadralok* communal politics.[16] Muzaffar was to witness a scene of intense acrimony between rival groups at a Special Youth Conference in Dhaka, where he spoke against revolutionary terrorism and advocated class-conscious politics as an alternative to middle-class militancy.[17] But the ideological hold of Hindu revivalism and the cult of heroic self-sacrifice persisted, and continued to attract middle-class youth to the idea of a Hindu *bhadralok*-led revolution from above.

A small minority among the younger generation, disgusted by the factionalism of leaders and impressed by mass upheavals from below, rejected the political culture of secret societies and joined the PWP/WPP. There were others who were not immune to the lure and lores of revolutionary nationalism: they tried fusing the politics of individual terror with the aim of building socialism. This tiny stream, known as 'terro-communism', could not make much headway.[18] Shachindranath Sanyal published a red leaflet drawing on both terrorism and communism.[19] Batukeswar Datta, involved in the Howrah scavengers' strike, was convicted for throwing a bomb in the

Assembly alongside Bhagat Singh in April 1929. Inspired by the Russian Revolution, and strikes in Calcutta, Bombay and Kanpur, Datta, Bhagat Singh and others had formed the Hindusthan Socialist Republican Army.[20] As yet, 'socialism' as interpreted by these revolutionaries excluded the masses. The radical pull of terrorist and socialist methods from two directions made Datta choose the former. His ideological outlook and social programme were significantly different from those inspired by religious revivalism since he had first-hand knowledge of workers' struggles; nevertheless, he subscribed to the idea that a small band of revolutionaries could effectively overthrow the existing order through acts of individual terror.

Potential activists were searching for a political cocktail of mass politics and romantic violence. Saroj Mukherjee, who later became a leading communist from Bengal, was drawn to Congress nationalism, revolutionary terrorism and socialist initiatives. His friend Benay Chaudhuri, who also later emerged as a legendary communist and peasant leader, was attracted to socialism but became enmeshed in terrorist activities at this stage. Abani Chaudhuri, a fringe member of the first socialist nucleus and a communist organizer during the early 1930s, harboured deep reservations towards his cousin Benay Chaudhuri's associates. When they first met in Abdul Halim's presence in 1931, Abani made it clear to Mukherjee that people who maintained links with the politics of 'bombs and pistols' had no place in the communist party. [21] Many were drawn towards communism but returned to the terrorist fold during the late 1920s. Satis Pakrasi was to join the CPI after his release from prison in the late 1930s, having convinced himself that Muzaffar and Halim were better revolutionaries. Yet in 1928 he believed that socialist and communist thinking could be combined with mainstream Congress and revolutionary nationalist methods. [22]

The attempted merger of Jugantar and Anushilan in the later half of the 1920s also stopped the flow of ex-terrorist cadre into the communist party.[23] One of the preconditions to unity set by the Anushilan leaders was termination of all connections with communism. Consequently, Bhupendrakumar Datta, a prominent figure of the first socialist nucleus in 1922, despite their personal friendship, never saw Muzaffar again. By that time the early communists had been clearly identified by the *dada*s (terrorist leaders) as their ideological rivals.[24]

Communalism

Rising communalism, a vital ingredient of Swarajist, Hindu *bhadralok* revolutionary and Muslim *jotedar*-dominated *praja* politics, was gaining ground during the second half of the 1920s. As organized sectarian violence buried the coalition among different class segments, the expansion of the leftist current suffered. The defects in the left's campaign against communal forces were intertwined with its weak political base and restricted practical reach. The leftists were competing with more entrenched formations, socially and politically institutionalized under colonial rule. Though the communists analysed the social content of these ideologies in order to resist them,[25] a left mass base was non-existent in 1926, when major rioting engulfed Calcutta. By 1928, WPP activists were involved in campaigns to prevent communal clashes in working-class areas of the city where they had gained entry through strike-actions. However, the rural areas of Bengal remained virtually untouched since the political presence of the left there was either non-existent or very weak. Though ideologically committed to fight communalism, the PWP/WPP was not organizationally strong enough to stem the rising tide of exclusivist religious mobilization. Its potential political constituency displayed increasing signs of polarization; the inability to build a mass movement on class lines which could replace and resist other formations meant that those whom the leftists were unable to reach would be organized along communal lines.

Serajur Rahman's political conundrum indicated the growing marginalization of non-communal forces. Serajur informed Muzaffar in 1928 that his refusal to accommodate communal politics had isolated him from both Hindus and Muslims. *Desher Bani*, a nationalist paper that had displayed sympathy for Bolshevism in the early 1920s, which Serajur helped edit, was taken over by local Hindu Mahasabha elements in Noakhali. Forced to leave, Serajur was unable to publicize his expulsion lest it encourage Muslim communal forces.[26] The first socialist organization antagonized all sections of rural proprietor interests by declaring war against 'the government, the zamindars, the mahajans, the brokers, the lawyers and the mullahs'. While mobilization on vertical lines by Muslim *jotedar* elements obstructed left inroads among the share-croppers and the landless,[27] the Hindu communal press projected the PWP as a conspiracy by Muzaffar and other communists to downplay and defend Muslim communalism; they were able to convince their readership that class struggle was an alien concept invented to attack Hindu *bhadralok* interests.

Opposition to communalism directly affected the circulation of the socialist journal. The initial popularity of *Langal* among the Hindu Bengali intelligentsia fell sharply when the paper attacked *bhadralok* nationalism and Hindu communal politics. After the communal riots of 1926, to regain Hindu readers who were prejudiced against a paper edited by a man with an Arabic name, Pyarimohan Das's name was strategically inserted alongside Muzaffar's, although Das did not have any role in the paper. In 1928, police reports observed: 'The *Langal* had at first a large circulation which rapidly dwindled, and now the *Ganabani* has to be distributed free to be widely

read.'[28] Soumendranath reported to the Comintern that *Langal* was pheno-
menally successful among students and the middle classes in Calcutta. Sales
dropped in the city in the climate of Hindu–Muslim riots as the paper
refused to accommodate communal politics.[29]

Other Obstacles to Print Communism

Despite their radical anti-state content, *Langal* and *Ganabani* initially es-
caped prosecution. Internal reports of the police complained: '"Ganabani",
the organ of the WPP, Bengal, since reappearance, is carrying on its usual
tirade against a capitalist form of Govt and exploitation . . . quoting several
Bolshevik leaders. . . . The tone of the paper is distinctly objectionable but is
not considered actionable by the Public Prosecutor.'[30]

One reason why 'action' may not have been taken by the judiciary was
the temporary lull in censorship. This relaxed attitude of the state was abandoned in the face of renewed and vigorous anti-colonial opposition in 1929.[31]
That year, *Lal Paltan* stopped publication after Bimal Ganguly, its editor,
was jailed; it had started in 1928, following the Lilooah strike, to consolidate the communist influence over workers.[32]

Financial crises proved more difficult to overcome. Despite a promising
start, lack of funds contributed to *Langal*'s eclipse in early 1926.[33] *Ganabani*
too had 'a chequered career'.[34] The paper's poor finances during the rising
tide of communalism made Muzaffar extremely anxious in late 1926. Consequently, its publication was suspended[35], till it reappeared again in April
1927.[36] After its name was changed to *Ganabani*, the paper's circulation
dwindled to 1,000;[37] the loss of a communalized Hindu *bhadralok* readership in the city and distaste for class struggle among those turning to Muslim *praja* politics in the countryside meant that sales suffered. The 'Annual
Report' of the CPI in 1927 expressed the hope that, despite financial difficulties and the 'wrecked health of Muzaffar', *Ganabani* would 'go a long
way in promoting the proletarian cause in the province'.[38] Yet, after October 1927, printing was again suspended. The paper reappeared in June 1928,
but by the end of that year, it had ceased publication altogether.[39] Muzaffar
wrote to Soumendranath in September 1928 that this irregularity alienated
readers who were unwilling to subscribe, and advertisers were also no longer
interested. He despaired that people had 'lost faith in it'. He implied that
many were afraid of associating with a political journal under constant
scrutiny of the law.[40]

Lack of personnel also plagued the paper. Kali Sen, who replaced Das
and became its co-editor in 1928, displayed a more active interest;[41] still,
the pressure of running the publication often had to be shouldered solely by
Muzaffar. When the CPI entrusted the Calcutta communists to publish a

central organ of the CPI in December 1928, it acknowledged the importance of the work done by the Bengal PWP/WPP to promote radical journalism. Muzaffar was given an additional political duty of offering a Marxist
critique of popular Bengali and Hindi papers in its pages, since he was
already active in this field through *Ganabani*.[42] However this project too
drowned, alongside many other programmes of expansion, in the turmoil
of the Meerut arrests.

Differences

Differences over ideology and political direction generated constraints. The
trade union movement became a site of contest, leading to ruptures with
non-communist labour leaders. Intensification of hostilities between the
nationalists and the communists over class, property and future social organization strengthened the left perspective on an alternative decolonization.
At a practical level, responsibilities became a source of tension among the
principal activists within the organization. Muzaffar's relationship with the
former Anushilan activists was severely strained during this period, resulting
in their aborted attempts to replace him as the leading figure within the
Bengal WPP and the CPI. The tussle over leadership also revealed differences over strategy; absence of clear-cut mechanisms to tide over factional
strife; and confusion over what constituted the 'inside' and the 'outside' of
the CPI at a time when the actual size of the party was minute. Lack of
coordination between exiled communists from India and communists in
India, exacerbated by the ever-present state surveillance, also contributed to
misunderstandings and disagreements. The CPI differed with prominent
members of the CPGB who visited India. Muzaffar expressed this collective
displeasure to the Comintern, and also disagreed with M.N. Roy over organization, strategy and the situation on the ground. These complicated encounters overlapped, creating additional pressures to the expansion of the social
base of communism through the WPP.

At the Factory Gates
Each strike-action threatened to become a battle for hegemony. Communists and socialists belonging to the WPP often found themselves at odds
with independent and nationalist trade unionists, since they differed on
ways of fighting capital and mobilizing workers. There were personal differences too; these, however, were epiphenomenal, rooted as they were in political divergences over class politics. Muzaffar's critical observations in the
court, as the principal defendant at Meerut, on his non-communist, trade
unionist colleagues, contributed in no small measure to their acquittal. As
before, communists viewed a section of the syndicalists as allies; others were

seen as opponents during 1927–28. Huda, Muzaffar and Halim felt that Mohammad Daud and Mukundalal Sarkar deliberately obstructed the WPP's influence among seamen.[43] K.C. Mitra opposed the formation of a democratic union managed by a strike committee; Muzaffar interpreted this as a sign of despotism. Mitra's telegram to the Profintern, the trade union front of the Comintern, requesting immediate financial assistance for the Lilooah strike, and using Spratt's and Muzaffar's name without their permission, was perceived as misappropriation of funds to line his own pockets.[44] Halim felt that Mitra partially contributed to the failure of the Lilooah strike.[45] Huda informed the Comintern that the failure was due to Mitra's tactlessness and autocracy, and felt that money should be sent only after prior consultation with local comrades.[46]

Muzaffar regarded the role of the nationalist trade unionists as less than satisfactory when it came to advocating working-class interests. He felt that Kishorilal Ghosh and Mrinalkanti Bose, who were active in the Scavengers' Union and lawyers by training, should have advised the workers, who had faced extreme harassment in the course of the strike, to take proper legal precautions when negotiating with the Calcutta Municipal Corporation; instead, they had been keen on engineering a compromise. Muzaffar also accused Ghosh of misusing funds for his personal expenses during the Bauria strike; Ghosh denied this.[47] As one of the accused at Meerut, Ghosh claimed that he saw himself as a socialist and was willing to cooperate with the communists. However he was not ill-disposed towards evolution through political reforms. Muzaffar in turn emphasized that his difference with Ghosh 'was certainly not on a personal matter'. Repudiating the prosecution's 'sudden brain-wave' of projecting Ghosh as his 'personal enemy', he pointed out that their disagreements were political, and that *Ganabani*, under his editorship, had published articles such as 'Senseless Leadership' and 'Amritabazar Patrika's Love for Birla' where Ghosh was criticized.[48] In a letter to Spratt in January 1928, Muzaffar mentioned the 'obstructions' placed by Daud and Ghosh, who, despite 'differences amongst themselves', were 'quite at one in keeping communists . . . out of the labour movement'.[49]

Shibnath Banerjee, an independent socialist working with the AITUC, was accused by Muzaffar of gross negligence which resulted in the arrest, imprisonment and deportation of George Allison. Muzaffar suspected Shibnath's friend and president of the Bengal Jute Workers Association (BJWA), Kalidas Bhattacharya, 'a man suffering from great want', as the person most likely to have tipped off the police.[50] Nalini Gupta also held Kalidas and Shibnath responsible for Allison's arrest.[51] During the Bhatpara Conference of 1928, Kalidas was among those who tried to prevent Muzaffar from becoming general secretary of the WPP.[52] When Kalidas joined the WPP and affiliated the BJWA to it, Shibnath furiously opposed this. He felt that no help could be obtained from the All-India Trade Union Congress (AITUC) if the Association was connected with the WPP. By 1929, regular quarrels with Shibnath in this connection and the absence of any concrete benefit convinced Kalidas to resign from the party.[53]

Definition and Distribution of Work

Within the WPP, the definition and distribution of political work generated serious tensions. In Muzaffar's opinion, Kutubuddin, Hemantakumar and A.R. Khan were unable to fulfil their organizational duties as office-bearers; the day-to-day running of the organization and its journal had become an enormous responsibility, which no one save Halim was willing to share with him.[54] Nalini Gupta, in a letter to Roy in 1927, denounced most of his comrades as money-grabbing and incompetent.[55] Muzaffar thought that Nalini was a source of endless 'pain' and that he probably acted as a police informer before departing for Europe. Anushilan activists who joined the PWP also earned Muzaffar's antipathy.[56] Anushilan championed Hindu communalism as daily social practice by consciously excluding Muslims through a special clause in its constitution.[57] This may have added to Muzaffar's sense of discomfort, along with his knowledge of the factional character of Bengal terrorism. Activists with an Anushilan background tried, though unsuccessfully, to prevent Muzaffar from becoming the General Secretary of the Bengal WPP. Muzaffar thought that Goswami and others deliberately fostered a rift at the behest of the Anushilan leadership.[58] In his report to the Comintern, Huda declared that he was pleased with the Labour Secretary (Goswami) but 'extremely disappointed with the work of the General Secretary of the Bengal Party' (Muzaffar).[59] Huda also complained, at the secret CPI Conference held in Calcutta, that he felt 'neglected' by Muzaffar who tended to unfairly charge him with making 'mistakes'. Spratt and Bradley were entrusted to look into his complaint.[60] Spratt thought that those from Anushilan acted as a bloc to break up the All-India WPP Conference for factional rather than 'doctrinal' reasons.[61] Contemporary police reports suggested the possibility of a 'serious split' during the conference spearheaded by 'a section of the Bengal group, led by Goswami and Gopen Chakraborty': 'These two have, for some time past, expressed dissatisfaction with Muzaffar Ahmad's conduct of the Party's affairs. Though temporary reconciliation was effected between the rival groups, it would appear that personal jealousies and petty dissensions are hindering the smooth working of the Party and may lead later to an open breach.'[62] Chakraborty later held that the WPP Conference nearly broke up over the choice of leadership, though 'unity' prevailed in the end.[63]

The confrontations at the conference generated further bitterness. Hemantakumar's letters to Muzaffar in January 1929 revealed a mood of despair over the infighting. However, Hemantakumar displayed willingness to 'openly' talk to the discontented elements, which may have helped restore 'unity'. Gopal Basak, in his letters to Muzaffar in February and March 1929, agreed that every member had defects and that grievances needed to be aired to clear the atmosphere. He was therefore 'shortly coming over to Calcutta to meet you all'.[64] This goodwill visit never happened. Basak met his argumentative comrades not in Calcutta but in Meerut, when they stood forcibly united at the dock, charged as conspirators aiming to deprive the King-Emperor of his sovereignty over British India.

Via Europe

The coordination between the CPI, the CPGB, the Comintern and Indian communists abroad sparked confusion and dissatisfaction. The CPI members working in India, Roy from his bases in Berlin and Zurich, the Foreign Bureau of the CPI manned chiefly by Mohammad Ali in Paris, the CPGB trying to establish communication with India, and the Comintern executive with headquarters in Moscow, were all supposed to function as complementary units. In practice, as mentioned above, they suffered from chronic gaps in communication and analysis. Colonial censorship and surveillance enforced clandestine functioning, increasing the scope for misunderstanding and distrust.

The initial conflicts between the CPGB and Roy over work in India[65] convinced Roy that the British communists, particularly Saklatvala and Allison, were deliberately ignoring the work started in India at his initiative on behalf of the Comintern. Saklatvala's visit to India and interactions with the CPI leadership further complicated matters. In a letter to Roy in January 1927, Muzaffar complained that Saklatvala refused 'to acknowledge the existence' of communists in India and advocated the formal dissolution of the CPI; and that the 'British comrades' were against direct communication between the CPI and the Comintern. According to Muzaffar, the Indian communists belonged to an organization which, though not formally affiliated to the Comintern, had paid dearly for its connections with the international movement; they were unwilling to be 'exploited' any further. He declared that if the Comintern shared the British viewpoint that they should operate as a section of the CPGB, 'self-respect' demanded an honourable parting of ways between the communists of India and the Third International. The CPI could function as an independent body and still remain ideologically consistent.[66] This criticism had an immediate impact. C.P. Dutt and Mohammad Ali's report in March 1927 on organizational work in India observed that the Indian communists had accused British comrades, particularly Allison and Saklatvala, of trying to subordinate the Indian communist movement to the CPGB; unless the relationship between the CPI and the Comintern improved, the CPI leaders 'do not see why they should accept instructions from any outside body'. Concrete steps were taken to redress these grievances. In September 1927, a Comintern analysis of the relationship between the CPI and the CPGB emphasized that under no circumstances should the former be made subordinate to the latter. The CPI should be directly connected with the Comintern through cooperation between Indian and British comrades, and this was 'not a question of personalities' but 'a question of principles and tactics'.

Soumendranath's report to the Comintern in May 1928 also indicated some progress on that front. He summarized the episodes chronologically, beginning with when Campbell/Allison came to India and started work with non-communist leaders of the Bengal Federation of Labour. Campbell's reading of the contemporary situation made him suggest that Indian comrades should not communicate with the Comintern independently of the CPGB. This proposal was rejected. Soon after, he was arrested and deported. Saklatvala initially displayed the same attitude. When the CPI requested him to preside over their second party conference, he refused on the bureaucratic ground that the CPGB had not given him permission to do so. Meanwhile, he met and cooperated with 'bourgeois leaders of the Swaraj Party'. He finally agreed to attend the second Bengal WPP conference held in Calcutta in March 1927.[67] A copy of his letter declining the invitation to preside over a proposed conference of Indian communists appeared in the press, forcing an embarrassed CPI to temporarily give up the idea of organizing the event. Subsequently, Saklatvala himself requested a meeting with the CPI leadership. He 'had considerably changed his attitude by that time', acknowledging the importance of having a communist party in India.[68] In 1928, Roy informed the Indian communists that the Saklatvala–Campbell episode was to be considered as closed. He advised the CPI to become affiliated to the Comintern.[69] Saklatvala's differences with Roy and the Indian communists may have stemmed from his theoretical position that peasants and workers should form a common front with the Indian bourgeoisie against colonialism. By 1927–28, however, he was questioning his earlier position.[70] It was probably this turnaround that made Muzaffar, in his autobiography, omit any reference to the bitterness surrounding the trip. He admiringly mentioned Saklatvala as 'the best speaker' he had 'ever listened to', one whose speeches helped popularize communist ideas.[71]

Roy and Muzaffar

Muzaffar also had several disagreements with Roy during this period. In January 1927, several years after his arrest which had disrupted their correspondence from 1923, Muzaffar resumed corresponding with Roy. He wrote that he had been unable to communicate for so long because 'excessive' work pressure coupled with financial distress had led to a possible tubercular 'relapse' after his release and he had been bed-ridden for a while. Muzaffar felt that Roy had continued to maintain contact with opportunists in the meantime and sent money through people who misappropriated it. He also thought Roy was unfair in asserting that those accused at the Kanpur trial lacked sufficient 'courage.'[72] Despite the bitter tone, the letter revealed that the two shared a transparent relationship which allowed an open display of anger and dissatisfaction. Roy read this letter many months later, after his return from China, and his response reached India only in 1928. Intercepted and read out in the course of the debate on the 'Public Safety Bill' by government representatives on 10 September 1928, it earned fame as the 'Assembly letter', and came to be at the centre of a controversy that was both very public and internal.

Though addressed to Muzaffar, Roy's letter was for the CPI leadership as a whole, and dealt with organizations of the CPI and the WPP and relations between them; links with the Comintern; coordination between the Communists in India and emigré sections; and organizational finances.[73] After referring to disagreements with 'Edward', Roy defined their relationship as comrades, agreeing on the principles and programme of a revolutionary struggle for freedom.[74] Roy was critical of the way the Bengal WPP was functioning and accused Muzaffar of forging a coalition with the non-communist left through the organization. He was sceptical of the agrarian radicals, especially Nareshchandra Sengupta, whom he regarded as a 'landlord'. Roy also differed with Muzaffar over the formation of a legal communist party. He advised the Indian communists to form an underground organization to avoid state persecution. He stressed the need for coordination between emigrant Indian communists and the CPI through the 'Foreign Bureau' in Paris so that future cooperation would be possible.[75] On 10 May 1928, Muzaffar replied to Roy. His tone was conciliatory; he agreed with Roy on several issues, but argued that Nareshchandra Sengupta and Atulchandra Gupta were not pro-landlord elements for they had strongly opposed the Permanent Settlement. Muzaffar insisted that people like them were rare in Bengal, a 'zamindar-ridden province' where even 'proletarianized intellectuals' refused to sever social ties with the structure of landownership. He emphasized the urgency of working with non-communists in Bengal and felt that Roy often received 'wrong reports'.[76]

Unknown to Muzaffar, the inner world of the Comintern was changing. M.N. Roy's relationship with the Comintern was deteriorating.[77] A Comintern emissary disguised as a tourist met Muzaffar in Calcutta and Bombay, asking questions on the situation in India and on the functioning of the communist network. Muzaffar later thought the man had been sent to investigate Roy's claims regarding India and what the local communists made of him. The Comintern accused Roy of failing to offer proper guidance to the Chinese communists in 1927; of formulating a theory of 'decolonization' which argued that a situation was emerging whereby imperialism would voluntarily renounce power in the colonial world; of providing exaggerated reports of communist strength in India; and of advocating the expansion of the WPP, a 'two-class party', where the proletarian leadership was not clearly established. The process culminated in Roy's attempts to float a counter-Comintern opposition and his subsequent expulsion from the Third International in 1929.[78]

Also raging during this period were personal conflicts which had political repercussions. Usmani, the last among the Kanpur prisoners to be released, depended on Muzaffar's material assistance from outside. His demands and desperate requests were varied in range: from supply of clothes to publication of his articles, to a separate lodging as he was averse to staying in the overcrowded WPP office. Occasionally he jokingly complained about Muzaffar's 'indifference' and 'mute' non-response which outdid that of Gandhi. However he acknowledged that Muzaffar, despite his failing health and mental worries, had been very generous towards him. Muzaffar's reading of Usmani as 'a complex egotist' was probably strengthened during these interactions. Immediately after his release, when Usmani wished to travel abroad, Muzaffar told him that under no circumstances was he to leave India as the organization needed him. Ignoring Muzaffar, Usmani made his way back to Russia in 1928; and he attended the Sixth Congress of the Comintern as a delegate.[79] There he criticized Muzaffar and implied that no work was being done in India under his leadership. Soumendranath, who was also present, later claimed that Usmani had tried to discredit Muzaffar and others building an organization in India, and had been somewhat checked when invited to a 'thundering debate' by him.[80] Contemporary police reports observed that Usmani was received 'favourably by the Soviet authorities', but he 'fell somehow into disfavour, owing chiefly to Usmani's quarrelsome and arrogant behaviour'. Usmani returned to India after the Comintern Congress and attended the All India WPP Conference.[81]

Arriving in Calcutta in late December 1928, he met Muzaffar at a restaurant on Harrison Road and 'surrendered'. Usmani informed him that although criticisms directed against Muzaffar's leadership had surfaced in Moscow, they had not been entertained. Muzaffar correctly surmised that it was Usmani who had complained against him. Usmani also stated at the 'secret' meeting of the CPI held after the WPP Conference, that the Comintern wanted either Muzaffar or Ghate to join its central executive. The CPI decided to send Muzaffar to Moscow,[82] but he was never able to make the journey.

Against Nationalism

Having to remain within the united bloc against imperialism which was dominated by the nationalists also generated conflict and stress. There is an influential reading of the relationship between the CPI and the Comintern that is shared by US historians guided by the logic of the Cold War,[83] CPI historians influenced by revised readings originating from Moscow,[84] and Indian historians sympathetic to nationalism.[85] This reading argues that right up to the end of 1928, Indian communists had remained a part of the anti-imperialist united front, critical of the Congress but willing to work with it. In December 1928, however, the Sixth Comintern Congress executed a sudden sectarian 'Left' turn, and Indian communists cut off all connections with the non-communist left as well as the nationalist mainstream. The twists and turns in the relationship between the nationalists and the communists have been interpreted in other ways too. According to Sobhanlal Datta-Gupta and G.K. Leiten, the decision at the Sixth Comintern Congress was not unilaterally taken by the central, Moscow-based leadership. The massacre of Chinese communists by nationalist forces in 1927, and the growing rift between the German communists and social democrats played a decisive role. The Soviet representatives, Kuusinen and Martynov, were in favour of the idea of a united anti-imperialist front. But the Indian communists, supported by their British comrades, emphasized the difficulties of working with the Congress leadership.[86] The new strategy of the Comintern advocated severing organizational links with the Congress, cooperating with the Congress and other groups on specific issues and campaigns, building a party of the proletariat with a revolutionary class agenda, and creating a strong peasant front rather than perpetuating a 'two-class party' structure.[87]

Animosity between the WPP and the Congress at a time of growing left influence on the trade union front in Bombay and Bengal, as well as the possibilities of expanding the organization in the rural areas, made the new Comintern 'thesis' a welcome proposition to Indian communists. It was viewed as an acknowledgement of their experiences and their reading of the Congress leadership at various levels. A 'hardening of attitude' towards the nationalists,[88] coupled with an overestimation of the potential for class-conscious mass militancy, contributed to the making of the new 'line' and its application in India. Muzaffar had developed deep reservations about nationalism. The restraining influence of the Gandhian leadership on the mass struggle was one of the reasons that made him turn away from mainstream anti-colonialism. He openly stated that Gandhi was 'reaction incarnate', and that his programme of *charkha* and *khadi* were 'instruments of stupidity'.[89] Similarly, he claimed that Subhash Bose, after his return from Burma, had developed a habit of continually attacking Marxism. Bose's extremely 'objectionable remarks' at a Provincial Congress Committee meeting forced Muzaffar to invite the 'champion orator' to a debate. Either due to 'contempt' or 'arrogance' Bose ignored the challenge, and Muzaffar was relieved since he regarded himself as lacking in any public-speaking skills.[90] He felt especially marginalized within the Provincial Congress Committee, as people influenced by the Hindu Mahasabha had 'captured' it.[91] Thus Muzaffar shared Roy's reservations about the Congress. In a letter to Roy in May 1928, he observed: 'We may become members of A.I.C.C., Provincial Congress Committees and even members of the Executive Committee', but there was no point in 'accepting office' as this could only mean committing to 'things which we must not do on principle'.[92] In August the same year, he publicly declared the existence of two parallel anti-colonial movements: one, the nationalist movement led by the capitalists and aimed at achieving 'Dominion Status', and two, class struggle for complete independence.[93] The division was deepened by the communists' demand for complete independence as an immediate goal and the refusal by the Congress leadership to adopt this resolution at successive Congress sessions.[94]

The 'Political Resolution' presented before the First All India WPP Conference in 1928 emphasized the separation of the WPP from the Congress when the time was ripe. It was argued that as long as the WPP was relatively weak, it needed to follow the policy of agitating within the Congress in order to expose its 'reactionary' leaders and to attract the revolutionary sections of the petit-bourgeoisie from the nationalist ranks towards the WPP. The resolution cited the class sympathy of the Indian bourgeoisie to the 'White Terror' of the Chinese bourgeoisie as reported in the nationalist press during the late 1920s.[95] The change in the Comintern line was not yet known. The message sent by the Comintern to the All India WPP arrived after the conference and the CPI Central Committee meeting were over.[96] The message affirmed that separation from the Congress was necessary and encouraged the communists to form a mass party of the proletariat.[97]

Day after Day

Muzaffar and his colleagues led a materially precarious and marginalized social existence. From police surveillance reports, political correspondence and memoirs, the picture of daily life that emerges is one of chronic poverty, overcrowded living spaces, ill-health, financial crisis, house searches, police raids and arrests; replicated day after day, this impeded activism.[98]

Empty Pockets

When Muzaffar returned to Calcutta in 1926, he found himself sharing the PWP office premises at 37 Harrison Road with Shamsuddin Hussein, Abdul Halim, Nalini Gupta and Manimohan Mukherjee. A police agent reported: 'Muzaffar Ahmed has been suffering from tuberculosis, Halim from appendicitis and Nalini Gupta from cancer' (though the actual nature of Nalini's illness was never ascertained). When Spratt later joined their commune, Muzaffar observed that he worked hard and became 'much reduced in health'.[99] Financial difficulties restricted access to treatment. Muzaffar consulted Bidhan Chandra Roy, well-known physician, Congress leader and Chief Minister of West Bengal after independence, 'free of charge'. However, he could not afford the injections needed to treat his tuberculosis. Nazrul was also ill and a 'Europe-returned' doctor in Krishnanagar bore his medical costs.[100]

Financial difficulties restricted movement. Muzaffar's 'bankrupt' condition made travel for organizational purposes difficult though not impossible;[101] he managed to take part in strikes in and around Calcutta, travelling by tram and local train, and to visit comrades and attend party meetings in northern and western India as well as Congress and AITUC conferences.[102] A bitter letter sent to the Foreign Bureau of the CPI in Paris by Jatin Mitra, a recruit of Nalini Gupta, stated that 'the boys here' led a semi-starved existence while Roy lived comfortably in Berlin.[103] David Petrie, Director of the Intelligence Bureau, held that the Bengal PWP 'never succeeded in becoming a force in the political world because it laboured under an ever-present threat of bankruptcy'.[104] Nalini, in a letter to Roy in 1927, pointed out that work was at a standstill due to lack of funds; the house-rent was not being paid and the paper had stopped publication.[105] Muzaffar wrote to Roy in early 1927 that acute financial difficulties facing the organization and its activists had reduced him 'to beg at the door of friends'.[106] Police informer '531' reported on 10 June 1927:

> The WPP maintains the organization from the subscriptions and donations raised from members and sympathizers. They are in great financial difficulty. I know that Muzaffar Ahmad and Halim were without food for 2 or three days when I and Saumandra Tagore paid them Rs 10/-.
>
> . . . They say a good deal about establishing branches all over Bengal and in every mill area and to do away with the aristocracy and also about Lenin and Trotsky. But so long as they have got no money even for their food, I don't think that they could do anything.[107]

Huda wrote to the Comintern in October 1928 that the WPP badly needed money. It was suffering hardship and indebtedness as money had to be spent on strikes, propaganda and demonstrations.[108] In a letter to a friend, Muzaffar mentioned 'a lady', the wife of a friend, from whom he had borrowed money, and wondered how he could repay her.[109] The correspondence between Muzaffar and Soumendranath during the latter's stay in Berlin also revealed financial worries as a constant problem plaguing the activists in Bengal. Their discussions touched on daily shortages made acute by chronic illness, court cases and arrests, inability to pay house-rent and difficulties in running *Ganabani*. Despite Soumendranath's promise, monetary help from Europe could not reach the organization. Muzaffar's initial exasperation and later impatience made way for the correct surmise that the money had been intercepted by the police.[110] He wrote to Ghate in February 1929: 'There is no end of pecuniary difficulties. Comrade Spratt has wired for his allowances, but nothing has reached him as yet.'[111] The hazards of urban life caught up with them when Spratt's pocket was picked, increasing their collective desperation.[112]

Attempts to mobilize resources and raise funds only brought temporary relief. Muzaffar and Halim sometimes travelled outside Bengal to collect money for the organization.[113] The 'starvation of colleagues' like Muzaffar and Halim as well as the 'obstruction to activism' prompted Soumendranath to organize a 'Spring Festival' at Albert Hall in 1926.[114] A police agent recorded a 'variety performance' for fund-raising by the Bengal PWP on 6 March 1926, where Nazrul performed politically 'objectionable songs' and, in a short speech, appealed for money to support the PWP. The agent was struck by the 'high standard' of the ballet and music, and in the tone of a seasoned columnist, held that the programme announcement 'included dances by a well known European dancer (the German wife of Ram Bhattacharji); this attracted an audience of about 500 persons and a sum of Rs. 400/- is said to have been realized by the sale of tickets.'[115] Encouraged by this success, Soumendranath organized a ballet at the University Institute Hall, a daring social event since cultural performances including 'respectable women' were uncommon at the time. This challenge to conservative social taboos earned the organizers, particularly Soumendranath, a barrage of insults from 'moralists' who attacked them in the vernacular press.[116] Soumendranath's report to the Comintern mentioned the group's dependence on charitable contributions from friends and on cultural performances to raise money.[117] R.P. Dutt sent some roubles from Moscow to help the republication of *Ganabani* in 1928[118] in response to Muzaffar's urgent appeal.[119] The duty of distributing funds collected for the activists devolved on Muzaffar.[120] Dange sent money on behalf of the Girni Kamgar Union to help the Bauria strikers, which provided short-term relief. After the Bauria strike was over, Dange asked Muzaffar to spend the money on what he thought was best for the organization. Muzaffar spent it on his colleagues, including Spratt, since they were suffering great hardship.[121]

A 'Questionable Society'

The search for public donations was probably hampered by a degree of disapproval directed against the heterogeneous religious, ethnic and linguistic origins of the PWP members. These highlighted their distance from the dominant identity politics and mainstream middle-class social values. A Special Branch officer reported on 22 January 1927, after a search of the PWP office room at 37 Harrison Road: 'On enquiry from the manager and from other boarders it was learned that the occupants of room number 10 . . . were generally disliked by others, on account of their questionable society.'[122] Muzaffar faced benign mockery from Hindu *bhadralok* police officials at the Special Branch after being arrested on the eve of the Meerut trial alongside Ayodhyaprasad, Spratt and Huda. He was asked where he had found a 'character' like Huda and why he had not yet converted Ayodhyaprasad to Islam since they possessed common food habits, such as the consumption of beef.[123] There are indications that both the nationalists and the communal elements shunned communists socially. When invited to lunch by Moinuddin, his old contact who worked for the weekly journal *Satyasroyee*, Muzaffar made it clear that he wished to avoid any unpleasantness at Moinuddin's work place. He knew that the editor of the journal, Abdullah Hel Kafi, a nationalist Congressman, orthodox Wahabi and Muzaffar's contemporary in the world of Muslim literary activism, would not approve of his visit. After being assured that the office would be empty that afternoon, he accepted the invitation.[124] When Shachinandan complained that their group was ridiculed and condemned for its associations with field-hands and coolies, Muzaffar quoted from Tagore's poetry on the insults reserved for those stripped of all social status; he advised Shachinandan to ignore the bourgeoisie and the petit-bourgeoisie.[125]

The unconventional appearance of some of the younger members of the socialist circle did not quite fit the standards of middle-class respectability either. During his first visit to 37 Harrison Road in early 1926, Soumendranath sported a carefully cultivated irregular 'look': he went without shoes, wore shaggy, long hair, and dressed only in *khadi*. He was met by an atypical collective that impressed and attracted him in various ways: Muzaffar, 'a small, thin man with a pale face' who spoke to him about the aims of the group; Nalini Gupta, 'a tall skinny chap' whose incredible stories and 'wicked' sense of humour he later learnt to appreciate; Halim, 'a young lad' with an air of quiet dedication; Hemantakumar, a man of 'razor-sharp intelligence'; Nazrul, whose songs bowled him over.[126]

The communitarian living conditions and cultural climate at Harrison Road, and later European Asylum Lane, replicated those of the Bengal Muslim Literary Society Office in the late 1910s and early 1920s. 37 Harrison Road was a large mansion located on a busy thoroughfare; this was one of the main arteries of Muzaffar's old neighbourhood, the College Street area. The first socialist organization rented two rooms to run its office and paper, and to provide shelter to homeless, 'starved or half-starved' activists who suffered from 'insomnia' due to 'torn mattresses, pillows and blankets'. In November 1927, the office shifted to European Asylum Lane. The immediate neighbourhood, with its cross-class character, was eminently suitable for relocation. It had a history of Muslim working-class activism that could be traced back to the anti-colonial upsurge and the formation of unions. In 1920, the 'Inland Steamship and Flat Employees' Association' had emerged in the adjacent Alimuddin Street, while the 'Calcutta Hackney Carriage Drivers' Association' had set up office on European Asylum Lane in 1923.[127]

The address 2/1 European Asylum Lane, where Muzaffar and his com-

2/1 European Asylum Lane, now Abdul Halim Lane: the office of the Peasants' and Workers' Party moved to the first floor of this building in 1927

A closer view of the PWP office building at
2/1 European Asylum Lane

rades took up residence, belonged to a three-room apartment on the first
floor of a two-storeyed building in central Calcutta.[128] While one of the
rooms served as the office, the other two functioned as living quarters. The
floors were covered with straw-mats and the rooms were sparingly furnished.
Most of the residents slept on the floor in cramped conditions.[129] Muzaffar
slept on a camp-bed or in the corner, separating himself from the others, as
he was afraid of infecting them with tuberculosis.[130] Residents and visitors
enlivened the mood at the office. Police informer '531' recalled in June
1927: 'Nalini Gupta was a good story teller and he used to entertain the
boys with stories about his adventures in Russia and other foreign countries.'[131] Nazrul, Manimohan, Soumendranath and Spratt often lifted the
gloom with songs and laughter. Nazrul reportedly translated the 'International' in the course of a single day; Soumendranath recalled that he was
among those who locked up the poet in a room before a conference in order

to force him to compose songs, and released him only after he had completed the task.[132] Spratt's father's sermons from England, warning him to stay away from 'wine, woman and politics', were read out to generate amusement.[133] Apart from the permanent residents, relatives and friends visited and stayed at the PWP/WPP premises, which was an occasional source of strain since the presence of 'outsiders' required greater caution. Kutubuddin's residence, 7 Moulavi Lane, remained a meeting place for the activists; Muzaffar continued to visit his old friend in search of assistance and counsel.[134]

The activists often found themselves in social situations of serio-comic dimensions. Soumendranath was 'in a state' and 'shivering' like a 'malaria-patient' when forced to deliver his first public speech at Krishnanagar in 1926; the audience, moved to pity, urged him to sing instead, a request to which he responded immediately. After the conference, he took Kutubuddin on a short tour to explore the cultural ambiguities of local Vaishnava communities. Soumendranath disguised Kutubuddin in the garb of a religious Hindu so that the latter would be not attacked by the communally vigilant, and they conversed at length with Lalita Sakhi, a male cross-dresser who had organized the Hindu mob during the most recent riot.[135] Once, when summoned to negotiate during the scavengers' strike, the WPP leaders had to meet the Mayor of Calcutta in drenched clothes as they had been caught in the rain on their way,[136] unintentionally conforming to their image as atypical individuals. Experiences such as these added a lighter touch to their activism.

The engagements of WPP activists were entwined with the social geographies of urban radicalism: the intellectual milieu of the College Street area, the cosmopolitan neighbourhoods of Harrison Road/European Asylum Lane, the mass protests in the Chowringhee area, and the working-class slums and suburbs in and around Calcutta. While walking through familiar streets, Muzaffar often ran into acquaintances who dragged him to teashops for some 'adda'. His discussions with friends at the office ranged from the esoteric to the prosaic: he conversed with Nazrul on themes of gay love in Persian poetry; with Aftab Ali, on the problems posed by financial hardship.[137] Certain patterns that had emerged during the days of the first socialist nucleus continued: while police agents trailed the principal activists like shadows, unknown but sympathetic working-class people such as postal workers surreptitiously offered help.[138] With their meagre resources, the activists tried to look after each other as well as visitors who arrived suddenly. Soumendranath posted bail for Allison when the latter was arrested.[139] The activists ate together, when they could afford meals, in cheap Muslim restaurants, since Hindu establishments refused to admit Muzaffar and Halim.[140] Acquaintances from Muzaffar's early days as an organizer still asked after him; Moinuddin and Abani Chaudhuri remained in touch. In a letter to Halim in 1928, Abani, who was living away from Calcutta, described Halim as Muzaffar's 'chief support' in very trying times.[141] Though his original ambition to be a writer on Islamic culture and civilization had been long abandoned, Muzaffar retained his social links with the milieu where he had become an activist. He published news of the Bengal Muslim Literary Society in *Ganabani*.[142] Abdul Sovan, an assistant lecturer in Arabic and Islamic Studies at Dhaka University, invited Muzaffar to attend a conference organized by the society in 1929. The conference was to be held on 30 March; Muzaffar was in Meerut by then.[143]

Watching the Detectives

State repression posed a continuous impediment which the PWP/WPP and the communists could not overcome. Muzaffar and his colleagues were under constant surveillance; this made coordination with contacts outside Bengal extremely difficult. Connections with the Comintern and CPI members in other regions were repeatedly obstructed by mail interceptions, a policing technique that contributed in no small measure to gaps in communication. The opening and copying of all correspondence, undercover and open systems of keeping watch, the planting of agents and informers, searches, arrests, deportations, and the suppression of activities through legislative and judicial measures were routine. All this was to culminate in the Meerut Conspiracy Case and the consequent dissolution of the WPP.

Fearful Propaganda

Though Muzaffar was repeatedly referred to in police dossiers as 'the suspect', 'the well known Bolshevik agent', 'the ex-convict', the term 'Bolshevik agent' fell into relative disuse and the word 'communist' came to be applied more frequently from the second half of the 1920s. This reflected partial recognition of communism as a movement with local roots and an internationalist perspective rather than an artificial import from Russia. However the 'Bolshevik Menace' continued to be viewed with trepidation in official and non-official colonial circles. *The Englishman* reported on 9 July 1926 that Colonel M. Saunders, a 'prisoner of the reds' in 1917, while 'addressing a general meeting of the Calcutta Branch of European Association . . . referred in grave terms to the Bolshevik menace to the British Empire'. He emphasized the danger posed by the Third International and by 'Jewish criminals', capable of any atrocity, who have climbed 'to the top' after the 'wholesale destruction of the upper and middle classes in Russia'. 'The result of this', he claimed, with a generous dose of anti-Semitic fervour, 'is that the greater percentage of leading commissars to-day in Russia are

Jews.' He pointed at the 'Bolshevik' influence in South China through the 'Canton Soviet', which had 'seriously damaged British interests in Chinese waters'. He warned of a dangerous Soviet influence extending over Tibet and Burma, and affecting British India's borders, a situation that needed 'very careful watching'. Identifying 'propaganda' as 'the principal weapon of the Soviet, arms being the secondary one', he predicted a clash of arms between the British empire and Bolshevism 'within the present generation'.[144]

To prevent the inflow of communist literature and communications from abroad, counter-measures were strictly enforced. A circular issued by the Finance Department of the Government of India stated:

> In exercise of powers conferred by section 19 of the Sea Customs Act of 1878 . . . the Governor-General in Council is pleased to prohibit the bringing into India of any copy of a publication issued by or emanating from (a) the Communist International or (b) any organization affiliated to or controlled by, or connected with the Communist International.[145]

Indian connections with the British Communist Party and attempts by communists to organize Indians in Britain, particularly sailors, were closely observed. London sources recorded the emergence of a 'red' Indian Seamen's Union (ISU) at the initiative of C.P. Dutt, Upadhyay and Saklatvala. On 6 November 1926, a social evening was hosted at the union's 88 East India Dock Road office to celebrate its formation; while only twenty sailors were present, the 'powder' of communism was added amid songs and refreshments through emphasis on labour combinations run by workers themselves. The organizers also met in central London, congregating at Clemens Palme Dutt's flat at 38 Mecklenburgh Square, to discuss ways of expanding their network among Indian seamen in London and Liverpool. These activities led to the fear that 'red' infiltration of seamen's unions in Calcutta and Bombay would lead to smuggling of banned literature and, ultimately, of arms. Mogal Jan, a sailor and leader of the ISU in Calcutta, was suspected of establishing connections with the ISU in London. Abdul Hakim, a sailor involved in the Assembly Letter controversy, was in touch with Upadhyay and the London ISU. Ships arriving in Indian ports were regularly searched and continued to yield 'results' in the form of proscribed communist literature.[146]

Checking Mail

Muzaffar's correspondence with organizations and individuals in Europe was carefully monitored. A system of cooperation through intelligence-sharing between colonial powers aided the British efforts to intercept and suppress communication. A letter dated 26 January 1928, in which Muzaffar signed himself as 'Edward', was found on Schikler, a communist of 'Austrian extraction', who was arrested in Paris the following month. The French police interrogated Schickler and his partner, a woman of Polish nationality. Their peripatetic image and non-institutionalized relationship were used to justify the treatment they received; British intelligence noted, 'he and his mistress were expelled from France the same day'. Intended for Mohammed Ali, the letter gave an address where communist literature could be sent. In May 1928, a letter written to Roy in response to the Assembly Letter was intercepted at Howrah.[147]

To smoke out 'illegal' literature and potentially 'seditious' material, raids were conducted at regular intervals.[148] A Special Branch officer reported in January 1927 that the office room of the PWP at 37 Harrison Road was searched in the presence of witnesses while the regular occupants were away; and that some papers and books were seized.[149] Muzaffar referred to intrusive visits from the police in a letter to Spratt.[150] The European Asylum Lane office was again searched in February 1929 while Muzaffar and others were away at the Kusthea Peasant Conference. The intention was to collect incriminating evidence that would enable the prosecution to prepare a court case at Meerut.[151] However, preparations for a major case had started much earlier. From late 1927, as the PWP entered labour politics, the routine vigilance over communist correspondence and activism acquired a new sense of urgency. In December 1927, the police noted that Muzaffar had requested Halim while in Lahore to send 'Sylhet Oranges' and 'dry Coconuts' for circulation 'amongst my friends here'.[152] Deciphering this as a coded reference to the distribution of banned literature, the police continued to keenly read letters of 'important members of the communist party' in Bengal. In the letter from Muzaffar to Mohammad Ali in Paris, found on Schikler in 1928, Muzaffar had asked after 'our long haired Comrade'; this, the police quickly worked out, was none other than Soumendranath Tagore, residing in Berlin. Some letters were suppressed, while others were photographed and then delivered to unearth the wider implications of communist strategies. Agents watched Muzaffar and Halim, particularly when they were posting letters; this was viewed as important as it led immediately to the detection of communist correspondence.[153]

Occasionally, the 'battle on the postal front' subverted the smooth procedures of mail censorship. Although the police checked everything, Muzaffar devised ways of communicating with the Comintern. The use of new names and addresses till they were discovered by the police and abandoned for a new set of names and addresses was a time-tested method followed since 1922. The cat-and-mouse game to evade or widen the censorship net continued without either of the two sides giving in. As before, unexpected acts of solidarity helped the communists. A postman secretly delivered the Comintern's message to the All India WPP Conference. During the Meerut trial, intelligence officials were intrigued that the letter, evading them, had managed to reach the accused. [154] However, meagre resources prevented the communists from wholly overcoming the state's attempts. Special Branch agents were present each day at the local Park Street post office to take away 'sacks' of material which had arrived for the residents of European Asylum Lane. There were protests at the Bhatpara Conference of 1928 against the interception of correspondence. [155]

Shadows

Freed from prison on account of his tuberculosis in late 1925, Muzaffar quickly rejoined politics. Fever, weight loss and throwing up of blood had convinced the prison doctor that the disease might prove fatal. David Petrie, Director of the Intelligence Bureau, expressed serious reservations over the 'wisdom' of the decision to release him early. Decades later, Muzaffar was to remark in jest that he was not able to oblige Petrie by dying and had even outlived him. [156] Muzaffar thought that Petrie's anger at his release was probably triggered by his article 'Bharat Kano Swadhin Noy?' (Why is India Not Free?), which appeared in *Langal* on 14 January 1926, indicating his return to activism. [157] The Central Intelligence Bureau never lost sight of Muzaffar and those who associated with him.

Shadowing the movements of the principal figures was another way of monitoring the PWP and CPI. Muzaffar's request to travel abroad, a few months after his release, was turned down. The fear that he would establish close contact with the Comintern had returned. [158] Though the Bengal intelligence agents of Indian origin were disappointed when refused a financial reward for their role in Muzaffar's arrest in the Kanpur Conspiracy Case (1924), they did not slacken their vigil. It was no accident that R. Gupta, a senior Special Branch officer with fifteen years' experience, declared during the Meerut trial: 'I know Muzaffar Ahmad well.' [159] One of the reasons for shifting the office from the busy Harrison Road to the quiet European Asylum Lane was to avoid police agents. [160] Police officials made discreet enquiries and collected information from an occupant of the ground floor at 37 Harrison Road. The watch reports between March and June 1926 reflected the everyday routine of the PWP activists and their urban social setting. Young men who met them were physically described in detail for procedural purposes. Once, a casual meeting with someone on a motorcycle attracted curiosity. [161]

Occasionally, the police operatives were confronted by their targets. When an agent caught sight of Muzaffar, Halim and some others at a north Calcutta park while on his 'rounds' in June 1926, Muzaffar allegedly charged him with 'spying' and asked whether they could enjoy the open air in the public garden without interference. In response to this 'accusation', the agent indignantly denied watching them and came away.[162] An informer (whom we have already noted under the code name '531') became a PWP member and reported on what transpired at the Harrison Road office. The police successfully installed their agent, Jankiprasad Bagerhatta, a participant in the Kanpur Communist Conference of 1925, as the general secretary of the CPI; though he provided valuable information for a year, Muzaffar eventually became suspicious and Bagerhatta was forced to resign in 1927. From as early as July 1926 aspects of his behaviour had seemed irregular to Muzaffar. Bagerhatta's role as a police agent became fully known during the Meerut Conspiracy Case. By then he had withdrawn from politics. He was to later re-emerge as a scriptwriter of popular films, which he invited his former 'comrades' Muzaffar and Halim to see.[163]

Sometimes, steps were taken to physically obstruct surveillance. Soumendranath and Campbell often 'fooled' police agents by successfully slipping away and gleefully observed their frantic search from hidden corners. Once Campbell surreptitiously deprived two sleeping police agents of their blankets. The articles were retained by Soumendranath as a 'trophy' and ultimately provided comfortable bedding to his terrier.[164] In December 1927, the police watcher deputed to observe Ben Bradley, who was visiting his colleagues in Bengal, 'could not do so owing to Godbole who was keeping a keen watch on us'.[165] During the Bhatpara Conference, CID officers were prevented from entering by Muzaffar and Kalidas at the suggestion of Atulchandra Gupta, on the ground that the event was for members only. The details of the proceedings could only be learnt through an informer who was posted inside. Often agents were allowed to enter conferences but were made to pay a high entry fee; the policemen posted at the Kusthea Peasant Conference purchased tickets, and were irritated to notice that 'students' and 'youths' were being allowed to walk in and out as they wished.[166]

Communist Deluge and Colonial Capital

Despite vigilance, or because of it, the state was aware that the communists and socialists were unable to undertake any major activity during the first two years of the PWP's existence. The 'Annual Report' of the CPI observed in 1927 that the government had so far avoided direct collision, and concentrated instead on mail censorship, surveillance and harsh imprisonment for many activists, particularly those in the North West Frontier Province.[167] Knowing that the Bengal PWP was crippled by financial difficulties and ideologically isolated, the colonial authorities did not regard its activists a major threat. Till the end of 1927, the party was regarded as an organization that had made 'little progress' beyond the 'spasmodic' publication of a weekly paper.[168]

Greater alarm was registered once the organization started participating in strikes, with the affiliation of the Bengal Jute Mill Association to the PWP in 1927 and full-fledged work on the labour front from 1928.[169] The official reading of contemporary labour relations produced the context of a major offensive against communists and leading trade unionists. A report on the contemporary working-class upsurge observed:

> 'Down with Imperialism', 'Land for the Peasants and Bread for the Workers', 'Long Live the Soviet Revolution' etc. have been dinned into their ears. In their processions they now carry red flags bearing Communist devices, and the spirit of violence has manifested itself on frequent occasions. The indigenous Communist leaders, by their reckless advocacy of Leninist doctrines, have brought into being forces which they can no longer control. . . . Conflicts with the police and frenzied attacks on property . . . are symptomatic of the grave unrest brought about by a handful of local Communist agitators. The dire results of their activities will be viewed with gratification by Headquarters in Moscow, for everything has worked according to Plan.
>
> The creation of unrest, or a preliminary to the 'workers' revolution' has been the avowed policy of the Communist International not only in India, but in every other country where they have attempted to gain a footing.[170]

Complaints from individual capitalists acclerated government plans for a crackdown. 'A private letter from a Calcutta merchant' was given immense importance by the Secretary of State for India. Identifying himself with 'those of us who are entrusted with the management of large and hitherto prosperous and contented concerns', the letter-writer argued that in the light of communist-led industrial disturbances, 'We are all wondering what "the Government concerned" conceive to be "their responsibilities" to which they are so "fully alive"! The atmosphere out here just now is highly charged and pregnant with trouble – a deep feeling of insecurity on our side and arrogant insolence on the other.'[171]

The police interpreted the Bhatpara Conference as presaging a violent threat to the existing social order. They were alarmed by the fact that while the means to the end in 1925–27 was 'non-violent mass action', by 1928 it was 'rallying of the people to mass action'.[172] L.H. Colson, D.I.G, Bengal Intelligence, and an old advocate of swiftly dealing with the 'potential Bolshevik threat' even when it was not visible in the industrial suburbs of Calcutta,[173] remarked in July 1928:

> I submit herewith a dossier prepared in this office on the Workers' and Peasants' party, Bengal Branch. It seems to me that this party with its existing branches . . . constitutes a serious menace to the public peace . . . fomenting, procuring and managing recent labour disputes and disturbances. . . . What has been done hitherto is merely a first essay in class warfare and it appears to

me that Government should arm themselves with adequate powers to deal with persons who openly proclaim and publish their intentions to destroy the existing Government by mass agitations, mass organisation and mass disturbances.

The militant mood of the workers was a cause of rising concern and special powers were requested in order to counter them. Colson observed:

> At the present time under the existing law the police have no legal right to compel organizers of strike meetings or meetings of this subversive association to give facilities for reporting the speeches these agitators choose to make. . . . If these persons are permitted to go on organizing, inciting and training ignorant workers in ways of violence and sedition the damage to public safety and property generally may easily be immense at no distant date.

Colson suggested an official scheme to counter the WPP's intended all-India activities, 'which have only just begun'.[174]

By late 1928, the government was already preparing the ground for a major suppression of communism. The correspondence between the Viceroy and the Secretary of State for India suggested that the process of initiating a conspiracy case against the communists was being speeded up. The two discussed deporting Spratt and Bradley through the 'Removal from India Bill' at length, as well as the immediate need to instruct Home Department officials at Simla to prepare 'an elaborate trial for conspiracy'.[175] In September 1928, photographing and retaining intercepted communist mail was being greatly recommended as evidence to be produced in court. The emphasis was on proving 'guilt by association'.[176] The state's belief of imminent communist dominance over the working class was strengthened by industrial actions which gave legitimacy to leftist strategies and occasional monetary help received by the strikers from Russia.[177] The police detected the 'evil influence' of WPP members behind the militancy of these strikes,[178] and noted the strong presence of communists and 'sympathizers' among the office-bearers elected at the Jharia Conference of the AITUC in December 1928.[179] Simultaneous campaigns in the districts stressing the need to establish workers' and peasants' control over factories and landed property also alarmed the state. In April 1928, a circular from the Intelligence Bureau, Government of India, suggested that the communists had been instructed by Moscow to mount propaganda among landless peasants and 'support every kind of Muhamedan conspiracy in India'.[180]

Despite its pivotal role in checking the advance of communism and socialism, the system of colonial surveillance and repression was plagued by lapses in intelligence, exaggerations and distortions, as well as hurdles erected by its targets. Information 'derived from most delicate sources' was often proved wrong.[181] A report from Metiabruz noted in 1929: 'No news of mill-hands going to demonstrate against Simon Commission on their arrival in Calcutta tomorrow. The leaders probably could not convene such an idea as no meeting could be held.' Yet the next day a sizeable contingent arrived from the area to demonstrate, led by the very leaders who had apparently failed to mobilize them.[182] The police surmised, from Muzaffar's connections with politically disillusioned Congressmen in Noakhali such as Serajur Rahman and Khitish Roy, that 'Muzaffar Ahmad is not only connected with Bolshevik and communist movements in India and abroad but he is very intimately associated with some of the local organizations and commands considerable hold on them. He appears to be financed by these organizations too.' This was clearly exaggerated since very little was done in terms of concrete organizational work and mobilization in the districts.[183] However, overemphasizing the communist strength had its uses. It strengthened the structures of surveillance and repression.

To Curb Communism

The first major step to curb communism was the introduction of a Public Safety Bill in the Legislative Assembly. In official circles, it was tellingly referred to as the 'Removal from India Bill', designed to expel British communists active in India. H.E. Hansen, Deputy Commissioner of Police, Calcutta Special Branch, held: 'A distinct advance is possible because of the activities of Spratt and Bradley alone. It is high time the Deportation Bill was passed into law.'[184] It was in this context that M.N. Roy's letter was intercepted; used to press for the passage of the Bill, it created a stir in the Legislative Assembly.[185] The Bill sought wider powers even if deportation as a tool was already in use, as evident from the expulsion of Campbell and later Johnstone.[186] The second step was to introduce the 'Trade Disputes Bill', which was interpreted in radical trade union circles as a method of crushing labour militancy. The 'Public Safety Bill' was defeated by a narrow margin. Many members, unconvinced by the government's claim that it targeted communists only, feared it could be extended to all those who were sympathetic to anti-colonial movements in India. However, the 'Trade Disputes Act' was passed in early 1929.[187] The Congress officially opposed both Bills, but the capitalist links of individual Congress members were evident during the debate and voting.[188] The defeat of the 'Public Safety Bill' in the Legislative Assembly in September 1928 hastened the launching of the conspiracy case in Meerut the next year.[189]

The CPI leadership was alert to the system of surveillance that could lead to arrests. By March 1929, a significant increase in the number of watchers had caused disquiet to Muzaffar and his comrades. However they were not prepared for the scale of the repression. On 20 March, at 3 in the morning,

Portrait of 25 of the Meerut prisoners taken outside the jail. Back row (left to right): K. N. Sehgal, S.S. Josh, H. L. Hutchinson, Shaukat Usmani, B. F. Bradley, A. Prasad, P. Spratt, G. Adhikari. Middle Row: R. R. Mitra, Gopen Chakravarti, Kishori Lal Ghosh, L. R. Kadam, D. R. Thengdi, Goura Shankar, S. Bannerjee, K. N. Joglekar, P. C. Joshi, Muzaffar Ahmed. Front Row: M. G. Desai, D. Goswami, R. S. Nimbkar, S. S. Mirajkar, S. A. Dange, S. V. Ghate, Gopal Basak.

The Meerut prisoners

the residents of 2/1 European Asylum Lane were woken by loud knocks at the door, accompanied by the announcement that an urgent telegram had arrived. Halim, who lived in the office room closest to the front door, unlocked the latch, expecting a postman. Instead he found a large posse of officers and constables from the Special Branch. Forcing their way in, they demanded to know where Muzaffar was. Though Halim tried to warn Muzaffar, it was too late. As far as Muzaffar, Spratt, Huda and Ayodhyaprasad were concerned, their stay at the WPP office and their engagement with the first socialist organization were over.[190]

Collapse and Renewal

The passage of the repressive labour legislation was timed to coincide with the beginning of the Meerut trial against thirty-one communists and trade-union activists charged with sedition. The double-edged crackdown led to the collapse and dissolution of the WPP in Bengal. With the arrest of the principal organizers, the energies of those who remained outside was claimed by the mammoth task of organizing the legal defence, in what proved to be the most long-drawn out and elaborate conspiracy case in colonial India. Steps were initially taken to keep the organization running on a day-to-day basis; financial worries, increased state repression, and the parting of ways between communists and many of the independent socialists on ideological and organizational grounds made them unsustainable. Signs of recovery could be registered from the early 1930s in the shape of the Calcutta Committee of the CPI which developed a following among segments of workers engaged in strikes and the young intelligentsia alienated by the social content of nationalism. The committee also established connections with rural struggles against zamindari oppression. This created the ground for the emergence of communist-led mass politics in the region from the late 1930s.

Halim's Trials
State repression took its toll on the first round of leftist radicalism. From Bengal, Muzaffar Ahmad, Shamsul Huda, Philip Spratt, Ayodhyaprasad, Dharani Goswami, Gopen Chakraborty, Gopal Basak, Radharaman Mitra, Kishorilal Ghosh and Shibnath Bannerjee stood trial. The last three were acquitted in the end since they were not directly connected with the CPI. Muzaffar as the principal accused received the longest sentence among those convicted of conspiracy. By the end of 1933, all were released except those considered most dangerous: Muzaffar, Dange and Usmani, the three veterans of the Kanpur Conspiracy Case, and Spratt. Muzaffar was not allowed to rejoin political activism before 1936.[191]

Immediately after the Meerut arrests, Halim was formally put in charge

'Dhaka House', 41 Zakaria Street: the office of the 'Calcutta Committee' of the CPI was located here in the early 1930s

of running the organization at the initiative of the non-communist members of the WPP. Payment of rent and other dues, networking with members, attempts to retain the organization's bases, coordinating the defence of the Meerut accused, correspondence with the Comintern, and other such duties devolved on him. In their search for evidence, the police stripped the office of everything except bare furnishings. The landlord filed a law-suit over unpaid rent and eventually the European Asylum Lane office had to be vacated. Halim tried to hold on to a skeletal organization despite these obstacles but was sentenced to one year's rigorous imprisonment in 1930. By then, constant police harassment, financial hardship and organizational disarray had virtually aborted all his efforts.[192]

The collapse of the WPP made the agrarian socialists Nareshchandra Sengupta and Atulchandra Gupta look for other organizations that opposed the Permanent Settlement. They joined the Praja Party which had emerged in 1929 in response to the debates and polarization surrounding the tenancy amendment. Led by Akram Khan, Abdur Rahim and Fazlul Haq, it was primarily a forum of Muslim *jotedar* interests in which agrarian radicals and socialists had little influence.[193] Non-communist members of the WPP continued to help the communists in various ways. Nareshchandra presided over a thousand-strong meeting at Albert Hall on 2 October 1929, to raise money for the Meerut prisoners. Speaking as a legal practitioner, he labelled the Meerut Conspiracy Case as 'false' and 'based on evidence fabricated by Government spies'. He insisted it was a political 'duty to arrange for the defence and expose the tactics of the Government'.[194] Atulchandra maintained links with Halim and the rest of the communist nucleus, trying to help in 'every way'. Bhupendranath and Hemantakumar continued to offer assistance in organizing youth and peasants.[195] Signs of communist revival were apparent from the early 1930s when Halim, Ranen Sen and Somnath Lahiri renewed organizational efforts through the 'Calcutta Committee' of the CPI. This body re-established connections with the Comintern and paved the way for expansion of the communist influence in Bengal from the second half of the 1930s.[196] Though the communists were now building their own party and the WPP had dissolved, they continued to maintain links with many friends and associates from the earlier period.[197] Some joined the CPI; Abani Chaudhuri, Muzaffar's contact and member of the first socialist nucleus, became a communist activist in the early 1930s. Saroj Mukherjee had attended the All India WPP Conference in December 1928; he joined the CPI in 1931 after Bhupendranath asked him to get in touch with Halim.[198]

Among Workers of the World

The communist presence within trade unions was weakened but did not evaporate overnight as the government had hoped. They continued to be active among the segmented working class and even established contact with those untouched by their activism so far. Aftab Ali's support for the ISU decision not to boycott the Royal Commission and Prabhabati's advocacy of halting the jute general strike in order to negotiate with employers alienated them from the communists in the course of 1929.[199] Yet the process of building red unions continued. In 1930, the scavengers went on strike again in the Calcutta–Howrah region.[200] In April 1930, Abdul Momin organized a successful carters' strike in Calcutta; a former Non-Cooperator and Khilafatist, he had been jailed with Halim and A.R. Khan during the mass upsurge of 1921–22, and become a *muhajir* and then a communist during his travels in the 'Muslim World'. The carters erected barricades, fighting a pitched battle with the police during which a sergeant was killed. The event was intimidating enough to make the Calcutta Police Commissioner, Charles Tegart, the most able persecutor of the middle-class militant nationalists of Bengal, to advise the government to negotiate with the strikers.[201] Momin and Bankim Mukherjee, who were sentenced to one year's imprisonment for their role in the disturbance, joined the CPI. Halim, also jailed for the publication of a 'seditious handbill', met Saroj Mukherjee after being released in 1931 and asked him to work with Somnath Lahiri among railway workers.[202]

Genda Singh, a communist of Punjabi Sikh background who was already working with the WPP, and Abani Chaudhuri became active among transport workers.[203] Mohammad Ismail, an Urdu-speaking journalist-turned-communist trade union leader who organized tram workers, joined their efforts. Communist organizers were visible among the Hindi and Urdu-speaking Muslim tobacco workers, tailors and cotton-mill workers of Metiabruz, and the port and dock workers of Kidderpore. Ranen Sen was active among the Lilooah railway workers and the Wimco Match Factory workers of Maniktala, Calcutta. A match factory worker nicknamed 'Mastan' became Sen's principal associate. His assertive 'sloganeering and shouting' attracted public attention during meetings and marches. Many workers organized themselves, assisted by the CPI. A Muslim working-class woman, Gulbahar Bibi, formed a union among the predominantly female rice-mill workers of Tollygunge. Known for her militant confrontations with the police, she was a regular visitor to the CPI office on Zacharia Street during the early 1930s.[204]

Calcutta's status as an international port-city facilitated interactions between the CPI, and migrant Asian communists and workers. John Jameson, an exiled Chinese communist from Canton who had evaded Kuomintang persecution, established contact with Halim and the 'Calcutta Committee'. Jameson created a communist nucleus among Calcutta's Chinese cobblers and wrote leaflets addressed to them on behalf of the CPI. He was arrested and deported by the British authorities in 1932. His Indian comrades in Calcutta suspected that he was killed after reaching China.[205] Some Malaysian communists also established contact with Indian and Chinese communists in the city in 1930; their report, probably to the Far Eastern Bureau of the Comintern, mentioned the weakened state of the communist movement in Calcutta as an outcome of state persecution and arrests.[206]

A Residual Radicalism

Desperation among the depression-hit working-class people in and around Calcutta made them resort to militant confrontation with the forces of law and order under communist leadership; this incensed the colonial authorities. During the early 1930s, unlike the nationalists and non-communist socialists, communists in prison came to be treated like ordinary criminals. They were denied the special privileges extended to political detainees. As a mark of protest against being assigned the status of 'third-class prisoners', twenty-one communists went on a hungerstrike in Alipore Central Jail in 1934.[207] They turned their imprisonment in their favour, though, as they rapidly realized that it facilitated recruitment. Many of the Bengali militant nationalists, recognizing the elitism and weakness of secret revolutionary cells, started reading Marxist literature in jail; they joined the CPI *en masse* upon release in the late 1930s.[208]

Some Congressmen who had come into contact with communists in the course of strike-actions joined them. Jiban Maiti, who helped organize the Howrah scavengers, became a communist in the late 1930s after being released from prison. Another veteran of the Howrah scavengers' strike, Agam Datta, was a communist supporter. Jogesh Dasgupta, secretary of the Howrah Municipality, who had done his utmost to crush the strikers, also became a communist sympathizer in his old age, having lost all illusions about the Congress.[209] Among Muzaffar's district contacts, Khitish Roy of Noakhali joined the CPI. He was active in Calcutta and Noakhali in 1946 during the communal riots as a peace campaigner, and remained in East Bengal after partition as a political organizer and popular figure among the local Muslim poor.[210] Manmathanath Sarkar, a defence counsel of the revolutionary nationalists, met Muzaffar in the late 1920s while experiencing the dual pull of communism and revolutionary terror. In 1929, he helped Halim to organize legal aid for Muzaffar and others. In the late 1930s he was among those nationalist revolutionaries who, upon release from long imprisonment, met Muzaffar and joined the CPI.[211] A schoolboy, Smritish Bannerjee, impressed by the striking railway workers who were marching along the Ganges strand under communist leadership in 1928, took them home and offered refreshments. A few years later he joined the CPI but then left to follow Gandhi; he was killed while trying to prevent riots in 1946.[212]

Communist journalism had eclipsed, but reappeared. Halim's brief biography of Muzaffar appeared in *Jagaran* in February 1930, as part of a larger publicity feature on the Meerut accused. Launched at Hemantakumar's initiative, it was entitled 'An Introductory Note about the Meerut Prisoners'.[213] Halim kept left publishing initiatives alive. Though *Ganabani*'s last appearance was in 1928, it was succeeded by several short-lived papers which repeatedly suffered from the post-1929 censorship of the communist press. Old associates of the first communists, Nazrul, Atulchandra, Nareshchandra and Pabitra Gangopadhyay, as well as individual members of the *Kallol* circle, contributed to these efforts.[214] Though the WPP's rural mobilization was negligible, it prepared the ground for militant struggles in the countryside. Organizational activism in Mymensingh led to the emergence of a branch of the Young Comrades League (YCL) in the district. In 1930 some YCL members organized the peasants of Kishorganj and launched a movement against local moneylenders that culminated in an agrarian uprising. The following year, similar efforts in Malda met with suppression.[215]

These movements and efforts pointed to a residual radicalism from an earlier period and possibilities of future expansion. Though left activism was thrown into disarray by the Meerut arrests, the left regrouped and tried to repair the losses. While some connections were irrevocably lost, new networks were created. In this sense, the unrealized aims of the first socialist organization, expressed through opposition to the state and the structure of private property, were again articulated. The following was symptomatic of the renewed left politics that became visible from the second half of the 1930s: when Faizuddin led a march of poor Mymensingh peasants in 1937, apart from targeting oppressive landlords, the slogans raised were, 'Lift the Ban on the Communist Party' and '*Inquilab Zindabad*' (Long Live the Revolution).[216]

Under Muzaffar Ahmad's leadership, the PWP/WPP emerged as the first socialist organization in Bengal with a radical programme of mass mobilization. The contradictions confronting it exercised constraints on expansion. If one is to assess the impact of these constraints on the eventual collapse and dissolution of the organization, several entangled issues need to be considered, which touch on internal differences. Even though they were confined to the male intelligentsia, the principal activists created a social basis of political praxis, reflected by communitarian living and action; they went beyond the familial. Could it be that the heterogeneity of the activists, rooted in the social divergences of their earlier politics, contributed to factionalism, weakening the organization? Was Muzaffar's inability to present himself as an effective leader to a substantial group of activists a major blow to the organization's prospects of expansion? Was factionalism more significant than the repression unleashed by the state?

Factional differences among the leading activists stemmed from political perceptions rather than differences in social backgrounds. How else can we explain the support Muzaffar received as the principal organizer from those who did not share his social origins? Among those who reposed their full confidence in his leadership were the agrarian socialists Nareshchandra Sengupta, Hemantakumar Sarkar and Atulchandra Gupta, former nationalist-turned-radical Soumendranath Tagore, and the British communist Philip Spratt. Similarly, Muzaffar's chief antagonists within the organization, Gopen Chakrabarty and Dharani Goswami, received the approval of A.R. Khan and Huda who had more in common with Muzaffar in terms of background. It seems that Muzaffar's insistence on retaining and increasing the representation of agrarian socialists in major posts of the organization contributed to disputes over leadership, an indication of differences over political perceptions and strategy. He was unwilling to theoretically de-emphasize the original aim of building a rural base even though the vast agrarian hinterland outside the limits of the city remained overwhelmingly unreachable at this stage.

Despite factionalism, the organization grew. In 1928, when his detractors repeatedly expressed dissatisfaction over Muzaffar's leadership and internal strife reached its height, the potential for creating a mass base among workers, peasants and youth emerged for the first time. A related feature of communist politics in this period was the tendency to criticize and go beyond Comintern directives. This tendency emerged under Muzaffar's leadership as labour struggles and communal violence became ideological sites for confronting nationalism. The Comintern's acknowledgement of gaps in its understanding, based on critical insights offered by Muzaffar and others who came to be regarded as key communist figures in the contemporary colonial world, implied that local autonomy was not to be interfered with.

It would therefore seem that state repression, rather than fissures arising from differences over decision-making and activism at various levels, led to the collapse of the WPP. The floating of 'conspiracy theories' from above acted as a ruling strategy to overcome opposition and took on a life of its own. As a device, it protected a security state wrapped in liberal imperialism and careful to ward off accusations of excess even while committing them. 'Surgical' strikes against those identified as the most dangerous malcontents, through the operations of colonial law and judiciary, helped manufacture, segregate and criminalize opponents. With the physical removal of some of the main organizers, the functioning of the organization, work in affiliated unions, coordination with other groups and individuals, and contact with the outside world were dealt a blow; the WPP, given its small size, never recovered from this. The checks offered by the competing ideologies of nationalism and communalism in the period of organizational weakness and decline also created barriers in the path of communist and socialist efforts to build a left mass-base in Bengal. The first socialist organization, by offering a new political alternative, represented a departure in Bengal politics. Focusing on class, it tried to overcome the deliberate occlusion of the social interests of the exploited in mainstream politics. Despite the contradictions impeding its expansion, the early communists and socialists were on the verge of making a breakthrough in trade-union politics, and developing wider contacts in the sphere of agrarian movements, when their activities came to a sudden halt. Had the communist leadership remained active, in keeping with the changes in the Comintern's position, was there a strong likelihood that the structure of the organization would have changed, and mutated into worker and peasant fronts of the communist party? Although counterfactual questions cannot be answered, all existing evidence suggests that political initiatives and social possibilities of widening left activity in several forms were present. The Meerut Conspiracy Case acted as a brake, effectively postponing another cycle of radical social protest involving workers, peasants and the intelligentsia to the second half of the 1930s.

Notes and References

1 IB 320/26 (310/1926).

2 Taj ul-Islam Hashmi, *Pakistan as a Peasant Utopia: The Communalization of Class Politics in East Bengal, 1920–1947*, Oxford, 1992, pp. 113, 176.

3 IB file number censored.

4 Moinuddin, 'Ekti Sangrami Jiban: Ekti Adorsho' (A Life of Struggle: An Ideal), in Mazharul Islam (ed.), *Muzaffar Ahmad: Shango o Proshango* (Muzaffar Ahmad: Reflections and Essays), Calcutta, 1989, p. 82.

5 IB 210/27 (23/1927).

6 IB 95/24 (41/1924).

7 IB 210/27 (23/1927).

8 Muzaffar Ahmad, *Amar Jiban o Bharater Communist Party* (My Life and the Communist Party of India), Calcutta, 1969, fifth edition 1996, pp. 471, 480–81, 494.

9 'Bhabishya Bharat' (Future India), *Ganabani*, 9 September 1926, reprinted in Muzaffar Ahmad, *Probondho Sangkalan* (Selected Essays), Calcutta, 1970, p. 12.

10 *Communists Challenge Imperialism from the Dock: The General Statement of 18 Communist Accused*, Calcutta, first edition 1967, reprint 1987, pp. 282–84, 289–90.

11 Muzaffar Ahmad, *Kazi Nazrul Islam: Smritikatha* (Kazi Nazrul Islam: Reminiscences), Calcutta, 1965, ninth edition 1998, p. 222. For a biographical note on Prabhabati Dasgupta, see Manju Chattopadhyay, *The Trail-blazing Women Trade Unionists of India*, Delhi, 1995, pp. 6–10.

12 Muzaffar Ahmad, *Bharater Communist Party Garar Prothom Jug* (The First Phase of the Communist Party of India), Calcutta, 1959, fourteenth edition 1997, p. 17.

13 Ahmad, *Amar Jiban o Bharater Communist Party*, pp. 484–85.

14 Statement of Muzaffar Ahmad, *Meerut Communist Conspiracy Case (1929) Papers*.

15 Ibid.

16 D.M. Laushey, *Bengal Terrorism and the Marxist Left, Aspects of Regional Nationalism in India, 1905–1942*, Calcutta, 1975, pp. 45–48. Sumit Sarkar, *Modern India 1885–1947*, Hong Kong, 1989, pp. 251–52. Ahmad, *Kazi Nazrul Islam: Smritikatha*, pp. 199, 201.

17 Ahmad, *Probondho Sangkalan* (Selected Essays), pp. 1–2. 'Krishak o Sramik ebong Shikkhito Jubak Samproday' (Peasants, Workers and the Educated Youth), a speech delivered by Muzaffar as president of the peasants and workers section on 19 August, later published in *Ganabani*, 25 August 1927.

18 Ranen Sen, *Bharater Communist Partyr Itibritta* (An Account of the Indian Communist Party), Calcutta, 1996, p. 18.

19 Muzaffar Ahmad, 'Amar Pointallish Bacharer Sathi' (My Friend for Forty-Five Years), in Abdul Halim, *Nabajibaner Pathe* (Towards a New Life), Calcutta, 1966, second edition 1990, p. 9.

20 Ahmad, *Amar Jiban o Bharater Communist Party*, p. 481. Subodh Chandra Sengupta and Anjali Basu (eds.), *Sansad Bangali Charitabhidan* (Dictionary of Bengali Biography), Vol. 1, Calcutta, 1994, pp. 327–28.

21 Saroj Mukhopadhyay, *Bharater Communist Party o Amra* (The Communist Party of India and Ourselves), Vol. 1, Calcutta, 1993, pp. 24, 48, 53–54.

22 Satis Pakrasi, *Agnijuger Katha* (The Burning Times), Calcutta, third edition 1982, pp. 127, 129, 188–89.

23 Laushey, *Bengal Terrorism*, p. 49.

24 Bhupendrakumar Datta, *Biplaber Padachinha* (Footprints of Revolution), Calcutta, 1999, pp. 209–10.

25 To the left activists, communalism was a powerful and vicious manifestation of material contradictions. It was read as a tool of class oppression and class aspirations, as well as a violent consciousness of social divisions, rather than as a cause-in-itself.

26 IB file number censored.

[27] Hashmi, *Pakistan as a Peasant Utopia*, pp. 106, 117.

[28] IB 320/26 (310/1926), in Ladlimohon Raychaudhuri (ed.), *The Seed-Time of Communist Movement in Bengal*, Calcutta, 2000, pp. 150–51.

[29] Purabi Roy, Sobhanlal Datta Gupta and Hari Vasudevan (eds.), *Indo-Russian Relations 1917–1947, Select Documents from the Archives of the Russian Federation, Part I: 1917–1928*, Calcutta, 1999, pp. 299–300.

[30] IB 210/27 (23/1927).

[31] N. Gerald Barrier, *Banned: Controversial Literature and Political Control in British India, 1907–1947*, Columbia, 1974, p. 66.

[32] Gita Chattopadhyay, *Bangla Samayik Patrikapanji (List of Bengali Periodicals), 1915–1930*, Calcutta, 1994, p. 341.

[33] Muzaffar Ahmad, *Samakaler Katha* (Story of My Times), Calcutta, 1963, fourth edition 1996, p. 56.

[34] IB 320/26 (310/1926).

[35] IB 210/27(23/1927).

[36] David Petrie, *Communism in India (1924–1927)*, Calcutta, 1972, p. 130.

[37] Roy, Datta Gupta and Vasudevan (eds.), *Indo–Russian Relations 1917–1947*, pp. 299–300.

[38] G. Adhikary (ed.), *Documents of the History of the Communist Party of India*, Volume III C, 1928, Delhi, 1982, p. 205.

[39] Anisuzzaman, *Muslim Banglar Samayik Patrika* (List of Bengali Muslim Periodicals), Dhaka, 1969, pp. 460–63. Chattopadhyay, *Bangla Samayik Patrikapanji*, pp. 240–41.

[40] IB 320/26 (310/1926).

[41] Ahmad, *Amar Jiban o Bharater Communist Party*, p. 339.

[42] Adhikary (ed.), *Documents*, Volume III C, p. 783.

[43] IB 320/26 (310/1926). IB file number censored.

[44] Ahmad, *Amar Jiban o Bharater Communist Party*, pp. 471, 478, 486, 491. Statement of K.C. Mitra (DW20), *Meerut Communist Conspiracy Case (1929) Papers*.

[45] IB 320/26 (310/1926). IB file number censored.

[46] Roy, Datta Gupta and Vasudevan (eds.), *Indo-Russian Relations 1917–1947*, pp. 342–46.

[47] Ahmad, *Amar Jiban o Bharater Communist Party*, pp. 471, 478, 486, 491.

[48] *Meerut Communist Conspiracy Case (1929) Papers*.

[49] IB 210/27(23/1927). *Meerut Conspiracy Case Papers*.

[50] Ahmad, *Amar Jiban o Bharater Communist Party*, pp. 370–71.

[51] Roy, Datta Gupta and Vasudevan (eds.), *Indo-Russian Relations 1917–1947*, pp. 223–24.

[52] Statement of Kalidas Bhattacharya (DW16), *Meerut Communist Conspiracy Case (1929) Papers*. IB 320/26 (310/1926). IB file number censored.

[53] Statement of Kalidas Bhattacharya, *Meerut Communist Conspiracy Case (1929) Papers*.

[54] Ahmad, *Amar Jiban o Bharater Communist Party*, p. 347.

[55] Roy, Datta Gupta and Vasudevan (eds.), *Indo-Russian Relations 1917–1947*, pp. 223–24.

[56] Ahmad, *Amar Jiban o Bharater Communist Party*, pp. 346–49, 351, 464–68.

[57] Ibid. pp. 399–400.

[58] Ibid. pp. 346–49, 351, 464–68. Sen, *Itibritta*, p. 24. IB 320/26 (310/1926), in Raychaudhury (ed.), *The Seed-Time of Communist Movement in Bengal*, p. 157.

[59] Roy, Datta Gupta and Vasudevan (eds.), *Indo-Russian Relations 1917–1947*, p. 341

[60] Adhikary (ed.), *Documents of the History of the Communist Party of India*, Volume III C, pp. 782, 785.

[61] Philip Spratt, *Blowing up India: Reminiscences and Reflections of A Former Comintern Emissary*, Calcutta, 1955, p. 44.

[62] Subodh Roy (ed.), *Communism in India, Unpublished Documents, 1925–1934*, Calcutta, 1998, p. 120.

[63] Interview with Gopen Chakraborty, in Gautam Chattopadhyay, *Communism and Bengal's Freedom Movement*, Bombay, 1970, pp. 141–42.

[64] IB 320/26 (310/1926). IB file number censored.

[65] IB 320/26 (310/1926).

[66] CPI (M) Archives, Calcutta.

[67] Roy, Datta Gupta and Vasudevan (eds.), *Indo-Russian Relations 1917–1947*, pp. 234–35, 238, 240–41, 300–01.

[68] G. Adhikary (ed.), *Documents of the History of the Communist Party of India*, Volume III C, 1927, Delhi, 1979, p. 204.

[69] Adhikary (ed.), *Documents*, Volume III C, 1928, pp. 225–43.

[70] Mike Squires, *Saklatvala: A Political Biography*, London, 1990, pp. 144–55.

[71] Ahmad, *Samakaler Katha*, pp. 65–66.

[72] CPI (M) Archives, Calcutta.

[73] Horace Williamson, *India and Communism*, edited by Mahadevprasad Saha, Calcutta, 1976, p. 128.

[74] IB 320/26 (310/1926), in Raychaudhury (ed.), *The Seed-Time of Communist Movement in Bengal*, pp. 153–55.

[75] Adhikary (ed.), *Documents*, Volume III C, 1928, pp. 225–43. IB 320/26 (310/1926).

[76] IB 320/26 (310/1926).

[77] Roy, Datta Gupta and Vasudevan (eds.), *Indo-Russian Relations 1917–1947*, pp. 347–54.

[78] Ahmad, *Amar Jiban o Bharater Communist Party*, pp. 365, 374–75, 395, 397–98, 406.

[79] IB file number censored.

[80] Soumendranath Tagore, *Jatri* (Voyager), Calcutta, 1975, p. 221.

[81] Roy (ed.), *Communism in India*, pp. 118–19.

[82] Ahmad, *Amar Jiban o Bharater Communist Party*, pp. 459–61. IB file number censored. Adhikary (ed.), *Documents*, Volume III C, 1928, p. 783. Williamson, *India and Communism*, edited by Saha, p. 132.

[83] G. D. Overstreet and M. Windmiller, *Communism in India*, Berkeley, 1959, p. 119. David N. Druhe, *Soviet Russia and Indian Communism, 1917–1947, With an Epilogue Covering the Situation Today*, New York, 1959, pp. 96–99.

[84] Chattopadhyay, *Communism and Bengal's Freedom Movement*, Bombay, pp. 118–19.

[85] Aditya Mukherjee, 'The Workers' and Peasants' Parties, 1926–30: An Aspect of Communism in India', in Bipan Chandra (ed.), *The Indian Left: Critical Appraisals*, New Delhi, 1983.

[86] Sobhanlal Datta-Gupta, *Comintern, India and the Colonial Question, 1920–1937*, Calcutta, 1980, pp. 115–67; G.K. Leiten, *Colonialism, Class and Nation: The Confrontation in Bombay around 1930*, Calcutta, 1984, pp. 102–03, 104–05. For a recent treatment of the relationship between the Comintern and communism in India, see Sobhanlal Datta-Gupta, *Comintern and the Destiny of Communism in India 1919–1943: Dialectics of Real and a Possible History*, Calcutta, 2006.

[87] Datta-Gupta, *Comintern, India and the Colonial Question*, pp. 115–67. Irfan Habib, 'The Left and the National Movement', *Social Scientist*, Volume 27, Nos. 5–6, May–June 1998, p. 12.

[88] Leiten, *Colonialism, Class and Nation*, p. 107.

[89] Statement of Muzaffar Ahmad, *Meerut Communist Conspiracy Case (1929) Papers*.

[90] Ahmad, *Amar Jiban o Bharater Communist Party*, pp. 475–76.

[91] IB file number censored.

[92] IB 320/26 (310/1926).

[93] Statement of PW 212, *Meerut Communist Conspiracy Case (1929) Papers*.

[94] IB 320/26 (310/1926), in Raychaudhury (ed.), *The Seed-Time of Communist Movement in Bengal*, p. 148. Ahmad, *Bharater Communist Party Garar Prothom Jug*, pp. 22–23. Ahmad, *Samakaler Katha*, pp. 88, 90–91. Ahmad, *Amar Jiban o Bharater Communist Party*, p. 373. Leiten, *Colonialism, Class and Nation*, pp. 110–11.

[95] Jyoti Basu (ed.), *Documents of the Communist Movement in India*, Volume I: 1917–1928, Calcutta, 1997, pp. 381–84.

[96] Ahmad, *Bharater Communist Party Garar Prothom Jug*, p. 17.

[97] Ibid.

[98] Ahmad, *Amar Jiban o Bharater Communist Party*, pp. 510–12. Shachinandan Chattopadhyay, *Muzaffar Ahmad Smriti* (Memories of Muzaffar Ahmad), Calcutta, 1988, pp. 28–48 .

236　　　　　　　　AN EARLY COMMUNIST

[99] IB 320/26 (310/1926).
[100] IB 93/26 (1/1926).
[101] Ibid.
[102] IB file number censored. Ahmad, *Amar Jiban o Bharater Communist Party*, pp. 346, 348, 353.
[103] Ahmad, *Amar Jiban o Bharater Communist Party*, p. 343.
[104] Petrie, *Communism in India (1924–1927)*, p. 129.
[105] Roy, Datta Gupta and Vasudevan (eds.), *Indo-Russian Relations 1917–1947*, pp. 223–24.
[106] CPI (M) Archives, Calcutta.
[107] IB 320/26 (310/1926).
[108] Roy, Datta Gupta and Vasudevan (eds.), *Indo-Russian Relations 1917–1947*, pp. 342–46.
[109] IB file number censored.
[110] IB 320/26 (310/1926).
[111] IB file number censored.
[112] Ahmad, *Amar Jiban o Bharater Communist Party*, p. 491.
[113] IB 210/27 (23/1927).
[114] Tagore, *Jatri*, pp. 90–91.
[115] IB 67/1924 (105/24). IB 320/1926 (310/26).
[116] Tagore, *Jatri*, pp. 90–91.
[117] Roy, Datta Gupta and Vasudevan (eds.), *Indo-Russian Relations 1917–1947*, p. 300.
[118] IB 320/1926 (310/26).
[119] IB file number censored.
[120] Moinuddin, 'Ekti Sangrami Jiban: Ekti Adorsho', in Islam (ed.), *Muzaffar Ahmad: Shango o Proshango*, p. 82.
[121] Ahmad, *Amar Jiban o Bharater Communist Party*, p. 491.
[122] IB 320/26 (310/1926).
[123] Ahmad, *Amar Jiban o Bharater Communist Party*, p. 512.
[124] Moinuddin, 'Ekti Sangrami Jiban: Ekti Adorsho', in Islam (ed.), *Muzaffar Ahmad: Shango o Proshango*, p. 83. Sengupta and Basu (eds.), *Charita-bhidhan*, Vol. 1, p. 50.
[125] Chattopadhyay, *Muzaffar Ahmad Smriti*, pp. 34–35.
[126] Tagore, *Jatri*, p. 86.
[127] IB 51/21 (318/1921). IB 150/22 (189/1922).
[128] Ahmad, *Kazi Nazrul Islam: Smritikatha*, p. 215. Abdul Halim, 'Bidrohi Banglar Kobi' (Rebel Poet of Bengal), in *Nabajibaner Pathe*, pp. 138–39.
[129] Ahmad, *Kazi Nazrul Islam: Smritikatha*, p. 190. Ahmad, *Amar Jiban o Bharater Communist Party*, pp. 347, 509–12.
[130] Chattopadhyay, *Muzaffar Ahmad Smriti*, p. 43.
[131] IB 320/26 (310/1926).
[132] Ahmad, *Kazi Nazrul Islam: Smritikatha*, pp. 98–99, 190, 204, 215, 224, 227. Ahmad, *Amar Jiban o Bharater Communist Party*, p. 331. Halim, 'Bidrohi Banglar Kobi', in *Nabajibaner Pathe*, pp. 138–39. Tagore, *Jatri*, pp. 86–88.
[133] Chattopadhyay, *Muzaffar Ahmad Smriti*, p. 45.
[134] IB file number censored. Ahmad, *Amar Jiban o Bharater Communist Party*, pp. 509–10.
[135] Tagore, *Jatri*, pp. 87–90.
[136] Ahmad, *Amar Jiban o Bharater Communist Party*, pp. 476, 484.
[137] Ahmad, *Kazi Nazrul Islam: Smritikatha*, p. 151. Ahmad, *Amar Jiban o Bharater Communist Party*, p. 510.
[138] Ahmad, *Samakaler Katha*, pp. 37–38.
[139] Ahmad, *Amar Jiban o Bharater Communist Party*, pp. 371, 373–74.
[140] Chattopadhyay, *Muzaffar Ahmad Smriti*, p. 33.
[141] IB 210/27 (23/1927).
[142] *Ganabani*, 1, 9, B 1334/1927.
[143] IB file number censored.

[144] IB 35/26 (2/1926), in Raychaudhury (ed.), *The Seed-Time of Communist Movement in Bengal*, pp. 174–79.

[145] IB 117/27 (2/1927). Among the organizations listed were the CPGB, the Pan-Pacific Trade Union Congress, the National Minority Movement, Young Communist League, Labour Research Department, Workers Welfare League of India, Indian Seamen's Union (London), Colonial Bureau of the Comintern, Foreign Bureau of CPI, Chinese Information Bureau, Tass News Agency.

[146] IB 75/27 (34/1927). Ahmad, *Samakaler Katha*, pp. 34–36.

[147] IB 320/26 (310/1926), in Raychaudhury (ed.), *The Seed-Time of Communist Movement in Bengal*, pp. 153–155. IB file number censored.

[148] Statement of PW 245, *Meerut Communist Conspiracy Case (1929) Papers*.

[149] IB 320/26 (310/1926).

[150] IB file number censored.

[151] Ahmad, *Kazi Nazrul Islam: Smritikatha*, p. 222.

[152] IB 210/27 (23/1927).

[153] IB file number censored. IB 210/27 (23/1927).

[154] Ahmad, *Samakaler Katha*, pp. 33–34, 36–39. Roy (ed.), *Communism in India*, p. 47. Statement of PW 235, *Meerut Communist Conspiracy Case (1929) Papers*. IB 320/26 (310/1926).

[155] IB 320/26 (310/1926). IB file number censored.

[156] Ahmad, *Amar Jiban o Bharater Communist Party*, pp. 321–31. Petrie, *Communism in India*, pp. 165–66. Roy (ed.), *Communism in India*, pp. 3–5.

[157] Ahmad, *Probondho Sangkalan*, pp. 1–2.

[158] IB file number censored.

[159] Statement of PW 245, *Meerut Communist Conspiracy Case (1929) Papers*.

[160] Chattopadhyay, *Muzaffar Ahmad Smriti*, pp. 40–41.

[161] IB file number suppressed.

[162] IB 210/27 (23/1927).

[163] IB 320/26 (310/1926). IB file number censored. Ahmad, *Amar Jiban o Bharater Communist Party*, pp. 352–56. Tagore, *Jatri*, pp. 92–93. Mike Squires, *Saklatvala*, p. 153.

[164] Tagore, *Jatri*, pp. 97–98.

[165] IB 93/26 (1/1926).

[166] IB 95/24 (41/1924).

[167] Adhikary (ed.), *Documents*, Volume III C, 1927, p. 207.

[168] IB 320/26 (310/1926), in Raychaudhury (ed.), *The Seed-Time of Communist Movement in Bengal*, pp. 147, 150.

[169] Ibid, p. 150.

[170] Roy (ed.), *Communism in India*, p. 62.

[171] Ibid, pp. 40–42.

[172] IB 320/26 (310/1926), in Raychaudhury (ed.), *The Seed-Time of Communist Movement in Bengal*, pp. 149–50.

[173] Colson's suggestions on combating the 'Bolshevik Menace' have been discussed in Chapter Three.

[174] IB 320/26 (310/1926), in Raychaudhury (ed.), *The Seed-Time of Communist Movement in Bengal*, pp. 145–46.

[175] Roy (ed.), *Communism in India*, pp. 64–70, 28–33, 33–37.

[176] IB 93/26 (1/1926).

[177] Ahmad, *Amar Jiban o Bharater Communist Party*, pp. 496–502.

[178] IB file number censored. IB 320/26 (310/1926), in Raychaudhury (ed.), *The Seed-Time of Communist Movement in Bengal*, pp. 150–51.

[179] Roy (ed.), *Communism in India*, pp. 59–60.

[180] IB 93/26 (1/1926).

[181] Ibid.

[182] IB 210/27 (23/1927).

[183] IB file number censored.

[184] IB 210/27 (23/1927).

[185] Ahmad, *Samakaler Katha*, pp. 34–36.

[186] The circumstances of Campbell and Johnstone's deportation have been discussed in Chapter Four.

[187] IB file number censored.

[188] Sarkar, *Modern India*, pp. 271–72.

[189] Roy (ed.), *Communism in India*, p. 39.

[190] Ahmad, *Amar Jiban o Bharater Communist Party*, pp. 458, 509–11.

[191] Pramita Ghose, *Meerut Conspiracy Case and the Left-Wing in India*, Calcutta, 1978, pp. 82–84, 147–48. Spratt, *Blowing up India*, pp. 58–59. IB file number censored.

[192] IB 210/27 (23/1927).

[193] For a critical account of *praja* politics from an insider, see Abul Mansoor Ahmad, *Amar Dakha Rajnitir Panchash Bachar* (Fifty Years of Politics as I Saw It), Dhaka, 1968. Naresh-chandra Sengupta, 'Atmakatha' (My Story), in *Jugoporikrama* (Survey of an Age), Volume 1, Calcutta, 1981, pp. 15–16.

[194] Roy (ed.), *Communism in India*, p. 123.

[195] Mukhopadhyay, *Bharater Communist Party o Amra*, p. 54.

[196] Somnath Lahiri, *Rachanabali* (Collected Writings), Vol. 1, Calcutta, first edition 1985, reprint 1995, pp. 68–69. Sen, *Itibritta*, pp. 236–43.

[197] IB 210/27 (23/1927).

[198] Mukhopadhyay, *Bharater Communist Party o Amra*, pp. 16, 46, 48.

[199] IB file number censored.

[200] Mukhopadhyay, *Bharater Communist Party o Amra*, p. 35.

[201] Tanika Sarkar, *Bengal 1928–1934: The Politics of Protest*, Delhi, 1987, p. 104.

[202] Mukhopadhyay, *Bharater Communist Party o Amra*, pp. 35, 46, 51, 54.

[203] Ibid, p. 61.

[204] Ibid, pp. 54, 58, 62–63. IB 210/27 (23/1927). Amitabha Chandra, *Abibhakta Banglay Communist Andolan: Suchana Parbo* (Communist Movement in Undivided Bengal: The First Phase), Calcutta, 1992, p. 9.

[205] Sen, *Itibritta*, p. 243. Interview with Ranen Sen, Calcutta, 13 and 16 August 1999.

[206] IB 93/26 (1/1926).

[207] Mukhopadhyay, *Bharater Communist Party o Amra*, pp. 76, 78, 84–85. Sen, *Itibritta*, pp. 51–52.

[208] Muzaffar Ahmad, 'Santrasbadi Biplobira Bharater Communist Partyte Elen – Bangla o Bihar' (Revolutionary Terrorists Join the Communist Party – Bengal and Bihar), in *Nirbachito Rachana Sangkalan*, pp. 136–44. Pakrasi, *Agnijuger Katha*, pp. 161–81, 188. Laushey, *Bengal Terrorism*, pp. 86–120. Similar patterns could be detected elsewhere in Asia; communist drives in colonial prisons of Vietnam during the 1930s led to mass recruitment from the ranks of underground activists belonging to the nationalist and secret society networks. See Peter Zinoman, *The Colonial Bastille: A History of Imprisonment in Vietnam, 1862–1940*, Berkeley and Los Angeles, 2001, pp. 200–39, 267–96.

[209] Ahmad, *Amar Jiban o Bharater Communist Party*, pp. 482–84.

[210] Sengupta and Basu, *Charitabhidhan*, Vol. 1, p. 117.

[211] Muzaffar Ahmad, 'Amader Manmathanath' (Our Manmathanath), *Nandan*, *Poush-Magh* B 1380/1974, pp. 1082–84.

[212] Interview with Gopen Chakraborty, in Chattopadhyay, *Communism and Bengal's Freedom Movement*, p. 139.

[213] IB file number censored.

[214] Mukhopadhyay, *Bharater Communist Party o Amra*, pp. 66, 84.

[215] Chandra, *Abibhakta Banglay Communist Andolan*, pp. 8, 98–103.

[216] Mukhopadhyay, *Bharater Communist Party o Amra*, p. 166.

Class, Language, City

'The dead have their own tasks.'
– Rainer Maria Rilke, 'Requiem for a Friend'

Munshi Alimuddin had died long before Muzaffar Ahmad arrived in Calcutta. Yet the nineteenth-century Urdu writer's unobtrusive shadow seems to have followed Muzaffar from the beginning to the end of his time in the city. During the 1910s, Muzaffar found employment as a private tutor and stayed in the house of Alimuddin. Whenever the spectre of destitution visited in the early 1920s, he could seek asylum there. Towards the later decades of his life, this association was strangely rekindled when a CPI commune and office were set up at a street named after the dead writer; it became the Bengal headquarters of his party from the 1960s. Following Muzaffar Ahmad's death, the office was moved to a new building named after Muzaffar on the same street. When Muzaffar had come to the city in 1913, his ambition was to be a writer. What Munshi Alimuddin became in nineteenth-century Calcutta eluded him. The dialectical interplay between his social being and social consciousness took him in directions he could not have envisaged at the moment of his arrival.

Prose

Muzaffar Ahmad's emergence as a polemical communist writer from the second half of the 1920s mirrored a break with his earliest intellectual engagements. An advocate of a distinct language which was rare in the 1920s, his prose style, shaped by radical modernist perceptions, attracted only a small left readership even if other writers acknowledged its significance later.[1] During his career as a Bengali Muslim cultural polemicist, Muzaffar supported Islamic content but not Islamization of form, opposing artificial arabicization or aanskritization. As his political outlook changed, his rejection of attempts to communalize the Bengali language became even more pronounced. Muzaffar refused to do away with Arabic and Persian words which had been part of the Bengali vocabulary, and to spell certain Bengali words in ways that delinked them from their Arabic and Persian roots. Simultaneously, he wrote in a modern style which originated from the great nineteenth-century Hindu *bhadralok* writers. He also mastered a reticent humour through his sentence structures; this acted as a tool of sub-version while the prose was adapted to put forward the social interests of the lower orders of society. His writings were examples, therefore, of radicalism in the formal sense as well.

The Question of Class

From 1926 to 1928, Muzaffar expanded the thematic content of his political prose in the pages of *Langal* and *Ganabani*.[2] A continuation of the Marxist critique of class society begun in 1922, the articles aimed to project socialism as the only alternative to nationalism and communalism before middle-class readers. 'Class' was stressed as a radical model of theory and action. Muzaffar shifted and challenged the terms of existing political discourse on the anti-colonial struggle to transform the discourse itself. Some of the key ideas that went into the making of the new interpretative framework intersected with and drew on the analytical reservoir built by the Roys, the Dutt brothers, Spratt and others, though they could not be seen simply as 'derivative'. Muzaffar treated and created contemporary left issues of the day with examples drawn from wider political events as well as developments in his immediate surroundings. The interactions between nationalism and communalism, and their class dimensions, were central to his concerns. This meant breaking away from the existing perspectives and substituting them with radically new ones, achieved through the prism of 'class'.

One way of arriving at class-based politics was through an interpretation of 'freedom' and, more importantly, by identifying its enemies. In 'Bharat Kano Swadhin Noy?' (Why is India Not Free?'), Muzaffar offered a taxonomy of class forces that were obstructing 'freedom' for the vast majority of peasants and workers. His focus was on those with vested interests who kept existing class relations in place: imperialists who represented British colonial capital and operated through the bureaucracy of the colonial state; Indian capitalists, landlords and usurers who were keen to emerge as future ruling classes, and acted through the ideology and politics of nationalism; Hindu and Muslim theologians, priests and clerics who played a crucial role in communal mobilization, which undermined the development of class solidarity.[3] He was to repeat this argument.[4]

The categorization of exploiters, in turn, led Muzaffar to develop other key concepts along Leninist lines. While analysing the rule of colonial capital, he distinguished between 'empire' and 'imperialism'. Arguing that imperialism went beyond the concept of a formally constituted territorial empire, he stressed that British rule in India was representative of a system which other capitalist countries also imposed over their colonies and semi-colonies. He identified France and the United States of America as two of the foremost imperialist countries guided by the interests of their respective bourgeoisies, and engaged, like Britain, in the formation of imperialism. This was linked to his projection of imperialism as a global process against which the Indian anti-colonial struggle had to be situated;[5] India and the world could only be free if liberated from imperialism and the exploitative conditions it created.[6]

Applying an internationalist comparative perspective to local conditions, Muzaffar focused on the specific modes of imperialist oppression. Contrasting India with China, he argued that while the latter was officially a politically independent, 'free' country, the economic stranglehold of imperialism placed it firmly within the boundaries of the colonial world.[7] In 'Rajodroho' (Sedition), he offered a critique of the colonial legal lexicon. He defined anti-state activities in India as 'sedition against imperialist oppression', the appropriate phrase for accusing political prisoners; the king of England, a mere figurehead, was not the principal executor of imperialism. Muzaffar argued that the charge of 'sedition against the king' which led to his conviction at Kanpur was ridiculous. Violation of the colonial law was not really an offence against the monarchy; such actions harmed British colonial capital and Indian owners of large property who were protected by the law.[8] Muzaffar linked imperialism to some of the contemporary ultra-right political formations and strategies evident in Europe. 'Bhadrasrenir Manabikata' (Humanity of the Bhadralok) described fascism in Italy as a ruling-class offensive linked with empire-building, to crush the struggle of ordinary people and rob them of their entitlements. 'British Labour Party-r Adhahpatan' (Degeneration of the British Labour Party) criticized the Labour leadership for displaying social-imperialist and pro-capitalist tendencies which betrayed the interests of the British working class as well as the colonized subjects of Britain.[9] Clearly, the experience of the anti-colonial struggle and the complex variations within it were also instrumental in shaping the language used in these articles.

Exposing Mainstream Anti-Colonialism
It was the second category of exploiters, those protected under the cloak of nationalism, who received the lion's share of Muzaffar's critical attention. The need to form an alternative political struggle informed by class analysis and to go beyond mainstream anti-colonialism formed his perspective. He argued that the idea of a 'nation' free of class divisions was the master

strategy of the ruling class in waiting; the guiding principles and strategies of nationalist politics were based on the denial and suppression of class politics; the attempts to dissolve and diffuse class conflict could take various forms. 'Krishak o Sramik Andolan' (Movements of Peasants and Workers) challenged the claims of 'spiritual' unity and equality advanced by the nationalist leaders; these idealist manoeuvres suppressed class struggle by persuading the oppressed to cooperate with their oppressors.[10] 'Sreni Sangram' (Class Struggle) dissected the nature of middle-class opposition to the state and capital which took on reformist, 'humanitarian' and nationalist forms; a shared fear of class struggle characterized all. 'Politicians, non-politicians, humanitarians and a-political elements' ignored, suppressed, denounced and projected 'class' as an alien force introduced by socialists and communists to 'destabilize' the existing society. Muzaffar sarcastically observed that some of these people even 'worshipped' communist theoreticians 'from Marx to Lenin' but regarded class struggle as inimical to 'Indian interests'; they laid stress on 'postponing' class struggle till the colonizers were forced to leave despite 'acknowledging the oppression' inflicted on 'the Indian peasants by the Indian landlords' and by 'the Indian capitalists on the Indian workers'. They felt that class oppression had to be tolerated 'as long as the British remain in our country'. That 'class struggle exists in society because classes exist' was ignored. The fact that 'workers and peasants' were never called 'capitalists and landlords' indicated that there were differences in their class positions and class interests. Otherwise, the need to separately name different categories of people in society would not have arisen.[11]

The occlusions of mainstream nationalism made Muzaffar turn towards the social character of colonial prisons, humanist claims and elite resistance. 'Karagar Sambandhye Desher Oudashinyo' (The Indifference of the Country to Prisons) exposed upper-class leaders who did not regard ordinary people as 'human'. Only a small percentage of the jail population were political prisoners, but a disproportionate focus on their 'human rights' was advanced by mainstream political leaders. This reflected the solidarity among members of the possessing classes of society. These very leaders chose to ignore the 'human rights' of 'ordinary prisoners' who committed crimes against the rule of private property and were subjected to a brutal prison regime.[12] 'Kon Pathe?' (Which Way?) argued that the 'formation of secret societies' acted as yet another way of denying class struggle. 'Terror' was necessarily a method explored by middle-class and lower-middle-class activists who suffered from a 'hidden sense of aristocratic elitism' which kept them away from the masses. The Hindu *bhadralok* terrorists, Muzaffar affirmed, had singularly failed to achieve freedom for India as their ideology and actions excluded ordinary people.[13] Despite the enormity of his

Muzaffar Ahmad (*third from left*) after his release from prison in 1951

'self-sacrifice', the terrorist, rooted in middle-class opposition to colonialism, conformed to self-interest by failing to join the masses in their struggles
against the imperialists and Indian proprietor interests.[14]

Muzaffar accused the leaders of different political parties of abandoning
the people unhesitatingly if class interests so demanded, though they claimed
to be concerned with the welfare of the masses. He regarded the Indian
National Congress as being consistent in this respect.[15] Focusing on the role
played by the nationalist leadership in perpetuating the oppression faced by
workers and peasants, he criticized the All India Trade Union Congress
(AITUC) and its affiliated organizations, run by 'parasitic' middle-class leaders
or humanitarian activists led by charitable motives. To Muzaffar, they were

ideologically incapable of regarding the working class as leading agents in the freedom movement and as harbingers of 'revolutionary trade union-ism'.[16] He highlighted the contradictions embedded in nationalism. He criticized the nationalists for speaking against British 'bureaucracy' and 'empire' controlled by colonial capital, while refusing to oppose capitalism. Citing C.R. Das and Gandhi as examples, he argued that they were aware of class struggle in society, and that they chose to side with the capitalists armed with this foreknowledge. Muzaffar analysed the speech delivered by Das at the Lahore session of AITUC in 1923, to show that although he acknowledged the validity of class conflict, Das did not propagate it as he did not wish to repudiate his ties with capital.[17] The Swarajists opposed even the claim of workers to a minimum wage.[18]

A similar case could be made, according to Muzaffar, regarding the relationship between nationalism and the peasantry. He observed that land-lordism, the social prop of imperialism in the countryside, was no longer economically profitable to British imperialism; the government could extract far greater revenue if the landlords disappeared as intermediaries between the state and the cultivators. Greater material benefits, which were dependent on maintaining control over the rural folk, prevented colonialism from doing away with the system. The Bengal Congress, guided by landlord interests, also could not be expected to stand by the peasantry. The Congress programmes of 'village reconstruction' and 'returning to the villages' were totally useless as they bypassed concrete questions regarding the sources of agrarian exploitation and poverty. Muzaffar wrote: 'It is rank hypocrisy to remain silent on the land question and oppose imperialism. The two are intertwined. If one is condoned, then both are supported automatically.'[19] The Swarajists displayed their alignment to the landlords by opposing the Bengal land tenancy reforms.[20] An extension of this continued betrayal of the people was the tendency to compromise with imperialism.[21] The 'bourgeois, landlord and petit-bourgeois composition' of the Congress prevented the organization from demanding and struggling for anything more than 'Dominion Status'. [22]

Muzaffar concentrated on the dominant form of anti-colonialism in Bengal. In 'Bhadrasrenir Manabikata' (Humanity of the Bhadralok), he argued that nationalism in Bengal was based on a Hindu *bhadralok* identity. This equipped the *bhadralok* radicals to embrace martyrdom 'with a smiling face' while stridently defending their narrow self-definition of 'gentility'. To drive home his point on the elite core of nationalist politics, Muzaffar noted and condemned the contemporary craze for Mussolini as a model nation-builder in the pages of *Amrita Bazar Patrika*. He felt that contemporary accounts of fascist atrocities, including the one offered by Dilip Roy after returning from Italy, were being deliberately ignored to shower praise on a vicious dictator. The attachment in the nationalist quarters of Bengal to the kind of 'patriotism' which projected members of the '*bhadralok*' classes as higher beings, or as natural leaders of those engaged in manual work (the Bengali term for the latter, a pejorative one, being '*chotolok*'), acted as a bridge between fascism and *bhadralok* nationalism.[23]

The Story of the Bhadralok

Muzaffar was to repeat this understanding of the relationship between *bhadralok* identity and sympathy for fascism in his court statement on revolutionary nationalism during the Meerut Conspiracy Case:

> I would further like to explain how the Workers and Peasants Party and I, as a Communist, looked at the Terroristic activities prevalent in certain parts of India, especially in Bengal. . . . Terrorism . . . had been a purely sectarian movement of educated youths belonging to the Hindu religious thought. All the pioneers of this movement had come from the Bhadralog class of Bengal which in fact has never been a class in the real sense. . . . This so called class consists of all sorts of people from landlords to proletarianized intellectuals.
>
> Young intelligentsia drawn from such a meaningless class joined together in a movement . . . out of mere romanticism and a platonic ideal of courage. . . . I must admit that the Terrorists have sacrificed a great deal since the very beginning of their movement. The gallows, transportation for life, sentences to imprisonment and detention without trial have always fallen to their lot and boldly they have stood all these miseries of life. Every revolutionary will certainly appreciate the sacrifice made by the Terrorists, but are the Terrorists revolutionaries? I must say, they are not. They have never believed in the real revolutionary social elements – the workers and the peasants. In their ideal, they have never visualized the social changes to come. . . .
>
> In short, having failed to be analysts of social conditions and economic forces, the Terrorists have remained today where they had been 27 years ago.
>
> Pure Terroristic movement like this could not achieve any success in any country. Mere romanticism will not lead the Terrorists very far. There is one extreme possibility however which is worth taking into consideration. As the Terrorists have got social affiliation with the landowning class they will join hands with this class when the actual revolutionary situation will develop. In that case they will come to play a counter revolutionary role like the Social Revolutionaries in Russia and the Fascists in Italy. Of course it is probable that a small section of them will understand the revolutionary significance of the main struggle and will join it.[24]

Muzaffar's earlier analysis indicates that he was consistent in his reading of the *bhadralok* as a class. Responding to his old polemical opponent Sudhakanta Raychaudhuri, Muzaffar was to re-emphasize his critique of the 'bhadralok class position'. Sudhakanta had written an 'Open Letter' in *Birbhumbani* (Voice of Birbhum) where, according to Muzaffar, he expressed dissatisfaction over repeated attacks on the 'bhadralok and the educated' in the pages of *Ganabani*; he had wondered if the communists who wrote and ran *Ganabani* did not see themselves as 'educated bhadraloks', and suggested that the paper should display less 'anger, disrespect and sarcasm' towards those who constituted its readership. Muzaffar replied that the *bhadralok* as a class were unique; an identical social formation was not be found anywhere. Held together on the basis of consciousness of class rather than common material interests, they were peculiar. This consciousness was realized in social practice through a shared contempt for 'non-respectable' people. Some belonging to the *bhadralok* ranks were 'poor, often pauperized'. Despite this they tended to identify with the upper classes, regarding the masses as inferior. Although they gained nothing from the existing social order in material terms, they clung to it as to their gentlemanly values. This could be linked to their love of larger-than-life authority figures such as C.R. Das and Gandhi. They regarded 'respectability' as the touchstone of their own existence while having no respect for the ordinary people on whose labour their survival rested. Muzaffar acknowledged that the communists were 'educated' people, but their education had taught them to oppose the culture and politics of the '*bhadralok*'. This was because the communists had consciously sided with and refused to despise the primary producers, commonly labeled as '*chotolok*'.[25]

A Hidden Chronicle of Divisions

Muzaffar also focused on the entangled structures of class and communal conflict. He regarded communalism from above as a double-edged strategy of the possessing classes, a method of maximizing the internal bargaining power of various upper-class fractions while weakening the collective bargaining power of the poor. The masses, on the other hand, responded to communal politics precisely because they faced dispossession and deprivation under the existing property regime. Communalism from below reflected aspirations to fight dispossession.

Muzaffar upheld these arguments, from the second half of the 1920s, through a series of articles reacting to the deteriorating communal climate.[26] 'Kothay Protikar?' (Where Lies Redressal?) held the nationalist and Khilafatist leaders responsible for the revival of communal politics with the waning of the Non-Cooperation Movement. It predicted major communal riots and destructive social polarization that could only go against the interests of the 'starving workers and peasants' who constituted the majority of the population. Muzaffar questioned the concept of 'Hindu–Muslim unity' on the grounds that the leaders who forged this alliance assumed that the

Communist Party members drawn from the ranks of Muslim workers of Calcutta, 1939

interests of ordinary people could only be expressed in religious terms. This implicated them in the social project of dividing the people and exposed their communal perceptions. The Lucknow Pact, the Non-Cooperation Movement, the formation of the Swarajya Dal and other political examples of attempted 'unity' were fundamentally flawed as they were all guided by a 'mentality of communal separation' (*samprodayik bhedbuddhi*); the same mentality provided an impetus to communal movements such as 'Hindu Mahasabha, Hindu Sangathan, Suddhi Andolan, Khilafat, Tabliq, Tanzeem and Muslim League'.

Though primarily interested in probing the social roots of communal politics rather than the religiosity of the people, Muzaffar did reveal the communist position on matters of faith. He did not 'wish to go into the fundamental basis of religion' but declared that, though religion projected itself as the 'congealed' 'love of humankind', it sought justification through the 'slaughter of humankind'. He also treated the contradictions inherent in the manipulation of religious symbols which acted as points of mobilization during communal conflict.[27] He described festivals based on religious symbols as harmful, and opposed those who regarded them as beneficial and constructive.[28] In 'Akkhani Patra' (A Letter), Muzaffar agreed with the correspondent Daud Ali Datta that the unfolding of communal violence was painful, but stressed on their hidden class content. The poor who plundered the property of the rich were motivated as much by class interests as by communal ones. The mainstream media, representing proprietor interests, suppressed this.[29] Muzaffar argued that the only method by which the upper classes could project themselves as victims was by labelling class rage from below as 'communal'. The real victims were rising against the regime of property. The oppressed were not necessarily aware of the forms their rising assumed; still, these were socially desperate actions reflecting a desire to be free which remained unfulfilled. If the people took their rage beyond communal forms and closed ranks, they could liberate themselves.[30] 'Akkhani Patra' suggested that men of religion such as *mullah*s and priests (*mullah–purohit*), pillars of the existing social order, reinforced the oppressive conditions through communal strategies.[31] Muzaffar opposed pan-Islamism on political terms. Ridiculing the idea of a united Muslim fraternity as 'weak' and 'absurd', he referred to the differences among the Arabs and the Turks to hold that apparent religious solidarity was often undercut by other considerations.[32]

Violence and Representation
Muzaffar related contemporary representations of gender violence to communal politics. In 'Nari-Nirjatan' (Oppression of Women) and 'Ashol Kathata Ki?' (What is the Real Issue?), he argued that the realities of patriarchy were being deliberately distorted to suit the communal politics of the proprietor classes. He criticized attempts to project sexual assaults on women as attacks against the honour of the community; such communal representations were extensions of violent male chauvinism. Muzaffar asserted that the sensational stories published in the press were aimed at spreading religious hatred: by projecting Muslim men as violators of Hindu women during communal riots, the Hindu *bhadralok*-run newspapers sidestepped the trans-communal character of sex crimes. They effectively ignored the routine violence against Hindu women by Hindu men, and of Muslim women by Muslim men. Those who printed these stories were devoid of any concern for the victims. Their only interest was the symbolic manipulation of sexual assault to boost their communal agenda.[33]

The New Party
By promoting political alternatives to the rule of British colonial capital and to the future class rule of the Indian upper classes, Muzaffar argued for a 'proletarian leadership' over the anti-colonial, democratic bloc. This made him explain and advocate the formation of the first socialist organization in Bengal. In 'Nutan Dal' (New Party), he criticized existing political formations for betraying the poor, and aligning with Indian capitalists and land-

lords. Any worthwhile anti-imperialist movement had to uphold the struggle of the lower classes. It was therefore necessary to build a mass struggle against imperialism led by a new kind of people's party led by the proletariat (*sarbohara*) and including exploited peasants.[34] He stressed that the party would also draw recruits from the impoverished lower-middle-class segments who faced dispossession, were alienated by capitalism and displayed interest in mass movements.[35] 'Ki Kara Chai?' (What is to be Done?) propagated the programme of the Peasants and Workers Party of Bengal (PWP) to mobilize women and men from working-class, peasant and lower-middle-class backgrounds on the basis of certain political, economic and social demands.[36]

The strategy of this party was to dissociate itself from the dominant ideology and leadership of the Congress, rather than from its mass base. Muzaffar stressed that it opposed the type of class 'oligarchy' envisaged by the nationalists, and that it wished to see the transformation of the Congress, the largest anti-colonial platform, into an organization upholding mass interests.[37] Emphasizing the role of 'mass consciousness' (*jana-gana choitonyo*) as the only force behind every struggle,[38] he argued that this consciousness could emerge through militant trade unionism and peasant movements. The workers, he thought, must be made aware of the damaging role played by reformists and opportunists in trade union politics, so that the working class could protect itself.[39] A radical peasant association was needed to implement a 'land to the tiller' programme through militant struggles.[40]

Politics of Disaffiliation

Muzaffar urged Hindu *bhadralok* and Muslim middle-class youth in search of political freedom to move away from hierarchical self-definitions which bound them to their class origins, asking them to uphold the interests of workers and peasants rather than capitalists and landlords. He asked political activists from the possessing classes who had sincerely devoted themselves to the cause of the country's freedom to consider where the interests of the majority of their compatriots lay, and unlearn the sense of social superiority they had inherited. He also stressed that lower-middle-class people facing dispossession could expect little from the future class rule of Indian capitalists and landlords. 'Akkhana Patra' (A Letter), addressing anonymous revolutionary terrorist 'friends', argued that they would be unable to bring about revolutionary transformation if they failed to identify with the masses.[41] Middle-class youth in search of complete freedom were asked to join the new party upholding mass interests, since freedom rested only in liberation from exploitation.[42] In 'Krishak o Sramik Ebong Sikkhito Jubo Samproday' (Peasants and Workers and the Educated Youth), a speech Muzaffar delivered at the Special Youth Conference in Dhaka as secretary of the section on Workers and Peasants, he appealed to the *bhadralok* youth to give up the politics of terror since it was closely linked with communal forms, and to adopt socialism as the most radical route to politics.[43] Elsewhere, he specifically urged Muslim middle-class youth to move away from exclusivist identity politics which was tied with propertied interests.[44]

Marxism in Context

Muzaffar's arrest in early 1929 ended a period of pioneering socialist journalism. Though his essays did not gain widespread popularity in the 1920s, they represented interventions which were to find a resonance later. Muzaffar's political prose was both new and significant, for it was the first systematic attempt to adapt Marxist–Leninist ideas to the Bengal context. Inspired by the Bolshevik Revolution (1917) and Leninism, revolutionaries in many countries were motivated to apply Marxism to local conditions. In this sense, Muzaffar's reading of class contradictions in Bengal and India can be situated in a broad stream of contextual Marxist interpretations. These came from some of the leading figures of his generation in the international movement such as Ho Chi Minh (1890–1969), Antonio Gramsci (1891–1937) and Mao Tse-Tung (1893–1976), as well as the neglected Peruvian communist Jose Carlos Mariategui (1894–1930). Muzaffar's prose, though functional and programmatic, generated a lucid vocabulary for the Marxist–Leninist left. Through his articles in *Langal* and *Ganabani*, Muzaffar initiated a new political language for Bengal by emphasizing terms such as 'class' (*sreni*), 'class struggle' (*sreni-sangram*), 'capitalism' (*dhanatantra*), 'imperialism' (*shoshonbad*), 'fascism' (*fascibad*), 'proletariat/dispossessed' (*sarbohara*), 'mass consciousness' (*janagana choitanyo*). Despite their restricted impact on the intelligentsia at the time, these words came to be associated with movements, organizations and protests which involved the illiterate poor, thereby paving the way for wider reception in the future. Simultaneously, Muzaffar expanded the meanings of terms popularized by the mainstream anti-colonial struggle and used them for the purposes of a socialist political strategy. By offering redefinitions of words such as 'nation' (*jati*), 'country' (*desh*), 'people' (*janagan*), 'freedom' (*swadhinata*) and 'popular interest' (*jana swartha*), he invested them with class dimensions and counterposed them to their mainstream usage.[45] Muzaffar arrived at several original interpretations of culture and politics in Bengal while seeking to popularize communism: a social critique of the *bhadralok* culture and mentality; the entrenched social weight of language to promote class exploitation in society; the overlapping class projects of nationalist politics and communal divisions; the communalization of the agrarian class struggle; the communal uses of patriarchy. Though anti-fascist politics in India, conventionally, is dated back to the 1930s, Muzaffar initiated anti-fascist polemics in the

Bengal context almost a decade earlier. Among the communists in the colonial world, he was one of the first to write on and perceive fascism and imperialism as episodes in the enmeshed lives of class and capital. There was a dialectical relationship between the political climate of his age and the 'language of class' he spearheaded, rooted in the conviction of revolutionary change.

Memoirs

Though Muzaffar continued to write, his next major engagement with prose came in the form of his political reminiscences. They treat of the times which set the stage for the early communist movement in which he was to play the role of a principal actor. Muzaffar turned to the autobiographical genre in the late 1950s. The three monographs recalling his days as the leading figure on the left in Bengal were mainly written and published during the last ten years of his life (1963–73). They exhibit a dialectical interplay between the time-frame of the memoirs themselves and the times in which they were written. This process finds its way into Muzaffar's narrative and the politics of his self-portrayal.

Context
Muzaffar's first attempt at recounting the past was through *Samakaler Katha* (Story of My Times), published while in prison on 5 August 1963, on his seventy-fourth birthday. The first edition contained six essays; three more were added to the 1988 reprint.[46] Individually published in different leftwing journals in the late 1950s and early 1960s, in the turbulent period just prior to the split of the Communist Party of India (CPI), the themes explored were influenced by a climate of heightened ideological struggle wherein the past had become a source of controversy.

Muzaffar's emphasis on documents to support his version was motivated by a desire to give his narrative a sense of historicity even though he was adamant that it was a recollection of his political past. Even memory had to be protected from accusations of amnesia and projected as more than the subjective perceptions of an infirm old man. Only the first two essays deal with personal experiences. They briefly outline Muzaffar's life and times before and immediately after he became a communist. The rest are polemical exercises, descriptive sketches and reproductions of old records. They revolve around fragments that constituted what he regarded as the political past: old letters, policy documents, the structure of police surveillance, socialist journalism, the Peasants and Workers Party as the first socialist organization, and the class character of the Indian National Congress. They could be regarded the raw material which shaped his political self: versions of the circumstances and currents that influenced the emergence of the communist movement from the late 1910s to the 1920s.[47]

Though released from prison in late 1963, Muzaffar was rearrested on the charge of threatening national security a year later. This was to be his last stretch in prison. Despite his poor health, the government kept him in jail till the middle of 1966. It was during this period that he wrote *Kazi Nazrul Islam: Smritikatha* (Kazi Nazrul Islam: Recollections),[48] published in late 1965. He had earlier written a booklet and short articles on Nazrul, which he revised and enlarged extensively. In the process, he arrived at what many regard as a minor masterpiece in literary recollection.[49]

Smritikatha is an exercise in the reconstruction of a literary age through reflections on his friend and a major Bengali poet, Kazi Nazrul Islam. It is also an indirect attempt to recount Muzaffar's early career as a literary activist. It contains a quaint and humorous portrait of his association with the intellectual circles of the 1910s and 1920s, a period of cultural and political transition. Through a description of his friendship with Nazrul Islam, Muzaffar unravelled the dynamic social sphere of the uprooted intellectual who was turning from literature to radical politics. *Smritikatha* remains a vintage study of the modernist avant-garde as well as conservative writers, and provides insights into the cultural backdrop of his own transition. In this sense, it complements his own memoirs where he attempts to locate his transformation and activism in the political currents of the same period. Muzaffar started working on them from 1965. Prison was proving to be a productive environment for him, even though he had to rely on friends to supply material from outside.

His comrades, Mahadevprasad Saha, Subodh Roy and Dwijendra Nandy, collected material from the National Archives of India, which helped Muzaffar prepare his version of the past. Roy edited and published Cecil Kaye's *Communism in India* alongside other secret British documents on Indian communism. Kaye, Director of Criminal Intelligence between 1919 and 1924, was in charge of containing communist networks in their early stages. Under his supervision, former *muhajirs* who had tried to return secretly from the Soviet Union and start communist activity inside India were captured and prosecuted. The Kanpur Conspiracy Case of 1924 was the last and most important event in Kaye's career as an expert on ways to counter Bolshevism. In 1925, the year marking his retirement, Kaye wrote a document authorized by the Indian government for exclusive circulation among British officials in charge of monitoring communist activities. Subodh Roy republished this document along with other surveillance reports compiled by the Intelligence Department under Kaye's directorship.[50] Saha wrote the introduction to Roy's anthology, and extended the project by introducing and republishing a similar document by Kaye's successor, David Petrie. Petrie's directorship lasted from 1925 to 1927. Based on the experiences of those years, Saha wrote an official sequel to Kaye's work which had the same title.[51]

Since Muzaffar figured prominently in these books as one of Moscow's chief 'agents', he made use of the material to refresh his memory. Saha also assisted Muzaffar in locating material from other sources, as he had done earlier while *Smritikatha* was being written. Muzaffar also received help from Devendra Kaushik, an Indian scholar, and Robert C. North, an American academic who sent him copies of Comintern documents. Other friends and comrades, some of whom were based in London with access to libraries and archives, also sent records.[52] Muzaffar paid great attention to data collection. Judging from his correspondence with those who helped him, it would seem that he often went to extraordinary lengths to locate a single detail. For instance, in a letter to one of his contacts in London, he enquired if any information could be gathered about one Abdul Kadir Khan, a police agent who had travelled with the *muhajir*s to the Soviet Union. Khan's cooperation had allegedly earned him a lecturership in Pashtu at the School of Oriental Studies (later SOAS) in London.[53]

The language of Muzaffar's autobiographical writings reflects the syncreticism that had evolved during the early decades of the twentieth century. It avoids and opposes the dual attempts to 'sanskritize' and 'Islamicize' the Bengali language, processes which led to a conscious purging of words in common usage from the vocabulary. A self-critical and reticent humour also characterizes these writings. These elements marking Muzaffar's prose can be related to the wider theme of the way the self was projected in his recollections.

Muzaffar Ahmad's memoir titled *Amar Jiban o Bharater Communist Party* (My Life and the Communist Party of India) remains unfinished. As he had anticipated, old age, illness and death intervened and prevented him from completing the most significant writing project of his lifetime. *Amar Jiban* was published in two phases. The first part, numbering 430 pages, was published during the author's lifetime. Muzaffar took two-and-a-half years, between 1965 and 1967, to finish this. The second part, which is only 67 pages long and incomplete, was published posthumously in 1974. It recounts the trade unionization and labour upsurge of the late 1920s which directly contributed to the arrest and trial of leading communists in 1929. Various portions of it, like his earlier autobiographical works, had already been printed before it appeared in book form.

Later, the two volumes were combined and reprinted. *Amar Jiban* incorporated, expanded and went beyond the themes collected and published in 1963 as *Samakaler Katha*. The work has an unusual, 'unstructured' form. Prison life, dependence on others for supply of source material and old age were some of the physical factors which shaped the book's unconventional thematic organization.

Content

The content of the book had a crucial impact on its form. An examination of the themes reveals that the memoir was primarily concerned with routes and episodes that went into the making of the early communist movement. The author's recollections are not consistently structured around his own role in the movement. Rather, the detailed narrative resembles a gigantic mosaic wherein Muzaffar's own career as a political activist is located among other careers and incidents. The author withdraws and reappears many times .in the narrative. In some episodes he does not figure directly; these are then interspersed with events where he does. Large sections are devoted to the details of the formation of an emigre communist party under M.N. Roy's leadership in Tashkent, which emerged out of the *muhajir* contingents who had travelled to Soviet Central Asia through Afghanistan after their exodus from India. Roy and his rivals, especially the Berlin Group who were seeking recognition of the Comintern, are dealt with in detail. Muzaffar also concentrated on the earliest communist documents prepared by Roy; these were circulated among the Congress delegates by his contacts at INC sessions in the early 1920s. He recorded the repression and imprisonment of the returning ex-*muhajir*s. He described the growth of early communist nucleuses in other cities of India and the principal figures involved therein. The wider setting of his activities had been shaped by these events. Other sections of the book are devoted to Muzaffar's early career as a struggling Bengali Muslim writer; his transformation into a political activist through contact with the labour movement and his entry into radical journalism; his first contacts with the Comintern; the attempts to set up an early communist network in Calcutta; his arrest, trial and conviction at Kanpur; release from prison and resumption of political activity through an all-India communist network; re-establishment of links with the Comintern; the first socialist organization in Bengal; radical journalism and the labour upsurge of the late 1920s.

The Act of Recollection

From recollection, Muzaffar was moving towards reconstruction. The process of recovering experiences obliterated from memory led him to write of his life and times on the basis of primary sources. He believed that recollection alone could not help him recover the past. He recognized that memory unsupported by other sources was open to criticism as selective and partial representation. Hence the search for a 'recovered' memory and 'accurate' reconstruction in order to render his version of events 'authentic'. He emphasized the fallibility of the act itself. The opening essay, 'Amar Smritikatha' (My Recollections), in *Samakaler Katha* begins with these perceptions:

> I do not believe that anyone can write of what happened forty-one/forty-two years ago on the basis of memory alone. I have completed my seventy-third year and am advancing towards seventy-four. Apart from my age, I have failing eye-sight. In these circumstances, who knows if I shall be able to complete writing [my] reminiscences?[54]

These lines lay bare the impetus behind, and the constraints on, the act of writing. They also account for his conscious dependence on primary and secondary sources, a method he relied on to project the historic dimensions of the times he lived through as an activist. In his introduction, entitled 'Amar Koifiyat' (My Excuse), Muzaffar wrote of his inability to extend his narrative beyond 1929 even though he had intended to cover the period up to 1934: 'There is a shortage of material. I refuse to write my reminiscences without reviving my memory with the help of documents.' He stressed that the work was already large in size even if he had been unable to do justice to all the material his friends had painstakingly supplied: 'I can only state one thing with confidence. I have done my best to amass correct data. I am aware that many would not find the information contained in this book to their taste. My only consolation is that I have collected genuine records that can be used by historians.'

Aware that he was probably letting down his friends and comrades by not living up to their expectations, he introduced a semi-defensive and humorous tone in 'Amar Koifiyat':

> Yes, this book is my memories of the Indian Communist Party. But under no circumstances can it be regarded as the history of the Communist Party. The Party did not ask me to write a book on the subject. . . .
>
> In order to write this book I have been in touch with many people, both in and outside India, seeking information. I have told all of them that I was writing my personal recollections of the Party and not its history. Yet everywhere it has been publicized that I am writing the history of the Indian Communist Party. I fail to see why. All this will only lead to the unnecessary disappointment of many comrades and friends.

Elsewhere, he wrote: 'I have a feeling that everyone will be disappointed by this book. Friends have expressed diverse expections. I don't think I shall be able to fulfil them.' He was anxious to establish that the conclusions he had drawn on the basis of documents stemmed from his subjective perception. It was his version of events rather than a directly political project or a scholarly text. He was aware that the material reproduced in his memoirs could be put to such uses and did not conceal his pride over this.

Yet, he was quick to emphasize that he was not a writer of history. There is a hidden warning to the uncritical reader in search of an 'authentic' and 'usable' past, in the distinction he draws between subjective reconstruction of memory based on primary sources and a work of history. He further hints at the limitations of a personal narrative when he points out that contradictions had crept into his account despite attempts to avoid them: 'It has taken two and half years for me to write this book. As a result, there are some discrepencies between earlier and latter portions. New facts have been added and are responsible for the disjunctions.'[55] Experiences 'recovered' through this method counted as 'reliable' memory, and encase a narrative journey through time with friends and enemies, organizations and individuals, the local and the international, state and society, nationalism and empire. It is at once a guide to the structure of the self and a key to the formation of a new political identity.

Classification
The links between recollection and reconstruction in *Amar Jiban* make it a text that cannot be classified as a conventional autobiography. Muzaffar's account conforms to all the characteristics required of a political memoir. There are reflective asides on contemporary political developments. There is an autobiographical aspect where the self is depicted through childhood, education, various phases of 'personal development' and in politics. There is a 'biographical element' which provides portraits of contemporaries who were known to him. Relations with those he came to know through his activism are depicted in semi-retirement, with observations that could benefit his 'political successors'. There is also the treatment, which some analysts of the autobiographical genre regard as the 'most ambitious mode' of recollection, of 'contemporary history', 'the times in which this career occurred'; a 'poly-genre' in the sense that it contains the 'tendency of the political memoir to invade neighbouring territories of autobiography, political science and historiography'. It also fits the category of an 'unconventional' memoir.[56] There is no attempt to evolve a 'self-oriented' discourse. Instead, there is a constant interplay between autobiographical elements and the wider context. There is a persistent need to 'situate' the self in a broad canvas. This narrative strategy is in marked contrast to the political memoirs written by some of Muzaffar's contemporaries. For example, the *praja* leader Abul Mansoor Ahmad's *Amar Dakha Rajnitir Panchash Bachar* (Fifty Years of Politics as I Saw It) or Jugantar revolutionary Bhupendrakumar Datta's *Biplaber Padachinha* (Footprints of the Revolution) share many or all of the characteristics that mark a political memoir.[57] However, both works

look at the surrounding events through the prism of the authors' own political careers and not the other way round. Where their narratives veer away from Muzaffar's account is in the method of self-projection. The conscious dialectic between the individual and the wider socio-political context in Muzaffar's memoir makes it step beyond the usual patterns of self-portrayal in political reminiscences. Descriptions of the personal are invariably attached to the social and the political. His narrative contains vivid and humorous descriptions of the socio-political reality in which he found himself. An example:

> My days were passing with this band of police-agents [assigned to watch over me]. One late afternoon, I decided to take a walk and went and sat down on the grass at Wellington Square. The watchers too settled themselves at a distance. Suddenly, I was possessed by a whim. Central Calcutta is a web of lanes and by-lanes. I thought it would be a worthwhile attempt to get rid of the watchers. I had familiarized myself with these alleys long ago. I stood up and immediately started walking. After a while, I increased pace, quickening my speed to the maximum. The watchers were not acquainted with these lanes. Almost all of them [soon] fell behind at the crossing of Mirzapur Street (now Surya Sen Street). I looked back to find that the Brahmin from Faridpur, sporting a 'tiki', was still at my heels. In this Bengal of ours, no one keeps a tiki. But this Brahmin had a thick one attached to [the back of] his head. The man was infuriating. I decided that I shall make him take a bath that night. I led him along the narrow alleyways of Muslim slums in the Baithakkhana area. The inhabitants discharged the water used for cleaning utensils on those lanes. In those days slippers were not in common use in Bengal. People wore shoes. Otherwise, the man's feet would have been soaked from this polluted water. [By then] I was in a state of exhaustion. I reached College Square [Park] and rested for a long time. Then I started roaming very slowly inside the Square. The closing hours were approaching. The park gates were going to be shut soon. Suddenly a mad dog appeared from nowhere. One of those little furry specimens. At first, the dog tried to bite the police agent. But the man created such a ruckus that the dog left him and instead leapt up and bit me under the knee. By then he was hooked on to my clothes as his teeth had got stuck in them. I managed to shrug him off with some force. After this he bit several other people. All this took place within a single minute.[58]

This description illustrates how attempts to escape police surveillance in late February 1923 led to momentary satisfaction, but also placed him in a very awkward situation. The incident also ruined his immediate political plans. He had been entertaining the thought of secretly slipping away to Europe as colonial surveillance had virtually paralysed his movements. But the dog-bite ensured that he would have to look for treatment which was only available in Shillong at the time. Upon his recovery and return, he was arrested and remained in prison till late 1925. This anecdote and many similar asides, in a narrative pursuing a directly political thread, help to draw the reader into the narrator's vanished world.

Self-Portrait

Muzaffar's self-portrayal as a political activist is invariably accompanied by observations on contemporary social mores as well as political events. The title of his memoir testifies that 'My Life' and the 'Communist Party of India' were of equal importance to the author, and they converge in his narrative. Muzaffar had arrived in the big city from a remote rural background on the eve of the First World War. He had desisted from direct engagement with politics during the war years, and was a 'cultural' activist involved in religio-ethnic identity politics with a broad sympathy towards anti-colonialism. The roots of his radicalization lay in the local and global anti-imperialist and anti-capitalist upsurge of the late 1910s and early 1920s. The 'mutation' of the self is hinted at, though not carefully recorded, in his memoirs. An example:

> I cannot say that the workers' strikes etc left me completely unaffected. While managing the newspaper, *Nabajug*, I was drawn to problems faced by workers to some extent. I was in the habit of mixing with sailors in Calcutta. However, I did not engage with them to organize a movement. People from Sandwip, my birth-place, worked in large numbers in ships during those days. This was the real reason for my roaming among them. But circulation among them made me become aware of different problems they faced. I wrote quite a bit on the demands of the seamen in *Nabajug*.[59]

This example offers insight into the experiences and observations which went into the making of the 'political self'. They are brief, fragmentary and selective glimpses. Self-censorship guided by hindsight, unavoidable gaps in memory, limited writing time, scarcity of personal written records and subjective restrictions on self-understanding may have led to the omission of some crucial aspects.

The 'political self' projected in these narratives is a public and social one. Muzaffar's personal links were confined to friends and colleagues who peopled the political and intellectual circles he frequented. This self is not rooted in a private sphere but wider, familiar social spaces. Some of its characteristics are shared lodgings with fellow cultural and later political activists; transformation of the organizational office-space into living quarters; and the absence of family life. The 'political self' is propelled by the consistent need to build a communist organization which would rally the masses against the rule of property. It is therefore an 'anti-establishment self' with a radical outlook, characterized *inter alia* by a subversive attitude towards the colonial surveillance network that significantly restricted his and the party's movements. Another aspect of this self stemmed from his political rejection of the principles and practice of the nationalists, including the advocates of 'revolution':

> The emergence of the revolutionary terrorists was a memorable event in Bengal. . . . Given my mental state during the second decade of this century, and the romantic aura of the terrorist movement, it would not have been unusual for me to have joined it. But there were hurdles. . . . The terrorist movement was without doubt an anti-British movement. But it was also a movement of Hindu Revivalism': it was aimed at re-establishment of a Hindu Kingdom. . . . From the 1920s, a change in outlook was initiated among revolutionary terrorists. Even then, while in prison during 1923–24, I had seen one of their big leaders order an imposing picture of the Goddess Kali from the jail office in the morning. He had arrived in prison the evening before.[60]

Elsewhere, he wrote in a humorous tone that he knew from personal experience that the older generation of 'revolutionary leaders', known as the movement's 'elder brothers', practised chastity and asceticism. They exercised srict cultural censorship over younger recruits by preventing them from learning about sex and socialism. The first dissent in the ranks of the younger terrorists came in the 1920s when some of them started reading literature on sexuality; this was followed by socialism. However, the influence of the elders was still strong enough to prevent any rupture with the terrorist movement. During the 1930s, the young terrorists again resumed study of the two subjects in prison. This time the moral strictures could no longer be imposed. After reading Marxist books 'banned' by their leaders, many joined the communist movement.[61]

Past and Present

A complex geography of socio-political relations based on identity and difference within the left is evident from Muzaffar Ahmad's memoirs. He played a crucial role by reopening old wounds. Bitterness endured in the past erupts with force in a narrative that is invariably marked by the contemporary scenario. Muzaffar is deeply derisive of Nalini Gupta who was sent as an emissary by M.N. Roy in order to establish contact with leftists in India in late 1921. Throughout his narrative, Nalini is depicted as a boastful, pretentious adventurer who occasionally acted as a police informant. Muzaffar is also extremely critical of Abani Mukherjee, Roy's former colleague in Moscow. Another visitor from Moscow, Shaukat Usmani, who was an ex-*muhajir*, is depicted as an ambitious, arrogant individualist. Muzaffar's narrative pays attention to the early Dange at regular intervals. Dange, the leading theoretician of the pro-Soviet ideological faction within the CPI, was a controversial figure while the memoirs were being written. He is projected in them as an arrogant, compromising and ambitious operator. Muzaffar even claims that Dange and Nalini signed a letter of apology to the state on the eve of the Kanpur trial to escape punishment. Janakiprasad Bagerhatta is aother person who figures in his list of 'shady' characters. Bagerhatta was the Joint Secretary of the communist party for a while during the late 1920s, and he left the party after Muzaffar exposed him as a police spy.[62]

In the Bengal context, Muzaffar concentrates his ire on Dharani Goswami and Gopen Chakraborty; originally from a revolutionary terrorist background, they joined the movement in the second half of the 1920s. Muzaffar thinks that they played a factional role by maintaining links with terrorist leaders interested in removing him from the leadership of the Workers and Peasants Party as well as the tiny communist organization active within it. Muzaffar had time and again expressed his willingness to work with those moving away from the ideology of militant nationalism and displaying an interest in class-based politics. Some of them had temporarily joined the socialist nucleus he briefly formed in 1922. His vocal criticism of the hierarchical, communal and caste character of the terrorist world-view and practice was well-known. An ideological battle with militant nationalists over the definition of real revolutionary activism was waged by Muzaffar throughout the 1920s. The conflict with Goswami and his friend Chakraborty was rooted, among other things, in this zone. Muzaffar thought they were more keen to work with Sibnath Banerjee, who had studied in Moscow, and with Radharaman Mitra. Banerjee and Mitra were independent socialists active in the labour movement. Muzaffar had disagreements with them on trade union work during the strike-actions of the late 1920s.

Not all of this can be explained on the basis of prejudice born from hindsight. Muzaffar's attitude towards Dange, Goswami and Chakraborty, who were part of the pro-Soviet CPI faction in the late 1950s and early 1960s, might have been guided by the political animosity generated within the communist movement during that period. However, he also linked people who were not part of the pro-Soviet faction with Goswami's and Chakraborty's initiative to oust him from leadership in the 1920s. For instance, Bankim Mukherjee, who became one of the leading communist trade union organizers, is depicted as someone who had sided with his two rivals. Mukherjee passed away in 1961 before the formal 'partition' of the communist party. The same is true of Muzaffar's attitude towards Shamsul Huda, an East Bengali sailor who had travelled via the USA to Moscow. Huda returned in the late 1920s, became an active communist organizer and sided with the anti-Soviet faction to which Muzaffar belonged in the 1960s. Not just hindsight, but the feeling of being cornered and frustrated by his comrades during the 1920s, played a role in shaping Muzaffar's narrative. This also proves that he was interested in projecting his role and experience as a clash and a contrast with that of others, including those who were with him at a decisive moment of the post-independence struggle. This explains why he insisted he was writing his memoir and not the history of the communist party. Had he set out to write such a history, people who were his comrades at the time could not have been projected in such a negative light.[63]

The sense of frustration, bitterness and isolation were primarily produced by faction-fighting. Muzaffar had hurled himself at the barriers erected by state and society, and stepped beyond them at a theoretical level, but found that they had to be continually tackled both inside the organization and in the outside world. Saddled with overwhelming odds, he struggled on but not without looking back in anger. He had mostly positive things to say of his early socialist associates who were part of the socialist nucleus formed in 1922: Nazrul Islam, Kutubuddin Ahmad, Abdur Rezzaq Khan and Bhupendrakumar Datta. Yet he does not hide moments when he questioned their judgement, had disagreements with them, or felt they were not doing enough for the movement. Abdul Halim, his life-long friend and closest colleague, whom he met in the middle of 1922, is possibly the only individual he does

Muzaffar Ahmad (*seated, right*) in 1966, when he was temporarily released from prison to attend Abdul Halim's funeral

not criticize. But then Halim was widely respected. Even the police officials in the 1930s and 1940s admired his abilities as a deeply dedicated organizer. The pro-Soviet sections also held him in great esteem even though some of them regretted that he 'refused to part from Muzaffar'.[64] Among Muzaffar's first colleagues, Abdur Rezzaq Khan was to join the pro-Soviet faction and came out very strongly against him. Possibly in memory of their early friendship, Muzaffar is not too critical of him. A similar 'personal' weakness creeps in when he speaks of Soumendranath Tagore, who was his close associate in the 1920s before leaving for Europe. After his return in the 1930s, Soumendranath became an early admirer of Trotsky and attacked his former comrades who remained within the Comintern, including Muzaffar. Despite this acrimonious divergence, Soumendranath is not projected in the same way as some of his other colleagues who joined the early left.[65]

This ambiguity is most evident in his relationship with M.N. Roy, his distant mentor. Roy had advised and offered support when Muzaffar started working as a left activist. They met only once, in 1939. Roy had long abandoned communism by then and saw himself as a 'Radical Humanist'. Roy and Muzaffar had associated with each other through a protracted correspondence during the 1920s. Their history of working together was marked by many disagreements. In the late 1920s, Roy had severe differences with the Comintern, and left. He was consequently expelled from the Communist Party of India. Muzaffar was critical of many of the decisions Roy made in the course of the 1920s and records them in his memoirs. He also differed with Roy over the latter's attempts to impose the Comintern's decision without informing himself of the problems in building an organization in India and Bengal. Roy's gender politics also dismayed Muzaffar. He felt that the early communist nucleus benefited considerably from the theoretical and organizational help offered by Evelyn Trent, Roy's first wife whom he divorced and whose contribution Roy never acknowledged. Roy was expelled from the Comintern in 1929, so there was no question of resuming contact afterwards. Despite this complete parting of ways, there is no denying the fact that a lingering regard for Roy remained. It finds its way into Muzaffar's narrative when he mentions his sole meeting with the man who had played such a crucial role in leading him to links with communism. Muzaffar was attending a political meeting when he heard that Roy and his second wife, Ellen Roy, were waiting downstairs in a car: 'I went down at once. I said, "I am Muzaffar. Please come upstairs with Mrs. Roy." It seems Roy was pleased. He turned to his wife and said "This is Comrade Muzaffar Ahmad." . . . That was my first and last meeting with Manabendra Nath Roy.'[66]

Roy had been a presence in his early years as an organizer and Muzaffar does not suppress this fact. Muzaffar also acknowledged Roy as one of the founders of the party when the CPI disregarded Tashkent and 1920 as the beginning of its formation. In this sense he was consistent in his claim that it was Roy, the ex-*muhajir*s and others who were the first to identify with communism, rather than those like himself. He did not see himself as a pioneer.

Familiar Spaces

There are also other interesting social dimensions to the kind of left identity that emerges from Muzaffar's depiction of the self. He made a conscious attempt to step out of the life-structures of a conventional middle-class individual. This is evident in his notions of communitarian living. Another characteristic is the rejection of state, family and private property on political, not moralistic, grounds. He mentions in passing while describing his early life that he was married off as a teenager by the village elders to stop him from running away, though 'marriage could not keep me tied to a family-life'. That is the only reference to his wife in his memoirs. She continued to reside away from him, mostly in Sandwip. Similarly, he mentions his brothers and his daughter only in passing,[67] though he did keep in touch with his daughter. A few of his letters to her were intercepted by the police and if they are anything to go by, they had a curiously formal relationship; he was aware of not having played the role of a parent. She claims that he sent her books and tried to keep himself abreast of her welfare from a distance. She regretted the fact that they never got to know each other well but did not hold this against him. Muzaffar himself writes that he was careful to keep himself away from the ties with which children can bind adults. He possibly liked children as he was very upset at the death of Nazrul's infant son while standing trial at Meerut. He also expressed concern and maintained close contact with Halim's children when the latter died in 1966, and he developed a close correspondence with his grandson.

Muzaffar's daughter claims that Muzaffar wanted his wife to divorce him and remarry, which she refused to do. From his daughter's account and from police records it would seem that he tried to help her out. At different points, from the 1920s to the 1950s, he sent her the meagre amounts he received as party wage or as royalty. He felt responsible and was concerned, but could not identify with these relationships as primary attachments. Private bonds were formed with those he worked with, on the basis of his association with them in public life. Prioritization of political work led to the creation of a private space shared with friends and acquaintances from political and literary circles. It could also be labelled as 'off-time' or leisure, an irregular part of the regular routine. After partition and the relegation of East Bengal, in his own words, to 'not just a foreign land but a distant foreign land', even occasional contact with relatives became increasingly difficult to maintain. He visited his friends and relatives in 1972, after Bangladesh was born. Apparently, despite an invitation from his daughter to stay on, he returned to Calcutta to stay with 'the comrades'.[68] This was a final gesture of farewell. He died the following year.

Though he personally rejected a conventional family life, Muzaffar was non-judgemental in his attitude towards love and sexuality. This is evident from his observations on revolutionary terrorist practices. In his early life he had held more or less conventional views on gender. But this changed from the early 1920s and by the time he was writing in the 1960s, he was, for example, challenging the male egotism of his mentor, M.N. Roy. Projection of the privations and joys of daily existence was another reflection of the less-than-usual mode of existence to which he became accustomed. There is no attempt to glorify suffering or to project a heroic image of self-sacrifice. Instances of personal hardship are described as irksome and miserable, as unpleasant situations he would have preferred to avoid.[69] These are interspersed with amusing anecdotes; they could involve colleagues who had ingloriously and accidentally created historic moments. This is his description of one of the earliest uses of the slogan 'Inquilab Zindabad' during a march in Calcutta in 1929:

> Aftab Ali had dressed really well that day and was marching at the very front. Mr. Gordon thought he was the leader and asked him to take down the two placards with those slogans. . . . Aftab Ali came and collected the placard entitled 'Long Live the Revolution' from my hand and 'Long Live Workers' and Peasants' Soviet Republic' from someone else. He then lost his nerve and could not lower them and started carrying both. Later Nripen Majumder took 'Long Live Workers' and Peasants' Soviet Republic' from Aftab Ali's hands. They walked along with the placards. The police arrested them in the street. . . . Both signed a letter of apology and promised good behaviour before the magistrate to secure their release.

Muzaffar even described the colonial police with humour. The following scene unfolded when the Workers and Peasants Party office was raided, Muzaffar and his colleagues were arrested and a search-list was drawn up to be presented as evidence at the Meerut trial:

> Mr. Hansen was in charge [of preparing the search-list] which seemed to continue for ages. He did not even treat us to a cup of tea let alone anything else. . . . These officers are always very keen to save money. . . . All day we went without food. I did not see the other police officers eat anything either except Mr. Hansen who had [some] chicken-soup.[70]

He often related his encounters with obscure individuals who displayed unexpected support. When travelling with police escorts to stand trial at Meerut, a sudden dinner invitation was offered and accepted:

> A Bengali gentleman (bhadralok) was sitting there. He had a bottle of alcohol under his arm. He stood up and welcomed us very warmly; and said we were to be his guests at the restaurant. This pleased the police-escorts as they could save on expenses. . . . He was fighting a case in Lucknow which someone had lodged against him for a sum of money he had left unpaid. . . . He paid for our dinner with that amount. . . . It had not been collected from him for some reason. . . . It's a great pity . . . I never . . . met him again.[71]

Corroborations, Confrontations

Despite attempts to furnish the reader with accurate and meticulous details, Muzaffar's personal and political dislikes over the course of his political career left their mark on his narrative. Several of his accusations against his opponents, outside but mainly within the communist movement, are supported by state documents, police files and communist literature preserved in the archives and other sources. Other narratives also claim that Nalini Gupta and Abani Mukherjee did play factional roles, and were not very stable, consistent or committed.[72] That Goswami and Chakraborty were trying to undermine Muzaffar's leadership is recorded not just in Muzaffar's memoirs but also by the police. A letter of apology in Dange and Nalini's name was preserved as a document by British Intelligence. Dange was to argue in the early 1960s that it was a forgery.[73] As the accusations and revelations became public, Muzaffar, from his prison-cell, felt an overwhelming political need to retaliate. Though many of his contentions are confirmed by other sources, past and contemporary antagonisms did prevent Muzaffar from being balanced in his judgement on certain matters. Goswami, Chakraborty, Huda and Bankim Mukherjee may have fallen out with him and questioned his leadership within the communist party. Still, along with him, they were the first generation of left trade unionists who introduced ideological militancy into the labour politics of Bengal at a time when the nationalist and communal leaders were attempting to 'restrain' workers. Similarly, whatever his character may have been, Dange was at the heart of the historic strikes that demonstrated the self-aware energy of working-class action to the mill owners of Bombay in the late 1920s.

Anger prevented Muzaffar from acknowledging these fully. Previous and ongoing animosities collapsed to create gaps in the narrative, and to project antagonists in a sometimes excessively unkind light. But then he was writing as a political prisoner, and of people he regarded as traitors and renegades. In this war, no side was giving any quarter to the others. Ironically, the records preserved by the state against which he had always fought provided Muzaffar and his opponents with the arsenal they needed in this battle. Old letters, leaflets, manifestos and surveillance reports conserved in the police dossier were dug up. Muzaffar emerged relatively unscathed from these exchanges.

Of Records

While the wide gap between the political circumstances which shaped his early career and the period in which he chose to glance backward also left its imprint on his versions, that he recorded them with the aid of factual material proves that Muzaffar was aware of their historic importance. Though the benefit of hindsight surfaced in his narrative, 'claims of descriptive accuracy' were supported by a considerable amount of primary research. His narrative reproduced archival material which had so far been unavailable. He also shed light on aspects of surveillance and political practice which matched official documents made accessible to the public long after his death. In this sense, his narrative is rich 'source-material'. Later historians were to benefit from this.[74]

Muzaffar's memoirs are also an interesting intervention on identity politics. He was possibly the only leading communist from Bengal to record the caste and communal dimensions of *bhadralok* nationalism, the dominant strain of the anti-colonial political identity, in his recollections. He was also the only figure on the left to focus on the role of former pan-Islamists in forming the first communist organization in Tashkent in 1920. The partition and the predominance of activists from a *bhadralok* background in the post-independence communist movement were perhaps responsible for the virtual eclipse from public memory of these early fighters on the communist left. Muzaffar was possibly prompted to project these ex-*muhajir*s as the first communists from India in reaction to the fact that most, though not all, of his younger colleagues who came from the terrorist tradition highlighted their 'militant' youth as a route to socialist revolution. He felt ideologically compelled to contest the tendency to project revolutionary nationalism as the only militant form of anti-colonial struggle. His most important work, *Amar Jiban*, is dedicated to the memory of the two early communists from a *muhajir* background whom he regarded as pioneers of communism in India.

His memoirs therefore offer a window to political currents and social processes obscured by time. They do not claim to be the autobiographical account of a mass leader, but of a marginal political actor whose attempts to promote a new political identity were severely restricted by the state, competing political formations and inner contradictions. That these forces were important in shaping the course of left politics in the 1920s cannot be denied. By focusing on the early communist movement, Muzaffar Ahmad provided an unusual record of a vanished but crucial era.

The City

Muzaffar's narratives centre around, veer away from and return to Calcutta. Communism in the city appears in the autobiographical accounts;[75] sometimes it is the focus of writing history.[76] It appears that segments of the young intelligentsia were responding to various radical currents in the early 1920s, manifest in the imperialized urban texture of two of the most important port-cities in the eastern half of Asia before the Second World War; from the available options, communism eventually emerged as the dominant ideological tendency. The ascendancy of communist politics in Shanghai in the 1920s facilitated mass radicalism, encompassing the revolutionary struggles of workers and intellectuals, women and youth. Right-wing nationalist forces led by Chiang Kai-shek with generous support from the imperialist powers brutally crushed the left tendency in 1927. Though urban communism re-emerged in Shanghai in the 1930s, its former political strength could not be recovered.[77] By contrast, the communists in Calcutta were not a noticeable presence before 1928; they recouped their strength, despite the countrywide crackdown in 1929 and subsequent disarray, from the second half of the 1930s, and a mass party emerged in Bengal and in the city; communism grew in strength, capable of unleashing working-class and popular mass actions. After independence and partition (1947), the rise of the communist influence over the West Bengal countryside was accompanied by their dominance over the political landscape of Calcutta, especially from the 1950s and 1960s.

The repression of communists in various parts of Asia during the second half of the 1920s and the early 1930s triggered a retreat of the left: from Indonesia to China, from India to Vietnam.[78] However, in each of these countries, communism as a source of alternative decolonization recovered by the late 1930s, and acted as a powerful conduit of the post-Second World War mass upsurge against colonialism and imperialism; in the case of China and Vietnam, communism emerged as the strongest political force. The radical reorientation of communism in China at its moment of retreat meant that cities continued to be spaces of contestation till 1949, even while the vast countryside was rapidly coming under the left influence. This was not the outcome in India where communism could not ride over the challenges posed by nationalism and communalism either in the city or the countryside. Yet, the inroads made in some of the metropolitan centres and rural areas signalled its visibility as the most socially radical strand in the struggle against imperialism. As Bombay, Lahore and Calcutta registered intensified

left-led working-class and intellectual actions, the late colonial city came to
be identified as a site of radical self-transformations.

In this study, the revolutions in Muzaffar Ahmad's political consciousness serve as a prism. Rather than examining the amply recorded origins of
nationalist and communal politics in Bengal, the focus is the social origins
of the left as a political force, emerging from a search for radical alternatives
to conditions existing under colonial rule which the social content of
nationalist and communal formations disallowed. In order to unravel this
particular process of political transition, the specific social conjunctures which
encouraged a small section of the intelligentsia to turn leftward are investigated. Muzaffar was to become the representative figure of a minute class
'fraction' which emerged from the making and unmaking of political identities. His transformation involved the recognition of various contradictions between the linguistic, sectional and anti-colonial components that
went into the making of 'Bengali Muslim' middle-class intellectuals; and
between the communal and nationalist political projects, and the social
aspirations which underlined mass participation in sectional and anti-colonial movements. Also important were the differences in material resources
among the formally educated, which divided the intelligentsia and generated hatred within it, but also created a bridge between its marginal, semi-
destitute members and other underprivileged groups in society.

Why did Muzaffar and a few others turn to ideas of socialist transformation? Specific conjunctures shaped their political alienation from the interests of their own class and class segment. Major political events such as the
Bolshevik Revolution of 1917, and the post-war mass upsurge culminating
in the Khilafat and Non-Cooperation Movements, left an indelible imprint
on their consciousness. Was the process of transition smooth? It involved
complicated encounters, 'conflict of values', changing 'structure of feeling'
and decreasing reliance on the concept of a 'wholly knowable community'[79]
in a socially divided, cosmopolitan environment. The complexities manifested themselves as a dichotomy between a communal and a communitarian
consciousness, until the former was abandoned in favour of the latter. The
perception of Islam as a religion based on egalitarian values embracing all
Muslims was challenged by a recognition of social divisions existing within
the known community. Egalitarian and communitarian values, imbibed
through religious practice, were reconfigured to arrive at an understanding
of trans-communal oppressions.

Though originally sharing the social perceptions of the majority of Bengali
Muslim intellectuals, who regarded the Islamic identity as a given and attempted to develop this as the conduit of capitalist modernity, Muzaffar
moved away from this ideological position. While his initial goal was to be
a cultural rather than a political activist who would devote himself to the

uplift of Bengali Muslims, he was unable to commit himself totally to claims of Muslim exclusivity. He became conscious, as a marginalized lower-middle-class intellectual, of the hierarchical relationships existing within the community. Community identity proved difficult to reject; he was well aware of the hostility and derision with which Muslims were treated in Hindu *bhadralok* culture. Despite strong anti-colonial convictions, the Hindu revivalist symbols and contempt for Muslims which dominated all branches of Hindu *bhadralok*-led nationalism continued to alienate him. The immediate local context of Muzaffar's transition was provided by his post-war urban location. The militant strike-wave which swept through every industry and mobilization of the lower orders of society during the Non-Cooperation and Khilafat Movements generated a dialectical relationship between Muzaffar's subjective social experiences and wider trends in society. The working-class militancy on display persuaded him to question prevailing ideas on the political agency necessary for social change. As his involvement with working-class activism deepened, he was increasingly convinced by the transformative potential embodied in the Bolshevik Revolution. The self-emancipation of workers without appealing to their national origin or communal composition was a strongly persuasive idea in the context of the constraints on lower-class protest exercised by nationalist and pan-Islamist ideologies. Internalization of communist ideas meant moving away from available models of anti-colonialism and community consciousness.

There were others in Muzaffar's social and intellectual milieu who were sympathetic to the lower orders of society but continued to define themselves in existing political terms. The ideological divergence between them and Muzaffar was not rooted in the non-recognition of exploitation but in identifying the social agency of political change. Muzaffar was one of the very few in the 1920s to undergo a radical self-transformation, in contrast to those from a similar background who remained tied to entrenched political forms. His political trajectory was very different, for example, from that of Abul Hussain and Abul Mansoor Ahmad who, despite their concern for the dispossessed peasantry, could not detach themselves from the political options available to the Muslim middle classes of the region: a confusing mélange of secular anti-colonialism, ethno-linguistic considerations and sectional politics. Increasing Hindu *bhadralok* intransigence in the 1930s further strengthened the attachment of the Bengali Muslim intelligentsia to *jotedar*-led *praja* politics, a tendency that would merge with the support for the Muslim League in the 1940s.[80] Neither was Muzaffar's route similar to that of his prominent contemporaries such as Akram Khan or A.K. Fazlul Haq. The growing influence of Hindu communal forces on the Bengal Congress made Akram Khan retreat from anti-colonialism to a reactive communalism which remained with him till the end of his life.[81] Fazlul Haq was uncomfortable with the dominant strains of identity available to Muslims. Yet, being a mainstream politician, unlike Muzaffar, he was forced to negotiate and compromise in one way or another.

Adoption of a new political identity therefore signalled a rejection of the social politics of mainstream political identities. It contributed to the creation of a social space which facilitated alternative modes of locating the self in society. The texture of the communitarian, cosmopolitan existence of the early communists indicated this. As members of Bengal's minority intelligentsia, the radical intellectuals and activists from a Bengali Muslim background who first turned to communist and socialist ideas were not unused to socio-cultural marginalization. Transition to the status of a radical 'fraction' strengthened their self-perception as 'outsiders' in the existing society, a crucial factor that went into the making of left politics in the region.[82] This 'fraction' increased in size with the inclusion of alienated sections of the Hindu *bhadralok* intelligentsia during the second half of the 1920s.

The actual size of the left in Bengal remained very small. The first socialist organization made its presence felt during the second half of the 1920s, primarily among workers in the industrial suburbs of Calcutta. The failure to expand among the rural poor in the districts indicated the restricted practical reach of left activism. Plainly, the communists and socialists could not overcome the greater political appeal enjoyed by nationalist and communal formations. 'Class' came to be recognized. Why was the spread of a 'class'-based politics inhibited at this stage? In his later autobiographical writings, Muzaffar himself would focus on the fragility of the new political identity which was curbed by the state, which faced the hostility of more established political formations and which was riddled with inner contradictions. The difficulty of translating an ideological position into action lay in multiple and interconnected causes: state repression; prior existence of competing ideologies in organized forms; internal organizational crises stemming from differences over leadership and strategy, theoretical occlusions, dearth of activists, and inconsistencies in coordination and communication with communists in other parts of India and outside. Among these, however, persecution by the state more than any other factor directly contributed to the dissolution of the first socialist organization. Factionalism revealed internal weaknesses and competing ideologies obstructed expansion. The unfamiliarity of socialist concepts in an intellectual milieu dominated by the Hindu *bhadralok* intelligentsia, a vast majority of whom were attached to forms of nationalist consciousness inspired by Hindu revivalism, acted as a major hindrance. But it was state power which brought the organization's activities to a sudden halt.

The ban on communism, apart from a state of exception during the Second World War, remained in place throughout the colonial era. However, during the 1930s large sections of disenchanted, younger members of the revolutionary nationalist circles turned to Marxism while in prison. Their transition was facilitated by a material process: the shedding of all social links with landed property by a sizeable section of the Hindu *bhadralok* who, it has been claimed, became dependent on professions from this period.[83] Unlike Muzaffar Ahmad's colleagues in the first socialist nucleus, Bhupendrakumar Datta and Jibanlal Chatterjee, this generation's break with terrorism was to be permanent. Their entry influenced the waning of revolutionary nationalism as a tendency and converged with a widening of the CPI's mass-base among workers and peasants. The case of Mohammad Haris, an Urdu-speaking tobacco worker who became the first working-class member of the Calcutta district committee of the CPI and died of typhoid at a young age in 1942, indicated the growing interactions between the intelligentsia and the city proletariat which had shaped the emergence of left politics in the urban environment.[84] In a short obituary, Muzaffar projected Haris as the organic link between the party and the working class.[85]

Muzaffar Ahmad was chief among those accused at Meerut, a factor which enhanced the prestige of the Bengal communists in the 1930s and influenced their rapid growth. The increase in the size of the organization also meant the termination of Muzaffar's role as the central figure of the communist movement in Bengal. Nevertheless, the later communists still based their social ideas on an understanding of dispossession and exploitation inflicted on the masses under imperial rule, and connected with capitalist enterprise and colonial land relations. The advance of communism as the third largest political force was met with setbacks. 1947, the year of Indian independence, was marked by the bloodbath and displacements which accompanied the partition of the country. Bengal was divided, signifying the triumph of dominant identity formations. The following year, the CPI was banned in parts of India and Muzaffar was reimprisoned. Henceforth he was primarily active in West Bengal, and Calcutta, the capital of this province, continued to be his base. As a senior CPI central committee member in 1964, he advocated the formation of a new communist organization independent of Moscow and Peking. He faced incarceration for the last time in the same decade, when already in his seventies, and he died a few years later.[86]

Muzaffar and other early communists journeyed from obscurity in political wilderness to become radical veterans who paved the way for the later emergence of a mass party and movement. This study has sought to explain the particular routes they explored in order to arrive at this goal. Others took quite different directions. While incarcerated in a fascist prison, Antonio Gramsci contemplated writing the story of his political life but never did. He wanted to explain the 'accident' by which a man's life, 'similar to a thousand others', makes him take a route that others did not.[87] In May 1928, when Muzaffar Ahmad was suffering from 'failing health' and 'mental worries' inflicted by the 'accidental' route he had taken, Shaukat Usmani wrote to him: 'Biography of . . . pioneers is the history of trials and vicissitudes. It is only the opportunistic scalp that thrives under the Raj of Capital. . . . Have patience and confidence . . . better days are coming.'[88] Despite the consolation offered, 'trials and vicissitudes' continued to visit Muzaffar; they were not necessarily replaced by 'better days'. Yet, he remained attached 'to life which is lived only once'. Towards the end of his life, he remarked: 'My attachment to atheist materialism increases each day. It is said, as people grow older they become increasingly inclined towards the spirit. In my case, I notice the opposite. Each year I am becoming even more attached to [the world of] matter.'[89] This was but one of many realizations that came to him in a city that transformed him.

Muzaffar Ahmad (*standing, centre*) campaigning for a communist candidate of Nabadwip Assembly Constituency, 1952

Muzaffar Ahmad (*seated, right*) at a party meeting, 1968

Notes and References

1. For an admiring appraisal by a contemporary, see Sibram Chakraborty, 'Bangla Sahityer Bishishto Gadyo Bhangir Sroshta: Muzaffar Ahmad' (Creator of a Distinct Bengali Prose Style: Muzaffar Ahmad), in Mazharul Islam (ed.), *Muzaffar Ahmad: Shango o Proshango* (Muzaffar Ahmad: Reflections and Essays), Calcutta, 1989, pp. 127–32. For later writings on Muzaffar's political prose, see Nepal Majumdar, 'Probondho Sangkalan: Muzaffar Ahmad' (Selected Essays of Muzaffar Ahmad), in Chitta Mandal (ed.), *Muzaffar Ahmader Sahitya o Samaj Rajniti* (Muzaffar Ahmad's Literary and Social Politics), Calcutta, 1990, pp. 166–68. Haripada Das, 'Nirabachito Rachana Sangkalan: Ekti Rajnoitik Bisleshan' (Selected Writings: An Analysis), in Mandal (ed.), *Muzaffar Ahmader Sahitya o Samaj Rajniti*, pp. 189–90.

2. Muzaffar Ahmad, *Probondho Sangkalan* (Selected Essays), Calcutta, 1970, pp. 2–3. 'Alphabetical and Chronological List of Muzaffar Ahmad's writings', in Muzaffar Ahmad, *Nirbachito Rachana Sangkalan* (Selected Writings), Calcutta, 1976, third edition 1990, pp. 217–55. In terms of records, this is a rich period. The titles of seven of Muzaffar's articles which appeared in *Langal* and 225 which appeared in *Ganabani* during the 1920s have been located. Though some are no longer available, all the titles and the majority of the articles he wrote at this stage can be accessed.

3. 'Bharat Kano Swadhin Noy?', *Langal*, 14 January 1926, in Ahmad, *Probondho Sangkalan*, pp. 3–6.

4. 'Ispar ki Uspar' (One Way or the Other), *Ganabani*, 9 June 1927; 'Simon Commission', *Ganabani*, 5 July 1928; 'Gana-Andolan o Congress' (Mass Movement and the Congress),

Ganabani, 19 July 1928; 'Poripurno Swadhinata' (Complete Independence), *Ganabani*, 2 August 1928; 'Swarajer Swarup' (Reality of Self-government), *Ganabani*, 23 August 1928 – in Ahmad, *Probondho Sangkalan*, pp. 49–51, 56–60, 77–81, 89–92, 124–27, 128–33, 134–39, 140–43. 'Probesh Nisedh' (Banned Entry), *Ganabani*, 19 May 1927; 'Royal Commission', *Ganabani*, 14 July 1927; 'Bolshevik Atanko' (Bolshevik Menace), *Ganabani*, 23 August 1928 – in Ahmad, *Nirbachito Rachana Sangkalan* (Selected Writings), pp. 46, 54–55, 89–91. 'Bharater Bhobishyo Itihash' (Future History of India), *Ganabani*, 1, 16, B 1334/1927. 'Banglar Barai Kon Khane?' (Where Lies Bengal's Boastfulness?), *Ganabani*, 1, 25, B 1334/1927.

[5] 'Bharat Kano Swadhin Noy?', *Langal*, 14 January 1926.

[6] 'Mukti Sangram' (Freedom Struggle), *Ganabani*, 26 May 1927.

[7] 'Jamidari Prathar Ucched' (Abolition of Landlordism), *Ganabani*, 21 April 1927.

[8] 'Rajodroho', *Ganabani*, 12 October 1926.

[9] 'Mukti Sangram' (Freedom Struggle), *Ganabani*, 26 May 1927. 'Jamidari Prathar Ucched' (Abolition of Landlordism), *Ganabani*, 21 April 1927. 'Bhadrasrenir Manabikata' (Humanity of the Bhadralok), *Ganabani*, 16 June 1927, in Ahmad, *Probondho Sangkalan*, pp. 93–97. 'British Labour Party-r Adhopatan' (Degeneration of the British Labour Party), *Ganabani*, 9 August 1928, in Gautam Chattopadhyay (ed.), *Sanhati–Langal–Ganabani*, Calcutta, 1992, pp. 183–85.

[10] 'Krishak o Sramik Andolan' (Movement of Peasants and Workers), *Langal*, 18 March 1926, in Ahmad, *Probondho Sangkalan*, pp. 14–17.

[11] 'Sreni Sangram' (Class Struggle), *Langal*, 25 February 1926, Ahmad, *Probondho Sangkalan*, pp. 11–13.

[12] 'Karagar Sambandhye Desher Oudashinyo' (The Indifference of the Country to Prisons), *Langal*, 25 March 1926, in Ahmad, *Probondho Sangkalan*, pp. 18–20.

[13] 'Kon Pathe?' (Which Way?), *Ganabani*, 23 September 1926, in Ahmad, *Probondho Sangkalan*, pp. 35–38.

[14] 'Akkhana Patra'(A Letter), *Ganabani*, 2 June 1927, in Ahmad, *Probondho Sangkalan*, pp. 82–88.

[15] 'Janaganer Kaj' (People's Work), *Ganabani*, 30 September 1926, in Ahmad, *Probondho Sangkalan*, pp. 44–48. 'Gana-Andolan o Congress' (Mass Movements and the Congress), *Ganabani*, 19 July 1928.

[16] 'Nutan Dal' (New Party), *Ganabani*, 14 April 1926, in Ahmad, *Probondho Sangkalan*, pp. 52–55.

[17] 'Mukti Sangram', *Ganabani*, 26 May 1927.

[18] 'Gana-Andolan o Congress', *Ganabani*, 19 July 1928.

[19] 'Jamidari Prathar Ucched', *Ganabani*, 21 April 1927.

[20] 'Krishak o Sramik Dal' (Peasants and Workers Party), *Ganabani*, 22 September 1927, in Ahmad, *Probondho Sangkalan*, pp. 119–23.

[21] Ibid. 'Swarajer Swarup', *Ganabani*, 23 August 1928. 'Simon Commission', *Ganabani*, 5 July 1928.

[22] 'Ispar ki Uspar', *Ganabani*, 9 June 1927.

[23] 'Bhadrasrenir Manabikata', *Ganabani*, 16 June 1927.

[24] Statement of Muzaffar Ahmad before R.L. Yorke, Additional Sessions Judge, Meerut (10–30 June 1931), *Meerut Communist Conspiracy Case (1929) Papers*.

[25] 'Khola Chithir Jawab' (Reply to the Open Letter), *Ganabani*, 28 July 1927, in Ahmad, *Probondho Sangkalan*, pp.101–04.

[26] For discussions on communalism in Bengal of the 1920s, see Suranjan Das, *Communal Riots in Bengal 1905–1947*, Delhi, 1993, pp. 59–107. For an understanding of rural communal politics, see Sumit Sarkar, *Modern India 1885–1947*, Hong Kong, 1989, pp. 233–37.

[27] 'Kothay Protikar?' (Where Lies Redressal?), *Langal*, 28 January 1926, in Ahmad, *Probondho Sangkalan*, pp. 7–10.

[28] 'Samprodayik Anusthan' (Communal Festivals), *Ganabani*, 1, 2, B 1333/1926.

29 'Akkhani Patra' (A Letter), *Ganabani*, 17 September 1926, in Ahmad, *Nirbachito Rachana Sangkalan*, pp. 13–14.

30 'Samprodayikatar Bisham Parinam' (The Terrible Consequences of Communalism), *Ganabani*, 30 September 1927, in Ahmad, *Probondho Sangkalan*, pp. 39–43. 'Arthanitik Asantosh' (Economic Unrest), *Ganabani*, 28 April 1927, in Ahmad, *Probondho Sangkalan*, pp. 61–65.

31 'Akkhani Patra', *Ganabani*, 17 September 1926.

32 'Bishwa Muslim Congress' (World Muslim Congress), *Ganabani*, 1, 2, B 1333/1926.

33 'Nari-Nirjatan', *Ganabani*, 1, 3, B 1333/1926. 'Ashol Kathata ki?' (What is the Real Issue?), *Ganabani*, 12 May 1927, in Ahmad, *Probondho Sangkalan*, pp. 70–76.

34 'Nutan Dal'(New Party), *Ganabani*, 14 April 1926, in Ahmad, *Probondho Sangkalan*, pp. 52–55.

35 'Krishak o Sramik Dal' (Peasants and Workers Party), *Ganabani*, 22 September 1927.

36 'Ki Kara Chai?' (What Is to Be Done?), *Ganabani*, 30 June 1927, in Ahmad, *Probondho Sangkalan*, pp. 96–100.

37 'Forward o Amra' (Forward and Us), *Ganabani*, 1, 28, B 1334/1927.

38 'Janaganer Kaj' (People's Work), *Ganabani*, 30 September 1926.

39 'Goray Galad' (Bungled Beginning), *Ganabani*, 4 October 1928, in Ahmad, *Probondho Sangkalan*, pp. 153–55.

40 'Jamidari Prathar Ucched', *Ganabani*, 21 April 1927. 'Arthanitik Asantosh', *Ganabani*, 28 April 1927. 'Krishak Sangathan', *Ganabani*, 5 May 1927.

41 'Akkhana Patra', *Ganabani*, 2 June 1927.

42 'Ispar ki Uspar', *Ganabani*, 9 June 1927.

43 'Krishak o Sramik ebong Sikkhito Jubo Samproday' (Peasants and Workers and the Educated Youth), *Ganabani*, 19 August 1927, in Ahmad, *Probondho Sangkalan*, pp. 110–18.

44 'Khola Chithi – Shikkhito Tarun Muslimganer Barabare' (Open Letter – An Appeal to the Educated Muslim Youth), *Ganabani*, 1, 1, B 1333/1926.

45 'Bharat Kano Swadhin Noy?', *Langal*, 14 January 1926. 'Krishak o Sramik Dal', *Ganabani*, 22 September 1927. 'Gana-Andolan o Congress', *Ganabani*, 19 July 1928. Inversions of meaning to redefine existing political terms characterize each of these articles.

46 Indranath Bandopadhyay, 'Samakaler Swarthe Samakaler Katha' (Story of My Times for Our Times), in Mandal (ed.), *Muzaffar Ahmader Sahitya o Samaj Rajniti*, p. 119.

47 Muzaffar Ahmad, *Samakaler Katha*, Calcutta, 1963, fourth edition 1996.

48 Mortuza Khaled, *A Study in Leadership: Muzaffar Ahmad and the Communist Movement in Bengal*, Calcutta, 2001, pp. 99–102, 107–11. IB 168/22 (115/1922). IB 168/22 (2/1922). IB 168/22 (serial number missing/ History Sheet Folder 1935–1951).

49 Muzaffar Ahmad, *Kazi Nazrul Islam: Smritikatha*, 1965, ninth edition 1998.

50 Subodh Roy (ed.), *Communism in India by Sir Cecil Kaye with Unpublished Documents from National Archives of India (1919–1924)*, Calcutta, 1971.

51 David Petrie, *Communism in India (1924–1927)*, Calcutta, 1972.

52 Muzaffar Ahmad, *Amar Jiban o Bharater Communist Party* (My Life and the Communist Party of India), Calcutta, 1969, fifth edition 1996, pp. 15–16.

53 Letter to Biplab Dasgupta, 19.4.1968, in *Ganashakti* (People's Power), *Muzaffar Ahmad Janmoshatobarsho Sankhya* (Muzaffar Ahmad Birth Centenary Edition), Calcutta, 1989, pp. 210–11. Ahmad, *Amar Jiban o Bharater Communist Party*, pp. 155, 157. Abdur Kadir Khan's account, 'A Pupil of the Soviet', was serialized in the *Times* on 25, 26 and 27 February 1930. He was engaged as a Lecturer in Pashtu at the School of Oriental Studies at the time. In his own words, before embarking on *hijrat*, he was a 'lecturer in Pashtu and Hindustani to the R.A.F. Officers stationed at the Military Staff College, Mhow, Central India'. This is confirmed by K.H. Ansari, *The Emergence of Socialist Thought among North Indian Muslims (1917–1947)*, Lahore, 1990, pp. 42, 256, 450.

54 Ahmad, *Samakaler Katha*, p. 5

55 Ahmad, *Amar Jiban o Bharater Communist Party*, pp. 13–17.

56 George Egerton, *Political Memoir, Essays on the Politics of Memory*, London, 1994,

Introduction, pp. xii–xiii. Indu Saha, 'Rajnoitik Atmajibani o Communist Andolon' (Political Autobiography and the Communist Movement), in Mandal (ed.), *Muzaffar Ahmader Sahitya o Samaj Rajniti*, pp. 128–43.

[57] Abul Mansoor Ahmad, *Amar Dakha Rajnitir Panchash Bachar*, Dhaka, 1968. Bhupendra-kumar Datta, *Biplaber Padachinha*, Calcutta, 1999.

[58] Ahmad, *Amar Jiban o Bharater Communist Party*, pp. 265–66.

[59] Ibid., pp. 82–83.

[60] Ibid, p. 28.

[61] Muzaffar Ahmad, 'Santrasbadi Biplabira Bharater Communist Partyte Elen – Bangla o Bihar' (Revolutionary Terrorists Join the Communist Party – Bengal and Bihar), in *Nirbachito Rachana Sangkalan*, pp. 137, 139.

[62] Ibid, pp. 88–101, 119, 184–210, 215, 241–44, 290–91, 296, 306–21, 352–56.

[63] Ibid, pp. 342–52, 349, 371, 467, 491–92. Subodh Chandra Sengupta and Anjali Basu (eds.), *Sansad Bangali Charitabhidhan* (Dictionary of Bengali Biography), Vol. 1, Calcutta, 1994, pp. 326–27.

[64] Interview with Ranen Sen, Calcutta, 13 and 16 August 1999.

[65] Ahmad, *Amar Jiban o Bharater Communist Party*, pp. 321, 400.

[66] Ibid, pp. 401–06.

[67] Ibid, pp. 23–25.

[68] IB 168/22 (serial number missing). IB 168/22 (100/1922). IB 168/22 (2/1922). IB 168/22 (119/1922). Afifa Khatun, 'Abba Baro Gharer Sandhane Chilen Tai Choto Ghar Tanke Bandhte Pareni' (My Father Searched for a Larger Space), in Mazharul Islam (ed.), *Muzaffar Ahmad: Shango o Proshango*, pp. 15–16. Ahmad, *Kazi Nazrul Islam: Smritikatha*, p. 236. Muzaffar Ahmad, 'Amar Pointallish Bacharer Sathi' (My Friend for Forty-Five Years), in Abdul Halim, *Nabajibaner Pathe*, Calcutta, 1966, second edition 1990, pp. 2–3. Letter to Arati Dasgupta, 19.4.1968, *Ganashakti, Muzaffar Ahmad Janmoshatobarsho Sankhya*, p. 214. In this letter he wanted to find out, through a contact in London, if a grand-daughter was living there, and learn from her the news of his other relatives in East Pakistan. He maintained this keen interest despite the sombre, unsentimental reflection that he was 'forever estranged' from his relatives. Sumanta Hira, 'Kakababur Sannidhye Kayekti Bachar' (A Few Years with Muzaffar Ahmad), *Ganashakti, Muzaffar Ahmad Janmoshatobarsho Sankhya*, p. 121. Abdul Mannan Saiyad, *Comrade Muzaffar Ahmader Aprokashito Patrabali* (Unpublished Letters of Comrade Muzaffar Ahmad), Dhaka, 2004.

[69] Ahmad, *Amar Jiban o Bharater Communist Party*, p. 268. Ahmad, 'Amar Pointallish Bacharer Sathi', in Halim, *Nabajibaner Pathe*, p. 7.

[70] Ahmad, *Amar Jiban o Bharater Communist Party*, pp. 520–21.

[71] Ibid., p. 513.

[72] Bhupendrakumar Datta, *Biplaber Padachinha* (Footprints of Revolution), Calcutta, 1999, pp. 207–08. Bhupendranath Datta, *Aprokashito Rajnitik Itihash* (Unpublished Political History), Calcutta, 1984, pp. 38–39, 41–45.

[73] IB 320/1926 (310/1926). Ahmad, *Amar Jiban o Bharater Communist Party*, pp. 307–08. Muzaffar reproduced sections from Home (Political) File 421, preserved in the National Archives of India, to contend that Dange and Gupta had apologized to the colonial state during the Kanpur trial in the hope of securing early release.

[74] K.H. Ansari, *The Emergence of Socialist Thought among North Indian Muslims (1917–1947)*. Ansari dismisses Muzaffar, Abdur Rezzaq Khan and other early communists as activists who failed to evolve a strategy independent of Moscow and lacked a creative vision of party-building. Yet, he heavily relies on the information provided in Muzaffar's memoirs to develop his narrative. The footnotes mention the English translation of Muzaffar's memoir; there is no admission that the clues offered by Muzaffar on individuals and networks were followed by the author to reconstruct the past. He also uses the sources to which Muzaffar had limited or no access, thereby reinforcing some of Muzaffar's claims. Ansari's sections on the *muhajir*s in Tashkent, their trial in British India, and the communist centres in Lahore and Uttar Pradesh, follow the trail set by Muzaffar. He even confirms, perhaps without intending

to, the actions for which Muzaffar held some of his colleagues responsible. For instance, Ansari's research indicates that Muzaffar was correct in assuming that the SOAS lecturer who wrote on his life as a *muhajir* in the Soviet Union in the *Times* was the same man suspected of being a police informer in the 1920s.

[75] Alfred Rosmer, *Lenin's Moscow*, London, 1971. Also see Ahmad, *Samakaler Katha*; Ahmad, *Kazi Nazrul Islam: Smritikatha*; Halim, *Nabajibaner Pathe*.

[76] Mark Naison, *Communists in Harlem during the Depression*, Urbana, 2005. Randi Storch, *Red Chicago: American Communism at Its Grassroots, 1928–35*, Urbana, 2007.

[77] Stephen Anthony Smith, *A Road is Made: Communism in Shanghai, 1920–1927*, Richmond, 2000. Patricia Stranahan, *Underground: The Shanghai Communist Party and the Politics of Survival, 1927–1937*, Lanham, 1998.

[78] Ruth T. McVey, *The Rise of Indonesian Communism*, New York, 1965. Stranahan, *Underground: The Shanghai Communist Party and the Politics of Survival, 1927–1937*. Pramita Ghose, *Meerut Conspiracy Case and the Left-Wing in India*, Calcutta, 1978. Hue-Tam Ho Tai, *Radicalism and the Origins of the Vietnamese Revolution*, Cambridge, Massachusetts, 1996.

[79] Raymond Williams, *The Country and the City*, London, 1973, pp. 59, 165–66, 265.

[80] Joya Chatterji, *Bengal Divided: Hindu communalism and partition, 1932–1947*, Delhi, 1995. Taj ul–Islam Hashmi, *Pakistan as a Peasant Utopia: The Communalization of Class Politics in East Bengal, 1920–1947*, Oxford, 1992.

[81] Ranabir Samaddar, 'Leaders and Publics: Stories in the time of transition', *Indian Economic and Social History Review*, Vol. 37, No. 4, 2000.

[82] For a treatment of minorities in the Russian left context, see Robert J. Brym, *The Jewish Intelligentsia and Russian Marxism: A Sociological Study of Intellectual Radicalism and Ideological Divergence*, London, 1978. For an analysis of the role played by minorities in the making of a communist party, see Paru Raman, 'Being an Indian Communist the South African Way: the influence of Indians in the South African Communist Party, 1934–1952', unpublished Ph.D. thesis, University of London, 2003. For a study of the interactions between Muslim intellectuals and Russian communism, see Maxime Rodinson, *Marxism and the Muslim World*, Delhi, 1980.

[83] D.M. Laushey, *Bengal Terrorism and the Marxist Left: Aspects of Regional Nationalism in India, 1905–1942*, Calcutta, 1975. Partha Chatterjee, *Bengal 1920–1947: The Land Question*, Calcutta, 1984.

[84] Sengupta and Basu (eds.), *Sansad Bangali Charitabhidhan*, p. 403.

[85] Muzaffar Ahmad, 'Pache Amra Bhule Jai' (Lest We Forget), *Janajuddha* (People's War), 9 September 1942.

[86] For a documentary biography, see Mortuza Khaled, *A Study in Leadership: Muzaffar Ahmad and the Communist Movement in Bengal*, Calcutta, 2001.

[87] John M. Cammett, *Antonio Gramsci and the Origins of Italian Communism*, Stanford, 1967, p. 3.

[88] IB file number censored.

[89] *Ganashakti, Muzaffar Ahmad Janmoshatobarsho Sankhya*, pp. 119, 230.

Bibliography

PRIMARY SOURCES

Official Records

Administrative Records

Census of India, selected years.
Eastern Bengal and Assam District Gazetteers, Noakhali, Allahabad, 1911.
Final Report on the Survey and Settlement Operations in the District of Noakhali 1914 to 1919, Calcutta, 1920.
Imperial Gazetteer of India, Eastern Bengal and Assam, Calcutta, 1909.
India in 1920, A Report prepared for presentation to Parliament in accordance with the requirements of the 26th section of the Govt. of India Act (5 & 6 Geo. V, Chap. 61).
Noakhali District Gazetteer, Statistics 1901–02, Calcutta, 1905.
Report of the Committee on Industrial Unrest, 1921.
Report on Municipal Administration of Calcutta, selected years.
Report of the Police Administration of the Town of Calcutta and its Suburbs, selected years.

Surveillance Records

Annual Report on Indian Papers Printed or Published in the Bengal Presidency, selected years.
Bengal Intelligence Branch Records, selected years.
Report on Native Newspapers, selected years.

Judicial Records

Kanpur Communist Conspiracy Case (1924) Papers.
Meerut Communist Conspiracy Case (1929) Papers.

Non-Official Records

English Periodicals/Newspapers

Amrita Bazar Patrika
The Englishman
Indian Daily News
Modern Review
The Statesman

Bengali Periodicals/Newspapers

Al-Eslam
Bangiya Musalman Sahitya Patrika
Dhumketu
Ganabani
Janajuddha
Kohinoor
Langal
Moslem Bharat
Noakhali
Prabasi
Samyabadi
Saogat

Published Primary Sources

Selections from Official Surveillance Reports / Archival Records

Adhikary, G. (ed.), *Documents of the History of the Communist Party of India*, Volume 1: 1917–1922, Delhi, 1971.
——, *Documents of the History of the Communist Party of India*, Volume III C: 1927, Delhi, 1979.
——, *Documents of the History of the Communist Party of India*, Volume III C: 1928, Delhi, 1982.
Basu, Jyoti (ed.), *Documents of the Communist Movement in India*, Volume I: 1917–1928, Calcutta, 1997.
Communist Partyr Ardhashatak Purti Smarak Patra (Fiftieth Anniversary of the Communist Party), A Communist Party of India Publication, Calcutta, 1975.
Communists Challenge Imperialism from the Dock: The General Statement of 18 Communist Accused, Calcutta, first edition 1967, reprint 1987.
Majumder, Manju Kumar and Bhanudeb Dutta, *Banglar Communist Andolaner Itihas Anusandhan* (Search for a History of the Communist Movement in Bengal), Calcutta, 2006.
Petrie, David, *Communism in India (1924–1927)*, Calcutta, 1972.

Raychaudhury, Ladlimohon (ed.), *The Seed-Time of Communist Movement in Bengal*, Calcutta, 2000.

Roy, Purabi, Sobhanlal Datta-Gupta and Hari Vasudevan (eds.), *Indo-Russian Relations 1917–1947, Select Documents from the Archives of the Russian Federation, Part I: 1917–1928*, Calcutta, 1999.

Roy, Subodh (ed.), *Communism in India by Sir Cecil Kaye with Unpublished Documents from National Archives of India (1919–1924)*, Calcutta, 1971.

——, *Communism in India, Unpublished Documents, 1919–1924*, Calcutta, 1997.

——, *Communism in India, Unpublished Documents, 1925–1934*, Calcutta, 1998.

Saiyad, Abdul Mannan, *Comrade Muzaffar Ahmader Aprokashito Patrabali* (Unpublished Letters of Comrade Muzaffar Ahmad), Dhaka, 2004.

Williamson, Horace, *India and Communism*, edited by Mahadevprasad Saha, Calcutta, 1976.

Bengali Tracts

Bishi, Pramathanath, *Desher Shatru* (Enemy of the Country), Santiniketan, 1925.

Bishi, Shaileshnath, *Bolshevikbad* (Bolshevism), Calcutta, 1924.

Chakrabarty, Rajkumar and Anangomohan Das, *Sandwiper Itihas* (History of Sandwip), Calcutta, B 1330/1923–24.

Chakrabarty, Sibram, *Moscow banam Pondicherry* (Moscow versus Pondicherry), Calcutta, 1929.

——, 'Jakhan Tara Katha Bolbe' (The Day They Will Speak Out), in *Sibram Chakrabarty-r Granthaboli* (Sibram Chakrabarty's Works), Calcutta, date of publication unknown.

De, Pulakesh, *Bolsheviki Shankalpo* (The Bolshevik Project), Calcutta, date of publication unknown.

Ganguly, Priyonath, *Estar Bidroho o Gorila Juddho* (Easter Rising and Guerrilla War), Calcutta, 1929.

——, *Lenin o Soviet* (Lenin and the Soviet), Calcutta, 1929.

Ghosh, Nabakrishna, *Keranir Maskabar* (The Clerk's Month-End), Calcutta, 1921.

Ghosh, Phanibhushan, *Lenin*, Calcutta, 1921.

Ghosh, Sarojnath, *Rusiyar Pralay* (Apocalypse in Russia), Calcutta, 1920.

Guha, Nalinikishore, *Manushyattva* (Humanity), Calcutta, 1920–21.

——, *Banglay Biplabbad* (Revolution in Bengal), Calcutta, first edition 1923, reprint 1924.

Islam, Nazrul, *Jugabani* (Message of the Age), Calcutta, 1922.

Ray, Pramathanath, *Mussolini*, Calcutta, 1929.

Sanyal, Pramathanath, *Mandir o Masjid* (Temple and Mosque), Calcutta, 1926.

Sarkar, Hemantakumar, *Bandir Diary* (A Prisoner's Diary), Calcutta, 1922.

——, *Bhashatattva o Bangla Bhashar Itihas* (Linguistics and the History of the Bengali Language), Calcutta, 1922.

——, *Swaraj Kon Pathe?* (Whither Self-Rule), Calcutta, 1922.

——, *Biplaber Pancharishi* (Five Sages of Revolution), Calcutta, 1923.

——, *Swadhinatar Saptasurja* (Seven Suns of Freedom), Calcutta, 1924.

Sengupta, Nareshchandra, *Rajagi* (Royal Estate), Calcutta, 1926.

Memoirs/Reminiscences

Ahmad, Abul Mansoor, *Amar Dakha Rajnitir Panchash Bachar* (Fifty Years of Politics As I Saw It), Dhaka, 1968.

Ahmad, Muzaffar, *Bharater Communist Party Garar Prothom Jug* (The First Phase of the Communist Party of India), Calcutta, 1959, fourteenth edition 1997.

——, *Samakaler Katha* (Story of My Times), Calcutta, 1963, fourth edition 1996.

——, *Kazi Nazrul Islam: Smritikatha* (Kazi Nazrul Islam: Reminiscences), Calcutta, 1965, ninth edition 1998.

——, 'Amar Pointallish Bacharer Sathi' (My Friend for Forty-Five Years), in Abdul Halim, *Nabajibaner Pathe*, Calcutta, 1966, second edition 1990.

——, *Amar Jiban o Bharater Communist Party* (My Life and the Communist Party of India), Calcutta, 1969, fifth edition 1996. English translation published as Muzaffar Ahmad, *Myself and the Communist Party of India 1920–1929*, Calcutta, 1970.

——, 'Amader Manmathanath' (Our Manmathanath), *Nandan*, Poush-Magh B 1380/1974.

Bannerjee, Naresh, 'Prokhyato Communist Neta Comrade Bankim Mukherjeer Janmoshatobarsho Upolokhye Sradhargho' (My Respects to Comrade Bankim Mukherjee at the Centenary of his Birth), in Chittabroto Majumder *et al.* (eds.), *Biplabi Nayak Bankim Mukherjee* (The Revolutionary Hero Bankim Mukherjee), Calcutta, 1998.

Basu, Mrinal Kanti, *Smritikatha* (Recollections), Calcutta, 1949.

Chattopadhyay, Shachinandan, *Muzaffar Ahmad Smriti* (Memories of Muzaffar Ahmad), Calcutta, 1988.

Datta, Bhupendrakumar, *Biplaber Padachinha* (Footprints of Revolution), Calcutta, 1999.

Datta, Bhupendranath, *Aprokashito Rajnitik Itihas* (Unpublished Political History), Calcutta, 1984.

Ganashakti (People's Power), *Muzaffar Ahmad Janmoshatobarsho Sankhya* (Muzaffar Ahmad Birth Centenary Edition), Calcutta, 1989.

Gangopadhyay, Pabitra, *Chalaman Jiban* (Journey through Life), Calcutta, 1994.

Ghosh, Atulya, *Kashto-Kolpito* (Difficult Imaginings), Calcutta, 1980.

Haldar, Gopal, *Rupnaraner Kule* (By the Shores of the Rupnaran River), Volume 1, Calcutta, 1963, reprint 1992.

Halim, Abdul, *Nabajibaner Pathe* (Towards A New Life), Calcutta, 1966, second edition 1990.

Islam, Mazharul (ed.), *Muzaffar Ahmad: Sango o Prosango* (Muzaffar Ahmad: Reflections and Essays), Calcutta, 1989.

Lahiri, Somnath, *Rachanabali* (Collected Writings), Vol. 1, Calcutta, first edition 1985, reprint 1995.

Mukhopadhyay, Saroj, *Bharater Communist Party o Amra* (The Communist Party of India and Ourselves), Vol. 1, Calcutta, 1993.

Pakrasi, Satis, *Agnijuger Katha* (The Burning Times), Calcutta, third edition 1982.

Sen, Ranen, *Bharater Communist Partyr Itibritta* (An Account of the Indian Communist Party), Calcutta, 1996.

Sengupta, Achintyakumar, *Kalloljug* (Age of Kallol), Calcutta, 1960.

Sengupta, Nareshchandra, 'Atmakatha' (My Story), in *Jugoporikrama* (Survey of an Age), Volume 1, Calcutta, 1981.

Sinha, Mani, *Jiban Sangram* (Life Struggle), Dhaka, 1986.

Rosmer, Alfred, *Lenin's Moscow*, London, 1971.

Spratt, Philip, *Blowing up India: Reminiscences and Reflections of a Former Comintern Emissary*, Calcutta, 1955.

Tagore, Soumendranath, *Jatri* (Voyager), Calcutta, 1975.

Selections from / Lists of Bengali Periodicals

Ahmad, Muzaffar, *Probondho Sangkalan* (Selected Essays), Calcutta, 1970.

——, *Nirbachito Rachana Sangkalan* (Selected Writings), Calcutta, 1976, third edition 1990.

Anisuzzaman, *Muslim Banglar Samayik Patrika* (List of Bengali Muslim Periodicals), Dhaka, 1969.

Chattopadhyay, Gautam (ed.), *Sanhati–Langal–Ganabani*, Calcutta, 1992.

Chattopadhyay, Gita, *Bangla Samayik Patrikapanji* (List of Bengali Periodicals), 1915–1930, Calcutta, 1994.

Sarkar, Sipra and Anamitra Das (eds.), *Bangalir Samyabad Charcha* (Communist Thinking in Bengal), Calcutta, 1998.

Interview

Interview with Ranen Sen, Calcutta, 13 and 16 August 1999.

SECONDARY SOURCES

Books and Articles

Bengali

Bandopadhyay, Sibaji, *Gopal–Rakhal Dwandasamas: Uponibeshbad o Bangla Shishu-Sahitya* (The Gopal–Rakhal Dialectic: Colonialism and Children's Literature in Bengal), Calcutta, 1991.

Basu, Ajitkumar, *Kolikatar Rajpath, Samaje o Sanskritite* (Streets of Calcutta, In Society and Culture), Calcutta, 1996.

Bera, Anjan, *Sangbadik Nazrul* (Journalist Nazrul), Calcutta, 1998.

——, *Srishti Shukher Ullashe* (Joy of Creation), Calcutta, 1999.

——, *Banglay Marxbadi Prokashonar Prothom Parbo* (First Phase of Marxist Publications in Bengal), Calcutta, 2000.

Chandra, Amitabha, *Abibhakta Banglay Communist Andolan: Suchana Parbo* (Communist Movement in Undivided Bengal: The First Phase), Calcutta, 1992.

Das, Susnata, *Swadhinata Sangram o Abibhakta Banglar Communist Andolan* (Freedom Struggle and Communist Movement in Undivided Bengal), Calcutta, 2008.

Hasan, Zahirul, *Kazi Abdul Wadud*, New Delhi, 1997.

Mandal, Chitta (ed.), *Muzaffar Ahmader Sahitya o Samaj Rajniti* (Muzaffar Ahmad's Literary and Social Politics), Calcutta, 1990.

Mitra, Radharaman, *Kolikata-Darpan* (A Mirror of Calcutta), Calcutta, 1997.

Mohammad, Hassan, *Comrade Muzaffar Ahmad o Banglar Communist Andolan* (Comrade Muzaffar Ahmad and the Communist Movement in Bengal), Chattagram, 1989.

Sengupta, Subodh Chandra and Anjali Basu (eds.), *Sansad Bangali Charitabhidhan* (Dictionary of Bengali Biography), Vol. 1, Calcutta, 1994.

——, *Sansad Bangali Charitabhidhan* (Dictionary of Bengali Biography), Vol. 2, Calcutta, 1996.

English

Ahmed, Rafiuddin, *The Bengal Muslims 1871–1906: A Quest for Identity*, Delhi, 1981.

Ansari, K.H., 'Pan-Islam and the Making of the Early Indian Muslim Socialists', *Modern Asian Studies*, Vol. 20, No. 3, 1986.

——, *The Emergence of Socialist Thought among North Indian Muslims (1917–1947)*, Lahore, 1990.

Bagchi, Amiya Kumar, *Private Investment in India, 1900–1939*, Delhi, 1980.

——, *The Political Economy of Underdevelopment*, Cambridge, 1993.

——, 'Wealth and Work in Calcutta 1860–1921', in Sukanta Chaudhuri (ed.), *Calcutta: The Living City*, Volume 1, Calcutta, 1995.

——, 'Workers and the Historians' Burden', in K.N. Panikkar, Terence J. Byres and Utsa Patnaik (eds.), *The Making of History: Essays Presented to Irfan Habib*, Delhi, 2000.

——, *Perilous Passage: Mankind and the Global Ascendancy of Capital*, Delhi, 2006.

Banerjee, P., *Calcutta and Its Hinterland, 1833–1900*, Calcutta, 1975.

Banerjee, Sumanta, 'The World of Ramjan Ostagar: The Common Man of Old Calcutta', in Sukanta Chaudhuri (ed.), *Calcutta: The Living City*, Volume 1, Calcutta, 1995.

Barooah, Nirode K., *Chatto: The Life and Times of an Indian Anti-Imperialist in Europe*, Delhi, 2004.

Barrier, N. Gerald, *Banned: Controversial Literature and Political Control in British India, 1907–1947*, Columbia, 1974.

Basu, A.K., *Indian Revolutionaries Abroad, 1905–1922: In the Background of International Developments*, Patna, 1971.

Basu, Sanat, *Essays on Indian Labour*, Calcutta, 1996.

Basu, Subho, 'Emergence of the Jute Mill Towns in Bengal 1880–1920: Migration Pattern and Survival Strategy of Industrial Workers', *Calcutta Historical Journal*, Vol. 18, No. 1, 1996.

——, *Does Class Matter? Colonial Capital and Workers' Resistance in Bengal, 1890–1937*, Oxford, 2004.

Beinin, Joel and Zachary Lockman, *Workers on the Nile: Nationalism, Communism, Islam and the Egyptian Working Class*, Princeton, 1987.

Bernstein, Gail Lee, *Japanese Marxist: A Portrait of Kawakami Hajime 1879–1946*, Cambridge (Mass.) and London, 1990.

Bhattacharya, Debraj, 'Kolkata "Underworld" in the Early 20th Century', *Economic and Political Weekly*, Vol. 38, No. 38, 2004.

Bhattacharya, Sabyasachi, *Bande Mataram: The Biography of a Song*, Delhi, 2003.

Bhattacharya, Tithi, *The Sentinels of Culture Class, Education, and the Colonial Intellectual in Bengal (1848–85)*, Oxford, 2005.

Broeze, F.J.A., 'The Muscles of Empire: Indian Seamen and the Raj 1919–1939', *Indian Economic and Social History Review*, Vol. 18, No. 1, 1981.

Broomfield, J.H., *Elite Conflict in a Plural Society*, Berkeley, 1968.

Brym, Robert J., *The Jewish Intelligentsia and Russian Marxism: A Sociological Study of Intellectual Radicalism and Ideological Divergence*, London, 1978.

Cammett, John M., *Antonio Gramsci and the Origins of Italian Communism*, Stanford, 1967.

Chakrabarty, Dipesh, *Rethinking Working-Class History, Bengal 1890 to 1940*, Princeton, 2000.

Chakraborty, Upendra Narayan, *Indian Nationalism and the First World War (1914–1918)*, Calcutta, 1997.

Chandavarkar, Rajnarayan, *The origins of industrial capitalism in India: business strategies and the working classes in Bombay, 1900–1940*, Cambridge, 1992.

Chatterjee, Partha, *Bengal 1920–1947: The Land Question*, Calcutta, 1984.

Chatterji, Joya, *Bengal Divided: Hindu communalism and partition, 1932–1947*, Delhi, 1995.

Chattopadhyay, Gautam, *Communism and Bengal's Freedom Movement*, Bombay, 1970.

Chattopadhyay, Manju, *The Trail-blazing Women Trade Unionists of India*, Delhi, 1995.

Chattopadhyay, Suchetana, 'Misinterpreting Muzaffar Ahmed', *Economic and Political Weekly*, Vol. XXXIV, No. 13, 27 March 1999.

Das, Suranjan, *Communal Riots in Bengal 1905–1947*, Delhi, 1993.

Dasgupta, Alokeranjan, 'The Social and Cultural World of the Men of Literature in Calcutta', in Surajit Sinha (ed.), *Cultural Profile of Calcutta*, 1972.

Datta, Partho, 'Strikes in the Greater Calcutta Region, 1918–1924', *Indian Economic and Social History Review*, Vol. 30, No. 1, 1993.

Datta, Pradip Kumar, *Carving Blocs: Communal Ideology in Early Twentieth Century Bengal*, Delhi, 1999.

Datta-Gupta, Sobhanlal, *Comintern, India and the Colonial Question, 1920–1937*, Calcutta, 1980.

——, *Comintern and the Destiny of Communism in India 1919–1943: Dialectics of Real and a Possible History*, Calcutta, 2006.

Davis, Mike, *Dead Cities and Other Tales*, New York, 2002.

De, Amalendu, 'Bengali Intelligentsia's Attitudes to the Permanent Settlement', *Social Scientist* , Vol. 5, No. 56, 1977.

——, 'The Social Thoughts and Consciousness of Bengali Muslims in the Colonial Period', *Social Scientist* , Vol. 23, Nos. 263–265, 1995.

d'Encausse, Helene Carrare and Stuart R. Schram, *Marxism and Asia*, London, 1969.

De Haan, Arjan, *Unsettled Settlers, Migrant Workers and Industrial Capitalism in Calcutta*, Calcutta, 1996.

Dey, Amit, *The Image of The Prophet in Bengali Muslim Piety (1850–1947)*, Calcutta, 2006.

Dirlik, Arif, *The Origins of Chinese Communism*, Oxford, 1989.

Druhe, David N., *Soviet Russia and Indian Communism, 1917–1947, With an Epilogue Covering the Situation Today*, New York, 1959.

Eaton, Richard M., *The Rise of Islam and the Bengal Frontier, 1204–1760*, Berkeley, 1993.

Edman, Irwin (ed.), *The Works of Plato*, New York, 1956.

Egerton, George, *Political Memoir: Essays on the Politics of Memory*, London, 1994.

Ellinwood, D.C. and S.D. Pradhan, *India and World War I*, Delhi, 1978.

Fisher, John, 'The Interdepartmental Committee on Eastern Unrest and British Responses to Bolshevik and other Intrigues against the Empire during the 1920s', *Journal of Asian History*, Vol. 34, No. 1, 2000.

Foster, John, 'The Declassing of Language', *New Left Review*, 150, March/April 1985.

Gafurov, B.G. and G.F. Kim (eds.), *Lenin and National Liberation in the East*, Moscow, 1978.

Ghose, Pramita, *Meerut Conspiracy Case and the Left-Wing in India*, Calcutta, 1978.

Ghosh, Tapabroto, 'Literature and Literary Life in Calcutta: The Age of Rabindranath', in Sukanta Chaudhuri (ed.), *Calcutta: The Living City*, Volume 2, Calcutta, 1995.

Gordon, Leonard A., *Bengal: The Nationalist Movement 1876–1940*, New York, 1974.

——, *Brothers Against the Raj: A Biography of Sarat and Subhash Chandra Bose*, Delhi, 1990.

Habib, Irfan, 'Colonialization of the Indian Economy 1757–1900', in *Essays in Indian History: Towards a Marxist Perception*, Delhi, 1995.

——, 'The Left and the National Movement', *Social Scientist*, Vol. 27, Nos. 5–6, May–June 1998.

Haithcox, J.P., *Communism and Nationalism in India: M.N. Roy and Comintern Policy 1920–1939*, Princeton, 1971.

Harris, George S., *The Origins of Communism in Turkey*, Stanford, 1967.

Hasan, Mushirul, 'Religion and Politics in India: The Ulama and the Khilafat

Movement', in Mushirul Hasan (ed.), *Communal and Pan-Islamic Trends in Colonial India*, Delhi, 1981.

Hashmi, Taj ul-Islam, *Pakistan as a Peasant Utopia: The Communalization of Class Politics in East Bengal, 1920–1947*, Oxford, 1992.

Hatcher, Brian, 'Indigent Brahmans, Industrious Pandits: Bourgeois Ideology and Sanskrit Pandits in Colonial Calcutta', *Comparative Studies of South Asia, Africa and the Middle East*, Special Issue: *Divergent Modernities*, 16, 1, 1996.

Hauser, Arnold, *The Social History of Art*, Volume 4, London, 1983.

History Commission of the Communist Party of India (Marxist), *History of the Communist Movement in India, Vol. I: The Formative Years 1920–1933*, Delhi, 2005.

Hoare, Quintin and Geoffrey Nowell Smith (eds.), *Selections from the Prison Notebooks of Antonio Gramsci*, London, 2003.

Hobsbawm, Eric, *Revolutionaries*, London, 1999.

——, *Uncommon People: Resistance, Rebellion and Jazz*, London, 1999.

Josh, B., *Struggle for Hegemony in India 1920–47: the colonial state, the left and the national movement*, Volume Two, Delhi, 1993.

Joshi, P.C., 'Lenin: Contemporary Indian Image', in P.C. Joshi, Gautam Chattopadhyay and Devendra Kuashik (eds.), *Lenin in Contemporary Indian Press*, Delhi, 1970.

Joshi, S., *Struggle for Hegemony in India 1920–47: the colonial state, the left and the national movement*, Volume One, Delhi, 1992.

Khaled, Mortuza, *A Study in Leadership: Muzaffar Ahmad and the Communist Movement in Bengal*, Calcutta, 2001.

Laushey, D.M., *Bengal Terrorism and the Marxist Left: Aspects of Regional Nationalism in India, 1905–1942*, Calcutta, 1975.

Leiten, G.K., *Colonialism, Class and Nation: The Confrontation in Bombay around 1930*, Calcutta, 1984.

Lenin, V.I., *On the Intelligentsia*, Moscow, 1983.

MacKinnon, Janice R. and Stephen R. MacKinnon, *Agnes Smedley: The Life and Times of an American Radical*, London, 1988.

McGuire, John, *The Making of a Colonial Mind: A Quantitative Study of the Bhadralok in Calcutta, 1857–1885*, Canberra, 1983.

McPherson, Kenneth, *The Muslim Microcosm: Calcutta 1918 to 1935*, Wiesbaden, 1974.

McVey, Ruth T., *The Rise of Indonesian Communism*, New York, 1965.

Meiksins Wood, Ellen, 'Modernity, Postmodernity or Capitalism?', in Robert W. McChesney, Ellen Meiksins Wood and John Bellamy Foster (eds.), *Capitalism and the Information Age: The Political Economy of the Global Communication Revolution*, Kharagpur, 2001.

Menon, Dilip M., *Caste, Nationalism and Communism in South India: Malabar 1900–1948*, Cambridge, 1994.

Mitra, Priti Kumar, *The dissent of Nazrul Islam: poetry and history*, Delhi, 2007.

Mukherjee, Aditya, 'The Workers' and Peasants' Parties, 1926–30: An Aspect of

Communism in India', in Bipan Chandra (ed.), *The Indian Left: Critical Appraisals*, New Delhi, 1983.

Murshid, Tanzeen M., *The Sacred and the Secular: Bengal Muslim Discourses 1871–1977*, Calcutta, 1995.

Naison, Mark, *Communists in Harlem during the Depression*, Urbana, 2005.

Nakazato, Nariaki, *Agrarian System in Eastern Bengal, 1870–1910*, Calcutta, 1994.

Newman, Richard, *Workers and Unions in Bombay 1918–1929: A study of organization in the cotton mills*, Canberra, 1981.

Nigam, Aditya, 'Marxism and the Postcolonial World: Footnotes to a Long March', *Economic and Political Weekly*, Vol. XXXIV, Nos. 1 and 2, 2–8 and 9–15 January 1999.

Overstreet, G.D. and M. Windmiller, *Communism in India*, Berkeley, 1959.

Popplewell, R.J., *Intelligence and Imperial Defence: British Intelligence and the Defence of the Indian Empire, 1904–1924*, London, 1995.

Ray, Pratap Kumar, 'The Calcutta Adda', in Sukanta Chaudhuri (ed.), *Calcutta: The Living City*, Volume 2, Calcutta, 1995.

Ray, Rajat, *Urban Roots of Indian Nationalism, Pressure Groups and Conflict of Interests in Calcutta City Politics, 1875–1939*, Delhi, 1979.

——, 'Revolutionaries, Pan-Islamists, Bolshevists: Maulana Abul Kalam Azad and the Political Underground of Calcutta', in Mushirul Hasan (ed.), *Communal and Pan-Islamic Trends in Colonial India*, Delhi, 1981.

——, *The Felt Community: Commonality and Mentality before the Emergence of Indian Nationalism*, Delhi, 2002.

——, *Nationalism, Modernity and Civil Society: The Subalternist Critique and After*, Calcutta, 2007.

Robb, Peter, 'The ordering of rural India: the policing of nineteenth century Bengal and Bihar', in David M. Anderson and David Killingray (eds.), *Policing the Empire, Government, Authority and Control, 1830–1940*, Manchester, 1991.

Rodinson, Maxime, *Marxism and the Muslim World*, Delhi, 1980.

Samaddar, Ranabir, 'Leaders and Publics: Stories in the time of transition', *Indian Economic and Social History Review*, Vol. 37, No. 4, 2000.

Sarkar, Chandiprasad, *The Bengali Muslims, A Study in their Politicization (1912–1929)*, Calcutta, 1991.

Sarkar, Sumit, *Swadeshi Movement in Bengal 1903–08*, Delhi, 1973.

——, 'Rammohun Roy and the Break with the Past', in *A Critique of Colonial India*, Calcutta, 1985.

——, *Modern India 1885–1947*, Hong Kong, 1989.

——, *Writing Social History*, Delhi, 1997.

——, 'From Class-Struggle to Identity Politics: Problematizing a Transition', *Calcutta Historical Journal*, Vols. 19–20, 1997–98.

——, *Beyond Nationalist Frames: Relocating Postmodernism, Hindutva, History*, Delhi, 2002.

Sarkar, Tanika, *Bengal 1928–1934: The Politics of Protest*, Delhi, 1987.

——, *Hindu Wife, Hindu Nation: Community, Religion and Cultural Nationalism*, Delhi, 2001.

Schlor, Joachim, *Nights in the Big City: Paris, Berlin, London 1840–1930*, London, 1998.

Schorske, Carl E., *Fin-de-Siecle Vienna: Politics and Culture*, New York, 1981.

Sen, Sukomal, *Working Class of India, History of Emergence and Movement, 1830–1970*, Calcutta, 1977.

Seth, Sanjay, *Marxist Theory and Nationalist Politics: The Case of Colonial India*, Delhi, 1995.

Shah, Mohammad, *In Search of an Identity: Bengali Muslims 1880–1940*, Calcutta, 1996.

Smith, Stephen Anthony, *A Road is Made: Communism in Shanghai, 1920–1927*, Richmond, 2000.

Squires, Mike, *Saklatvala: A Political Biography*, London, 1990.

Stedman Jones, Gareth, *Languages of Class: Studies in English Working Class History 1832–1982*, Cambridge, 1983.

Storch, Randi, *Red Chicago: American Communism at Its Grassroots, 1928–35*, Urbana, 2007.

Stranahan, Patricia, *Underground: The Shanghai Communist Party and the Politics of Survival, 1927–1937*, Lanham, 1998.

Tai, Hue-Tam Ho, *Radicalism and the Origins of the Vietnamese Revolution*, Cambridge (Massachusetts), 1996.

Visram, Rozina, *Asians in Britain: 400 Years of History*, London, 2002.

Williams, Raymond, *The Country and the City*, London, 1973.

——, *Problems in Materialism and Culture*, London, 1980.

Zabih, Sepher, *The Communist Movement in Iran*, Berkeley, 1966.

Zinoman, Peter, *The Colonial Bastille: A History of Imprisonment in Vietnam, 1862–1940*, Berkeley and Los Angeles, 2001.

Unpublished Ph.D. Theses

Berwick, John, 'Chatra Samaj: The Social and Political Significance of the Student Community in Bengal *c.* 1870–1922', University of Sydney, 1986.

Dasgupta, Rajarshi, 'Marxism and the middle class intelligentsia: culture and politics in Bengal, 1920s–1950s', University of Oxford, 2003.

Gourlay, S.N., 'Trade Unionism in Bengal before 1922: Historical Origins, Development and Characteristics', University of London, 1983.

Jones, Jean, 'The Anti-Colonial Politics and Policies of the Communist Party of Great Britain: 1920–1951', University of Wolverhampton, 1997.

Raman, Paru, 'Being an Indian Communist the South African Way: the influence of Indians in the South African Communist Party, 1934–1952', University of London, 2003.

Index